DESIGN AND MAKEUP
of the
NEWSPAPER

Johannes Gutenberg

DESIGN AND MAKEUP
of the
NEWSPAPER

By ALBERT A. SUTTON, *Ph.D.*

Professor of Journalism; Chairman,
Graphic Arts Department

MEDILL SCHOOL OF JOURNALISM, NORTHWESTERN UNIVERSITY

New York
PRENTICE-HALL, INC.

PRENTICE-HALL JOURNALISM SERIES

KENNETH E. OLSON, EDITOR

First Printing.................June, 1948
Second Printing...............May, 1949

To Lenore

Preface

MODERN NEWSPAPERS BEAR LITTLE RESEM-
blance to those printed in colonial days in this country. Since that
early period, the great increase in our population and complex changes
in social and economic conditions—including the discovery of advertising as an important source of revenue—have had a tremendous influence on the size and character of the newspaper.

Editors and publishers have come to realize that the way in which
news and advertising are displayed has much to do with the success of
their ventures, since the nature of the design and makeup employed
directly affects readership. As a result, serious attention is being given
to the application of scientific procedures in this phase of newspaper
production.

No longer are people satisfied with pages that are dull, gray, and
hard to read. They want their news presented so they can find it
quickly and get a summary of important stories in a hurry. They also
have become more discriminating in their tastes for advertising, which
should be planned with extreme care if it is to attract and hold the
interest of readers.

Consequently, newspaper workers and those planning to enter the
profession of journalism should attempt to learn as much as possible
about the principles and techniques involved in this specialized phase
of newspaper making.

Although the direction of design and makeup usually is centered in
one or two individuals on most publications, every member of the staff
should have an understanding of typography and the important work
involved in translating written words into printed pages that are attractive and interesting. The effectiveness and quality of the finished
product are dependent largely upon efficient and intelligent cooperation.

The purpose of this book has been to bring together significant information that is essential to an understanding of the basic problems
involved in the design and makeup of the newspaper. Not only has
it been planned as a textbook for use in colleges and universities giving

instruction in journalism, but also for practicing newspapermen and others interested in developing more proficiency in the subject.

Most of the material presented also is applicable to magazines, house organs, and other types of publications directed toward reading publics, and should be of service to workers in these related fields.

The physical appearance of the newspaper has undergone much improvement during the past two decades. This improvement has been brought about by the introduction of fresh, legible types, new styles of headlines and makeup, and a growing consciousness on the part of editors of the great value of harmonious and well-planned display. It is hoped that this book will make a useful contribution toward furthering the desire for newspapers that are more interesting and inviting to readers everywhere.

The author expresses his deep gratitude to Dean Kenneth E. Olson, of the Medill School of Journalism, Northwestern University, who encouraged him to undertake the writing of this book, read the completed manuscript, and gave much valuable advice during its preparation.

Grateful acknowledgment also is made to Professor Charles L. Allen, of the Medill School of Journalism, Northwestern University; Albert J. Krohn, of The Goss Printing Press Company; Walter B. Patterson and his associates, of the Mergenthaler Linotype Company; and F. A. Resch, executive newsphoto editor of The Associated Press, who read parts of the manuscript and made helpful comments and suggestions in the interest of accuracy; and to Professor Thomas F. Barnhart, School of Journalism, University of Minnesota, who read and criticized the first two chapters. Although citations and references to works used in gathering material for this book are acknowledged in appropriate footnotes, special mention should be made of the valuable information gained from Kenneth E. Olson's *Typography and Mechanics of the Newspaper,* published by D. Appleton and Company in 1930. To these and to all other authors and publishers of books and articles from which important data were obtained, I want to express my appreciation.

Sincere thanks also is extended to the many newspaper publishers and others who furnished useful information and illustrative material. Of particular value was the assistance given by the American Type Founders Sales Corporation, The Associated Press, N. W. Ayer & Son, Inc., the Babcock Printing Press Manufacturing Company, the Duplex Printing Press Company, Mr. J. L. Frazier of *Inland Printer,* The Goss Printing Press Company, Harris-Seybold Company, R. Hoe & Company, Inc., the Intertype Corporation, the Lake Erie Engineering Corporation, Lanston Monotype Machine Company, Ludlow Typograph Company, the Mergenthaler Linotype Company, Pontiac Engraving & Electrotype Company, H. B. Rouse & Company, the Sta-Hi Corporation, the Teletypesetter Corporation, Vandercook & Sons, Inc., and the Wood Newspaper Machinery Corporation.

Deep appreciation also is expressed to my wife, Lenore W. Sutton, who helped with editing and assisted in many other ways; to Miss Elizabeth Macpherson, who typed the manuscript; to Miss Charlotte Ryde, who prepared some of the illustrations; to Miss Eleanor F. Lewis and other members of the staff of the Charles Deering Library, Northwestern University; and to all others who aided in the preparation of this book.

Contents

DESIGN AND MAKEUP
of the
NEWSPAPER

I

A Brief History of Printing

No human endeavor has contributed more to the progress of civilization than the art of printing. Over the long stretches of time from the prehistoric era, man's ability to keep records in lasting form has made possible a gradual accumulation of knowledge that has helped guide his climb upward from primitive life to our present high level of social and economic development.

History undoubtedly will reveal that no generation has witnessed more striking evidence of the tremendous power of the press in shaping and directing the destiny of mankind than our own, and the horizons of the future for people everywhere who still are groping for peace and goodwill are brightened by the promise and the hope inherent in the printed word.

Even prehistoric man sensed the primary importance of a dependable method of communication and foresaw the necessity of devising some tangible means of recording ideas. Nobody knows how long man was content with a language made up of gestures and sounds, but out of the dim past have come evidences of his first crude attempts to combine with these a series of signs and symbols which gradually developed into a complex system known as the alphabet.

Evolution of the Alphabet

The evolution of the alphabet, which began in an era referred to by historians as prehistoric because of the absence of written records, is marked by four distinct stages of development.[1]

The first stage is referred to as the Mnemonic, or Memory-Aiding, Stage, in which real objects were used to serve as records or messages between people who were too far apart to communicate by sounds or gestures.

---

[1] Edward Clodd, *The Story of the Alphabet*, page 35. New York: D. Appleton and Company, 1918.

A "quipus," or series of knotted cords, was used extensively by the ancient Peruvians, the Chinese, and even by more recent primitive tribes to commemorate important happenings, to transmit orders in times of emergency, to serve as reckoning devices, and to preserve records of dead tribesmen.

The more elaborate "quipu" consisted of one main cord, to which were attached others of varying sizes and colors, each having its own particular meaning.   The character of the knots tied in any given strand also bore special significance.   For instance, a single knot might mean one thing; a double knot, another; and a triple knot, still another. Thus, a rather involved system was developed which necessitated the appointment of special officers whose duty it was to tie and to interpret the knotted cords.   Wampum-belts of handmade beads or of shells, arranged in meaningful patterns on dried skins of animals or on some other suitable material, served a similar purpose among the Indian tribes of New England, and notched sticks and tally sticks were employed by primitive people in some parts of the world.

The second stage was the Pictorial Era, in which the story or information to be imparted was given by means of pictures of objects. Preserved on the walls of caves and on rock slabs in Europe are crude drawings.   In some places are paintings of animals and human beings which were placed there by the paleolithic cave dwellers some 50,000 years B.C.   Pictures also were inscribed on weapons, on utensils made of bone, metal, and stone, and on other articles of value, for the purpose of identifying them.   Some of these pictures have been interpreted quite readily; others never have been explained.

These early pictographs, which were suggestive in meaning and served as aids to memory, underwent further refinements as the centuries passed.   The next step was a realization of the value of associating various pictographic symbols with objects and ideas.

This led rather logically into the third stage, known as the Ideographic Stage, in which pictures were used to represent ideas rather than mere objects—a discovery that was of momentous importance. However, as a result, the meaning of characters became more obscure, since the pictures suggested, rather than actually depicted, the objects, thus presupposing a knowledge of a fact or an event which the sign recalled.

All available evidence seems to indicate clearly that whenever writing has been developed, its earliest form was ideographic.   By combining these conventionalized pictures, our remote ancestors, as well as primitive people in more recent times, were able to tell stories covering a wide range of activities. The American Indians developed an ingenious system of ideographic writing by combining pictures and symbols to relate stories of battles, to record the deeds of their braves, and to tell of other significant happenings within their tribes. Many interesting stories carved on wood or bark, painted on hides and rocks, and woven into blankets have been discovered and preserved. What are thought to be the oldest specimens of true writing ever to be discovered are on two black stones about four inches square which came from Mesopotamia. Although nobody can say with certainty how old they are, they probably were made about 6,000 B.C.[2]

The most elaborate and best developed early system of picture writing was that of the Egyptians. Known as hieroglyphics, or sacred carvings, it started several thousand years before the birth of Christ. These carvings have been found in greatest abundance on palace walls, tombs, monuments, and temple walls. The earliest of these Egyptian inscriptions on stone yet found is preserved in the Ashmolean Museum of Oxford University. Referred to as the Send inscription, it probably was done about 4,000 B.C.

Finally, the fourth stage—the Phonetic Stage—was reached when the picture became a sign which represented a sound, either for a whole word, for syllables within the word, or for each letter contained in the word. With this development, the first phonetic, or spoken, alphabet was born.

The practice of associating a sound with a sign still is followed today in children's picture books, designed to teach them the letters of the alphabet. They learn, for instance, that "A" is for apple; "B" is for baby; "L" is for lion; and other similar combinations.

Many centuries passed before a means of deciphering early picture writing was discovered and the veil shrouding the historical secrets of many generations of human endeavor was lifted. This key was a slab of black stone, containing identical inscriptions in three different systems of characters—hieroglyphics, demotic Egyptian, and Greek. It was discovered in the year 1799 near the Rosetta mouth of the Nile River by French soldiers as they dug among the ruins of an ancient fort, and it became known as the Rosetta stone.

From it, Jean François Champollion, a French scholar and antiquarian, discovered the key to hieroglyphics, which made it possible for himself and others to interpret these early writings. Later, the Rosetta stone was placed in the British Museum in London.

[2] Douglas C. McMurtrie, *The Book*, page 9. New York: Oxford University Press, 1943.

INTRODUCTION OF WRITING MATERIALS

By about 3,000 B.C., the Babylonians, who inhabited the rich valley between the Tigris and the Euphrates rivers known as the Plain of Babylonia, had invented a system of writing which was called cuneiform writing, a name derived from the Latin words *cuneus,* meaning wedge, and *forma,* shape.

Cuneiform writing consisted of wedge-shaped characters and modified hieroglyphics which were impressed or punched by means of a stylus into lumps of soft clay. These then were hardened by baking and were used in keeping records and carrying on correspondence with the Egyptians.

Eventually, the lumps of clay were replaced by tablets of the same substance, which were marked by means of pointed sticks, tools of stone, bronze, or copper, each bearing a wedge-shaped mark or a modified picture representing a word or syllable. Clay slates or bricks used by school children of Babylonia, great earthenware jars, and libraries consisting of numerous bricks, tablets, and cylinders which belonged to Babylonian kings have been unearthed by excavators and archeologists. From these cuneiform records has come evidence of a civilization antedating the Egyptians; this civilization had been using a crude written language as early as 6,000 B.C.[3]

The development of the language of the Babylonians followed the same pattern as that of the Egyptians in that it went successively through the stages of pictograph, ideogram, and phonogram. Although cuneiform writing never reached the alphabetic stage, in the syllabic phonogram stage it consisted of an unwieldy system of about 500 characters.

As progress continued toward the development of a usable alphabet, the need arose for a medium more suitable than stone and clay tablets for record keeping. The difficulties involved in preparing, assembling, and transporting records of any length are readily apparent, and the limitations placed on the spread of information and its preservation in any large quantities were severe.

The discovery by the Egyptians of papyrus—the first paper—helped to relieve the situation. They found that the pith of a tall reed which grew along the Nile River could be treated, pressed out into sheets, and made into an excellent material for conveying written messages. Since it withstood decay for long periods of time if handled carefully, this

---

[3] Kenneth E. Olson, *Typography and Mechanics of the Newspaper,* page 9. New York: D. Appleton and Company, 1930.

first paper was well adapted to the keeping of important records. Although it would not be regarded as a good substitute for modern paper, it filled a definite need and served for many years.

The oldest papyrus rolls which have been found were taken from mummy cases dating from about 3,500 B.C.[4]

A pointed reed was used as a pen, which was dipped into a writing fluid, the basic ingredients of which were soot, gum, and an acid added to give it bite.

With the discovery of an acceptable paper, a pen, and ink, the stage was set for the development of a more simple alphabet, but it did not arrive simultaneously and full-blown. Long years of experimentation were required for its perfection.

Despite many conflicting theories regarding the origin of the alphabet, there seems to be quite general agreement that it was derived, at least in large part, from the hieroglyphics of the Egyptians. The most recent discoveries indicate that an ancient culture existing between the Phoenicians and the Egyptians on the Sinai Peninsula was responsible for the Semitic symbols which made up the first primitive alphabet that was carried by the currents of migration and trade to the Phoenicians. This Sinaitic origin of the beginning of the Phoenician alphabet, which is regarded as the first to appear, has been quite satisfactorily established. The early Sinai inscriptions date from between 2,000 and 1,500 B.C.

The Phoenicians made use of both hieroglyphics and cuneiform writing, undertaking the task of simplifying existing signs and assigning to each a definite phonetic value. By eliminating many unnecessary pictographs and ideograms, they succeeded in greatly reducing the number of letters in their alphabet, all of which were consonants, that were considered the essential part of a word.

The Greeks borrowed the Phoenician alphabet and remodeled it by adding separate letters to represent vowels and by combining some of the signs used by the Phoenicians to make up an alphabet of their own —one for people living in the eastern part of their country and another for those in the western section. In turn, the Romans adopted the Greek system, and after discarding, adding, and combining certain letters, they finally completed an alphabet with twenty-three letters, in which our J, U, and W were missing. Finally, the Anglo-Saxons took all the Roman letters and added to them the J, U, and W, to complete an alphabet of twenty-six letters such as we have today.

Europe was denied papyrus because of the conquest of Egypt by the

---

[4] McMurtrie, *The Book*, page 13.

Arabs. During the so-called "Dark Ages," which continued almost without interruption from the fifth to the twelfth century, knowledge was practically stamped out by war, suspicion, ignorance, and superstition.

The Greeks and the Romans, who were without this writing material, wrote their messages on tablets covered with wax, and the Romans developed new kinds of writing materials. One, made from the skins of sheep and goats, was known as parchment; another, which was from calf skin, was called vellum. Both were expensive but very durable, and they have remained in use to some extent ever since.

The year A.D. 105 usually is set as the date of the invention of paper,

		EGYPTIAN	PHŒNICIAN	GREEK					LATIN			HEBREW
1	Eagle	🦅	⟨	△	A	A	λ	α	A	A	λαa	א
2	Crane	🐦	𐤁	𐤁	𐌁	B	Β	β	Β	B	Bb	ב
3	Throne	▱	𐤆	𐤂	1	Γ	Γ	ΓΥ	⟨	C	{C GCSS	ג
4	Hand	◠	𐤃	△	△	△	δ	δ	D	D	δδd	ד
5	Mæander	🔲	𐤌	∃	∃	E	Є	ε	Ε	E	ee	ה
6	Cerastes	🐍	𐤅	Y	Y	YF		F	F	F	Ff	ו
7	Duck	🦆	𐤆	𐤆	𐤆	I	Z	ΖC	⫯	Z	z	ז
8	Sieve	◉	𐤇	𐤇	𐤇	H	H	h η	𐌇	H	hh	ח
9	Tongs	⟅	⟆	⊕	⊕	⊙	Θ	θ ϑ	⊗			ט
10	Parallels	\\	𐤉	𐤉	𐤉	I	I	ι	I	I	ij	׳
11	Bowl	◠	𐤊	Y	𐤊	K	K	Kκ	K	K	k	כ
12	Lioness	🐆	𐤋	L	V	∧	λ	λ	L	L	Ll	ל
13	Owl	🦉	𐤌	𐤌	M	M	Μ μ	μ	M	M	m m	מ
14	Water	〰	𐤍	𐤍	M	N	N	μ ν	M	N	n n	נ
15	Chair-back	⊢	⊣	𐤎	𐤎	Ξ	ξ	ξ	⊞	+	x x	ס
16	....			O	o	O	O	o	O			ע
17	Shutter	🎴	𐤐	𐤐	⌐	Γ	π	π ϖ	P	P	p	פ
18	Snake	🐍	𐤑	𐤓	M	M	ϡ		𐤓			צ
19	Angle	△	𐤒	φ	φ	φ			Q	Q	q q	ק
20	Mouth	⟨⟩	𐤓	𐤓	P	P	P	ϱ ρ	ρ	R	Rr	ר
21	Inundated Garden	〰	𐤔	W	⟩	⟨	C	⊂ σ	⟩	S	ſ ſ s	ש
22	Lasso	⟋	𐤕	+	T	T	T	Τ	T	T	τ t	ת
		i	ii	iii	iv	v	vi	vii	viii	ix	x	xi

Figure 1. Chart showing origin of letters in the alphabet. (From *The Story of the Alphabet,* by Edward Clodd, copyright, 1938, by D. Appleton-Century Company, Inc., reproduced by permission of the publishers.)

for in that year Ts'ai Lun, of China, reported his discovery of paper to the Emperor.[5]   Before this time, writing in China was done on bamboo or on pieces of silk, but neither material proved satisfactory.

From China, the use of paper moved gradually westward, reaching Egypt about A.D. 900; Spain, in 1150; Italy, about 1270; and Germany, in 1390.[6]   But paper did not come into common use in Europe until the fourteenth century, when the first paper mill was erected in Germany.   Until that time, vellum and parchment remained the most popular materials.

First Efforts at Bookmaking

The first crude attempts at bookmaking were made by writing on long sheets of papyrus, which were rolled up from each end onto sticks to aid the reader.   These were called scrolls.

The earliest scrolls were written the narrow way of the paper and were unrolled by turning the handles from the top downward.   Later, the writing was done the long way of the sheet and it was divided into pages or columns.   This development was the first step leading to the preparation of books made up of separate pages.

In the first century A.D., the rolled books, or scrolls, of papyrus and parchment were replaced by the codex, or book, consisting of small sheets bound together in much the same way as a present-day volume. Codices came into general use about the fourth Christian century, when jurists decided they were more convenient than the rolls for their law-books.

The first real books were made of vellum or parchment sheets, placed one on top of the other and folded in the middle.   Then the practice was started of stitching these sheets up the back along the fold. Finally, board covers, attached over the first and last pages, were introduced, and the book as we know it today became a reality.

The Christian church, as well as the jurists, helped materially in popularizing the codex, since the old *volumen,* or roll, had become associated with literary works of a pagan culture which the church leaders were anxious to supplant.

The development of books was largely the work of monks of the Christian church in medieval times.   During the Dark Ages, from the fifth to the twelfth century, while the common people were kept in ignorance, and even nobles and kings were hardly able to write, the

---

[5] Thomas Francis Carter, *The Invention of Printing in China,* page 2.   New York: Columbia University Press, 1925.

[6] McMurtrie, *The Book,* page 63.

entire world was dependent upon the work of the monks to keep their records and to preserve valuable learning of the past.   The making of books became almost exclusively a monastic function.   At first, the monks spent most of their time copying the Bible and other religious works, but gradually they began devoting more and more time to the copying of the best ancient classics.

Usually, the monastic scribes did their work in a large room in a monastery known as a "scriptorium," or "writery."   Generally, this was a large room containing benches and desks at which the writing was to be done.   In case more than one copy of a given work was to be made, as many scribes as there were books to be produced would write simultaneously as the words were called out slowly by a reader stationed on a platform in the front of the room.   Professional scribes became highly skilled penmen, and they produced written books in lettering almost as perfect as our best modern printed works.   In fact, the first types to be made were fashioned after the handwriting of the monks.

Bookmakers also became expert in fashioning beautiful covers for their books.   Hand-carved wood, ivory, and plates of silver were used to enhance the product and frequently the covers were studded with gems and precious stones.   Such books were greatly treasured and kept under guard in the monasteries, castles, and homes of the rich.

Many of these early books also were highly illuminated with large colored initials and artistically decorated headbands and borders. Kings and princes often employed scores of scribes and illuminators to copy and prepare books of the highest quality.

These early manuscript books form the very foundation upon which our cultural development is established.   Through the slow-moving pens of the ancient scribes, the works of Plato, Aristotle, Euclid, Virgil, Horace, and many other great men of that early period became a part of our cultural heritage.

Only the wealthy were able to afford the luxury of these early books. The common people did without and consequently were held in ignorance.   However, with the revival of learning following the Dark Ages, this condition commenced to change.   The great masses of the people began to see the advantages of learning as a means of breaking the fetters that had shackled them for so long, and gradually a widespread desire for books arose.

IMAGE PRINTS AND BLOCK BOOKS

To meet this growing need, a method of production was sought which would be faster and cheaper than writing by hand.   Block printing, or xylography, was seized upon as the initial answer, and block books came into being. They were printed from blocks of wood on which the material to be reproduced was engraved in relief by hand. The form then was inked and any desired number of impressions was taken upon sheets of paper.

Books of this kind were printed in the Orient nearly six centuries earlier than in Europe. Printing from seals or stamps, which were inked and pressed against paper to give an impression, was practiced in China as early as the fifth or sixth century of the Christian Era.

First, seals were used for purposes of identification of documents; then came the printing of charms, and finally block printing. The oldest examples of printing from blocks of wood are paper charms, said to have been made in Japan about A.D. 770. Evidence seems to indicate that printing of a similar nature was done in China long before this, but the earliest established date of the beginning in that country is A.D. 868.[7]

The oldest printed book now extant, dated May 11, 868, is the so-called *Diamond Sutra,* one of the most treasured of the Buddhist scriptures, which now is a possession of the British Museum. It consists of a roll about sixteen feet long and about one foot wide, made up of seven sheets of paper pasted end to end, with six sheets of text and another shorter one on which the woodcut appears. It was printed entirely from wood blocks.

In Europe, the earliest form of block printing came in the form of playing cards, which had great influence in awakening a desire for learning. By making use of engraved blocks of wood, these cards could be produced in large quantities, and by the fourteenth century card playing was very popular in many parts of Europe—a condition which the clergy denounced but were unable to abolish.[8] Whether or not this practice was transmitted from China is not definitely known, but it is certain that cards were being used in China as early as A.D. 969, if not earlier.

Following playing cards, the next step toward printing in Europe was the use of engraved wood blocks for the production of pictures of saints. The figures were carved in relief in the wood blocks, then stained or inked so the image could be transferred to paper when rubbed.[9] The resulting prints from these woodcuts were crude but could be used effectively by the clergy in teaching the common people,

---

[7] McMurtrie, *The Book,* page 86.

[8] Theodore L. De Vinne, *The Invention of Printing,* page 100. New York: Francis Hart and Company, 1878.

[9] Olson, *Typography and Mechanics of the Newspaper,* page 15.

Figure 2. Earliest dated woodcut, the *St. Christopher*, of 1423. (From *The Book* by Douglas C. McMurtrie. Copyright 1943 by Douglas C. McMurtrie. Used by permission of Oxford University Press.)

since they were familiar with the pictures of saints and Biblical characters shown in stained glass windows, paintings, sculptures, and carvings within the churches.

At the start, pictures were printed on single sheets, with no lines of explanation. Later, carved words were added to help explain the story or to describe the character depicted. And finally, the practice of collecting these single sheets for binding into book form was begun. One of the best-known of these block books was the *Biblia Pauperum,* which appeared about the year 1425. Consisting of forty-two pages printed on rough paper in brown ink, with all explanations in Latin, this book dealt exclusively with Biblical history. The second edition was enlarged to seventy pages, and eventually it went through eleven printings.

The next development was that of combining manuscript pages of text, written by copyists, with the image prints used for illustrations. Although it apparently was considered too expensive to engrave large amounts of the text on the wood blocks, one famous book, known as the *Donatus,* an abridgment of a Latin grammar, containing no pictures, was done in this manner. This book of thirty-four pages was used extensively, since it served as a useful primer in preparatory schools of the time. More than fifty editions are said to have been printed.[10]

Despite the fact that block books were poor examples of printing, they became very popular during the period from 1440 to 1470 and had wide circulation among the common people, who were hungry for any kind of learning. However, the educated classes regarded these block books with disdain and gave no encouragement to their production.

INVENTION OF MOVABLE TYPE

The invention of the wood block for printing was a big step forward, since it made possible the production of books in large quantities at a price within the reach of an ever-increasing number of people. The result was a far-reaching intellectual awakening which the ruling classes were unable to forestall.

Fear and superstition gradually were replaced by hope and belief in a future that held more promise for even the lowliest. Civilization was on its march upward, and, as time passed, new and better ways of preserving records and spreading information were demanded.

Writing by hand and the preparation of wood blocks were found to be too slow and costly. This realization led to a search for ways and

---

[10] Olson, *Typography and Mechanics of the Newspaper,* page 16.

means of overcoming such handicaps. Throughout Europe, men interested in the art of printing and bookmaking began experimentation
which resulted in a satisfactory answer to the problem—the invention
of movable type.

However, more than four hundred years before the first printing of
this kind was done in Europe, the Chinese had made the discovery.
The inventor was Pi Sheng, who made his types from baked clay; then
the Chinese tried types of tin, and later of wood, which first were engraved in a block and afterward sawed apart and arranged in a case.
But these types were *word* types, not *letter* types, and apparently
proved unsatisfactory, as the practice fell into disuse. In Korea,
also, a half century before the invention in Europe, books were printed
from cast metal type, but here, again, it was not made up of single letters, and the eventual refinement was left for the printers in Europe.

Although historians have made a diligent search for the answer, no
one can say with definiteness what man was responsible for the invention of printing from movable type as we know it today. Like other
great inventions, it evolved as a result of the cumulative efforts of
several men, and because conclusive evidence is lacking, only circum-
stantial evidence can be relied upon to furnish a basis for determining
the true claimant of the distinction. This condition exists because of
the failure of the earliest printers to date their works and to give the
name of publishers.

The earliest examples of printing in Germany are in the form of fragments, containing no identification of the printers, places, or dates of
publication. The most primitive of these is a scrap of paper on which
is printed a sibylline poem in German. This is generally referred to
as the *Fragment of the World Judgment,* since it deals with the Last
Judgment.

The first *dated* piece of printing is known to have been produced in
1454, when four different issues of a papal indulgence were issued in
printed form, but the name of the printer who did the work still is
shrouded in mystery.[11]

Since the controversy began, almost every country in Europe has
laid claim to the invention of printing, but in almost every case, the
inspiration has been one of national pride rather than one based on
sound proof. Outstanding among these is the claim of Lourens Jans-
zoon Coster of Haarlem in the Netherlands, who is said to have begun
to print with movable types at Haarlem around the year 1430. However, the work supposedly that of Coster consists only of fragments,

---

[11] McMurtrie, *The Book,* page 147.

none of which bears the name of the printer, the date, or the place in which it was done.

The greatest weight of evidence points to Johann (John) Gutenberg as the inventor of movable types of metal cast in matrices, which constitute the important foundation of printing as we know it today. He is credited with printing what is regarded as the world's first printed book, the Gutenberg Bible, also known as the 42-Line Bible or Mazarin Bible, which was completed in the year 1456, or earlier, in the city of Mainz, Germany. Furthermore, the claim that Gutenberg also was responsible for the printing of books of which only fragments exist to-day—including the *Fragment of the World Judgment*—seems to be well-founded.

THE GUTENBERG BIBLE

The Gutenberg Bible was a magnificent book, printed in Latin from text type resembling the handwriting of the monks. It contained 1,300 pages, 12 x 17 inches in size, and the type for each page was set in two columns, each 42 lines in depth, which led to its being referred to as the 42-Line Bible. It gets the name Mazarin Bible from the fact that the first copy was discovered in Paris in the library of a French cardinal named Mazarin.

Some of the copies were printed on vellum; others were on paper. It is believed that the paper copies are the earliest. A brilliant black ink, which has retained its color through the years, was used, and the hand-made, illuminated letters of great beauty were furnished by expert rubricators.

The date of the completion of the book was determined by a notation at the end of two copies which said that the rubrication was completed on August 14, 1456. However, the printing, which must have required several years, undoubtedly was finished before that date. How much sooner, is a matter of conjecture.

Gutenberg became interested in printing long before his famous Bible was published, and he spent several years experimenting with the materials he eventually used in its production. His first type was made of wood, each letter being cut out separately and assembled by hand into lines which were held together by strings run through holes in the bottom of the type. Next he invented a frame to hold the lines firmly in place.

The press on which the printing was done resembled a wine press, but Gutenberg found that the wood type had a tendency to break when pressure was applied, and that the letters wore down. So he then

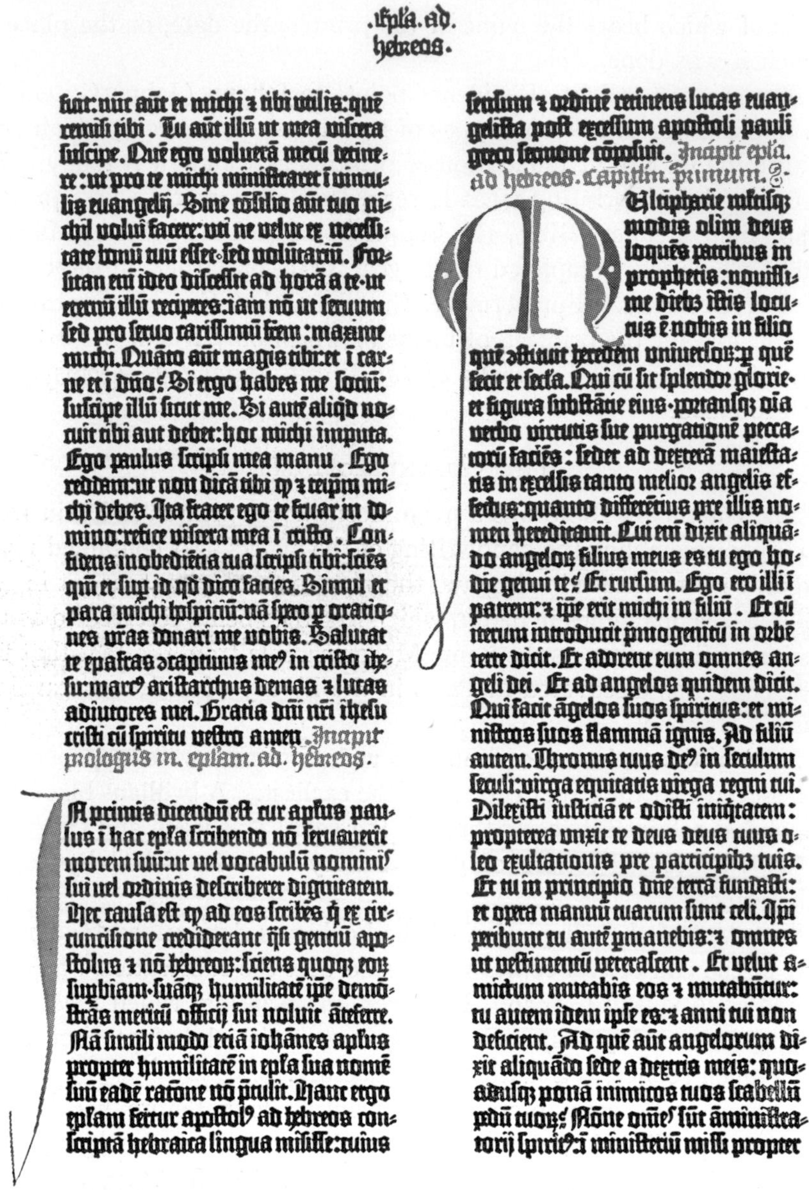

Figure 3. Page from the Gutenberg Bible of 42 lines. (From *Pages from the Gutenberg Bible of 42 Lines*. Reproduced by courtesy of The H. W. Wilson Company.)

tried cutting type out of metal. This experiment finally resulted in his invention of a brass mold, which made it possible for him to produce individual letters much faster and in far greater quantities than had been possible by the earlier method.

The metal he used—an alloy of lead, tin, and antimony—was basically the same as that used in present-day types. Likewise, the ink which he manufactured out of lampblack and oil contained the same basic elements as the present-day black printing inks. Thus, along with the invention of movable type, Gutenberg developed a suitable press and printing ink, all of which contributed to the success of the first printed book.

Since none of Gutenberg's works bore his name or gave any information about his activities, historians have had to search elsewhere for their facts concerning him. Much of this data has been discovered in public records, the most valuable of which dealt with lawsuits involving the collection of debts incurred by Gutenberg to finance his ventures in printing. These documents indicate that Gutenberg borrowed substantial sums of money from Johann Fust, who sued him when he was unable to repay the loans when they came due. As a result, Gutenberg was forced to turn over to Fust most of his printing equipment. Fust used this equipment in setting up an establishment of his own in partnership with Peter Schoeffer, his son-in-law, a former employee of Gutenberg.

Fust and Schoeffer became the outstanding printers of Mainz, and many bibliographers believe they were the men who either wholly produced or at least brought to completion the famous 42-Line Bible, rather than Gutenberg. During their partnership, which lasted from 1455 until 1466, Fust and Schoeffer produced more than a hundred books.[12] The most famous of these was the first edition of their Psalter, which appeared in 1457. This book was the first ever to be dated and signed, and it also was the first to be printed in colors.

From this time forward, the practice of identifying the printer of a book and its place and date of issue was followed, and, as a result, printing emerged from anonymity.

After turning over his equipment to Fust, Gutenberg again succeeded in borrowing more money and established another press, where he printed fifty or more books and pamphlets before his death in February, 1468. Although he had played a leading part in laying the foundations of an art which revolutionized the world, Gutenberg died hopelessly in debt and almost friendless.

---

[12] Olson, *Typography and Mechanics of the Newspaper,* page 24.

THE SPREAD OF PRINTING IN EUROPE

Gutenberg, Fust, and Schoeffer kept their activities secret and guarded their work with great care, since the invention could not be patented. Nevertheless, news of it leaked out.

In the meantime, other rival printing houses were established in Germany. John Mentelin, in partnership with Adolph Rusch, set up an office in Strasbourg, and Ulrich Zell began one in Cologne, an important educational center. Both of these men had worked with Gutenberg and were experienced craftsmen.

When Mainz was sacked in 1462 by Adolphus Nassau, he banished the printing trade and scattered the workmen. Some of these fugitive printers, who had learned the art under Gutenberg and Schoeffer, established presses of their own elsewhere, and the new art spread rapidly into several European countries. Two of these printers, Conrad Sweynheym, of Mainz, and Arnold Pannartz, of Prague, crossed the Alps into Italy and set up a press in Subiaco in 1464, the first to be established outside Germany.[13]

They first issued a *Donatus,* or Latin grammar, which was followed by four other volumes. They then moved their press to Rome, where they continued in partnership until the end of 1473. Altogether, they produced fifty-two different works and did much to popularize printed books in Italy and throughout the world.

The next country in modern Europe to have printing was Switzerland, where its first *dated* book was produced in Basel in the year 1474 by Berthold Ruppel. Although conclusive proof is lacking, the first printing office is believed to have opened in Basel, which at that time still was a part of Germany, about the year 1467.[14]

The new art reached France in 1470, when a press was set up in Paris through the efforts of Johann Heynlin, a rector and librarian of the Sorbonne in that city, and Guillaume Fichet, professor of philosophy and rhetoric. They induced three German printers to do the work, which consisted largely of the production of books for the use of scholars.[15]

In Holland, the first dated and signed Dutch books were produced by Geradus Leempt and Nicholaus Ketalaer at Utrecht in 1473.[16] Printing also was being done in the area comprising present-day Bel-

---

[13] Olson, *Typography and Mechanics of the Newspaper,* page 27.
[14] McMurtrie, *The Book,* page 188.
[15] McMurtrie, *The Book,* page 190.
[16] Olson, *Typography and Mechanics of the Newspaper,* page 33.

gium, where the first press was established in the town of Alost during this same year by Johann of Paderborn, also known as John of Westphalia..

In this region also, at Bruges, the first book ever to be printed in the English language was produced by William Caxton, a wealthy merchant, and Colard Mansion, a young printer, whom he enlisted as an associate. In 1469, Caxton gave up the management of a great trading company in Bruges to become secretary and financial adviser for the Duchess of Burgundy so he could devote more time to translating and printing literary works. His first book—a landmark among English-speaking peoples of the world—was a translation of Le Fevre's *Recueil des Histoires de Troies*. It was printed about 1475.[17]

The earliest product of the Spanish press is believed to have come in the form of an indulgence, in the Spanish language, which was issued by Cardinal Rodrigo Borgio under a papal bull which bears the date of March 5, 1473. The name of the printer and the place of publication are not known. For the most part, the first printers in Spain and Portugal were wandering Germans, who took the knowledge of the new art to the Iberian Peninsula, as they did to many other parts of Europe.[18]

The last important European country to establish printing was England, where the first press was set up near Westminster Abbey in the outskirts of London in 1476 by William Caxton, who brought his equipment to his homeland from Bruges, where he and Mansion had produced the *Histories of Troy* the year before.,

Encouraged by the success of his first venture, Caxton set out to furnish his people with books in the English language, presenting the best literature of the period. Altogether, he produced one hundred books, many of which were his own translations. Among the best-known books to come from his press were the works of Chaucer, including the famous *Canterbury Tales,* a volume of 374 pages, which appeared in 1478, Malory's *Morte d'Arthur*, the *Chronicles of England, The Golden Legend,* and *Myrrour of the World*. The last of these, which appeared in 1481, was the first of Caxton's books to contain woodcut illustrations. The pictures apparently met with considerable approval, since *The Golden Legend,* printed in 1483, contained seventy.[19]

William Caxton was not a fine printer. He was more interested in

---

[17] Olson, *Typography and Mechanics of the Newspaper*, page 35.

[18] Daniel Berkeley Updike, *Printing Types: Their History, Forms, and Use*, Vol. I, page 99. Cambridge: Harvard University Press, 1927.

[19] Olson, *Typography and Mechanics of the Newspaper*, page 35.

the content of books and their wide distribution than in artistic typography and technical perfection.   However, his contribution to English literature and to the enlightenment of the masses of the people was of tremendous importance.   When Caxton died in 1491, his business came

Figure 4.   The Caxton portrait invented by Bagford.   (From *Caxton, Mirrour of Fifteenth-Century Letters,* by Nellie Slayton Aurner.   London: Philip Allan & Co., Ltd.)

into the hands of his chief workman, Wynkyn de Worde, who continued to print in the same plant with the types that Caxton had been using.[20]

During the fifteenth century, printing also was started in several of the smaller countries in Europe, and by the end of the century scores of books had been produced. Before the year 1500, 2,835 books had been published in Venice, 925 in Rome, 751 in Paris, 526 in Strasbourg, 530 in Cologne, and 130 in London.[21] Most of them averaged 300 copies an edition. Thus, less than fifty years after printing first took root in Germany, it grew into a flourishing industry, and its importance to mankind increased as the years passed.

Several European families of printers carried on the traditions of their founders and became famous. Outstanding among them was the family of Estienne—three generations of fathers and sons who printed in Paris and Geneva from 1502 to 1664—and the Didots, who distinguished themselves in France during the eighteenth century. Colard Mansion, the Plantins, and the House of Elzevir gained renown in the Low Countries.[22]

BEGINNING OF PRINTING IN AMERICA

Less than a century after the invention of printing, the first printing press to reach America was established in Mexico City in 1539, or perhaps earlier. Juan Pablos is credited as America's first printer. He was sent to Mexico City by Juan Cromberger, the leading printer of Seville, Spain, to open a branch of his main office. The first work of his press is said to have been the printing of cartillas, or primers, for the education of children.

The earliest printed book was the *Breve y mas compendiosa doctrina christiana,* which appeared in 1539. Although its authenticity has been established, no copies are known to exist today. As in the case of Gutenberg in Europe, the claim that Juan Pablos was the first printer in the New World has been disputed, but no clear record to the contrary has been established.

In 1638—only eighteen years after the landing of the Pilgrims on Plymouth Rock—the first printing press arrived in the colonies of North America. Reverend Jose Glover, of Sutton in Surrey, England, may be regarded properly as the father of printing in the United States,

---

[20] Henry R. Plomer, *A Short History of English Printing,* page 20. London: Kegan Paul, Trench, Trubner, and Company, Limited, 1900.

[21] Olson, *Typography and Mechanics of the Newspaper,* page 27.

[22] Olson, *Typography and Mechanics of the Newspaper,* page 33.

because it was through his efforts that the first press was established.[23]
Glover was a clergyman who came to this country after being suspended from his pastorate because of nonconformity with the principles
of the Church of England.

In New England, he became interested in a proposal to found an
educational institution to be known as Harvard Academy, and he returned to England for the purpose of raising funds for the enterprise.
Included in the plans was a decision to start a printing plant as a part
of the venture, and Glover set about purchasing the necessary type and
equipment.

To manage the press, he engaged Stephen Day (or Daye), a lock-
smith, who was an able mechanic.   Day brought with him his two sons,
and it is probable that the younger Day, Matthew, is the one who actually printed the first works to be produced by the Cambridge Press.[24]

Glover and Day, with their families, began the voyage in the mid-
summer of 1638, but Jose Glover did not live to see the new press
established; he died on the trip over.   However, Day went ahead with
the plans after he reached New England.

The new press was located in Cambridge, Massachusetts, in 1639,
and during this year the *Freeman's Oath*—the first piece of printing to
be done in what is now the United States—was published.   This was
followed in the same year by *An Almanack,* and in 1640 the first real
book, generally referred to as the *Bay Psalm Book,* made its appearance.

The widow of Jose Glover married Rev. Henry Dunster, president
of Harvard College, in 1641.   Dunster thereafter became responsible
to the Glover heirs for the management of the property.[25]

Early records of this first press in the colonies seem to indicate
clearly that Matthew Day, one of Stephen Day's sons, was this country's first printer, rather than the father, who was responsible for the
establishment and management of the concern until his death but was
not capable of doing the actual printing.

When Matthew Day died in May, 1649, Samuel Green was chosen to
succeed him.   He published several books, among which was the first
Bible to be printed in America.

---

[23] Isaiah Thomas, *History of Printing in America,* Vol. I, page 222.   Worcester:
Press of Isaiah Thomas, June, 1810.

[24] George Parker Winship, *The Cambridge Press, 1638-1692,* page 13.   Philadelphia: University of Pennsylvania Press, 1945.

[25] John Clyde Oswald, *A History of Printing,* page 47.   New York: D. Appleton
and Company, 1928.

In 1676, the second press was set up in Boston by John Foster, under license from Harvard, but this soon came under the control of Bartholomew Green, a son of Samuel. The first newspaper to appear in America, *Publick Occurrences Both Foreign and Domestick,* was printed on September 25, 1690, in Boston by Benjamin Harris. However, it was

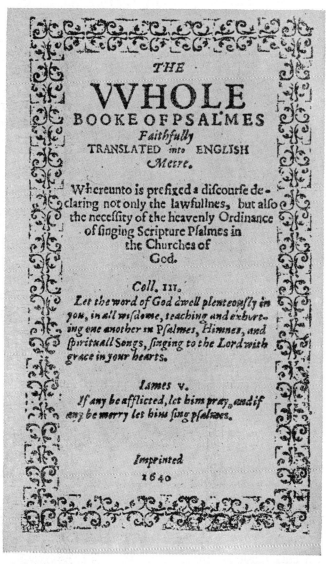

Figure 5. Page of first book printed in colonial America. (From *Printing in the Americas,* by John Clyde Oswald. New York: The Gregg Publishing Company, 1937. Reproduced by courtesy of the publishers.)

discontinued after only one issue by order of the Governor and Council.

Fourteen years later, John Campbell established the Boston *News-Letter* on April 24, 1704. This newspaper, the first to meet with success in this country and the second to be published in the colonies, continued under the management of Campbell until 1722, when it was turned over to the printer, Bartholomew Green. When Green died, the paper was inherited by his son-in-law, John Draper, also a printer, who served as publisher until his death in 1762; then his son, Richard, became the owner.

The second colony to have a press was Virginia, where printing was started by William Nuthead in 1682. Three years later, in 1685, a press was begun in Philadelphia by William Bradford, who later introduced the first newspaper in New York, the *New York Gazette*, which he continued for nineteen years.[26]

In most cases, early colonial newspapers were edited and published by men who knew the printing trade and thus were able to keep labor costs at a minimum. Entire families often were engaged in the work, and newspaper and printing establishments in some cases continued under family management for several generations. Some of the most famous were the Greens, the Bradfords, the Franklins, and the Sowers —all well known for their printing activities during this period.

One of the truly outstanding figures in the history of printing during colonial times was Benjamin Franklin, who began his career as an apprentice in the shop of his brother, James, publisher of the first issue of the *New England Courant*, which was started on August 17, 1721. However, the two brothers did not get along well together, and Benjamin left. He later established a printing office in partnership with Hugh Meredith, who withdrew from the firm when it was faced with financial difficulties. Under the management of Franklin, the business survived and prospered.

One of his most important undertakings was the *Pennsylvania Gazette*, for which he did some brilliant writing. Another was his *Poor Richard's Almanac*, well known to all students of early American literature.

Like many other colonial printers, Benjamin Franklin made type molds and cast his own lead type. He also manufactured his printing ink and contrived a copperplate press to print paper money, ornamented with cuts made by himself.

Another famous colonial printer was Isaiah Thomas, who in 1770, at the age of twenty-one years, founded the *Massachusetts Spy*, a news-

---

[26] Oswald, *A History of Printing*, page 106.

paper devoted to the cause of the colonial patriots. He also is noted for writing and publishing a book entitled *History of Printing in America,* the first general work on early printers and printing in the United States.

DEVELOPMENT OF PRINTING IN THE UNITED STATES

Printing did not experience rapid expansion in the colonies. Difficulties involved in securing type, paper, and ink were severe, and subscription lists were small. Furthermore, major attention naturally was given by these early settlers to the serious business of establishing homes in a strange, new land.

Events leading up to the Revolutionary War did much to change the situation. Increasing political agitation created a need for better media of expression and resulted in the founding of several newspapers, which played leading roles in molding public opinion in America favorable to the break with England. By April, 1775, thirty-seven newspapers were being printed in the colonies.[27]

After the war, continued political dissension added new impetus to the trend, and when the pioneers began their march westward in search of new land, they took with them their printing presses. By 1814, presses had been established as far west as Illinois, Indiana, and Michigan, and by 1929 a total of 14,942 newspapers were being printed in this country.

During the nineteenth century, the work of Theodore L. De Vinne, who printed *Century Magazine* in his printing establishment in New York City, was of special significance in this country. De Vinne was the first to use surfaced paper for magazine work and fine bookwork, and his experiments led to great improvement in the reproduction of illustrations. He also helped to design a type known as Century Expanded, which was used on *Century Magazine* for many years and found its way into a large number of printing plants throughout the country. In addition, De Vinne was the author of several books on printing, including *The Invention of Printing Types* and *Plain Printing Types,* both important contributions to literature on the subject.

Another American who became famous as a printer and type designer was the late Frederic W. Goudy. He was a native of Bloomington, Illinois, where he was graduated from high school in 1883. His occupational career began as an accountant, but later he served as an apprentice printer in small-town shops in the Middle West. In 1895, he became a partner of C. Lauren Hooper in the operation of the Came-

---

[27] Oswald, *A History of Printing,* page 228.

lot Press in Chicago. While there he developed his first type face, Camelot, which he offered to sell for $5.00 to the Dickinson Type Foundry in Boston. This firm paid him twice that amount, and by their acceptance, they launched America's foremost type designer on a notable career.

In 1903, he designed an alphabet which was used widely by a leading national advertiser, and with the proceeds he bought a small hand press and type to establish his Village Press at Park Ridge, Illinois.

Before his death on May 11, 1947, at the age of 82, Goudy had designed more than 100 type faces, the better known of which are Kennerly, Forum Title, Goudy, Goudy Old Style, Deepdene, and Garamond. Stressing beauty and simplicity of design in printing, he won world-wide fame as one of the greatest typographic artisans of all time.

Figure 6. Frederic W. Goudy, wearing doctor's robes when granted honorary degree by a university in this country. (Courtesy of Lanston Monotype Machine Company.)

In recognition of his valuable contributions to the graphic arts in America, he was awarded the gold medals of the American Institute of Architects, the Architectural League of New York, and The American Institute of Graphic Arts, and he had many other honors bestowed upon him by other groups.

He was the author of several books, including *The Alphabet, Elements of Lettering, Capitals from the Trajan Column at Rome,* and *Typologia.* A collection of typographical material and works by Frederic W. Goudy now is on permanent display at the Library of Congress.

R. Hunter Middleton, of the Ludlow Typograph Company, and W. A. Dwiggins, for Mergenthaler Linotype Company, also have made important contributions in the field of type design.

Since the beginning of the twentieth century, many notable private presses have been established in the United States, and the fine printing produced by them has been a source of inspiration and benefit to members of the graphic arts.

Outstanding among these are The Village Press, located at Marlborough-on-Hudson, New York, which was founded by Frederic W. Goudy in 1903; the press, At the Sign of the Charobates, conducted by Carl Purington Rollins, of New Haven; the Overbrook Press, maintained by Frank Altschul and operated by Margaret Evans, at Stamford, Connecticut; Hawthorn House, the imprint of Edmund B. Thompson, of Windham, Connecticut; and the Peter Pauper Press and the Black Cat Press, both of Chicago, which have grown into printing and publishing enterprises but still maintain much of the private press tradition.[28]

This country also has produced several distinguished masters of typography, whose work has received wide acclaim. One of the most widely known is Bruce Rogers, who did his first noteworthy work at the Riverside Press, in Cambridge, Massachusetts. An artist of ability, Rogers draws his own decorations, designs and casts his type, creates typographical arrangements with great skill, and plans the kinds of bindings to be employed.

Another was the late Daniel Berkeley Updike, of the Merrymount Press, in Boston, who not only won fame as a designer of fine books, but also developed a successful, high-quality printing office. Unlike Rogers, Updike relied almost exclusively on type alone to accomplish his most effective work. His book, *Printing Types: Their History, Forms, and Use* (in two volumes), is of great value in the field of printing.

Other outstanding figures in the American movement toward betterment of the graphic arts are Dr. John Henry Nash, John Clyde Oswald, W. A. Dwiggins, Bruce McCallister, J. L. Frazier, Frank McCaffrey, Edwin and Robert Grabhorn,[29] and the late Douglas C. McMurtrie, who wrote numerous books on the history of printing. Many others are doing work of great value in the graphic arts.

By 1945, a total of 11,877 newspapers and 5,880 periodicals were being published in the United States,[30] and many book publishing houses and commercial printing plants added to the tremendous volume of printing. The Government Printing Office alone does an annual business far in excess of the combined output of early colonial printers.

At a meeting held by the Advertising Club of New York in 1938, Augustus E. Giegengack, Public Printer of the United States, drew

---

[28] McMurtrie, *The Book*, page 480.
[29] McMurtrie, *The Book*, page 480.
[30] *N. W. Ayer & Son's Directory of Newspapers and Periodicals*, page 111. Philadelphia: N. W. Ayer & Son, Inc., 1945.

some comparisons between the past and the present in the printing industry. He said:

If Benjamin Franklin could step into the Government Printing Office today, he would see a plant occupying thirty-five acres of floor space. Busy in the different sections would be a working force of 6,000 employees, or almost exactly the population of Boston at the time of Franklin's birth. . . .

This master of hand composition would see 406 machines setting and casting type faster than the eye can follow, and would doubtless recall that he once worked all night resetting a small pied page. . . .

He would see presses ranging from small platens to huge rotary web presses, which are a maze of wheels and rollers; 187 presses in all. The total number of chargeable impressions from all these presses in one year amounted to four billion. . . .

Of ordinary postal cards we print five million each day, or two and a half billion a year. . . . These cards represent a great many pennies—and Franklin tells us what to do with pennies.[31]

Today newspaper printing and publishing ranks as the ninth leading industry in the United States, with an annual volume of business of almost a billion dollars.[32]   In addition, commercial printing products exceed one-half billion.

John Gutenberg must have envisioned some changes in Europe as a result of his invention of movable type, but it is unlikely that he could foresee, even in his most fantastic dreams, the tremendous impact his work was to have upon the world at large.

NEED FOR HISTORICAL STUDY

The satisfaction and pride which a person takes in his chosen field of endeavor are among the first requisites of success in any profession. Consequently, anyone planning to enter journalism or related fields in the graphic arts, as well as those now engaged in such work, should make a careful study of the history of printing.   This "art preservative of all arts" has a glorious past, filled with a wealth of information that not only commands respect and admiration, but also helps to guide the efforts of those interested in its advancement and their own welfare.

In addition to a good historical background, an understanding of the tools and materials which are used in the production of newspapers and other printed material is of primary importance.   Even the indi-

---

[31] Augustus E. Giegengack, "The Amazing Benjamin Franklin," *Who's Who in the Composing Room*, February, 1938 (Supplement).

[32] *The World Almanac*, 1945.

vidual who plans to devote himself to writing soon finds that a knowledge of types and the technical aspects of printing is essential. Since types are basic to all printing, they are the logical starting point for a study of typography.

II

Printing Types: Their Structure, Design, and Classification

FUNDAMENTALLY, PRINTING TYPES OF TODAY are very similar to the first ones ever cast by John Gutenberg and his contemporaries in Germany and the Low Countries five centuries ago. They are made by the same basic method. Letters are cast by forcing hot metal into molds or matrices containing imprints of the characters desired. In the beginning these molds were made of clay or sand; later, metal matrices were employed, which were formed by impressing the form of the letter into a brass blank by means of a hard steel punch that was cut by hand. Then, in 1884, Lynn Benton, of Milwaukee, invented a punch-cutting machine which completely displaced the earlier methods and led to the development of the Linotype and other type-casting machines. However, all early types were cast by hand, and even down to the first part of the nineteenth century, hand type-molds were in use.

Today printing types are made almost exclusively by machines. Modern type-casting machines are capable of infinitely greater production, and the possibilities of imperfections are minimized.

The metal used in the present-day printing types is practically the same as that from which Gutenberg's type was cast. It is an alloy of lead, tin, and antimony that may vary in proportions according to the size of the type being produced or the purpose for which it is made.[1]

Development of a metal suitable for printing types that had to be pressed against soft paper with great pressure in order to get a good impression was no simple matter. First of all, a metal was sought that would fill the mold perfectly and would not shrink appreciably when cooled. Furthermore, it had to be fusible at a low temperature, dura-

---

[1] Kenneth E. Olson, *Typography and Mechanics of the Newspaper*, page 49. New York: D. Appleton and Company, 1930.

ble, and hard, but at the same time soft enough so that the type would not pierce the paper when printed.

PARTS OF A PIECE OF TYPE

A piece of type consists of a rectangular block, usually of metal, which has cast in relief on its surface the letter to be produced.   Since the character is transferred to paper or to some other surface, it is made in reverse so that it will not print backwards.   This is why in reading type it is necessary to view it with the bottom of the letter facing away—or "upside down."

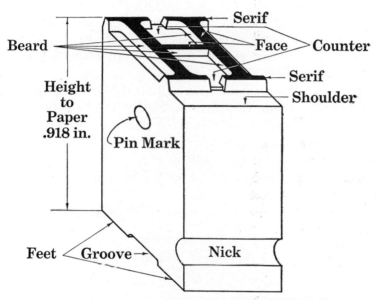

Figure 7.   Drawing of a piece of type.   (Courtesy of American Type Founders Sales Corporation.)

The various parts of a piece of type are shown in Figure 7.   The *body*, or shank, is the main part of the piece of type, which supports the face and extends from the shoulder to the extreme bottom of the feet.   The term "body" also is used sometimes to denote the size or thickness of spacing material and borders on which varying designs have been cast.

The *feet* are the projections at the bottom on which the type stands. They are separated by the *groove*, or open space in between them.

The *nick* is a rounded-out impression on that side of the body which runs up to the bottom of the character to be printed.   The number of nicks and their placement on the body vary according to the kind and size of type, and they serve as an aid to the printer in distinguishing the different faces produced by a given foundry.   Type of a given size and kind will have the same nick, or combination of nicks, and these will not be the same as those found on another.   Nicks also enable the printer to tell which side should be placed facing away from him when he is setting type.

On one side of the body is a small, circular depression known as the *pinmark,* which is made by a pin used to hold the mold together when the type is cast.   Some types do not have this mark.

The upper part of the body on which the face rests is known as the *shoulder.*   The *face* itself is the flat surface at the top which consists of the letter to be printed.   It is made up of *light elements,* or the fine strokes of a letter; *heavy elements,* or the heavier strokes; and *serifs,* the cross-lines at the end of elements which are added to give refinement or individuality to many type faces.

In some types, the serifs are thin and straight; in others, they are bold and blunt.   Again, they may be curved and heavily bracketed. In fact, the nature of the serifs, in those types which carry them, has much to do with establishing tone or feeling, and they are a great aid in helping to distinguish one type from another.

The face is supported by the *neck,* or *beard,* sloping from the outside edge of the face down to the shoulder.

Depressions, or hollow areas, between elements of the letter are called *counters.*

EARLY TYPE FOUNDERS

John Gutenberg and other early printers in Europe cut their own punches, made their matrices, and poured molten metal into the molds to cast the types which they used for printing.   This practice continued until about the middle of the sixteenth century, when type founding was started as a separate branch of the graphic arts.

One of the earliest and most famous type founders was Claude Garamond, who established his type foundry as an independent enterprise in France between 1536 and 1540.   The cutting of his first type was ordered by the king, Francis I, for use in the printing of Greek classics. Later, Garamond produced Italic and Roman types which were sold and imitated by many printers in France, England, and America.[2] The type face which bears his name, Garamond, still is regarded by many experts as one of the most beautiful ever designed.

---

[2] Olson, *Typography and Mechanics of the Newspaper,* page 31.

William Caslon was England's first public type founder to gain last-ing fame and wealth.   The types which Caslon designed met with im-mediate favor throughout Europe and were the most popular among early colonial printers.   Caslon also designed and produced many ar-tistic ornaments, or "flowers," which sprang from the design of the type itself, and when used with borders resulted in pages of great beauty and delicacy.

John Baskerville was another great English type founder of the eighteenth century whose type was a departure from the Oldstyle Ro-mans which had come into use largely through the efforts of Caslon and Garamond.   Baskerville types were more geometric in design, with less contrast between light and heavy elements and with serifs that were more pointed.   His types were the first modern, or near-modern, faces to be produced, and they served as an inspiration for the types made by Giambattista Bodoni, of Parma, Italy, which will be discussed later in this chapter.

Another English type designer and printer of note was William Mor-ris, who in the 1890's cut one type face resembling the first Roman, which he called Golden, and others he named Troy and Chaucer.[3] However, his main interest was in the production of books of artistic design, and his fame is based more on the fine printing which came from his Kelmscott Press than on the types he made.

DEVELOPING THE POINT SYSTEM

After the establishment of type founding as a separate branch of the printing industry, printers began buying some of their types from the type founders.   However, in the beginning, each type founder cast types according to his own measurements, mainly to guard against the possibilities of losing customers to another firm in an effort to protect his own business.   As a result, printers found it extremely difficult to use satisfactorily together the types of their own casting and those purchased from foundries.   Journeymen printers often were forced to use cardboard and wood strips in order to make the various types fit properly into a form.   Results frequently were not good.

These difficulties were overcome largely when a French printer by the name of Fournier in 1737 devised a plan for making all types a standard size.[4] His scheme of measurement became known as the point system, since it was based on the smallest unit, which was referred

---

[3] Daniel Berkeley Updike, *Printing Types: Their History, Forms, and Use*, page 207.   Cambridge: Harvard University Press, 1927.

[4] Olson, *Typography and Mechanics of the Newspaper*, page 59.

to as a *point*.   Thereafter, all type founders in France were required by law to cast their types according to the Fournier system.

The Didot family of printers in France later modified the Fournier point so it would conform with the French inch, and it still is being followed in European countries.   This system eventually was adopted by printers and type founders in England, and it came into use in this country in 1887.   Known here as the American Point System, it displaced all other schemes of measurement for printers and brought about much-needed uniformity.

The smallest unit in this system is the point, which is about 1/72 of an inch in length—0.01384 of an inch, to be exact.   Measurements in the point system used throughout this country, for all practical purposes, are stated as follow:

> 72 points equal 1 inch
> 6 picas equal 1 inch
> 12 points equal 1 pica
> 6 points equal 1 nonpareil
> 72 picas equal 1 foot

All type produced in the United States, Canada, England, and most of the South American countries is cast to the uniform height of 0.918 of an inch.   However, many different heights are in use in Europe, and much confusion still exists there and in Russia as a result.   Nineteen countries, including the United States, today are using type cast to the standard height of 0.918, but there still is considerable lack of uniformity.

The ruler used by the printer for measuring purposes is known as the *line-gauge*.

Type sizes are expressed in terms of points, the measurement being taken across the body of the piece of type from the edge of the shoulder at the top of the letter to the extreme bottom edge.   Thus, a type which measures 36 points (or $\frac{1}{2}$ inch) from the top of the body to the bottom would be designated as 36-point type.

All letters and other characters in the alphabet of a given size, or font, of foundry type are cast on the same size body, but every letter does not extend from the top of the shoulder to the bottom because of variations in shapes of letters.   For instance, the letter "e" takes up only a portion of the body size; the letter "l" extends to the top of the shoulder in some type designs, but it requires no space on the bottom part of the shoulder; and the letter "y" generally runs almost to the bottom.   That portion of the letter which extends above such small letters as the "e," "a," and "o," is known as the *ascender;* that which extends below is called the *descender.*

In deciding upon the size of a given type that already has been printed, the measurement should be taken from the top of the highest ascender to the bottom of the lowest descender.   If no descenders or ascenders appear in the printed line, allowance must be made for them just the same.   A common error in determining the size of type that has been used in printing a line of all-capital letters is that of measuring the face itself, without taking into consideration the additional space occupied by the shoulder at the bottom of the pieces of type from which the line was printed.

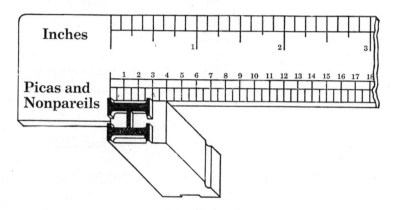

Figure 8.   Section of a line gauge measuring a piece of type.
(Courtesy of American Type Founders Sales Corporation.)

The length of lines is measured in picas by the printer, rather than in inches.   For instance, a line that is two inches long would be twelve picas long, according to the printer's system of measurement.   The depth of a type form also is taken in the same manner by the printer. Consequently, it is essential that the student of printing learn the point system thoroughly so that he will be acquainted with the proper terminology and equipped to measure type and type forms in the proper way.

For many years before the point system came into general use, type sizes were given names.   An examination of the following list discloses that some of these were direct derivatives of the point system itself. A few of these names for type sizes still persist.   Those most frequently mentioned in some printing plants today are Agate, Nonpareil, Brevier, and Pica.

EARLY NAMES FOR SIZES OF TYPES

Name	Size	Name	Size
Diamond	4½ point	English	14 point
Pearl	5 "	Great Primer	18 "
Agate	5½ "	Paragon	20 "
Nonpareil	6 "	Double Pica	22 "
Minion	7 "	2-line Pica	24 "
Brevier	8 "	2-line English	28 "
Bourgeois	9 "	2-line Great Primer	36 "
Long Primer	10 "	2-line Double Pica	44 "
Small Pica	11 "	Canon	48 "
Pica	12 "		

LINING SYSTEM FOR TYPES

Another difficulty experienced by printers for many years was that of getting faces of different types cast on the same body size to "line up," or align across the bottom when set together. This lack of alignment made it necessary to improvise by using strips of paper or metal above and below letters to get the desired results—a practice which was both inefficient and time-consuming. To overcome this problem, a method of standardization was adopted by leading type founders and manufacturers of type-casting machines. The lining system, as it is called, is used in the casting of all type by type founders in Canada, the United Kingdom, and the United States.

All type is made "point line," which means that faces will align systematically with one another at the bottom, irrespective of size, by the use of leads, slugs, and other spacing material that also is cast according to the point system. This, of course, does not apply to superior and inferior figures and letters, which will align with themselves. Superior characters are above the main line of letters, and inferior characters are below. There are three common lines: standard, art, and title.

Most type faces having lower-case, or small, letters in the alphabet are made on *standard line,* and all of these cast the same size will align at the bottom, regardless of the design. Thus, it is possible to use together most types of differing designs or faces providing they are of the same size, and the lines will align as perfectly as though all of them were of the same style of type.

Art line types differ from those cast on the standard line only in one respect: they have more shoulder at the bottom, which is required to take care of very long descenders found in some designs. Cursive type and swash letters that sweep far below the main line usually are cast art line.

Title line is used for types which have no lower-case, or small, letters, and consequently require very little shoulder at the bottom.   Consequently, close spacing is possible between lines.   Many of the early headline types, consisting of only capital letters, were cast this way, and a few present-day types still are of this kind.

Regardless of the line on which type is cast, it can be brought into alignment quite easily with any other face by merely adding leads or slugs.

The adoption of the Fournier point system and the standardization of the casting of type on the "point line" have been of immense value to printers and publishers.   These developments have simplified typesetting problems and have resulted in greater efficiency throughout the industry as a whole.

MATERIALS USED IN TYPE

Most type in use today is made of metal.   There are three kinds of metal type: foundry type, type slugs, and type cast on the Monotype.[5]

Foundry type is so called because it is cast in type foundries.   Each letter is cast on a separate piece, or body, with the exception of certain combinations such as the "ffl," "ffi," "fl," "fi," and "ff," and others, which are known as ligatures.

Type slugs differ from foundry type in that an entire line of words is cast on a single, solid body known as a slug.   Most of the type used in the production of newspapers and magazines is cast in this way on slug-casting machines, the most common of which are the Linotype and the Intertype.   *Monotype type* is made on a machine known by this name, which casts each letter on a separate body and assembles them into lines automatically.

In addition to metal types, some also are made of wood.   Large sizes of type, such as those used for the printing of posters and billboard advertising, frequently are cut out of specially prepared wood in order to reduce the weight and cost of production.   However, regardless of the material used in their manufacture or the manner in which they are made, all types are cast to standard height in this country.

DESIGN OF TYPES

From a structural standpoint, types have remained practically the same since their origin in Germany about the middle of the fifteenth century, but type designs have undergone many changes.   Several hundred kinds have been introduced during the intervening years.

---

[5] Olson, *Typography and Mechanics of the Newspaper,* page 50.

This development was inevitable. As the art of printing spread from one country to another, the type forms naturally took on the expression of different cultures and reflected the peculiarities of handwriting found in manuscripts after which the forms had been modeled. Furthermore, as printing became more popular for the production of books in larger and larger quantities, the type designs were made to conform to a smaller format and to lend themselves to greater condensation.

Type designs that were suitable for large pages, such as those used in the Gutenberg Bible and other early works, were not well adapted to the classics and more popular editions planned and printed on a more economical basis for the masses. Likewise, type designs that appealed strongly to the people of one nation did not satisfy the tastes of those in another who had different temperaments. And just as fashions in wearing apparel undergo transformations from one era to another, so do fashions in type style. Yet out of all the wide experimentation which took place, there emerged only a few well-defined patterns of design around which most of the others were fashioned.

Type can be classified into five great races: *Text, Roman, Italic, Gothic,* and *Script and Cursive.* Each of them is distinctly different from the other, possessing certain characteristics that identify it unmistakably, in most instances, with the parental form from which it originated. An acquaintance with these five races of type is fundamental for the student of printing and journalism, since such a knowledge is the starting-point in gaining a workable understanding of types.

The first step in the identification, or recognition, of a given type face is that of determining the race to which it belongs.

TEXT TYPE

The oldest race of type is Text, or Black Letter, which was the first type-form employed in Germany and the one used in printing the Gutenberg Bible. A highly decorative design, this type was fashioned after the handwriting found in manuscripts of that early period. Although it was partially displaced by other designs in Germany and Italy before the end of the fifteenth century, it was the only one used in England until well into the sixteenth century.

All our present-day Text faces sprang from the fifteenth century type-forms that were referred to as Gothics. However, they have been given the name of Text in American terminology, although incorrectly.

These early designs might be divided roughly into three categories: namely, the Pointed, which sometimes is called *lettre de forme;* Round,

Domine omnipotens, Deus patrum nostrorum Abraham, et Isaac et Jacob, et seminis eorum justi, qui fecisti coelum et terram cum omni ornatu eorum; qui ligasti mare verbo praecepti tui; qui conclusisti abyssum, et signasti eam terribili et laudabili nomine tuo; quem omnia pavent et tremunt a vultu virtutis tuae, quia importabilis est magnificentia gloriae tuae, et insustentabilis ira comminationis tuae super peccatores; immensa vero et investiga=

8. *Lettre de Forme*

Domine omnipotens, Deus patrum nostrorum Abraham, et Isaac et Jacob, et seminis eorum justi, qui fecisti cœlum et terram cum omni ornatu eorum; qui ligasti mare verbo præcepti tui; qui conclusisti abyssum, et signasti eam ter// ribili et laudabili nomine tuo; quem omnia pavent et tremunt a vultu virtutis tuæ, quia importabilis est magnificentia gloriæ tuæ, et insustentabilis ira com// minationis tuæ super peccatores; immensa vero et investigabilis misericordia promissionis tuæ: quoniam tu es Dominus, altissimus, benignus, longaminis, et multum misericors, et pœnitens super malitias hominum. Tu, Domine, secundum multitudinem bonitatis tuæ promisisti pœnitentiam et remissionem iis, qui peccaverunt tibi, et multitudine miserationum tuarum decrevisti pœni// tentiam peccatoribus in salutem. Tu igitur, Domine Deus justorum, non posu// isti pœnitentiam justis, Abraham, et Isaac et Jacob, iis, qui tibi non peccave// runt; sed posuisti pœnitentiam propter me peccatorem, quoniam peccavi, super

9. *Lettre de Somme*

Domine omnipotens, Deus patrum nostrorum Abraham, et Isaac et Jacob, et seminis eorum justi, qui fecisti cœlum et terram cum omni ornatu eorum; qui ligasti mare verbo præcepti tui; qui conclusisti abyssum, et signasti eam terribili et laudabili nomine tuo; quem omnia pavent et tremunt a vultu virtutis tuæ, quia importabilis est magnificentia gloriæ tuæ, et insustentabilis ira comminationis tuæ super peccatores; immensa vero et investigabilis misericordia promissionis tuæ: quoniam tu es Dominus, altissimus, benignus, longaminis, et multum misericors,

10. *Lettre Batarde*

Figure 9. The three styles of fifteenth-century Gothic type-forms. Types of similar design today are called Text. (From *Printing Types: Their History, Forms, and Use,* by Daniel Berkeley Updike. Cambridge: Harvard University Press, 1927.)

37

also known as *lettre de somme;* and Vernacular Cursive black-letter, similar to the French *lettre batarde.* They represented the formal, less formal, and cursive manuscript hands of the Roman period, and they bear the same resemblances that appeared in manuscripts of that period which immediately preceded the invention of printing.[6]

The Pointed version was used for headlines and important words; the smaller, rounder type, which was less studied and less formal, gave a less massive effect and came nearer to the more modern ideas; and the Vernacular was intended primarily for the printing of books in German, but it also was used for the printing of many Latin books. The tendency was to shift gradually toward the letter forms which are associated with German Text of today.

Text type frequently is referred to as Old English, since it was used by William Caxton, the first English printer, and served for so many years as the only type for printing in England. One of the more common Text families also bears the name of Old English Text.

Several explanations have been given for the introduction and early popularity of Text type. In the first place, it was quite logical for the designers to try to imitate the beautiful and ornate writing found in the manuscripts which were the chief source of record keeping of that period. Secondly, these early printers knew that they would have to produce books in types that would meet with greatest approval if they were to succeed in their enterprises, and they were wise enough to realize that the kind of letter forms which people were accustomed to reading would be the most readily acceptable.

Furthermore, these early printers attempted to make their books resemble the handwritten manuscripts as closely as possible in the hopes that the people would not suspect they had been produced by some other method.

This is Wedding Text type

This is Cloister Black type

Today, Text, or Black Letter, type faces are used sparingly. They are employed mainly for the printing of material of a religious nature, such as church announcements and programs, greeting cards for religious holidays, and occasionally wedding announcements and calling cards.

---

[6] Updike, *Printing Types: Their History, Forms, and Use,* page 60.

Among the present-day Text types that are in common use are **Wedding Text** and **Cloister Black**. There are several others.

Many early newspapers bore name plates printed in **Text type, and** the practice still is followed by some present-day editors, partly because of the desire to carry on a tradition of long standing and also to obtain the harmonious contrast that can be had by using this rather dignified design along with other less decorative types.

ROMAN TYPE

The second main race, and by far the largest, is that known as Roman type. This kind of type was being used in Italian books printed before the end of the fifteenth century.

The first real departure from Text came with the introduction of a type by Sweynheym and Pannartz in 1465 which was neither Black Letter nor Roman, but a mixture of the two. Used for the printing in their establishment in the monastery at Subiaco near Rome, this new type was almost Roman in form, but it had the tone, or color, of Black Letter. Fashioned after humanistic characters that were the style in Italian manuscripts, these types were revivals of the Carolingian bookhands of the early scribes. This style of writing was inspired by the Renaissance, which awakened the classical feeling.

Italian designers expressed themselves in writing that was graceful and highly decorative, and the beauty of these early Renaissance books reached a stage of perfection that never has been surpassed.

Other printers in Italy, among them Wendelin de Spire, produced many Roman types of varying degrees of purity, but credit for development of the first true Roman type face is given to Nicolas Jenson, who started printing in Venice in 1468.

Jenson was a native of Sommevoire, France. He started as a die cutter in the royal mint in Paris, and in 1458 was sent by King Charles VII, of France, to Mainz, Germany, to learn the secrets of printing. Before he returned to Paris, the king died, and Jenson devoted his attention to publishing. He established a printing office in Venice in 1468 and produced his first Roman letter in 1470.[7]

Like the semi-Romans which preceded it, Jenson's type was inspired by the humanistic manuscripts of the period. But it was more readable, mellow in form, and resulted in an evenness of color when used in mass. This first type produced by Jenson has served as the accepted model for many Roman type designs developed since that time.

---

[7] Olson, *Typography and Mechanics of the Newspaper,* page 28.

ſuas oſtendunt.His cæterisq; huiuſmodi niſi contentioſus ſis cōcedas
oportet diuina uniuerſum hunc mundum prouidétia gubernari.Hæc
a Philone compédioſius ſumpſi:tum ut oſtendā quales hebræi etiam
iuniores uiros habuerunt:tū ut pia de deo ſentétia iudæoꝗ appareat.

VNC Autem teſtimonia etiam exteriorum de ipſis
diligenter citabimus.Illuſtriſſimi enim etiā græcorū
nō imperiti omnino iudaicæ philoſophiæ alii uitam
eorū ſcriptis ſuis approbaſſe uidentur:alii theologiā
quantū potuere ſecuti ſūt.Sic eim diſces nō temere
ſed abſoluta exquiſitaq; ratione iudaicā philoſophiā gentilibus nugis
præpoſitam a nobis fuiſſe.Primum igiť ea ponā quæ de uita iudæorū
præclariſſimi græcorum teſtantur.Theophraſtum igitur audias:cuius
nōnullos textus Porphyrius in his libris poſuit quos de abſtinendo a
carnibus cōſcripſit:his uerbis iudæi ad hæc uſq; tépora Theophraſtus
ait animalia quomodo ſacrificant:ut ſiquis nos ad imitatione illorū
hortaretur audire non pateremur.Non enim comedūt ex ſacrificatis:
ſed mel atq; uinum noctu infūdunt holocauſta facientes:nihilq; inde
relinquentes:ut nec ille qui omnia perſpicit rem tam prauam iſpicere
poſſit:quod faciūt interim ieiunantes:ac quoniam philoſophi natura
ſunt de deo inter ſe colloquétes noctu aūt ſtellas aſpiciétes oratioíbus
deum inuocāt.Primi enim iſti omninm hominum & bruta & ſe ipſos
offerre cœperūt:nulla neceſſitate aut cupiditate id faciétes.Et ī quarto
eiuſdé negocii hæc a ſe ipſo ſcribit Porphyrius.Eſſæi iudæi genere ſūt:
hi alter alterum magis diligunt q̄ cæteri homines faciant:& uoluptaté
oém quaſi uitioſam aſpernanť:continétiā & ītegritaté animi ab omni
perturbatione remotā præcipuā putantes uirtutem.Vxores nō ducūt:
alienos aūt liberos teneros adhuc & ad oém aptos doctrinā adoptátes
pro ſuis educare ac moribus ſuis ſtabilire ſolent:quod faciunt non qa
matrimonium abominétur:ſed quia mulierum mores cauédos putāt.
Diuitias omnes adeo ſpernūt ut mirabilis quædā in eis cōmunitas ſit.
Nullus eorum præter cæteros aliquid poſſidet:oīa eis cōmunia ſunt.
Nemo alio ditior aut pauperior.Vna omibus quaſi fratribus facultas
eſt.Vngi oleo non patiuntur:ꝗ ſiquis forte oleo tactus fuerit diligéter
quaſi a magna macula corpus illi abſtergiť:non enim molles ſed aridi
atq; duri eſſe corpore cupiunt.Alba ſéper induunť.Electione cōmuni

Figure 10. Page from Nicolas Jenson's *Eusebius*, "*De Praeparatione
Evangelica*," Venice, 1476. (From *The Technique of Advertising Production*, by Thomas Blaine Stanley. New York: Prentice-Hall, Inc., 1940.)

Roman type differs from Text type in many ways. In the first place, it is much less decorative, lighter in tone, and more legible. Several characteristics common to Roman type which set it off definitely from all other races are these: it contains serifs, shadings within letters, and light and heavy elements—all of which were designed to promote ease in reading.

There are two kinds of Roman types in use today: Oldstyle Roman and Modern Roman. Both of these have the same common characteristics, but treatment is different.

In Oldstyle Roman types, the serifs are slanting or curved and are bracketed into the main stroke; in Modern Romans, the serifs are thin and straight. Contrast between light and heavy elements is much more pronounced in the Modern Romans, and shadings are perfectly balanced, giving the type a more chiseled, geometric appearance than Oldstyle Roman, in which the shadings may be off-balance, with a tendency to pull the letter either forward or backward, depending on the particular design. One of the best examples of Oldstyle Romans is Caslon Oldstyle.

This is Oldstyle Roman type
This is Modern Roman type

(The first line in the example above is Caslon Oldstyle; the second line is Bodoni.)

The most famous and widely used Modern Roman is a type known as Bodoni. It was designed by Giambattista (John the Baptist) Bodoni, who was born in Saluzzo, Italy, on February 16, 1740. The son of a master printer, Bodoni learned the trade at an early age and was summoned by the Duke of Parma in 1768 to take charge of his library and printing presses.

Dissatisfied with the type faces then available, Bodoni began cutting punches for new types, and, after several years, he issued his first complete book of type specimens, which contained a new design that became known as Modern Roman.

A crisp, clear type face that differed considerably in design from the Oldstyle Romans, Bodoni type has remained popular ever since, and it is used extensively by present-day printers and publishers. Other Modern Romans have been introduced since Bodoni's time, but none has yet achieved its fame or has been a serious rival.

Some Roman types, such as Baskerville, Century, and Scotch Roman, carry characteristics of both the Modern and Oldstyle versions, and these frequently are referred to as Transitional or Mixed Romans.

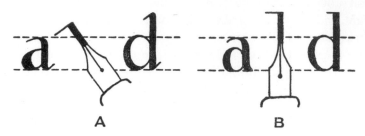

A   **B**

Figure 11. Example A shows pen's position in Old Style writing, and Example B shows its position in modern writing. (Adapted from *Type Lore*, by J. L. Frazier. Chicago: J. L. Frazier, 1925.)

ITALIC TYPE

The next oldest race of type in point of origin is Italic, the first example of which was produced in 1501 by Aldus Manutius, a famous printer of Venice. This new Aldine Italic was based on humanistic cursive handwriting of a somewhat earlier period, and it became the leading vernacular type of Italy.[8]

Unlike Text and Roman type-forms which preceded it, Italic type slanted to the right, was characterized by originality of letters, contained many tied letters, and the capitals, which were shorter than the ascending lower-case letters, were in Roman.

Aldus was a great scholar of the classics, and his invention of Italic type was the outcome of his desire to produce books that would be within the reach of everyone. To fulfill this ambition, he designed a condensed type for printing the first pocket-sized editions ever published—an Everyman's Library for the Venetians. Altogether he produced 123 different works, including school books, dictionaries, and the pocket-sized editions of Greek classics.

The punches for his types were cut by Francesco da Bologna, who also had designed Roman types for him. The Aldine character that he prepared became the model for most of the Italic types which have followed, and it was widely imitated by contemporary printers, some of whom called it Aldino, and others, Italic, in an effort to avoid identifying it with the rightful claimant to the invention.

---

[8] Updike, *Printing Types: Their History, Forms, and Use*, page 125.

Among the Aldine imitations was one produced by printers in Lyons, who were responsible for changing the Roman capitals used by Aldus to slanting characters which were adopted eventually for all Italic

IVNII IVVENALIS AQVINA
TIS SATYRA PRIMA.

EMPER EGO AVDITOR
tantum?nunquám ne reponam
s   V exatus toties rauci theseide
Codri ?
I mpune ergo mihireatauerit ille
togatus?
H ic elegos?impune diem consumpseritingens
T elephus?aut summi plena iam margine libri
S criptus, et in tergo nec dum finitus, Orestes?
N ota magis nulli domus est sua, quam mihi lucus
M artis, et æoliis uicinum rupibus antrum
V ulcani. Quid agant uenti, quas torqueat umbras
A eacus, unde alius furtiuæ deuehat aurum
P elliculæ, quantas iaculetur Monychus ornos,
F rontonis platani, conuulsáq; marmora clamant
S emper, et assiduo ruptæ lectore columnæ.
E xpectes eadem a summo, minimóq; poeta.
E t nos ergo manum ferulæ subduximus, et nos
C onsilium dedimus Syllæ, priuatus ut altum.
D ormiret-stulta est clementia, cum tot ubique
V atibus ocurras, perituræ parcare chartæ.
C ur tamen hoc libeat potius decurrere campo,
P er quem magnus equos Auruncæ flexit alumnus,
S i uacat, et placidi rationem admittitis, edam.
C um tener uxorem ducat spado, Meuia thuscum
F igat aprum, et nuda teneat uenabula mamma,
P atricios omnes opibus cum prouocet unus,
A ii

Figure 12.   Aldine Italic as used in *Juvenal and Persius*, Aldus, Venice, 1501. (From *Printing Types: Their History, Forms, and Use*, by Daniel Berkeley Updike. Cambridge: Harvard University Press, 1927.)

fonts. Thus, the "agreeable perpendicular movement" that was regarded by many early printers as one of the type's most desirable features, disappeared, and the Aldine printing house itself adopted the new style of capitals in 1560, less than fifty years after the death of Aldus.

Today there are hundreds of Italic faces from which to select. All of them slant to the right, are condensed in shape, and carry characteristics common to the Roman and Gothic forms after which they are modeled.

This is Caslon Oldstyle Italic

Although Italic type originally was used as a body type, it seldom is printed in large masses today because it is not easily read when used this way. Since it generally is lighter in weight, narrower, and more decorative than most Romans and Gothics, it is a weaker type and should not be used for printing that demands treatment denoting great strength.

SCRIPT AND CURSIVE TYPE

Types which most closely resemble handwriting belong to the Script and Cursive race. They are, in fact, direct descendants of handwriting of the scribes of the sixteenth and seventeenth centuries. In design, they look more like Italic than any of the other races, but they are characterized by a much greater freedom of design and an easy flow which is missing in the more formal type-forms. Most of these types are fashioned after writing which slants to the right; however, some lean to the left, in imitation of "back-hand" writing, and others are straight and rigid in form.

Some of them are in imitation of writing done with the pen, in which long, sweeping flourishes predominate; others resemble that of the brush, containing strokes that are heavy and black in appearance. Of all the races, Script and Cursive are the most temperamental and unpredictable.

This is Script type

This is Cursive type

Although both Script and Cursive type faces resemble handwriting, they differ in one respect: in true Script, letters are linked together as in handwriting; in true Cursive, the individual letters are not joined, but many designs are constructed so expertly that the gap between letters is bridged so easily by the eye that the casual reader is not conscious of this lack of continuity. Because of such close similarity, some manufacturers give the name Script to some types that are actually Cursive in design.

Today many Script and Cursive types are available, ranging from the most delicate designs to others that are crude and unattractive. However, the number in most common use is small.

Since these types do resemble handwriting so closely, they are used in the more personal and intimate kinds of printing, such as calling cards and stationery for women, social invitations and wedding announcements. They are employed appropriately in advertisements dealing with women's apparel, perfume, jewelry, and other products demanding light treatment. Pleasing contrast can be obtained by combining them with other races of type for display purposes in advertising for men, as well as for women, and for headlines in both newspapers and magazines.

Gothic, or Sans-Serif, Type

Another large group of types belongs to the Gothic, or Sans-Serif, race. These types are extremely plain in design. Most letters have no serifs, and they are open and blocky. Strokes are of approximately the same weight throughout, and there are no shadings within true Sans-Serif characters.

Gothic is a misnomer, however, since the design in no way suggests designs associated with architecture of such origin. Nevertheless, this name has become firmly established in printing nomenclature in the United States.

This is Gothic type

Sans-Serif, which in French means "without serif," is the correct designation and today is accepted widely in this country; but the mistaken name of Gothic still persists. In Europe, types belonging to this race are called Block Letter, Grotesque, Antique, and Sans-Serif.

Sans-Serif types have been in use for many years, but they were not employed widely or in any great quantities in this country until after World War I, when Germany introduced new designs based on some of the earlier forms. There the Sans-Serifs went through a period of rapid expansion, and several new type families of this race appeared. But the Nazi government did not look with favor upon the innovations in typography which the new types prompted, and experimentation by German designers came to an abrupt end.

In the meantime, the new concept of type design began to gain attention in this country, and such type faces as Kabel, Futura, and Erbar experienced rather sudden popularity.   Since their introduction, Sans-Serif types have undergone considerable refinement in design and several families belonging to this race today are in extensive use throughout the country.   In addition to those already mentioned, Bernhard Gothic, Metro, Tempo, Vogue, and many others are very popular.

Sans-Serif types are well adapted to modern design, which demands that "function shall determine form," stresses the importance of simplicity in layout, and encourages geometrical arrangements of type areas and illustrations.

Of all the five races of type, Sans-Serif suggests most strongly the use of ruler and pen by the designer.   Its plain, geometric simplicity and openness of letters promote readability when used for display purposes, but it is not so well suited for use in large masses.   Despite its legibility, readers accustomed to Romans in the text of newspapers, magazines, and books find the plainer design used in large areas monotonous and uninviting.

Although the first Sans-Serif types introduced in this country did not meet with great favor, but were regarded at the start as more of a fad that soon would pass, improvements in design and a better understanding of their possibilities led to rather wide acceptance.

Today many newspapers and magazines use Sans-Serif types for headlines.   Some of them have complete headline schedules in this style of type, in which they make use of the many variations available in a given family.   These types also are used in many kinds of advertisements for display lines and small blocks of copy.

Sans-Serif type also is suitable for a wide range of commercial printing jobs, such as letterheads, envelope corners, formal announcements, hand bills, and business forms.   Because of its plainness, it is not so versatile as Roman type, and care must be taken not to use it indiscriminately on jobs for which it is not adapted.

Stripped of the fine lines that are found in the Roman type faces, it is a sturdy, rugged type denoting strength and durability and will stand up under long wear and hard service.

SQUARE-SERIF GOTHICS

Another group of types, which has become known as Square-Serif, or Block-Serif, resembles the Sans-Serif very closely.   The only significant difference is that all the members in this group have serifs which are as heavy as the main strokes of the letters and "squared-off" at the ends.

These types are plain, open-faced, and the letters are without shadings.   Since they do have serifs—a characteristic common to the Roman race—they defy a clearcut classification; however, because of the extreme plainness and a design more similar to Gothics than to any other, they generally are regarded as belonging to the Gothic race.

This is Square-Serif type

Square-Serif types are derived from the so-called "Egyptian" faces of the period of decadence in type design which existed from about 1815 to 1840.[6]   Although the faces produced at that time were common-looking and unattractive, the newer versions introduced by skillful designers in recent years are greatly improved, with enough variations in weight, width, and structure to make them suitable for a wide range of uses.

Because of their plainness and precise geometric design, these types, like the more modern Sans-Serifs, are well adapted to typography of the machine age.   Although they are not truly Egyptian in design, the names of some of them are suggestive of the so-called period from which they came.   Among the most popular types in this group are Stymie, Karnak, Cairo, Memphis, and Girder.

FAMILIES OF TYPE

After a type face has been classified according to race, the next step in the process of its identification is that of determining its family relationship.

In any one of the five races of type, just as within the human races, there are many families.   For instance, belonging to the Roman race of types are the Caslons, the Garamonds, the Cheltenhams, the Goudys, and many others.   The characteristics common to these particular families are those which were mentioned in the foregoing discussion on the Roman race of type.

All of them have serifs, light and heavy elements, and shadings within letters.   However, the way in which these various elements are handled in each familial group is what sets one off quite distinctly from

---

[6] Thomas Blaine Stanley, *The Technique of Advertising Production*, page 140. New York: Prentice-Hall, Inc., 1941.

the other.   Each member of a given family bears certain resemblances peculiar to the parent-form that establishes its relationship.

A type family might be regarded as having a "family tree" similar to that boasted of by humans, with each branch representing a different member.   In some type families, there are many members, or branches.   The size depends upon the number of variants, or branches, which go to make up the entire "tree," or group.

Some type families are much larger than others.   One of the largest is Cheltenham.   Among the members of this family are Cheltenham Oldstyle, Cheltenham Oldstyle Italic, Cheltenham Wide, Cheltenham Bold, Cheltenham Bold Italic, Cheltenham Bold Condensed, Cheltenham Bold Extra Condensed, and several others.   In addition to having the same racial characteristics, the basic design remains essentially unchanged throughout and differences are slight, consisting mainly in variations in weight and width of face.

This is Cheltenham Oldstyle

This is Cheltenham Oldstyle Italic

This is Cheltenham Wide

This is Cheltenham Bold

This is Cheltenham Bold Italic

This is Cheltenham Bold Condensed

This is Cheltenham Bold Extra Condensed

SERIES OF TYPE

In each of the branches of a given type family, there are several sizes, ranging from very small to very large ones.   This spread of sizes usually is from around six point to seventy-two point or larger.

All the sizes going to make up one particular branch of a type family are known as a *series* of type.   For instance, all sizes of Goudy Catalogue—a member, or branch, of the Goudy family—would be referred to as a series.

72 Point

Sold

60 Point

Eight

48 Point

Dahlia

42 Point

Blandly

36 Point

Madrigal

30 Point

Rhapsodist

24 Point

Philanthropy

18 Point

BACKBONE
Monthly sales
are expanding

14 Point

LAST EDITION
The best books of
fiction seldom fail
to have good sales

12 Point

PRODUCTS SOLD
Men are interested in
all matters pertaining
to their own business

10 Point

SELECTED CLERK
Expensive handmade
papers are much used
at the present time for
the finest sort of work

8 Point

EXCITING QUESTION
Newsprint is consumed in
enormous amounts by the
city newspapers especially
for the Sunday editions of

6 Point

COMPLICATED MACHINES
The wood pulp used for making
newsprint contains the original
impurities present in the wood;
that is why our newspapers turn

Figure 13. Different sizes making up a series of Goudy Catalogue type.

FONT OF TYPE

Each of the sizes of a series of type is kept in a separate case.   Cases are placed one below the other in the same stand or cabinet, with the smallest size at the top and the larger sizes at the bottom.   An assortment of all of the characters going to make up one size of one particular branch of a given family, which is stored in a single type case, is known as a *font* of type.

This arrangement helps to explain what is meant when someone remarks or indicates that a letter in a line that has been set is "wrong font."   He means that the letter in question belongs to some other font, or in some other case of type, and consequently is out of place.

WIDTH AND WEIGHT OF TYPE FACES

All members of a type family are not of the same width.   On the contrary, some of them may be very wide, while others may be very narrow or thin.   Many of the type faces adapted for display purposes in advertising and headlines are available in five widths: namely, extra-condensed, condensed, regular, expanded, and extended.

Night Hawk

Buys Engine

Navigator

Daughter

Hybrid

Figure 14.   Example of five widths of type faces.   Reading from the top: Cheltenham Bold Extra Condensed, Cheltenham Medium Condensed, Cheltenham Medium (Regular), Cheltenham Medium Expanded, and Cheltenham Bold Extended.

Extra-condensed type is very narrow; condensed is narrower than that ordinarily used for large masses; regular is the width of face commonly used for text material, since it is the most legible; expanded is somewhat wider than the regular or normal face; and extended is much wider than regular.

Because of the great irregularity of extra-condensed and expanded types, they should be used sparingly and with great care.

Every family does not contain types of all these five widths, but most of them have more than one from which to choose, depending upon the purposes for which they were designed.

Types also vary according to the lightness or heaviness of face, which is referred to as the *weight* of face.   The most commonly used Roman types usually are cast in two weights — regular and bold. However, a few of the Romans — notably, Cheltenham — and many of the Gothics are available in four variations: light, medium, bold, and extra-bold (heavy).

Athletic club here
Tempo Light

Popular tourist stop
Tempo Medium

Sets new record
Tempo Bold

Rate decreases
Tempo Heavy

Figure 15.   Four different weights of faces available in Tempo type.

Thus, it is possible to obtain very fine shadings of tone on a page or in a printed piece by selecting types that differ only in width and weight of face, even though all those chosen may come from the same family and carry the same basic design.   In like manner, great contrast between type masses, or even single lines, may be obtained.

WIDE SELECTION OF TYPE

Today we are not limited as were the printers and publishers in earlier periods, who could choose their types from only a few available designs.

On the contrary, there are hundreds of type families, each containing a wide variety of design, from which to select.   There are so many, in fact, that the beginner is very likely to become confused unless he obtains a basic understanding of the methods to follow in classifying a type face into its proper race and family.   He must realize early that the degree of his success is dependent upon his ability to recognize and employ skillfully the vast storehouse of types at his disposal.   However, the number of types in most common use today is relatively small, and since this is the case, special emphasis should be placed on a thorough study of the type families that are encountered most frequently.

III

Some Popular Type Faces

THE TYPOGRAPHY AND MAKEUP OF A NEWS-
paper or magazine have much to do with its popularity. Lively, spar-
kling copy in news articles, headlines, editorials, and advertisements
often is not enough to attract and hold the interest of many readers.
The way in which these messages are presented to the public in printed
form is of great importance.

Careful consideration should be given to the choice of types, since
in the final analysis, they are the vehicles of the thoughts to be expressed and consequently go to make up one of the controlling factors
over readership.

Every type "speaks its own language." No two of them are alike—
even members of the same family—and collectively they run the scale
from extreme femininity to rugged masculinity. In design, some of
them are light and airy, with a generous sprinkling of delicate strokes
and decorative endings; others are plain and heavy, entirely lacking in
aesthetic qualities, but denoting with unmistakable clarity a feeling of
strength and vigor.

By far the largest number of available type faces fall in between
these two extremes; but in every instance, slight variations in design
help to determine the feeling expressed, thus making it possible for the
designer of printing by careful selection to obtain fine shadings of tone,
on the one hand, or high contrast on the other.

The designer of printing has at his disposal a wide variety of basic
materials out of which to fashion his work, the quality of which is
limited only by his own ingenuity and his ability to choose and apply
them wisely.

The first prerequisite is an ability to recognize type faces and an understanding of how to use them appropriately. Since only a comparatively small number of the many hundreds of types available carry the
main load in present-day publications, the most logical plan is to con-

centrate on learning these, and to supplement this information as the need arises.

Types chosen for discussion in this chapter are from families that are in extensive use by newspapers and magazines in this country. When these have been mastered, the student will be well on his way in matters of type recognition, and by applying the methods discussed will be able to enlarge his knowledge of other types.

STEPS TO FOLLOW

When looking at an unfamiliar specimen of type, the first thing to do is to determine the race to which it belongs; then the family; and finally, the particular branch of that family. In order to recognize any given type face, it is necessary to become thoroughly familiar with certain characteristics which set it off from all others.

Differences between types may appear in the nature of the serifs, the shape of certain letters, variations in elements, unusual terminals or endings, the height of the lower-case letters, and the length of ascenders and descenders.

In every font of type, certain key letters should be checked closely, since ordinarily they differ greatly in many families and consequently serve as clues to correct identification. Among the most important ones to be watched are the capitals "A," "T," "R," "S," "G," "C," "E," "W," "P," and "B," and the lower-case "e," "y," "t," "k," "g," "m," "l," "i," and "d." However, other letters in the alphabet frequently vary widely from family to family, and the practice of inspecting the entire alphabet always is advisable.

Another desirable test is to see the type in question printed in a small mass, because often the tone or color of a face used this way will aid materially in its future recognition. This also will show what effect may be obtained when it is employed as body matter.

In addition to the classifications into races and families, types also may be divided up into groups, according to the countries or areas from which they spring. For instance, those based on Jenson's Roman and others cut in the latter part of the fifteenth century are called *Venetian;* the ones fashioned after the early designs produced in France are known as *French;* and type faces with designs similar to the first outstanding Roman types introduced in England are known as *English,* or *Dutch-English,* since the initial ones resembled early Dutch models.

CASLON OLDSTYLE

The most distinguished member of the *English* group is Caslon. None of the Roman types has experienced greater popularity or gained more lasting favor among printers and publishers than this type, which bears the name of the man who designed it—William Caslon, a famous English type founder.

Caslon began his career as a type designer in 1720 and issued his first specimen sheet in 1734. Although resembling Dutch types in many respects, his faces were marked by more thin, delicate strokes and a freedom and vigor that was typically Anglo-Saxon. Individuality is obtained by artistic touches and by letters that are not perfect in form, but when used together in mass, result in highly pleasing effects of rare beauty and refinement.

Caslon types were accepted enthusiastically in England and throughout Europe and were used extensively by colonial printers in America. Although their popularity waned during the first half of the nineteenth century, they were revived again in 1859 when an American type foundry imported Caslon Oldstyle matrices, and by 1900, leading manufacturers of types and type-casting machines in this country were producing this face in quantities.[1] Today, Caslon is one of our leading Oldstyle Roman families.

Caslon is one of the most versatile types available to the designer of printing. Because of the delicacy of many strokes, the graceful curves in the formation of serifs, and the fine endings of elements, it is adapted to the more feminine appeals, and its over-all weight gives it enough strength, especially in the bolder varieties, to furnish strong masculinity when desired.

Because of its great legibility, Caslon is popular as both a display and a body type in advertisements, pamphlets, folders, books, and other kinds of printed pieces. Although few newspapers use it exclusively for headlines, many of them include it in their head schedules, and a large number of magazines also use it this way. Except in the condensed version, it is a little too wide for satisfactory use in one-column headlines, but it is well adapted for heads of wider measure.

In none of its forms can Caslon be accused of being cheap or blatant, and it never should be employed where "shouting" seems desirable. It is characterized by enough restraint and, at the same time, sufficient strength and character to give a feeling of frank simplicity, honesty, dependability, dignity, and formality.

In the first place, the letters are tall and graceful, with generous ascenders and descenders. Characters are open and legible, with considerable contrast between light and heavy strokes. Serifs are pointed

---

[1] Kenneth E. Olson, *Typography and Mechanics of the Newspaper,* page 131. New York: D. Appleton and Company, 1930.

A B C D E F G H I
J K L M N O P Q R
S T U V W X Y Z

1

2

3

The "tramp printer" was a colorful figure in the history of American journalism. He learned his trade the hard way by serving an apprenticeship as a printer's devil. Then he harkened to the call of the open road and spent the rest of his life traveling far and wide over the country, stopping only long enough in any one place to earn sufficient money to pay his way on to the next.

He was famous for his tall stories, which he gathered from the many towns and villages he

6

7

8

12 POINT ROMAN

4

5

Anyone planning to enter the profession of journalism should learn as much as possible about the tools of his trade. Foremost among these are printing types, for it is through them that he will make his voice heard.

The invention of printing with movable type was one of the greatest discoveries of all time. It marked a great turning-point in the history of the world by providing a method for making the accumulated knowledge of the centuries available

9

0

12 POINT ITALIC

a b c d e f g h i j k l m
n o p q r s t u v w x y z

Figure 16. Caslon Oldstyle No. 337.

and those at the top of vertical elements slant upward to the right, whereas most serifs at the bottom of elements are straight across. Serifs have a tendency to curve out from the main stem, adding gracefulness to letters.

Certain letters are distinctive in form. The serifs on the cross-bar of the "T" sweep up at the ends; in the "A," the main element coming up from the right is chiseled out at the end. The endings of the "s" seem to be squared off to give it a very formal appearance. The "C" has distinctive serifs, with the one at the bottom pulling down below the main stroke forming the letter. The top and bottom cross-bars in the "E" swing far out, but the center bar is much shorter, ending in a triangular serif.

The "e" thickens at the end of the loop at the top, with a fine line coming across high up on the letter, leaving a comparatively small amount of white space on the inside; the "a" looks quite tall, since the loop is rather small and the stroke at the top leans far out over it. The "g" has an angular appearance because of the shape of the neck, which swings back and then far downward in a graceful stroke to form the bottom part of the letter in a loop that is oblong in shape and wider than the one forming the upper part. The smooth, oval, drop-like ear, which is joined to the letter with a thin line is repeated in the tips of such letters as the "a," "c," "f," "j," "r," and "y." Another interesting variation is the solid triangular serif, placed at the top of the letter "t."

Caslon Italic letters incline almost uniformly to the right with more slope than is found in some type families, but many of the characteristics common to the Oldstyle Roman version of the face carry through. Especially distinctive are the "swash" capitals, "A," "E," "M," and "N," which are available in some fonts.

Because of its extreme versatility, Caslon has been a very popular face from the time it was first introduced in England. It is a large family, and by making use of the various branches together, a wide variety of effects can be obtained.

GARAMOND OLDSTYLE

Foremost among the group of *French* types is Garamond. Like Caslon, Garamond is an Oldstyle Roman which bears the name of its designer, Claude Garamond, a distinguished French typographer, who began his work as a designer about 1540.

Garamond is an exceptionally clear and open type, with a quality of elegance, freedom, and quiet dignity that was a distinct and pleasing departure from the first Roman faces introduced in Italy.

Garamond's Roman and Italic types, known as *caractères de l'Université,* were cut during the French Renaissance at the order of François I for use in books for the royalty and the church.   One of the most beautiful Roman types ever designed, it has an air of haughtiness about it which suggests quality, dignity, exclusiveness, and grace.   It is somewhat less conservative and formal than Caslon, containing more decorativeness of design.

Because of its feminine appeal, Garamond is used extensively in advertising dealing with women's wear, fashions, specialties, and other kinds of quality merchandise.   It also is well adapted for feature headlines, women's and society pages in newspapers, and is one of the favorites in class magazines, especially those for women.   The bolder versions have a masculine flavor and can be employed in a wide range of advertising and other printing where strength, tempered with friendliness and reserve, is desired.

Less restrained and more decorative than Caslon, Garamond consequently is not quite so versatile.   A true Oldstyle Roman, it possesses more movement and grace than Caslon and greater freedom of design. There is less contrast between light and heavy elements, affording more warmth and color, and the greater variations in formation of letters give it a slightly more feminine tone.

Lower-case letters are quite tall, and descenders and ascenders are long, which results in slenderness and gracefulness of form that are very pleasing.

The "A" comes to a point at the top, has a high cross-bar, and is narrower than the one in Caslon.   Serifs at the bottom of elements appear to be slightly concave, and a slight unevenness along the edges of downstrokes in letters may be detected.   Those serifs coming at the top of elements are not uniform: some of them slant up to the right, as in the "h," while the ones at the end-strokes of the "u" are straight, and the "i" has one that appears to be chiseled out to accommodate the dot that is placed high above it.

In the "E," all three cross-bars are long, with the one at the bottom extending slightly beyond the other two.   The "D" is wide, and the line at the bottom of the loop curves up slightly just before it reaches the vertical element.   In the "W," there is a perfect "V" on the right-hand side, but the one on the left is not allowed to finish.   The "Z" is a very wide letter.

The "S" is narrow and a little severe.   The "N" is quite wide and the serif at the top on the left-hand side of this letter does not extend all the way across.   This same characteristic is apparent in both top serifs in

A B C D E F G H I
J K L M N O P Q R
S T U V W X Y Z

1

6

The "tramp printer" was a colorful figure in the history of American journalism. He learned his trade the hard way by serving an apprenticeship as a printer's devil. Then he harkened to the call of the open road and spent the rest of his life traveling far and

2

7

wide over the country, stopping only long enough in any one place to earn sufficient money to pay his way on to the next.

He was famous for his tall stories, which he gathered from the many towns and villages he visited on his journeys, and he loved to spin long yarns about

3

8

12 POINT ROMAN

4

9

Anyone planning to enter the profession of journalism should learn as much as possible about the tools of his trade. Foremost among these are printing types, for it is through them that he will make his voice heard.

5

0

The invention of printing with movable type was one of the greatest discoveries of all time. It marked a great turning-point in the history of the world by providing a method for making the accumulated

14 POINT ITALIC

a b c d e f g h i j k l m
n o p q r s t u v w x y z

Figure 17.   Garamond.

the "M," and the upright element on the left side slants noticeably to the right.

The "a" is narrower than the one in Caslon, and the loop is smaller. In the "e," the cross-bar at the bottom of the loop is high and very thin, with little white space inside it, which results in a very delicate letter. The "g" is slender and has a horn-like projection pointing straight out from the top part of the letter.

One of the most distinctive letters in Garamond is the "T," in which the serif on the right points straight down, while the one on the left slants to the right. Both serifs extend well above the cross-bar forming the letter at the top. Another unusual letter is the "y," in which the line at the right side extends well down below the main line, terminating in a "golf-club" ending that is distinctive.

The Italic in Garamond contains many more variations than Caslon, with several swash letters from which to choose, and the total effect of a line set in Garamond Italic, while slightly warmer in tone, is more decorative.

Cloister Oldstyle

Cloister Oldstyle is a member of the *Venetian* group of types, modeled closely after the first true Roman face designed in 1470 by Nicolas Jenson, who fashioned his type after the manuscript hands.[2]

Like other types in this group, Cloister possesses certain pen-drawn characteristics. It has an easy flow and freedom of design, but a slightly heavier appearance than Caslon and Garamond, which is accentuated by rather blunt, diagonal serifs that are bracketed into the main stroke, and a lack of much contrast between thin and thick strokes. Used in mass, the tone is considerably darker, which gives added warmth.

Cloister is a good type for advertisements and other kinds of printing where the purpose is to express richness, dignity, sturdiness, stability, and charm. The easy, smooth flow, together with its warmth of tone, adds a mellowness that is hard to equal. It is popular among advertisers of jewelry, perfume, and other quality merchandise, and it is found in abundance in the class magazines.

Cloister also is employed in headline schedules of many newspapers —especially for feature headlines—because of its compactness, which permits more unit counts to the line than many other Roman types.

Since it has the flavor of the old Scripts used in works dealing with the church, Cloister is employed widely for printing of a sacred nature,

---

[2] Olson, *Typography and Mechanics of the Newspaper*, page 136.

A B C D E F G H I J K L M N O P Q R S T U V W X Y Z

1

2

3

The "tramp printer" was a colorful figure in the history of American journalism. He learned his trade the hard way by serving an apprenticeship as a printer's devil. Then he harkened to the call of the open road and spent the rest of his life traveling far and wide over the country, stopping only long enough in any one place to earn sufficient money to pay his way on to the next.

He was famous for his tall stories, which he gathered from the many towns and villages he visited on his journeys, and he loved to spin long yarns about his varied experiences. Aside from being a skilled craftsman he was

6

7

12 POINT ROMAN

4

5

8

Anyone planning to enter the profession of journalism should learn as much as possible about the tools of his trade. Foremost among these are printing types, for it is through them that he will make his voice heard.

The invention of printing with movable type was one of the greatest discoveries of all time. It marked a great turning-point in the history of the world by providing a method for making the accumulated knowledge of the centuries available to the common people.

9

0

14 POINT ITALIC

a b c d e f g h i j k l m n o p q r s t u v w x y z

Figure 18.   Cloister Oldstyle.

and likewise is popular for wedding announcements, calling cards, and for many other social forms.

It is heavier in tone than Caslon or Garamond, and the contrast between light and heavy elements is slight. Lower-case letters are not so tall, and ascenders and descenders are very long. Serifs are heavy and blunt, and their slope to the right is more pronounced.

The curves of all looped letters and those at the top of the "n" and "m" give a pleasing, rounded effect, and the very close fit of characters results in a compactness that is highly desirable from the standpoint of unit count in a line.

Several letters are distinctive. The "e" is formed with a diagonal cross-bar, which comes to a point that projects out beyond the down-stroke. The serifs at the top of the "T" are almost straight, but pull slightly to the left. The right leg coming down to form the "R" slopes out into a thin, blunt ending, and is attached to the loop before the down-stroke reaches the vertical element on the left.

The "S" seems to be squared off at the bottom. Serifs at the top of the "M" are straight lines, without curves. The line slanting down between the two vertical elements in the "N" has a noticeable curve. The descender of the "y" thickens at the bottom into a blunt ending.

.The "W" is formed by two superimposed "V's," with a serif at the top of each of the four elements. The "J" falls below the main line of letters. The "Q," with its long, plain tail, also is unusual and distinctive.

Capitals appear to be quite short and wide, and shadings in the "o" and the "O" have a tendency to pull back strongly to the left.

Because of the wide selection of swash letters and the warm tone and regular flow of other characters, the Italic version of Cloister is feminine in appeal, but it is one of the most vigorous and beautiful Italics available.

GOUDY OLDSTYLE

Another Roman type that closely resembles the early *Venetian* faces is Goudy Oldstyle, which was produced by Frederic W. Goudy, America's foremost designer of type. One main difference between this type and that introduced by Jenson is in more generous serifs and greater contrast between light and heavy elements. Both are clearly modeled after the style of manuscript hands.

Although Goudy type has a warmth of tone like Cloister, it is more open in design, contains more decorative features, and possesses an easy, graceful flow that adds to its striking individuality. There is much greater freedom of design and a noticeable departure from the studied formality of Cloister, with a retention of enough of the classic to lend dignity and refinement.

Because of its decorative features, Goudy Oldstyle has a feminine appeal, and consequently it has experienced great popularity in advertising and in magazines directed toward women readers. It also is used extensively on women's pages, on feature and fashion sections in newspapers, and for feature headlines.

However, Goudy types, especially in the bold variety, have sufficient strength to make them suitable for many uses where masculine appeal is desired. In fact, some newspapers rely heavily on Goudy in their headline schedules, but its popularity as a headline type is not so widespread as when it was first introduced.

In the smaller sizes, it is very legible and serves well as a body type in advertisements, booklets, folders, and other small printed pieces. Because of its rich color, it is well suited for display purposes and can be used very advantageously with several of the other Roman types where close harmonious effects are desired. (Goudy Oldstyle is used for chapter headings in this book.)

One of the most outstanding individual features of Goudy—the feature that is most easily remembered—is the diamond-shaped dot over the "i" and "j." This characteristic is not found in any of the more common Roman types.

All the capitals are wide, open letters. Particularly distinctive are the "splash" endings in the "L" and "E," which assist in leading the eye easily along a line. The "O" and "Q" are very round. The bottom part of the loop forming the "P" does not quite reach the stem. In the "w," there is a perfect "v" on the right-hand side, but the line coming up to form the right side of the "v" on the left stops when it reaches the element slanting up from the other side.

The serif at the juncture of the elements at the top of the capital "N" does not extend all the way across, whereas the one on the vertical element on the right is equally divided on each side. Also, in the "M," serifs at the top extend outward, leaving a wide, unbroken white space in the center.

Serifs at the bottom of letters have a slightly concave, uneven appearance, carrying out still further the pleasing curve so noticeable in the "E" and the "L." The "a" has a ribbon-like ending on the curved line at the top of the letter, which also is apparent in the flag at the top of the "r."

These same characteristics are carried out in Goudy Italic, which is

A B C D E F G H I
J K L M N O P Q R
S T U V W X Y Z

1

2

3.

4

5

The "tramp printer" was a colorful figure in the history of American journalism. He learned his trade the hard way by serving an apprenticeship as a printer's devil. Then he harkened to the call of the open road and spent the rest of his life traveling far and wide over the country, stopping only long enough in any one place to earn sufficient money to pay his way on to the next.

He was famous for his tall stories, which he gathered from the many towns and villages he

12 POINT ROMAN

Anyone planning to enter the profession of journalism should learn as much as possible about the tools of his trade. Foremost among these are printing types, for it is through them that he will make his voice heard.

The invention of printing with movable type was one of the greatest discoveries of all time. It marked a great turning-point in the history of the world by providing a method

14 POINT ITALIC

6

7

8

9

0

a b c d e f g h i j k l m
n o p q r s t u v w x y z

Figure 19.   Goudy Oldstyle.

an attractive face.   It is very desirable for use in feature headlines, on women's and fashion pages in newspapers, and for contrast purposes for display lines in advertising.

Goudy Handtooled, one of the most recent members of this family, which made its appearance in 1923, is an artistic, decorative face that carries all the regular Goudy characteristics, and is given added distinctiveness by highlight effects brought about by tooling on the left

This is Goudy Handtooled

side of elements.   It is one of our best tooled types and is used for display purposes and for certain headlines where the feeling of quality and sophistication is desired.

BODONI

The most popular Modern Roman type in use today is Bodoni, which is fashioned closely after the face cut by Giambattista Bodoni during the latter part of the eighteenth century.   A crisp, vigorous, clean-cut type, Bodoni is more geometric in design than any of the Oldstyle Romans.   In many ways, it has the appearance of having been made with ruler and pen, but there are enough color and variety in design to avoid monotony.

Because of its preciseness of form, Bodoni has a quality of refinement and dignity which makes it an excellent type for use in the more formal kinds of advertising.   It is used widely by advertisers of high-class men's furnishings, formal wear, jewelry, and toiletries for gentlemen.   On the other hand, the fine-line serifs and delicate touches in some letters make it suitable for some of the more feminine kinds of advertising, where the accent is on fashion or reserve.

The warmth of tone and easy flow of the best Oldstyle Romans are missing, but a certain sparkle and orderliness about Bodoni give it great appeal.   Its popularity as a headline type for use in newspapers and magazines has increased rapidly in recent years.   In fact, many publications employ it exclusively in their headline schedules, making use of several branches of the family for the necessary variety.   Bodoni is an excellent choice for this purpose because letters fit closely together, and it has a clear, crisp appearance that is very pleasing.

Distinctiveness is obtained in several ways.   There is great contrast between light and heavy elements, and the serifs at the bottom of vertical strokes are very thin and straight-line.   Letters are open and legible but are slightly more condensed in design than most of the Oldstyles

A B C D E F G H I
J K L M N O P Q R
S T U V W X Y Z

1 **6**

The "tramp printer" was a colorful figure in the history of American journalism. He learned his trade the hard way by serving an apprenticeship as a printer's devil. Then he harkened to the call of the open road and spent the rest of his life traveling far and wide over the country, stopping only long enough in any one place to earn sufficient money to pay his way on to the next.

2 **7**

He was famous for his tall stories, which he gathered from the many towns and villages he

12 POINT ROMAN

3 **8**

Anyone planning to enter the profession of journalism should learn as much as possible about the tools of his trade. Foremost among these are printing types, for it is through them that he will make his voice heard.

4 **9**

The invention of printing with movable type was one of the greatest discoveries of all time. It marked a great turning-point

14 POINT ITALIC

5 **0**

a b c d e f g h i j k l m
n o p q r s t u v w x y z

Figure 20. Bodoni.

and fit closely together. Descenders and ascenders are very long. These characteristics contribute to the desirability of Bodoni as a headline type.

Shadings within the "o's" are perfectly balanced, as in other rounded letters, and the ending at the bottom of the "t" terminates in a thin upstroke, corresponding in weight and form to the bottom endings of the "c" and "e," which carry out a pleasing regularity of design.

Serifs on the "C" are similar to those found in Caslon, but the letter has a more chiseled appearance. The "G" has a short up-stroke which thickens as it comes up to meet the thin serif at the end. The right foot of the "R" swings down and out, ending in a thin stroke at line-level. None of the capitals is unnaturally wide.

The "c," "f," and "a" terminate at the top in distinct dot formations. The same characteristic is noticeable in the "g," in which the loop at the bottom is connected with a thin, angular neck. The "t" is chiseled out at the top, and the cross-bar is very thin. The "j" extends below the main line, and the "y" sweeps well below the line, terminating in a dot ending.

Bodoni Italic has much the same appearance as the regular face, except that it slants to the right and serifs are eliminated in some of the letters. It is open, clean-looking, and very legible—attributes which make it exceptionally well suited for use in feature headlines. Magazines, as well as newspapers, use it widely.

Bodoni Campanile

Another interesting member of the Bodoni family is Campanile. Although this face carries most of the regular characteristics of Bodoni, it is easily distinguished from the rest because of its extreme slenderness. Lower-case letters, as well as the capitals, are very tall, and this characteristic is accentuated by the shape and placement of serifs on some letters.

For instance, this type has distinct knob-endings on such letters as the "a," "f," and "y," which are attached to the main elements by thin lines. In the "g," this knob is placed high above the upper loop, giving emphasis to the upright appearance of the letter, and in the "f," the curve at the top is chiseled out to accommodate the ending.

Variation between light and heavy elements is great, and most of the serifs are thin and straight-line. Descenders are fairly long; ascenders are short. One outstanding characteristic is the pronounced bulge at the sides of the "o" and the "O," which is apparent also in other letters with elements that curve at the side.

A B C D E F G H I
J K L M N O P Q R
S T U V W X Y Z

1
6

The "tramp printer" was a colorful figure in the history of American journalism. He learned his trade the hard way by serving an apprenticeship as a printer's devil. Then he harkened to the call of the open road and spent the rest of his life traveling far and wide over the country, stopping only long enough in any one place to earn sufficient

18 Point Campanile

2
7

3
8

Anyone planning to enter the profession of journalism should learn as much as possible about the

30 Point Campanile Italic

4
9

5
0

a b c d e f g h i j k l m
n o p q r s t u v w x y z

Figure 21. Ludlow-set in Bodoni Campanile and Italic.

Because of its mechanical, extra-condensed appearance, Campanile must be used with caution. It can be employed successfully with other Bodoni faces and with Century, because of its thin, tall, geometric design, but it is not a good companion type for most of the Oldstyle Romans.

For purposes of contrast, it frequently is used appropriately with Gothic types. However, whenever this face is placed with types from other families and races, the matter of shape harmony must be considered carefully.

Campanile is used widely for display purposes in advertisements and for feature headlines, where emphasis through contrast is desired. Since it is too condensed to be highly legible, it is not very suitable as a body type, even in small masses.

ONYX

A type known as Onyx resembles Campanile so closely that the two frequently are confused. Letters are tall and slender, and, for the most part, are very similar to Campanile in shape and structure.

However, there are some very pronounced differences, only a few of which need to be remembered for purposes of identification. In the first place, contrast between light and heavy elements is greater than in Campanile. The cross-bar in the "A" is considerably lower, and letters such as the "O" and "D" do not have the pronounced bulge that is characteristic of Campanile. Consequently, most of the letters have a more rectangular appearance, which results in a slightly plainer effect.

Like Campanile, this type is used mainly for feature headlines and display in newspapers and magazines, and the same rules of harmony apply. Onyx can be combined best with Modern Roman and Gothic faces, and it should never be employed with the more ornate types which conflict in design.

BOOKMAN OLDSTYLE

Bookman is a very legible type, but it lacks the beauty of the other Oldstyle Romans. In design, it is much plainer, and when used in mass, it presents a slightly heavy appearance, which somewhat limits its usefulness. However, because it is sturdy and easy to read, it frequently is chosen for service in feature headlines and on special pages, but it seldom is found in any great amounts in most newspaper and magazine headline schedules.

Bookman gives the feeling of strength, honesty, dependability, simplicity, frankness, and reliability. It is exceptionally warm in tone, a

A B C D E F G H I
J K L M N O P Q R
S T U V W X Y Z

1
6

The "tramp printer" was a colorful figure in the history of American journalism. He learned his trade the hard way by serving an apprenticeship as a printer's devil. Then he harkened to the call of the open road and spent the rest of his life traveling far and wide over the country, stopping only

18 POINT ROMAN

2
7

3
8

Anyone planning to enter the profession of journalism should learn as much as possible about the tools of his

30 POINT ITALIC

4
9

5
0

a b c d e f g h i j k l m
n o p q r s t u v w x y z

Figure 22. Onyx.

characteristic that is obtained mainly by the weight of elements rather than by their variation. On the whole, it is not an attractive face, but it can be used effectively as a body type where depth of color is desired, along with some of the other more sprightly Oldstyles, and it is suitable for display lines in the smaller sizes.

Advertisers of the heavier and more masculine types of merchandise often find Bookman a good choice. However, there is nothing cheap or boisterous in its appeal, and it should never be employed where "shouting" seems desirable. It is adapted to messages that are straightforward and down-to-earth, but at the same time marked with an air of refinement.

At first glance, Bookman seems to be a plain-line type, but on careful examination it will be noted that there is some slight variation in weight of elements. This, together with the wideness of letter-forms, gives it a decidedly masculine appearance.

It has serifs which slant to the right, like other Oldstyle Romans, but they are squared off at the ends. Terminals of letters such as the "t" and the "e" also have this chopped-off effect—a distinct departure from Caslon, Goudy, and Garamond.

Another outstanding characteristic is the definite "back-pull" of the serifs on the "S," and "G." Several of the capitals are very wide, especially the "B," "D," "E," and "S." In the "W," the two elements at the top-center have a single serif.

The leg on the right side of the "K" joins the up-stroke at a point well away from the vertical element on the left. The "Q" is very unusual, and the "T," although designed somewhat like the one in Caslon, with serifs that rise above the main cross-line at the top, is much heavier and has less graceful curves than the Caslon letter.

Lower-case letters are quite tall and open, and descenders and ascenders are very short. The most unusual small letter is the "s," in which the serif at the top pulls back, as in the "S."

Bookman Italic, like the Oldstyle version, is very wide and plain, with the same characteristics carrying through without change, except for the slight slant of letters to the right. A few special swash characters, including the "A," "M," and "R," are available in the smaller sizes and add some liveliness when used.

CHELTENHAM

A widely used type family, consisting of more than thirty members, is Cheltenham. Designed in 1906 by Bertram Grosvenor Goodhue and Ingalls Kimball of the Cheltenham Press of New York, this type met

A B C D E F G H I J K L M N O P Q R S T U V W X Y Z

1

2

The "tramp printer" was a colorful figure in the history of American journalism. He learned his trade the hard way by serving an apprenticeship as a printer's devil. Then he harkened to the call of the open road and spent the rest of his life traveling far and wide over the country, stopping only long enough in any one place to earn sufficient money to pay his way on to the next.

He was famous for his tall stories, which he gathered from the many towns and villages he

12 POINT ROMAN

3

4

Anyone planning to enter the profession of journalism should learn as much as possible about the tools of his trade. Foremost among these are printing types, for it is through them that he will make his voice heard.

The invention of printing with movable type was one of the greatest discoveries of all time. It marked a great turning-point

12 POINT ITALIC

5

6

7

8

9

0

a b c d e f g h i j k l m n o p q r s t u v w x y z

Figure 23. Bookman Oldstyle.

with immediate favor among printers and publishers.   For some time
it was the most widely used type in the country, displacing temporarily
some of the older Roman types that had served for many years.[3]   In
time, its popularity diminished somewhat, but it continues to rank high
as a favored display type in American newspapers.

Cheltenham has both Oldstyle and Modern Roman features.   Serifs
that curve slightly, and variations in weight of elements would place
it in the Oldstyle classification; whereas the squared-off effects at the
top of vertical elements, balanced shadings, chopped-off endings in
some letters, and blunt serifs tend to put it in the Modern category.

However, it does not have the freedom and gracefulness of Caslon
and Garamond, or the crisp, clean-cut appearance of Bodoni.   It lies in
between these, and since it does have characteristics of both styles, it
is generally referred to as a Mixed Roman type.

Unlike most other Romans which are made in only regular and bold,
Cheltenham is available in three weights: light, medium, and bold.
Furthermore, there are four widths of faces from which to choose:
regular, wide, condensed, and extra-condensed.   Such a wide selection
of styles greatly increases the versatility and adaptability of this prominent type family.

Because of its heavy lines and rugged design, Cheltenham prints well
on newsprint, gives clear reproduction in stereotype plates, and can
withstand the tremendous pressure of mat-making machines better than
Roman types containing finer lines.   It is used widely in newspaper
headlines, for which it is particularly well adapted because of its compact structure, weight of characters, and large number of styles.

Some daily newspapers in this country still have complete head
schedules in Cheltenham type faces, in which they obtain wide variety
through careful selection of members from this big family.   However,
the trend for several years has been toward Bodoni, combinations of
Roman types of greater beauty and sparkle, and the more modern
Gothics.   As a display type for use in advertisements, Cheltenham is
popular, but here also the more artistic faces, such as Goudy, Garamond, Caslon, Cloister, and Bodoni, are taking preference.

Since Cheltenham is obviously a very masculine type, it is relied on
quite heavily for use in advertising for men and in other kinds where
emphasis is to be placed on sturdiness and durability.   In the bolder
versions, it denotes great strength, and consequently is adapted for use
in heavy display lines and large headlines.   Editors frequently use it

---

[3] Olson, *Typography and Mechanics of the Newspaper*, page 156.

A B C D E F G H I
J K L M N O P Q R
S T U V W X Y Z

1

2

The "tramp printer" was a colorful figure in the history of American journalism. He learned his trade the hard way by serving an apprenticeship as a printer's devil. Then he harkened to the call of the open road and spent the rest of his life traveling far and wide over the country, stopping only long enough in any one place to earn sufficient money to pay his way on to the next.

He was famous for his tall stories, which he gathered from the many towns and villages he visited on his journeys, and he loved to spin long yarns about

6

7

12 POINT ROMAN

3

4

5

Anyone planning to enter the profession of journalism should learn as much as possible about the tools of his trade. Foremost among these are printing types, for it is through them that he will make his voice heard.

The invention of printing with movable type was one of the greatest discoveries of all time. It marked a great turning-point

8

9

0

14 POINT ITALIC

a b c d e f g h i j k l m
n o p q r s t u v w x y z

Figure 24. Cheltenham Oldstyle.

very appropriately on sports pages, when proper attention is given to the choice of companion faces.

In the lighter face, Cheltenham is not objectionable as a body type in advertisements, but care must be taken not to use the bold versions in large masses. Although Cheltenham Oldstyle can be employed on women's and society pages provided enough of the Italic version is used to give a lighter touch, some of the true Oldstyle or Modern Romans would be more suitable.

The thick, heavy, and rather blunt serifs go to make up one of the most outstanding characteristics of Cheltenham. Although there is some contrast between light and heavy elements, the variations are slight as compared to other Romans, and, as a consequence, the type has a uniformly black appearance which is accentuated by chopped-off elements in several of the lower-case letters and squared-off serifs at the top and bottom of all vertical elements.

A most distinctive letter and one which will assist perhaps more than any other in identifying this face is the "g." It will be noticed that when the top part of the loop forming the upper portion of this letter is covered up, the lower part takes on the appearance of a figure "5." The "G" likewise is unusual, with a chin which protrudes like that of a pugilist.

In the "m" and "n," the vertical element on the left extends above the loop to which it is attached and ends in a squared-off serif at the top.   The "c" and "s" contain knob-endings.

The "A" somewhat resembles the same letter in Caslon, but differs in that the right-hand element which extends beyond the one on the left is not so chiseled out at the end and there is less contrast between light and heavy strokes.   The "E" is a very wide letter, with the bottom element extending beyond the two elements above it.   The serifs at the bottom of the "b" and at the top of the "q" are pointed and thus are out of harmony with serifs on other letters.   The main line of letters is moderately high.   Ascenders are quite generous, but descenders are very short.

Even in the Italic, Cheltenham looks heavy and masculine, particularly in the bold version.   With few exceptions, the characteristics apparent in the Roman varieties carry through.   One noticeable exception is the manner in which down-strokes on some letters—notably the "p," "m," and "n"—are chopped off in conformity with endings on other letters that terminate sharply as they swing upward.   Cheltenham Italic is used largely for display purposes and for feature headlines.

CENTURY

Century is a large type family that has experienced great popularity. Although it lacks the grace and beauty of some of the other Roman types, it is very serviceable, legible, and adaptable to a wide variety of uses.

Because of certain facial variations, Century cannot be classified strictly as an Oldstyle Roman; nor does it have all of the features of Modern Roman. Most of its members contain characteristics of both, and consequently, like Cheltenham, it may be regarded as a Mixed Roman.

The original face of Century was cut in 1895 by L. B. Benton, in collaboration with Theodore L. De Vinne, of *Century Magazine*.[4] Dissatisfied with the expanded body types then obtainable, De Vinne set out to design one that would be better adapted to pages with narrow margins, such as those used in the *Century Magazine*. Because of its slightly condensed appearance, Century was not adopted generally for use by other printers and publishers.

However, in 1900 a leading type manufacturer introduced Century Expanded, which has been used extensively as a body type because of its legibility and attractive design. Another member of this family, known as Century Schoolbook, has been a leading choice for the printing of schoolbooks for many years.

Because of the clear, orderly, and slightly condensed design, this type is used for headlines in many newspapers and magazines. Since it contains both Modern and Oldstyle characteristics, it will harmonize satisfactorily with types of either variety—a feature that increases its adaptability.

Some publications continue to prefer Century as a body type, but it has been displaced in many by other more recent faces designed especially by manufacturers as body type for newspapers.

In advertising, Century is employed for display in the bold and Italic versions, but it sees more service as a body type, often as a companion to some other face with a less restrained appearance. Most newspapers and printing plants have Century types and many use it generously because of its extreme versatility.

Some members of this family differ considerably from others, but certain characteristics are common to all branches. Lower-case letters are quite tall and open, with rather generous ascenders, but short

---

[4] Olson, *Typography and Mechanics of the Newspaper*, page 153.

A B C D E F G H I
J K L M N O P Q R
S T U V W X Y Z

1

2

3

4

5

The "tramp printer" was a colorful figure in the history of American journalism. He learned his trade the hard way by serving an apprenticeship as a printer's devil. Then he harkened to the call of the open road and spent the rest of his life traveling far and wide over the country, stopping only long enough in any one place to earn sufficient money to pay his way on to the next.

He was famous for his tall stories, which he gathered from the many towns and villages

12 POINT ROMAN

Anyone planning to enter the profession of journalism should learn as much as possible about the tools of his trade. Foremost among these are printing types, for it is through them that he will make his voice heard.

The invention of printing with movable type was one of the greatest discoveries of all time. It marked a great

14 POINT ITALIC

6

7

8

9

0

a b c d e f g h i j k l m
n o p q r s t u v w x y z

Figure 25. Century Schoolbook.

descenders. This, along with the fact that letters fit closely together, makes Century appear to be slightly condensed.

In the varieties of Century most easily distinguished, certain distinctive features are helpful in identification. For instance, the right-hand foot of the "R" terminates in a sharp up-swing. The "G" has a thin chin that extends slightly below the main line of letters.

Serifs on the "S" and "s" are vertical and pointed. The cross-stroke on the "e" is low, leaving considerable white space at the top of the letter, and the finial, which comes up high, has a chopped-off effect— a characteristic that is apparent in other letters with similar endings.

The "E," "F," and "T" have heavily bracketed serifs, and several letters, such as the "c," "f," "g," "j," and "y," have well-defined knob-endings.

Serifs at the top and bottom of vertical elements in lower-case characters are squared-off. This modern tendency is accentuated further by balanced shadings within letters that are somewhat more curved than those in Bodoni, and by considerable contrast between light and heavy elements.

Every member of the Century family does not carry all these characteristics, but some of the main features are apparent throughout. For instance, Century Oldstyle—one branch of the family—more nearly approaches true Oldstyle Roman, in that serifs at the top of vertical elements are sloped, with those in the "S" tending to pull back. There is less contrast between light and heavy elements, and the type does not have such a condensed appearance.

However, despite these features, which tend to soften the design and lend more grace, Century Oldstyle otherwise is very similar to other members of the family. At the same time, the problem of distinguishing it from other Oldstyle Romans, particularly Caslon, becomes more difficult.

Except for slight slanting to the right, the Italic versions of the face contain most of the main, outstanding characteristics, some of which are strongly stressed. Knob-endings are very decided, chopped-off effects are more numerous, and contrast between elements is greater.

Century Italic faces are not so decorative or flowing as the Italic versions of Garamond and Caslon, and consequently are not so well adapted to extremely feminine appeals.

RAILROAD GOTHIC

Of all the races, members of the Gothic race bear the closest resemblances to one another. Except in the case of isolated letters in some families, there are no serifs, and this feature, together with the absence of distinct shadings, contributes to a sameness in structure and appearance that is confusing.

However, the number of true Gothic families in common use today is comparatively small, with about fifteen meeting the general demand. Most publishers rely on two or three of these Gothics, supplemented usually by some modified forms which carry both Gothic and Roman characteristics, for use when special effects are desired. This limited employment helps to simplify the problem involved in identification.

Although the number of differences among Gothics is less than among Roman types, close study will reveal that each family within the race has certain characteristics, peculiar to it alone, which set it off from all the others.

One of the boldest and most blocky members of this race is Railroad Gothic. Available only in capitals, this type is used for heavy banner headlines in many newspapers, and it occasionally is employed for display lines in advertising in the smaller sizes. It also is used in sale bills, posters, handbills, and in large advertisements where great strength or the suggestion of cheapness is to be emphasized.

Railroad Gothic is rugged and durable, but unattractive. Because of its plainness and blackness, its usefulness is limited, and it gradually is being displaced by some of the more recent and more graceful Sans-Serif faces. All letters are plain and blocky, with lines almost uniform in weight and sharp, horizontal finials.

In some of the capitals, such as the "B" and "D," the curves are not smooth, but appear to have been formed by a rather abrupt trimming off of the corners.

The right leg of the "R" swings out and downward, ending in a horizontal line at the bottom. The "G" has a chin that extends down to the bottom of the letter. The cross-bar in the "A" is very low, which nevertheless leaves a very small amount of white space at the top, because of the extreme weight of elements. In the "K," the two elements which slant in from the right merge where they reach the vertical stroke.

Railroad Gothic contains no lower-case letters, but it is available in small, as well as larger, sizes.

Franklin Gothic

Another one of the older, more conventional Gothics is Franklin Gothic.

For many years it was used extensively by newspapers throughout

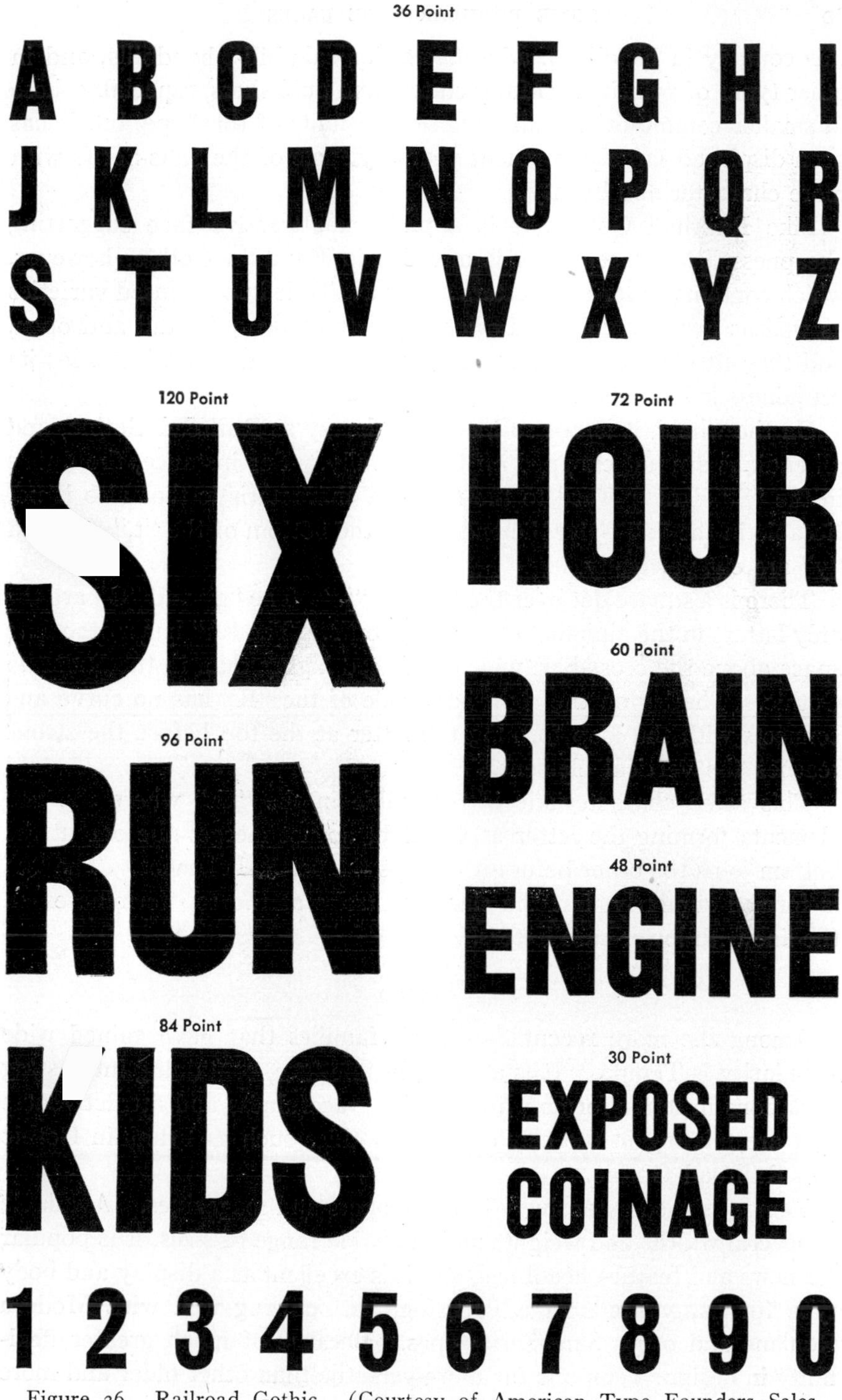

A B C D E F G H I
J K L M N O P Q R
S T U V W X Y Z

120 Point

SIX

72 Point

HOUR

60 Point

BRAIN

96 Point

RUN

48 Point

ENGINE

84 Point

KIDS

30 Point

EXPOSED
COINAGE

1 2 3 4 5 6 7 8 9 0

Figure 26. Railroad Gothic. (Courtesy of American Type Founders Sales Corporation.)

this country in headlines, advertisements, sale bills, handbills, and in other types of printing. Many editors and publishers, especially those in smaller communities, still have several fonts of this type, but it has been displaced largely in recent years by some of the Sans-Serifs with more character and beauty.

Like Railroad Gothic, it is a plain, unattractive face suggesting cheapness. More selection is afforded in Franklin Gothic, however, which contains lower-case letters and is available in condensed varieties as well as in the regular. Lower-case letters are quite tall and open, and they fit closely together, lending a compactness that increases its usefulness in headlines.

On the whole, it is not so black and heavy as Railroad Gothic, and all endings are not chopped off horizontally. For instance, the finials in the "S" slant upward to the right—a characteristic that also is noticeable in the "s"—and the endings at the bottom of the "t," "j," and "y" are cut vertically.

There is a square dot over the "i" and "j." The "g" and "G" are the only letters in the alphabet containing serifs. The "A" has more white space above the cross-bar, which is placed higher than in the Railroad Gothic. The leg on the right-hand side of the "R" has no curve and connects with the loop forming the letter at the top before the stroke reaches the vertical element.

This same characteristic is noticeable in the "K," where the two elements forming the letter at the right do not merge; the one at the bottom joins the other before it reaches the vertical element. The "k" is formed similarly, but the slanting stroke at the top terminates on the line with lower-case letters.

TEMPO

Among the more recent Sans-Serif families that have gained wide popularity is Tempo. It is a clean, legible face, containing interesting variations in letter-forms which lend a gracefulness and attractiveness that are missing in the conventional Gothics such as Franklin Gothic and Railroad Gothic.

Tempo is used extensively in newspapers and magazines. Available in several widths and weights and in a wide range of sizes, it is popular for news and feature headlines, and it is excellent as a display and body type for many kinds of advertising, harmonizing well with Modern Romans and other Sans-Serif types. Because of much greater flexibility in design, Tempo is far more versatile than other older and more conventional members of the Gothic race.

A B C D E F G H I
J K L M N O P Q R
S T U V W X Y Z

1

6

The "tramp printer" was a colorful fig-ure in the history of American journalism. He learned his trade the hard way by serving an apprenticeship as a printer's devil.   Then he harkened to the call of the open road and spent the rest of his life traveling far and wide over the country, stopping only long enough in any one place to earn sufficient money to pay his way on to the next.

He was famous for his tall stories, which

2

7

12 POINT ROMAN

3

8

Anyone planning to enter the profession of journalism should learn as much as possible about the tools of his trade.   Foremost among these are printing types, for it is through them that he will make his voice heard.

The invention of printing with movable type was one of the

4

9

5

0

14 POINT ROMAN

a b c d e f g h i j k l m
n o p q r s t u v w x y z

Figure 27.   Franklin Gothic.

A B C D E F G H I
J K L M N O P Q R
S T U V W X Y Z

1

2

The "tramp printer" was a colorful figure in the history of American journalism. He learned his trade the hard way by serving an apprenticeship as a printer's devil. Then he harkened to the call of the open road and spent the rest of his life traveling far and wide over the country, stopping only long enough in any one place to earn sufficient money to pay his way on to the next.

He was famous for his tall stories, which he gathered from the many towns and villages he visited on his journeys, and he loved to spin long yarns about his varied experiences. Aside from being a skilled crafts-

12 POINT TEMPO MEDIUM

6

7

3

8

4

Anyone planning to enter the profession of journalism should learn as much as possible about the tools of his trade. Foremost among these are printing types, for it is through them that he will make his voice heard.

The invention of printing with movable type was one of the greatest discoveries of all time. It marked a turning-point in the history of the

14 POINT TEMPO MEDIUM ITALIC

9

5

0

a b c d e f g h i j k l m
n o p q r s t u v w x y z

Figure 28. Ludlow-set in Tempo Medium and Italic.

Tempo is sturdy, durable, and much plainer than Roman types, but it does not suggest cheapness. On the contrary, it gives a feeling of cool refinement, quality, and dependability. In the heavier varieties, it is strong and masculine; but Tempo Light, although plain and simple in design, can be used very successfully where femininity is the dominant appeal.

Letters are well proportioned, open, and legible. In such characters as the "A," "N," "M," and "W," elements join in a sharp pointing effect, which is also carried out at the end of slanting elements in other letters.

In the "g," "m," "n," "p," "q," and "r," the vertical elements rise above the main parts of the letters at the top, giving the effect of serifs; and this same feature also is carried out at the bottom of the "u," "b," and "d."

The element forming the "a" at the top swings far back over the oblong loop. The "O" and "o" are very round, and so is the "e," which resembles a circle that is not quite completed.

Endings of the "s" and "S" slant uniformly to the right, but in the "e," the ending slants the other way. This lack of uniformity is noticeable in finials of other letters—a characteristic that adds liveliness to Tempo.

The cross-bar on the "t" extends farther to the right than to the left. The element forming the "g" at the bottom swings far to the left. The "i" and "j" each consist of a straight vertical line with a dot above, the only difference being that the "j" extends below the main line of letters. The "f" is very tall, with a low cross-bar.

Outside elements of the "M" slant inward, but they are straight in the "N." The formation of the "G" is unusual, with the short, horizontal finial pulling hard to the left. The "F" and "E" are narrow letters, with all cross-bars appearing to be the same length. The cross-bar at the top of the "T" and the bottom line of the "L" are short, giving these letters a condensed effect.

The tail on the "Q" is not centered on the body at the bottom and pulls to the right. The right-hand legs on the "R" and the "K" extend high on the vertical element.

In Tempo, as in most of the other more recent Gothics, certain letters are available in more than one style. This circumstance frequently adds to the difficulty in distinguishing one family from another. However, enough of the main variations are retained to make correct identification possible.

The Italic versions of this face carry most of the characteristics of the regular design, but a few additional variations are noticeable.   In several lower-case letters containing vertical elements, serifs are placed at the bottom, always on the right-hand side.   Although the slant to the right is not pronounced, a curved effect is apparent in many characters, resulting in an unusual and a more flowing design with some touches of femininity.

Although all Gothic types have some characteristics in common—especially that of plainness of design—a careful study of Futura, Vogue, Metro, Erbar, Spartan, and other members of this race will disclose many distinct differences which set one off from the other, and, at the same time, help determine their usefulness.

STYMIE

A typical example of the Square-Serif group of types is Stymie. Except for the addition of straight, square-ended serifs, this face resembles the Gothic forms.   It is geometric in design, uniform in weight, and the letters are wide and open.   Inherently, it is not a quality type, but its plainness, simplicity, and sturdiness make it useful in a wide range of advertising dealing with the more common kinds of products, where it is employed for both display and body matter.   It also is used for newspaper and magazine headlines, and for many kinds of commercial printing.

Stymie is available in four weights: light, medium, bold, and black (extra-bold).   Although this face is very plain, in the lighter versions it has a definite suggestion of femininity; however, the other three weights are strongly masculine in tone.

Because of its extreme plainness and the wideness of letters, which is accentuated by the rather long, straight serifs, Stymie—even in condensed varieties—is not so well adapted for headline usage as Sans-Serif and Roman types, but it can be used successfully if careful attention is given to the choice of companion type that harmonizes in design.

Stymie Bold and Stymie Black, when included in headline schedules, tend to give the page a spotted appearance because of their extreme blackness unless they are combined carefully with decks of lighter tone to afford the proper gradation.

Stymie harmonizes well with other Square-Serif faces and with most of the Sans-Serifs, but its use with Oldstyle or Mixed Romans should be restricted.   Modern Romans, which approach it more closely in design, sometimes may be used with Stymie, but the results are not entirely satisfactory.

As in the case of Gothics, members of this group resemble one an-

A B C D E F G H I J K L M N O P Q R S T U V W X Y Z

1

2

3

4

5

The "tramp printer" was a colorful figure in the history of American journalism. He learned his trade the hard way by serving an apprenticeship as a printer's devil. Then he harkened to the call of the open road and spent the rest of his life traveling far and wide over the country, stopping only long enough in any one place to earn sufficient money to pay his way on to the next.

He was famous for his tall stories, which he gathered from the many towns and villages

12 POINT ROMAN

Anyone planning to enter the profession of journalism should learn as much as possible about the tools of his trade. Foremost among these are printing types, for it is through them that he will make his voice heard.

The invention of printing with movable type was one of the greatest dis-

14 POINT ITALIC

6

7

8

9

0

a b c d e f g h i j k l m n o p q r s t u v w x y z

Figure 29. Stymie Light.

other very closely, and the fact that some letters come in more than one variety complicates matters of recognition. However, here again, each particular family contains certain characteristics that aid in its identification.

In Stymie, the serif at the bottom of the "t" pulls to the right, forming an L-shape, and the cross-bar on this letter appears to be almost evenly divided on each side of the vertical element. All letters containing loops have a very round appearance.

There is no slanting in serifs: they are either exactly horizontal or exactly vertical, giving the appearance of having been made with ruler and pen. The "G" has a generous chin, and the horizontal stroke in this letter extends far to the left of the up-stroke, but only slightly to the right.

Dots over the "i" and "j" are square, and the serifs at the top of these letters pull to the left. The "y" has a straight-line horizontal serif at the bottom. The "k" has an L-shaped ending at the top of the vertical element, with the serif on the left, and the slanting line going out from the main stem ends at the top of the main line of lower-case letters. Serifs at the top of the "M" do not extend all the way across, but pull out on each side.

The middle cross-bar in the "E" is shorter than the other two, and the cross-bar at the top of the "F" is the longer. The "Q" appears to be formed by the addition of a curved line across the bottom of a perfect circle. The line forming the "g" at the bottom swings to the left, but stops before reaching a point even with the extreme left side of the loop. The "j" extends below the main line of letters. Descenders in Stymie are very short, but ascenders are quite generous.

These characteristics also are found in the Italic versions. Stymie Light Italic is an attractive face, possessing a delicacy and simplicity of design that are distinctly feminine. These features make it suitable for use on women's pages and in advertising for women, when used along with the lighter versions of Stymie Regular or with other faces which harmonize.

RADIANT

Among the Gothic types that break away from the more conventional members of this race is one known as Radiant. Like the others, it is a plain, open design, without serifs, but the employment of light and heavy elements and a suggestion of shading within letters set it off definitely from the rest.

Except for the lack of serifs, it resembles the Modern Romans—

A B C D E F G H I
J K L M N O P Q R
S T U V W X Y Z

1

The"tramp printer"was a colorful figure in the history of American journalism. He learned his trade the hard way by serving an apprenticeship as a printer's devil. Then he harkened to the call of the open road and spent the rest of his life traveling far and wide over the country, stopping only long enough in any one place to earn sufficient money to pay his way on to the next.

He was famous for his tall stories, which he gathered from the many towns and villages he visited on his journeys, and he loved to spin long

12 POINT RADIANT MEDIUM

6

2

7

3

8

Anyone planning to enter the profession of journalism should learn as much as possible about the tools of his trade. Foremost among these are printing types, for it is through them that he will make his voice heard.

The invention of printing with movable type was one of the great-

14 POINT RADIANT HEAVY

4

9

5

0

a b c d e f g h i j k l m
n o p q r s t u v w x y z

Figure 30. Ludlow-set in Radiant Medium and Heavy.

especially in the heavy variety, where there is great contrast between strokes.   Shadings in Radiant are perfectly balanced, and it gives the impression of having been made with ruler and pen.

The ribbon-like effect in the curves of certain letters, such as the "s," "a," and "g," results in thickened, flag-like terminals that lend distinctiveness.

Radiant is a clear, clean, legible face that gives a feeling of simple dignity and dependable quality.   In the Medium variety, it has enough variations to suggest femininity, but Radiant Heavy is extremely masculine in design.

Lower-case letters are tall and open, with very short descenders but generous ascenders.   The "E," "F," and "T" are quite narrow. These characteristics, along with the fact that letters fit closely together, give the type a slightly condensed appearance.

The "G" is formed at the bottom with a short horizontal element that gives the suggestion of a serif, and the terminal on which it is placed does not curve, but rises vertically.

Vertical elements are squared off at both top and bottom, and in such letters as the "p," "q," "m," and "n," they extend above the loops forming them.   The "f" has a hook-like ending at the top, with a thin cross-bar underneath.

The "t" swings to the right at the bottom, and the "j" pulls back abruptly to the left.   The "Q" is formed at the bottom with the tail consisting of a diagonal line that extends to the inside of the letter.

In Radiant Heavy, these characteristics are much more pronounced than in the Medium version.   One slight variation is apparent in the dot over the "i," which is oblong in shape.

Although Radiant is not used so extensively as some of the more regular Gothics, it is an interesting face that can be employed successfully for display purposes where quality or simplicity are to be emphasized. Occasionally it is found in newspaper headlines.

Because of the many variations in elements and the plain, geometric appearance, both the Medium and Heavy versions harmonize well with Modern Romans as well as with other Sans-Serif types.

EDEN

Another unusual type of recent origin, and one that frequently is confused with Radiant, is Eden.   In this face, there is much contrast between light and heavy elements, shadings are perfectly balanced, and finials in several letters have a tendency to thicken as in Radiant.

However, the serifs in Eden place it in the Modern Roman classifica-

A B C D E F G H I
J K L M N O P Q R
S T U V W X Y Z

1

6

The "tramp printer" was a colorful figure in the history of American journalism. He learned his trade the hard way by serving an apprenticeship as a printer's devil. Then he harkened to the call of the open road and spent the rest of his life traveling far and wide over the country, stopping only long enough in any one place to earn sufficient money to pay his way on to the next.

14 POINT EDEN LIGHT

2

7

3

8

Anyone planning to enter the profession of journalism should learn as much as possible about the tools of his trade. Foremost among these are printing types, for it is through them that he will make his voice heard.

The invention of printing with

18 POINT EDEN BOLD

4

9

5

0

a b c d e f g h i j k l m
n o p q r s t u v w x y z

Figure 31. Ludlow-set in Eden Light and Bold.

tion.   The ribbon effect found in Radiant is not so distinct, and letters
are more rectangular in shape—a distinctive characteristic which is extremely helpful in identifying the face.

In letter-form, Eden resembles Square-Serif types more closely than
the Modern Romans.   Serifs are sharp, straight lines, which lack
curved effects.   Lower-case letters are tall and upright, with long ascenders and short descenders.

In such characters as the "O," the curves are short and sharp.   Both
the "K" and "k" are similar in shape.   The serifs at the bottom of the
"t" and "d" pull to the right, and the dot over the "i" and "j" is square.
All letters are wide and open and appear quite blocky when set together in a line.

Because of the great variation in weight of elements, and a slight
tendency toward decorativeness, Eden is not a particularly strong type,
and its rather plain, blocky design keeps it from being extremely feminine.   Consequently, it is somewhat limited in versatility.

Eden is used widely in advertising that deals with clothing, jewelry,
and other products where distinctiveness, rather than extreme strength
and beauty, is desired.   Occasionally it is found in feature headlines,
especially in the bold variety, but because of its unusual design, it does
not fit appropriately into many headline schedules which make use of
Oldstyle Romans.

Lydian

A novelty type family that has received considerable attention among
advertisers in recent years is one known as Lydian.   Like Eden, it is
a mixed design which does not fit into any single racial classification.

Lydian resembles Roman types in most respects, but it has no serifs
—a characteristic which is common to all members of this race.   On
the other hand, it is too decorative to meet the Sans-Serif requirements.
Lydian Italic, which slants slightly to the right, differs only slightly
from regular Lydian.

Letter-forms vary widely.   Some appear to have been made with
pen or brush and possess a pronounced ribbon effect that is very distinctive; others are plain and straight-line.

The dot over the "i" and "j" is diamond-shaped and placed horizontally.   Finials in such letters as the "e," "c," and "a" sweep out into
a sharp point.   Cross-bars on the "T" and "t" are chopped off at an
angle.   Both descenders and ascenders are quite generous.   The "W"
consists of two superimposed "V's," but in the "w" the elements in the
middle merge.

A B C D E F G H I
J K L M N O P Q R
S T U V W X Y Z

1

6

The "tramp printer" was a colorful figure in the history of American journalism. He learned his trade the hard way by serving an apprenticeship as a printer's devil. Then he harkened to the call of the open road and spent the rest of his life traveling far and wide over the country, stopping only long enough in any one place to earn sufficient money to pay his way on to the next.

2

7

He was famous for his tall stories, which he gathered from the many towns and villages he

12 POINT ROMAN

3

8

Anyone planning to enter the profession of journalism should learn as much as possible about the tools of his trade. Foremost among these are printing types, for it is through them that he will make his voice heard.

4

9

The invention of printing with movable type was one of the greatest discoveries of all time. It marked a great turning-point in the history of the world by providing a method for mak-

5

0

14 POINT ITALIC

a b c d e f g h i j k l m
n o p q r s t u v w x y z

Figure 32. Lydian.

Both Lydian and Lydian Italic are very feminine in design. They are not well adapted to use in large masses because of warmth of tone and the many unusual variations, which reduce legibility. Lydian types are unusual and attractive, but since they depart from the norms of both Roman and Gothic—the two races from which the design was drawn—their adaptability is limited.

Lydian is used mainly for display purposes in advertisements where distinctiveness of design is desired. Because of its eccentric characteristics, it is not very suitable for newspaper headlines and it should not be employed in large masses as a body type. The most desirable effects can be obtained by using Lydian and Lydian Italic together, but both faces harmonize reasonably well with Modern Romans, Sans-Serifs, and with other novelty faces of similar design.

CORONET

Although Script and Cursive types are not employed so extensively as members of the Roman and Gothic races, every publisher and printer have occasion to use them frequently.

Coronet is one of the most widely used members of this group of types. Since characters do not join, it is technically a Cursive type, but letters fit together closely, leaving such a small amount of white space between them that the eye bridges the gaps easily.

Except for the fact that letters are not connected, this type closely resembles the artistic specimens found in practice books used in teaching penmanship in grade schools. Graceful, flowing capitals and small, dainty lower-case letters containing many fine-line variations result in a delicate, informal face of great beauty.

Although no great emphasis is placed on decorative endings and ornamental flourishes, Coronet is a lively, refined face that is distinctly feminine in tone. It is used mainly for display in advertisements dealing with high-class merchandise, where quality or exclusiveness is stressed. Many magazines use it generously for headlines and some newspapers also include feature headlines set in Coronet in their headline schedules.

Since Coronet contains several characteristics common to Modern Romans, it harmonizes well with Bodoni. It can also be used successfully with good Sans-Serif types and with other Cursive and Script types of similar design. It is a good companion type for use with a wide selection of Italic faces.

One of the most distinctive features of Coronet is the white space

A B C D E F G H I
J K L M N O P Q R
S T U V W X Y Z

1

The "tramp printer" was a colorful figure in the history of American journalism. He learned his trade the hard way by serving an apprenticeship as a printer's devil. Then he harkened to the call of the open road and spent the rest of his life traveling far and wide over the country, stopping only long enough in any one place to earn sufficient money to pay his way on to the next.

2

He was famous for his tall stories, which he gathered from the many towns and villages he visited on his journeys, and he loved to spin long yarns about his varied experiences. Aside from being a skilled craftsman, he was well-informed about places and people from coast

14 Point Coronet

3

4

Anyone planning to enter the profession of journalism should learn as much as possible about the tools of his trade. Foremost among these are printing types, for it is through them that he will make his voice heard.

The invention of printing with movable type was one of the greatest discoveries of all time. It marked a great turning-point in the history of the world by providing a method for making the accumulated knowledge of the centuries available to the common people.

14 Point Coronet Bold

5

6

7

8

9

0

a b c d e f g h i j k l m
n o p q r s t u v w x y z

Figure 33. Ludlow-set in Coronet Light and Bold.

left between letters in a line. Capitals are large and flowing; lower-case letters are small. Ascenders and descenders are long.

The "f" has a loop at the top ordinarily found in handwriting, but the bottom part is formed by a thick, solid stroke. This same character-istic is apparent in the "b," "d," "h," "j," "k," and "p." However, the "g," "q," and "y" have open loops that conform with letters made with pen.

Among the capitals, all of which have a hand-drawn appearance, the "D," "F," "G," "P," and "R" are especially distinctive. The "s" is unusual in design, but the "v," "w," "x," and "z" are very plain.

This mixture of plain letters with others of greater finish results in a face that is very interesting and more legible than many other ornate members of the Script and Cursive race.

Mandate

Mandate is a good example of the bolder, masculine Script types which are adapted to more forceful display than Coronet. Although it closely resembles handwriting, with carefully joined letters and uniform elements, Mandate lacks the delicate, fine lines and easy flow of Cor-onet and other more feminine members of the race.

It is a plain, simple, rugged design that slants only slightly to the right. Letters are open and legible, containing little contrast between elements. There is more variety in capitals than in lower-case letters. The "C," "E," "P," "S," "T," and "X" are especially distinctive, ex-tending below the main line of characters.

Lower-case letters, for the most part, are tall and open. However, the "b," "h," "l," "p," "q," and "y"—letters which in handwriting ordinarily contain loops to form the vertical strokes—are filled in solid. This feature adds to the blackness of the face. Ascenders and de-scenders are very short, a characteristic which is emphasized in the "f," causing it to have a slightly top-heavy appearance.

The "O" is oblong in shape, with a small loop at the top which fails to connect with lower-case letters. The "r" rises high on the left-hand side, ending in a slight knob that is connected with the vertical element at the right with a line that slants sharply downward. Dots over the "i" and "j" are heavy and round.

Because of its weight and plainness, Mandate lacks the refinements and grace of Coronet. It denotes strength, forcefulness, and durabil-ity. It is used mainly for display purposes in advertisements dealing with the heavier or more masculine types of merchandise, and it also is employed to some extent in feature headlines in newspapers and in

A B C D E F G H I
J K L M N O P Q R
S T U V V W X Y Z

1

2

3

4

5

The "tramp printer" was a colorful figure in the history of American journalism. He learned his trade the hard way by serving an apprenticeship as a printer's devil. Then he harkened to the call of the open road and spent the rest of his life traveling far
18 Point Mandate

Anyone planning to enter the profession of journalism should learn as much as possible about the tools of his
24 Point Mandate

6

7

8

9

0

a b c d e f g h i j k l m
n o p q r s t u v w x y z

Figure 34. Ludlow-set in Mandate.

magazines, often along with some other face for contrast purposes.

Care should be taken in choosing a suitable companion face, since Mandate is plain and bold in design. It harmonizes fairly well with Modern Romans, but it can be used more appropriately with the plainer Sans-Serif and Square-Serif types in the heavier variety.

Mandate was designed by R. Hunter Middleton, of Chicago. He also designed Coronet, Bodoni Campanile, Eden, Radiant, and Tempo —all of which are discussed in this chapter.

BODY TYPES

A discussion of types would not be complete without some mention of those used in the main body of newspapers. However, problems in identification of the commonly used body-type faces found in present-day newspapers are very complicated, since most of them are offshoots of the Roman designs which preceded them and bear resemblances to one or more of the types already described.

One of the oldest body types is Roman No. 2, which was introduced before 1900, and which for many years was used widely by daily and weekly newspapers in this country. It was followed by Century Expanded, which experienced considerable popularity with the dailies because of its high legibility and sturdy, open design.

However, the ever-increasing speed of presses brought about the need for harder ink-rollers that would withstand greater wear. The wet, or steamed, stereotype matrix was replaced by a dry matrix which required far greater pressure in order to speed up the production of printing plates. The increased pressure required in the making of the dry matrix, which contains some moisture but not nearly so much as the wet matrix, was too great for Roman No. 2 and Century Expanded. As a result, the fine lines in these faces broke down, causing pages to appear too gray, and often too smudgy, for ease in reading—a condition which changes from a thin to a heavier flow of ink would not remedy. Consequently, composing-machine manufacturers began to give serious attention to the problem.

With the aid of expert type designers who based their work on scientific studies in legibility, the Mergenthaler Linotype Company introduced in 1926 a body type known as Ionic No. 5, which gained immediate popularity. Although this face in some ways resembled both Roman No. 2 and Century Expanded, it was a sturdier design, with heavier lines, more open letters to eliminate ink-traps, taller capitals, and lower-case letters almost as high as the capitals. The fine lines and thin endings of elements were eliminated. This achievement was recognized as of great importance and opened the way for further study and experimentation.

The Intertype Corporation soon afterward produced the Ideal News face, which was modeled after Century, but combined many of the better features of both this face and Ionic No. 5.

In the years that followed, several other re-designed types have made their appearance. Tests have shown these to be far more legible than the older newspaper body faces that preceded them and much better

The Army, working with power and precision, never gave the Navy a chance to set itself, but swept down the field with a short side reverse, two passes and a plunge to pile up a total in the first two periods on which they could ride through the rest of the game.

And although the Navy, trailing hopelessly, battered back through the first half by an Army line that was rugged and relentless, made a counter-attack that earned the respect and admiration of everyone, whether he wore the Navy blue or the Army's black, gold and gray, the Army was out of range.

EXAMPLE A.

The Army, working with power and precision, never gave the Navy a chance to set itself, but swept down the field with a short side reverse, two passes and a plunge to pile up a total in the first two periods on which they could ride through the rest of the game.

And although the Navy, trailing hopelessly, battered back through the first half by an Army line that was rugged and relentless, made a counter-attack that earned the respect and admiration of everyone, whether he wore the Navy blue or the Army's black, gold and gray, the Army was out of range.

EXAMPLE B.

The Army, working with power and precision, never gave the Navy a chance to set itself, but swept down the field with a short side reverse, two passes and a plunge to pile up a total in the first two periods on which they could ride through the rest of the game.

And although the Navy, trailing hopelessly, battered back through the first half by an Army line that was rugged and relentless, made a counter-attack that earned the respect and admiration of every one, whether he wore the Navy blue or the Army's

EXAMPLE C.

The Army, working with power and precision, never gave the Navy a chance to set itself, but swept down the field with a short side reverse, two passes and a plunge to pile up a total in the first two periods on which they could ride through the rest of the game.

And, although the Navy, trailing hopelessly, battered back through the first half by an Army line that was rugged and relentless, made a counter-attack that earned the respect and admiration of every one, whether he wore the Navy blue or the Army's black, gold and gray, the Army was out of range.

EXAMPLE D.

Figure 35. Four members of Linotype's Legibility Group of Body Types. Example A is Ionic No. 5; Example B is Excelsior; Example C is Opticon; and Example D is Corona. All these have been set 12 picas wide, 8 on 9. Although they have some common characteristics, each is distinctly different from the others.

adapted to the growing demands of fast newspaper production.   Among them are Excelsior, Textype, Paragon, Opticon, and Corona—all produced by Mergenthaler Linotype Company; and Regal and Rex faces, produced by the Intertype Corporation.

Body type in use today ranges in size from 6-point to 8-point, with the intermediate sizes of $6\frac{1}{2}$-, $6\frac{3}{4}$-, 7-, and $7\frac{1}{2}$-point available in some of the designs.   Although a few of the famous old papers still use 8-point type, most of the metropolitan dailies have changed to 7-point or $6\frac{3}{4}$-point for the main body of their newspapers.   The reduction of even a fraction of a point in size results in conservation of space. This saving was a factor of great importance during World War II.   As newsprint becomes available in greater quantities, however, the trend undoubtedly will be toward larger, rather than smaller, body type, since there are limits to which sizes can be reduced safely if legibility is to be retained.

Work of the Printer

A thorough acquaintance with some of the more common type faces is just a beginning in gaining an understanding of their use in printing. Such a study is basic, but of fundamental importance also is a knowledge of how type is assembled into lines and into printing forms, and an introduction to the materials other than type itself that are used in building the newspaper page.

Much can be learned by observing the printer at work and by questioning him, but the greatest value will be derived from learning, through actual practice, how type is set.   In this way, the student will become acquainted with the problems encountered by the printer with whom he must deal constantly.   He will discover both the limitations and the possibilities involved in hand composition, and he will have an opportunity to experiment with various type faces, singly and in combination, in various types of printed pieces which he may plan and execute himself.   He will thus have a chance to profit by experience.

IV

Elements of Hand Composition

THE GUTENBERG BIBLE WAS SET ENTIRELY BY hand. So were all other books, newspapers, magazines, and pamphlets produced before the invention of the Linotype near the end of the nineteenth century. More than four hundred years had elapsed before the introduction of the faster method.

The adaptation of type-casting machinery to the production of newspapers at the start was not rapid, but within a few years many of the large dailies had replaced the long rows of hand-compositors by machinery that could set type at a far greater rate of speed. Today, practically every newspaper in the country has such equipment, and the type used on newspaper pages is almost entirely machine-cast.

However, in producing type by machine most of the basic rules which govern the setting of type by hand are observed. The operator must have a knowledge of type faces, sizes, spacing, justification, indention, punctuation, and other matters required by the printer in his work. In fact, the best preparation a beginner on the Linotype can have before starting his apprenticeship is a thorough grounding in hand composition.

Furthermore, some sizes and faces of type often are not available on the type-casting machines and consequently must be set by hand, especially in the smaller newspapers and in job-printing departments. Whether cast by machine or set by hand, all type that goes into a newspaper page must be assembled by printers into forms before it can be locked up for the presses. Consequently, the only sure way to gain a thorough understanding of printing is to begin with a study of the elementary processes.

THE COMPOSING ROOM

In a newspaper plant, all the work of setting type and making up forms is done in what is known as the *composing room*. The workmen who set type are called *compositors*.

Four distinct, but closely related, operations take place in preparing type for the printing presses. The composing room, as a result, is divided up into a corresponding number of departments in order to assure efficient production.

First, there is the hand composition department, generally known as the *ad alley,* where all hand-set type is taken care of by the printers. Here all advertisements are made up and any headlines or other copy not to be handled by the machines are set.

Another section, where all the type-casting machines are located, is called the *machine composition department.* It usually is next to the hand composition department, since much of the type produced by machines must be passed on to the hand compositors for use in advertisements which they will complete. In this department also is located the desk of the *copycutter,* who holds one of the most demanding positions in a large composing room where many type-casting machines are in operation.

He is the first person to receive all copy for the main reading matter of the newspaper as it is delivered from the editorial rooms. His job is to divide this copy up into *takes,* to distribute it to the various operators, and to see that it is turned into type quickly and efficiently. Great responsibility for seeing that schedules are maintained with the pressroom rests on him.

The Linotype operators dump all type which they cast into galleys. The galleys are then placed on a surface known as the *bank,* where they remain until the bank boys are ready to take proofs. After this has been done, the type usually is stored on slides under the bank and the proofs are sent on to the next division.

This department is the *proofreading room,* which usually consists of a glassed-off space to reduce noise. All typographic errors found in the proofs are marked by the proofreader, who then returns them to the bank boys for distribution to the Linotype operators. They, in turn, cast new lines to replace those containing errors, and these new lines are inserted in their proper places in each galley of type.

After all corrections have been made and new proofs have been taken and O.K.'d, the type is taken to the *makeup department.* Here other printers, working under the direction of a makeup editor, arrange the type and the completed advertisements prepared in the ad alley into pages. The pages are locked securely into metal chases. Then these page forms are ready to be taken either directly to the pressroom or to the stereotype room, where metal plates are prepared for the presses.

THE CALIFORNIA JOB CASE

Type used in hand composition is stored in shallow wood or metal trays, known as *cases*.   Each case, designed to accommodate one font of type, is divided up into many compartments or boxes—one for each character.

Before type-casting machines were invented, when all type had to be set by hand, printers used a pair of cases (called *news cases*), both of which were placed on a stand, one above the other.   Capital letters were kept in the upper case; small letters, in the lower.   As a result, printers began referring to capitals as *upper-case* letters and to the small characters as *lower-case* letters.   These terms are still used throughout the printing trade.

These news cases were necessary when large quantities of one particular face of type were needed for the newspaper columns.   However, with the coming of the Linotype, the old news cases were almost entirely replaced by another kind, known as the *California job case,* which contains an entire font and is much more convenient and compact.   Because each will hold enough type of a given face for ordinary needs, California job cases have become the favorite in newspaper and printing offices.

These cases are stored in wood or metal cabinets, each of which is designed to accommodate several fonts of type.   Thus, it is possible to group together entire families of type, including various sizes and styles, for convenient and efficient handling.   At the top of the type cases, slanting working banks are provided, with lead-and-slug cases placed conveniently above them.

Other cases of special makes also are found in most newspaper and printing offices, but a knowledge of them is not necessary for the person who has no intention of following the printer's trade.   However, before any type is set, the lay of the California job case must be mastered.

LAY OF THE CASE

The California job case contains eighty-nine compartments of various sizes and shapes.   These compartments are sufficient to accommodate all capitals, lower-case letters, figures, special characters, and punctuation marks of one particular size and face of type.   The plan of arrangement for these is referred to by printers as "the lay of the case."

The case is divided up into three sections, with the capital letters and some special characters located in the one at the right-hand side. With the exception of the "J" and the "U," the capitals are arranged in alphabetical order, but these two letters come at the end. This inconsistency exists because the "J" and "U" were not included in the early alphabet, which contained only twenty-four letters, and the case at that time was planned for only twenty-four letters. In place of the "J," the "I" was used interchangeably as consonant and vowel; and the letter "V" was employed as a "U." Addition of the "J" and "U" first was suggested about 1585 by Louis Elzevir, a famous Dutch printer, who used the "v" and "j" regularly as consonants, and the "i" and "u" as vowels. He also adopted the capital "U" and the "J," placing them after the "Z" in the type case.[1]

However, dictionary makers did not adopt these two new capitals until 1822. When they did come into common use, makers of type cases followed Elzevir's plan of putting them at the end of the alphabet in order to avoid confusion, since early printers had learned their cases with these two letters missing from the alphabet.

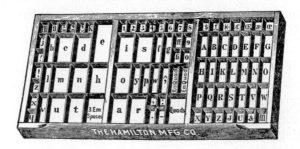

Figure 36. The California job case. (Courtesy of American Type Founders Sales Corporation.)

In the bottom row on the capital side of the case, the "U" is followed by the ampersand (&), or *and* sign, and the ligature, "ffl." The top row contains the dollar sign ($) and other special characters, which may vary, according to usage.

In learning this side of the case, it is desirable to memorize the characters found at the beginning and at the end of each line, since fewer "mental gymnastics" will be required in determining the location of a letter far down in the alphabet in the early stages.

Lower-case letters, punctuation marks, figures, and spaces and quads

---

[1] *I.T.U. Lessons in Printing*, Unit I, Lesson 5, page 4. Indianapolis: Bureau of Education, International Typographical Union, 1931.

are kept in the two sections on the left of the one containing the capitals. These letters are not located in alphabetical order; in fact, at
first glance, they appear to be badly jumbled. However, their arrangement has been planned in such a way that the most-used letters, occupying the largest boxes, are grouped together in the center so they can
be reached more conveniently by the compositor. For instance, the
"a," "r," "e," "t," "h," "i," "s," "n," and "d," are close to one another,
making it possible to secure quickly and easily those letters going to
make up common words such as "and," "is," and "the," and frequently
used combinations like the "-ed," "-el," and "-ant." Letters used infre-
quently are found around the outer edges.

Spaces and quads (spacing materials less than type-high that are
used to give white space between words, and at the beginning and end
of paragraphs or lines) are also found in the lower-case section. The
spaces occupy three compartments in the left section of the lower-case,
and the quads are contained in three boxes in the middle section.

Spaces are used to give white space between words; quads are for
the larger white areas at the beginning of paragraphs and at the end of
lines. The em quad, which always is the square of the type size, is the
unit on which all the others are based. It frequently is called a "mol-
lie" or "monkey" quad to distinguish it from the en, or "nut," quad,
which is just half the width of the em quad. The 2-em quad is two
times as wide as the em quad, and the 3-em quad is three times as wide.
It takes three 3-em spaces, four 4-em spaces, and five 5-em spaces to
equal the width of the em quad.

In addition to the spaces already mentioned, extra-thin spaces of
brass and copper, 1-point and $\frac{1}{2}$-point in thickness, respectively, sometimes are provided. However, by using the 3-, 4-, and 5-em spaces
separately or in combination, fine shadings of spacing can be obtained,
and the thinner spaces are unnecessary for ordinary purposes. Since
spaces do not print, they can be used interchangeably between cases
containing type of the same size.

A ligature is a piece of type which contains a face made up of two or
more letters. There are five boxes for such ligatures in the California
job case: the "ff," "fi," "fl," "ffi," and "ffl." These should be used in
setting up words which contain such combinations.

Letters which cause the most trouble are the "b," "d," "p," "q," and
the "n" and "u." These frequently are called "demons" because of
the trouble they cause beginners. However, it is comparatively easy
to identify any one of them correctly, if the piece of type is held face
up with the nicks facing outward, and if it is remembered that the letter

in this position appears "upside-down." To complete the test, place the thumb horizontally over the letter and imagine what the result would be if an imprint were taken and the thumb then lifted. Other letters which also cause difficulty may be tested in the same way.

The lower-case side of the California job case may be learned in alphabetical order, but the disorganized placement of characters makes this method rather difficult. A more desirable plan is to learn letters in combination by lines. For instance, learn the combinations "b, c, d, e," "l, m, n, h," "v, u, t, 3-em," and other groupings that fall naturally together. By breaking down the entire alphabet and character placements in this way, the location of letters can be recalled more rapidly and with greater ease. The entire case should be memorized thoroughly before the beginner starts to set type.

Other Spacing Material

In addition to spaces and quads, which are used within lines of type, other spacing material is needed for spacing between lines of type. Leads and slugs are used for this purpose. These are strips of metal, less than type-high, which are cut in graduated pica lengths and are kept in lead-and-slug cases, located above the inclined bank of type cabinets where the compositor works.

The regular lead is 2 points thick, which is the size that always is meant by the term "lead" (pronounced "lĕd") unless otherwise specified. Leads also are made in thicknesses of 1 point and 3 point, the thinner ones usually being made of brass to prevent breakage.

The regular slug is 6 points thick, and is the size that always is meant when referring to a slug unless otherwise specified. However, slugs are also available in 4-point to 12-point thicknesses.

In paragraph composition, leads 2 points in thickness ordinarily are used between lines. Type set in this manner is said to be "leaded." If no spacing material is used between lines, it is "solid."

Slugs are used when more space is desired between lines and groups of lines for display purposes, to fill out blank spaces between type masses and borders, and in other places within a form where considerable white space is desired. Leads also are used in this manner, along with slugs, when needed to give the correct amount of spacing, since both are cast according to the point system of measurement.

For many years, leads and slugs were cast in type foundries and sold either in 24-inch strips or in labor-saving fonts already cut in graduated lengths from 4 picas to 25 picas. However, today most newspaper offices are equipped with machinery which casts leads and slugs, as well

as borders and rules, in long strips out of the same metal as that used
for type.   These can be cut up into the desired lengths.

Other spacing material for blanking out larger areas of white spaces
also are provided.   Low blocks of wood and metal, known as "furniture," are used for this purpose.   Like leads and slugs, furniture is cast
or cut into accurate pica widths and lengths.   The common widths
range from 2 to 10 picas, and the most-used lengths, from 4 to 25 picas
and longer.   These metal pieces are less than type-high and are hollowed out to reduce their weight.   Metal furniture is made of iron,
steel, or Duralumin, which is extremely light and strong, and will not
shrink as a result of temperature changes.

Wood furniture, on the other hand, although very light in weight, is
less durable and is affected by humidity and temperature changes.   It
is used mainly for locking up forms for the press and usually is kept in
large cabinets made to hold fonts, graduated from 2 to 10 picas in width
and from 10 to 60 picas in length.   Larger sizes also are available, and
narrow strips, 6 or 12 points in thickness, known as "reglets," are used
in lockup.

The Composing Stick

Type is assembled by the compositor in a narrow, metal device
known as a *composing stick*.   It is so called because early printers
actually carved the first ones out of a stick of wood in such a way that
the type could be set up a piece at a time to form a line.   The main
difficulty was that it was not adjustable; consequently, type could be
set only one measure in width.   Furthermore, since the wood would

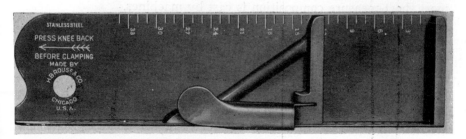

Figure 37.   The composing stick.

wear off and sometimes would warp slightly because of humidity and
changes in the weather, these first composing sticks were not entirely
satisfactory.

There are several styles of composing sticks, but those in use today
are very similar in design.   They are made in various depths and

lengths to accommodate lines of both short and very long measure.

The modern composing stick is made of metal. It is a precision tool, adjustable to pica and half-pica measurements which are marked off on a gauge along the foot, or outside edge. It can be set for the proper measure, or width, by raising a clamp at the side and moving an adjustable knee upward or downward to the desired position. At the opposite end is a fixed metal plate, of the same height as the head. Along the head, which extends the length of one side, are notches into which corresponding projections on the inside of the knee fit when it is clamped into position.

Composing Rule and Makeup Rule

The composing rule is a strip of smooth, thin metal, with an ear protruding on each end at the top, which is placed over a line after it has been set to aid the compositor in justifying the next one when leads or slugs are not used to separate lines. Thus, the difficulties that might arise from setting and justifying one line directly on top of another are overcome. It also is useful in removing type from a stick, for separating lines, and in tying up forms.

Another necessary tool is the *makeup rule,* or "humpback" rule, as it sometimes is called. It differs from the composing rule in that no ears protrude at the sides, and the top curves up into a "hump" for convenience in handling. Although it cannot be used successfully for separating lines of type while being set and justified in the stick, or for removing type from the stick, it serves all the other purposes of the composing rule. In fact, printers consider it more useful now that most short-measure composition is cast by machines.

How Type Is Set

Before starting to set type, the compositor first should collect all the material he will need so that he will be prepared to do his work most efficiently. Care must be taken when the case is removed from the cabinet. It should be pulled out a short distance against the body, and then grasped securely with one hand on each side. Then it can be taken off the slides and placed on the bank so that it rests firmly against the raised edge at the bottom.

If these precautions are not observed carefully, there is danger that the case will be dropped and the type spilled. Type which is mixed up in this way or is knocked down while being handled, is referred to by the compositor as "pi." Obviously, "pi-ed" type is very undesirable.

After positioning the case on the bank, the compositor sets his stick to the correct measure and places a slug of the right measure in it. He then stations himself a little to the left of the center of the case, so he will be able to reach the most-used letters with the least effort.

The composing stick is held loosely in the left hand, with its foot, or outer edge, up. The compositor's thumb should rest in a position just in front of the knee of the stick, next to its head, where the first letter will be placed. The fingers should be curved underneath and around the lower side.

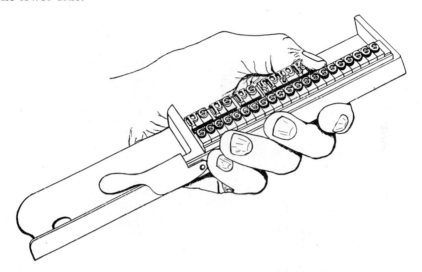

Figure 38. How to hold the composing stick. (Courtesy of American Type Founders Sales Corporation.)

If the copy calls for an indention to start the line, an em quad is taken from its box with the thumb and forefinger of the right hand. It is then placed upright in the lower left-hand corner of the stick under the left thumb, which is moved along so that it rests on the side of each succeeding letter as it is assembled, to keep the line in position. Otherwise, the letters would fall down and be pi-ed as the stick is moved over the case.

The compositor does not read each letter as he puts it into the stick, but he quickly looks for the nicks on the piece of type, picks it up, and rights it in his fingers as he carries it to position. Then his eyes travel immediately to the box containing the next letter, and he repeats the process.

In order to make the fewest possible motions, he follows the right hand, as it travels over the case, with his left, which holds the composing stick.   After each word, a 3-em (or common) space is inserted, and as many words are assembled as the line will hold.

It may be discovered that only part of the last word will fit.   In this event, the word is divided by placing a hyphen after a syllable—preferably the accented syllable.   The line then is read by the compositor, who corrects any errors that may have been made.

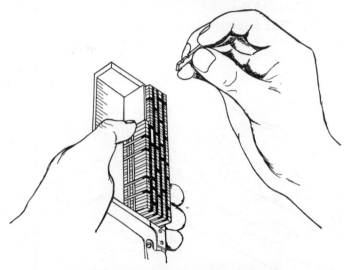

Figure 39.   How to place type in composing stick.   (Courtesy of American Type Founders Sales Corporation.)

The student should learn how to read type quickly and accurately. He will find that the letters appear to be "upside-down," which is somewhat confusing at the start, but with practice it is possible to develop the ability to read lines rapidly.

The stick is raised to a convenient position, with the open part still facing outward, and the line is read from left to right, as is all other type matter with which the compositor will deal.

Justifying the Line

Since it often takes as long, or even longer, to justify a line than it does to set the type, it is highly important that all necessary corrections be made first.

Making a line tight in the measure is known as *justification*.   This is accomplished by placing additional spaces between words if the letters do not quite fill the line out to sufficient length, or by slightly reducing the amount of space between words in order to admit the last word in the line.

It is not necessary to put exactly the same amount of spacing material between all words. On the other hand, the aim is to make spacing between words *appear* to be equal when the line is printed.

More space can be used between some words than between others, because of the shape of letters. For instance, if one word ends in a "w," and the one following it begins with a "v," less space would be needed than if the ending letter were a "d" and the beginning one a "b."

If enough room is left, a 5-em space might be added to the 3-em space that was used when the line was set, but it may be necessary to use some other combination between the various words. Frequently, it is necessary to remove the 3-em space and to substitute two 5-em or two 4-em spaces in order to fill the measure; or possibly 4-em spaces may have to be used in place of 3-em to permit the admission of a word at the end which would not otherwise fit. For best results, no space greater than an en quad should be used between words. As mentioned earlier, fine shadings of space may be obtained by using the spaces available separately or in combination.

Although some newspapers still follow the practice of placing an em quad after the period between sentences in a line, a better plan is to use the same space as that employed between words, since there is more white space around a period than around most letters in the alphabet, and the resulting page will have a more uniform appearance.

In case a sentence or paragraph is completed before the end of the measure is reached, the line is filled out with quads and spaces; the smallest ones are placed next to the period following the last word. This arrangement prevents their falling down and causing difficulty when the form is being handled.

The line should be made snug in the measure, but not so tight that spaces have to be forced down with great pressure. In order to avoid breaking the smaller spaces, the last letter or larger space at the end of a line may be removed, the thinner space inserted, and the letter or quad then replaced.

Insufficient space between words causes them to run together, and the line is difficult to read. On the other hand, too much space often results in "rivers" of white which also are very undesirable because legibility is reduced and the pages take on a streaked appearance. Consequently, close attention should be given to justification.

Spacing between lines is another important consideration. In paragraph composition, or straight matter, a lead ordinarily is used between lines. However, more space frequently is necessary when display lines are set in the larger sizes or when special effects are desired.

DUMPING THE STICK

When the stick is about half full, it is ready to be "dumped." This term means to empty the stick. First, a slug is placed after the last line, since a slug is heavier than a lead, and will not bend when the type is moved or lifted. Then the type is ready to be transferred to a galley.

A galley is a flat, rectangular metal tray, with raised edges less than type-high on three sides. Three kinds are used in most newspaper and commercial printing plants: the news galley, the book galley, and the job galley.

The news galley is about the length of a newspaper column and a little wider. It is made to accommodate Linotype slugs which go to make up the main reading matter of the newspaper.

The book galley is a little wider than the ordinary book page and about the same length as the news galley. As its name implies, it is used for holding type used in the pages of books.

The job galley is much shorter and wider than the other two. Job galleys are available in various sizes, adaptable for use with a wide variety of forms. This type of galley is the one used in the ad alley and in job-printing departments where most forms are wider than the news column.

The galley should be positioned on the bank always with the open end facing to the left. Then the composing stick containing the lines of type is placed in it, so that the head rests against the bottom edge of the galley and the open end faces away from the compositor.

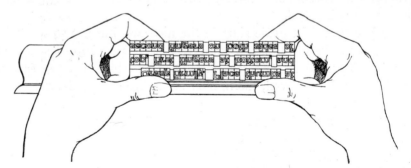

Figure 40. How to empty the composing stick. (Courtesy of American Type Founders Sales Corporation.)

The compositor now places his thumbs against the slug at the top of the type matter, his forefingers at the bottom, and the two middle fingers at the sides. While the middle fingers exert pressure to hold the stick from moving, the lines are pushed forward along the bottom of the stick with a slightly rolling motion, and, without lifting the type, it is shoved out toward the open end.

After the type has been moved far enough, a firmer hold should be taken on the lines by allowing the thumbs to go down to the bottom of the stick.   Then, placing his middle fingers so they will cover the ends of the lines as they come out of the stick, the compositor holds the type matter firmly as it is slid from the stick onto the bottom of the galley.

Keeping the fingers and thumbs in the same relative positions and pressing in firmly from all sides, the compositor now turns the type and slides it down into the bottom corner of the galley, raising his middle finger on the left hand high enough so it will clear the side.   When the type reaches the head of the galley, the compositor may remove his left hand and push the lines firmly together.   When the type has been positioned in this manner, the nicks will be facing toward the open end of the galley.   The compositor now should be standing at the head of the galley, facing to the left, so that the type can be read properly— "upside-down."

Tying Up the Form

The form now is ready to be tied.   Common string of good quality, but not too bulky, is used in tying up the type.   Enough should be used to go around the form five or six times.

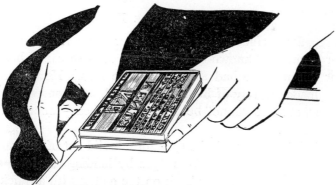

Figure 41.   How to tie up a form.

Grasping the end of the string between the thumb and forefinger of the left hand, the compositor then places it at the lower right-hand corner of the form, and with his right hand he tightly winds the cord clockwise all the way around, crossing the end held in the left hand on the first trip around in order to bind it securely.

Keeping the string taut, and pressing in with the left hand on the foot of the form, the compositor passes the string around the form until he reaches the end.   He then places the makeup rule alongside the string, pulls the end back around the rule's outer edge, and pushes the rule down between the layers of string and the type form.   The loop thus formed is drawn back tightly against the nearest corner, and the excess string at the end may be cut off by the sharp edge of the makeup rule.   The string is then pushed down by the makeup rule until it is in the center of the slugs, so that none will be protruding to get under the type form.

PULLING A PROOF

Now the compositor is ready to pull a proof of the form, so that he may see if any errors have been made.   He does this by taking an impression of the form on a piece of paper.   The print thus made is called a *proof*.

The importance of good proofs cannot be overstressed, since the type forms should be as perfect as possible when they are sent to the pressroom for printing.   In order to accomplish this, the proofs of original forms need to be clear and well printed so that the proofreader will have no difficulty in reading them.

Proofs may be pulled either by hand on the stone, or on a machine known as a proof press.   Taking the proof on the stone is the simpler, but also the slower, method.

PULLING A STONE PROOF

The large, flat-surfaced table on which forms are locked up in preparation for printing is known as the *stone*.   It is so called because old tables for this purpose had thick soapstone tops.   However, modern stones are made entirely of high-quality steel, and consequently withstand more wear and cannot be broken or nicked—common faults of the earlier stones.

In taking the stone proof, the type form is slid out of the galley onto the surface of the stone.   This is done by holding the form securely with the left hand and pulling back on the galley with a quick motion with the right hand until the form is free of the galley.

The form then is made level by placing a block of wood with a smooth surface, known as a *planer,* over the face of the type and by striking it gently with a wooden mallet.   After the form has been planed, it is inked by hand with a small ink roller, called a *brayer*.

Then a piece of newsprint paper, which may be dampened on one side, or dry proofing paper made especially for this purpose to insure a better impression, is placed carefully over the form.

When the paper is in position, the compositor gets a *proof planer,* which is another rectangular block of wood, similar to the one used for planing the form, except that the bottom surface which touches the type is covered with heavy felt. This he places carefully on the paper over the type, and holding it in position with his left hand, he taps it with a mallet in the right hand with just enough force to take a good imprint in the paper.

The proof planer then is tilted, lifted, and moved to another position on the form. This process is repeated until the entire form has been covered. After the form has been entirely planed, the paper is grasped at one corner and lifted from the type. It should not be slid off, or the ink will smear.

Pulling a Proof on the Proof Press

The simplest kind of press used for pulling proofs is one known as the *galley proof press.* This consists of a flat bed, mounted on metal legs, with tracks on each side of the frame. At the top of the frame runs a large metal roller used to gain the impression. This roller is cylindrical in shape, with a handle on each side, and its surface is covered with a heavy felt blanket. Underneath the bed is a small cabinet, in which proofing paper is kept within easy reach.

To take a proof, the galley of type is placed on the bed of the press, with the open end facing the roller. It is inked with a brayer, a strip of paper is put over the form, and the felt-covered cylinder is moved over the form by means of the handles at the sides. The paper then is removed.

Although this type of proof press is not entirely satisfactory, in that even impression over the entire form cannot be controlled, it is used in many newspaper offices and printing plants, since it is inexpensive, easy to operate, and permits proofs to be taken rapidly.

In order to meet the demands of printers and publishers for better proofs and more efficient machinery, manufacturers have developed many styles of precision-built proof presses, designed to produce good-quality work rapidly and easily. Some of them are very elaborate and expensive, but today excellent equipment within the reach of every newspaper is available. These modern proof presses are far superior to the older style and consequently have taken their places in most offices.

One common style found in many newspaper offices and printing plants today contains a large cylinder around which is placed the packing, made up of sheets of hard paper covered with a heavier wax-like sheet that is called tympan paper. The amount of impression can be controlled by increasing or decreasing the thickness of the packing.

This cylinder, which is held by stationary mountings at each side, rotates in bearings. The bed underneath is movable, so that it can slide backward or forward under the cylinder on tracks at the side supporting it. Attached to the cylinder is a handle which, when turned, causes the bed and cylinder to move in unison, and the impression is obtained as the bed with the form on it slides under the cylinder.

Some proof presses are equipped with grippers, which carry the sheet around the cylinder to avoid the possibility of its slipping, with automatic inking, and with beds large enough to accommodate a full-size newspaper page. Many of them are power-driven. Among the best-known and most widely used are the Potter and Vandercook proof presses.

Figure 42. The Vandercook No. 23 Safe Electric Proof Press. A newspaper proof press, electrically operated and geared to run up to 40 proofs (six columns wide) a minute. (Courtesy of Vandercook & Sons, Inc.)

Although it is impossible to describe how the many makes and models of these proof presses are operated, the fundamentals given can be supplemented by specific instructions regarding the machines that the students may find at their disposal.

First, the galley holding the type form is placed near the center of the bed, with the open end facing the cylinder. This is necessary so that the type lines at the bottom will not be pushed off their feet when the impression is taken.

The form is inked with the brayer, and the sheet of paper is placed accurately in position, either over the type form or on the cylinder, as the case may be. If it is put on the type form itself, it should not be moved until the proof has been taken, or the resulting imprint will be smudgy and hard to read.

The proof then is ready to be pulled by moving the type under the impression cylinder by means of the handle at one side.

In taking the paper off the type form, it should be grasped at one corner and lifted with a slow, steady pressure—not pulled across the type. The proof is now ready for the proofreader.

Washing the Type Form

As soon as the proof has been pulled, the form should be washed. Otherwise, the ink may harden, and the counters of letters eventually will be filled up. Furthermore, clean forms are more desirable to handle if corrections have to be made, and there is less likelihood of spreading ink over galleys and other working surfaces.

A rag is used for this purpose. It should be wadded up and then dampened with type cleaner. The form is washed by wiping the rag over the face of the type toward the closed end of the form. A type brush may be used to scrub out the counters of the type, but the form should first be gone over with the rag.

Making Corrections in the Form

When the type has been washed, the proof is read and all errors are marked. With few exceptions, the proofreading marks used in printing departments are standardized, and everyone who works on a newspaper should know what they are and how they are used. The proper method of marking proofs and the signs used will be discussed in another chapter.

Proofs are usually sent to the proofreading department, where this work is done. However, the compositor sometimes marks his own proofs and makes the corrections before sending them on to the proofreaders.

After the proof has been read by the proofreader, it is returned to the compositor for corrections. The galley of type is placed on the bank, and the form is untied. This is done by grasping the end of the string left protruding when the form was tied up and unwinding it counterclockwise on the spread fingers of the left hand, while holding the form in position with the right. The large loop thus formed is then placed over the forefinger and thumb of the left hand and the first two fingers of the right hand, with palms facing upward.

After stretching the looped string taut by pulling the hands apart, the right hand is twisted toward the body, forming the loop into a figure eight. Then with forefinger and thumb of the left hand, the compositor reaches over to take hold of the strings at the top on the right side and pulls them through the loop at the left, which slides down and forms a slip knot as the string is pulled tight.

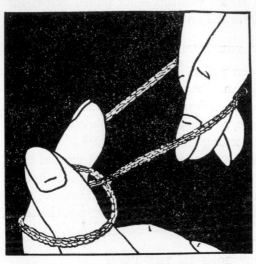

This is known as a *printer's knot* and always is used to tie string taken off forms so that it will not be thrown down loosely and become tangled. To untie the printer's knot, the sides of the loop at one end are grasped with the forefingers and thumbs and given a quick jerk; then the large loop is placed back on the spread fingers of the left hand. When the loose end is pulled with the fingers of the right hand, it unwinds easily and without becoming knotted.

Figure 43.   How to tie the printer's knot.

It is then ready to be used for tying up the next form.

Some corrections in hand-set matter can be made without putting the type lines back into the stick. For instance, if the letter to be substituted is of the same thickness as the one it is to replace, the change can be made by pushing in on the end of the line involved with the left hand to hold the letters tightly together, and lifting it slightly so the wrong letter can be taken out of the line with the thumb and forefinger of the right hand. Then the proper character is inserted in its place. Damaged characters and transpositions also can be handled in a similar way. However, where the letters to be replaced are not of the same thickness, the line to be corrected must be returned to the composing stick.

This is done by inserting the makeup rule with the right hand above the lead separating the incorrect line from the one below and sliding the lines below it down toward the end of the galley, while at the same time pushing in on the ends of the lines with the fingers of the left hand so that letters will not fall down. Then a slug is placed below the line to be removed, and two slugs may be placed above, one of which will be left, when the line is taken out, to keep the line above it from falling over.

Now the composing stick is placed either in the galley or on the inclined bank next to its outer edge, with the open end facing upward. The line is grasped with a middle finger at each end, the forefinger at the bottom and the thumbs at the top, and it is slid out of position into the open part of the galley.

Exerting pressure with the fingers and thumbs, the line is lifted with a quick motion so that it lies horizontally on the slug with the face of the type facing the compositor. It is then carried to the composing stick, which has been set for the correct measure, and is turned feet-down against the surface directly in front of the stick. The line is forced into the opening by "walking" it into place at the head, with a slight backward and forward motion.

The stick with the line in it is picked up and the slug at the bottom is removed, the correction is made, and the line is re-justified. Then the slug is replaced, and the line is removed from the stick and slid back into its former place on the galley.

The lower group of type lines now are moved back up into place against the top section; extra slugs that were used in the operation are removed; and the form is pushed together to take up the space occupied by them. The same process is repeated for other lines requiring a similar type of correction.

In correcting a form, the compositor always starts with the first line marked by the proofreader nearest the top, and works down the galley until all errors have been corrected. Then the form is re-tied, and another proof is taken. This is called a *revised proof*. If it is found to be free of errors, the form is ready for printing.

DISTRIBUTION OF TYPE

Although slugs of type cast on the machines are dumped and re-melted so that the metal can be used over again in the production of new type, all hand-set type must be placed back in the type cases. The returning of type to the proper boxes in the case is called *distribution*.

If there are any questions as to the kind and size of type that is to be "thrown in," they should be determined at the outset. There is a dependable method to follow in checking the identification of type, in case of doubt.

A piece of type from the form, preferably a wide letter, should be removed and compared with a similar character from the case which has been decided upon as the correct one. Then the nicks, the body size, the feet, width, and the face should be compared carefully. If they are the same in all respects, there is every reason to believe that the right case has been selected. In order to lessen the chance of error, a small lower-case letter should be inspected in the same manner. Just one of the checks is not sufficient, but if the pieces of type compared check on all the five points, it is certain that the correct case has been determined.

After the proper case has been located, one slug should be placed above and one below the last line, or group of lines, in the form. It is safer to begin with only one line, until the methods followed in distribution have been thoroughly mastered; then several lines can be taken in one "lift," as skill is developed.

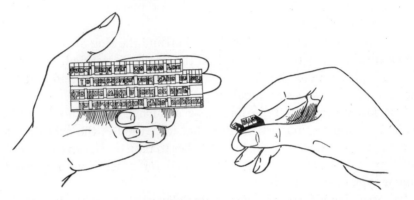

Figure 44. How to distribute type. (Courtesy of American Type Founders Sales Corporation.)

Type for distribution is taken from the galley in the same manner that it is removed from the composing stick. The forefingers are placed against the slug at the bottom, and the thumbs against the one at the top, while the middle fingers press in from each side on the ends of the lines.

The type is slid out into the galley, where it is gripped firmly and lifted quickly to a horizontal position a little lower than eye-level. Then it is tilted slightly to the right, so the lines rest against the middle finger of the right hand. When in this position, the left hand is removed and turned so that the forefinger rests under the bottom slug, the thumb on the left end of the lines, and the middle finger on the right end. This leaves the right hand free to take the type off and distribute it into the boxes of the case.

If several lines are being handled at once, they are held with the fourth and fifth fingers bent underneath to give more support at the bottom. The left ends of the lines rest farther down on the thumb, and the first and second fingers are curved around the foot of the type to the right side.

When lines of type are held in the proper position for distributing, the nicks are pointing upward and the face of the type is facing the compositor. It always should be held in this manner. Then it is tilted slightly to the left, so that it rests against the left thumb, and the top slug is removed by the right hand. The compositor then lifts his right hand and, placing his middle finger behind the letters of the last word at the right end of the line, he pushes them slightly forward toward him. Taking them between his thumb and the first two fingers, he slides them off the slug.

He reads the word, spelling it out as he places the letters one at a time into their proper boxes. The letters should be held close to the surface of the case, and, with a slight rolling motion of the thumb and forefinger, separated and dropped one at a time, with the middle finger tilting each one and the forefinger kicking it off into its box.

All words in the line are taken off one at a time or in groups, and distributed in the same manner. Then the lead over the next line is removed and the type is thrown in. The process is continued until all the type in the "lift" has been returned to the case.

If any words or lines are pi-ed they should be shoved aside and taken care of after the rest of the type has been distributed. Pi should be set up in the stick in the same manner as any other line, a letter at a time, with nicks facing out toward the open end. Then it can be distributed in the proper manner, with special care being given to reading letters correctly.

In distributing pi or in setting up a line of type out of the case, if a letter is found which is of the wrong size or of the wrong variety, it also should be placed aside. Such letters are referred to as "wrong font," and should be returned to the proper case after they have been accurately identified.

If the type form contains types of different sizes and styles, as might be the case in advertising composition, all lines of the same kind and size should be grouped together before distribution is started, so that they may be taken care of in an orderly fashion, thus saving time and effort.

PUTTING AWAY LEADS AND SLUGS

The job of distribution is not complete until leads and slugs have been returned to their proper places in the lead-and-slug cases. If furniture has been used, it should be returned to the cabinet from which it was taken.

The best plan is to return the furniture first, as it is the largest and will leave more working space in the galley. Then all the leads and slugs are stood up along the lower edge of the galley. Beginning at the head of the galley, they should be grouped according to length, with the longest ones at the top and the others in descending order. When the regrouping has been completed, each separate group should be measured to ascertain the length with accuracy. Then the leads and slugs should be separated and returned to their boxes in the lead-and-slug cases.

Need for Careful Workmanship

The beginner soon discovers that to become expert as a hand compositor, considerable practice is required. He also learns the absolute necessity of accuracy, the demand for attention to detail, and the desirability of searching for shortcuts to save steps and unnecessary motions, all of which contribute to greater efficiency.

Editors and publishers recognize the value of learning how to set type by hand. Many of them got their start at the type case and gradually worked their way up to positions of great responsibility. They have learned through experience that a knowledge of the work of the printer is useful to workers in every department of the newspaper.

V

Principles of Design and Layout

IN MANY RESPECTS, THE WORK OF THE DESIGNER of printing is much like that of the artist who stands before his canvas with brush and palette. Their tools are not the same, but the results of their efforts depend wholly upon their creative ability and the skill with which they employ the materials at their disposal. Neither of them can hope to succeed unless he becomes acquainted with certain fundamental principles of design—a part of the heritage that has been handed down through the ages by the great masters of the past.

In an art as old as printing, the evolution of many rules and conventions governing type display was inevitable. A thorough understanding of the basic ones is highly essential; however, they should not be regarded as an end in themselves, but rather the guiding principles on which to build.

FORMULATING THE IDEA

The principles which govern correct type display are applicable to every kind of printing. However, this discussion will deal mainly with advertising, since it is so vital to the newspaper and magazine and is a form of composition that is common to many other types of publications.

The success of an advertisement, or any other piece of printing, is largely dependent upon the nature of the copy and the exactness of the layout prepared. Often the same person who prepares the copy plans the typography and makes the layout. This is particularly true in the case of the advertising man on the smaller newspapers throughout the country.

His first job is that of visualizing an appeal that will meet with approval of both the advertiser and the reading public. The idea must come first. It will be conditioned by a thorough knowledge of the product itself, as well as the character, needs, purchasing power, and buying and reading habits of the prospective customers.   These considerations and others dictate the purpose which the advertisement must serve.   The copy that eventually is written and the way in which it is displayed will be the means of accomplishing that purpose.

After the idea has been developed and the copy written, the next step is to decide upon the kind of typographic display that will be the most effective in conveying the message.   This is where the principles of design and layout must come into play.   Types, borders, illustrations, and white space will be the materials with which the layout man now must deal, and the selections he makes and the manner in which he decides to place these elements upon the page will determine the effectiveness of the finished advertisement.

Once the size and shape of the advertisement have been decided upon, the problem becomes one of constructing a layout in which the elements are arranged in an orderly manner that will be pleasing to the eye, and, at the same time, will give the proper emphasis where it will accomplish the best results.

All designs of advertisements are not made according to set patterns which permit their classification readily into various well-defined categories.   Much depends upon the skill and judgment of the layout man. Given the same copy, no two of them will take exactly the same approach and emerge with identical layouts, because of the human elements which enter in.   However, several time-tested principles of design serve as guideposts to all of them in their work.

BALANCE

In every advertisement—as in every photograph or painting—there should be a frame.   This may consist of white space, border, or perhaps merely the tones or elements around the outer edges; but something should be there to confine the reader to the material to be presented.

Within the space allotted to a given advertisement, the various elements, including type masses, individual lines, white areas, and illustrations, are placed.   These will vary in size, shape, and color; the complexity of the design will be controlled to a large extent by the number of elements to be fitted into the frame.

In every such design, there is usually one main center of interest. It may be a display line, an illustration, a type mass, or some other feature that stands out above the rest.   Around it are grouped the subordinate masses, none of which is so prominent as to detract the attention of the reader from first being drawn to the most important area inside the frame.   The grouping should then lead the reader's eye

Personal or Commercial

- In *personal* banking, you can benefit from our exceptional variety of services...our individual attention to each customer, regardless of amount involved. For your *savings*, we offer maximum safety and convenience . . . bank entirely by mail if you choose.

- In *commercial* banking, you will find unusual satisfaction in the convenience we provide. Our credit procedure, for example, is purposely simplified; you can talk with an appropriate officer more readily; and you'll note his attitude is positive, constructive, helpful.

LA SALLE NATIONAL BANK

135 S. La Salle Street   *Chicago 3, Illinois*

FULL BANK AND TRUST SERVICE   FOR YOU OR YOUR BUSINESS

MEMBER FEDERAL DEPOSIT INSURANCE CORPORATION

Figure 45. An advertisement employing formal, or symmetrical, balance, with respect to both the vertical and horizontal axes. (Courtesy of the *Chicago Daily Tribune*.)

easily from this point to the other elements or masses one at a time until the entire advertisement has been scanned.

Orderliness is of primary importance. It is attained by arranging the various elements of a design so that each seems to take its place easily and without strain, giving the impression of correct distribution of mass or form or color in relation to a given point within the design.

The result is *balance,* which may be defined as an apparent feeling or condition of equilibrium between the various masses within a design. There are many kinds of balance, most of which can be classified as either *formal* or *informal.*

Formal balance is obtained when masses of equal weight are located at equal distances from the optical center, with the design so arranged that a straight vertical line would divide it into equal units which would be superimposed if one half were folded over the other. Masses on one side of the axis are exactly equal to those on the other side and are so arranged that the two halves are at rest.

This is the simplest type of balance. It is effective when the impression desired is one of perfect formality and when the material is of such a nature that it lends itself to this kind of treatment.

Among the works of Garamond, Bodoni, Caslon, and many other old masters of the art of printing, are to be found excellent examples of formal balance. Much of our present-day advertising of high quality is based upon this principle.

However, freedom of design is limited, and, because of the absence of action within the space occupied, layouts of this kind are quiet, restful, and somewhat static.

Practically all designs of this type are balanced on their vertical axis. If balanced on the horizontal axis, the lower half of the type design would have to duplicate exactly the upper half, but in reversed arrangement. This, of course, would be undesirable except in rare cases where such unusual effects are wanted for purposes of special emphasis.

Informal balance is the exact opposite of formal balance. It is a condition produced by placing masses of unequal size, shape, or tone in such a manner that no imaginary line could divide the design into equal halves. This scheme of arrangement is more flexible and is generally regarded as more pleasing than formal balance. Informal balance is employed to a far greater extent in contemporary advertising than the other, since it permits much more freedom of design.

Instead of directing the reader's eyes straight down the page, informal balance leads him from one mass to another by a path formed by elements which may vary greatly in character and structure.

Figure 46. An example of informal, or unequal, balance. (Courtesy of the *Chicago Daily Tribune*.)

The differences between formal and informal balance are easily demonstrated by the use of scales for weighing objects. Formal, or symmetrical, balance, is gained when objects of equal weight are placed on either side of the fulcrum at equal distances from the central point. Informal, or out-of-center, balance comes when a heavy object is placed close to the central point and a lighter one is moved away.

In the case of display in advertising, the design may require two or more small objects, because of their size or tone, on one side of the vertical axis to balance a larger mass on the other side; and a smaller mass, at the bottom, may have to be spaced far down in the frame in order to balance appropriately a larger mass at the top.

As long as the masses are arranged in an orderly manner in accordance with the principle regulating informal balance, elements of a wide variety of sizes and weights may be used together in a given layout. Thus, much greater liberty is allowed than in formal balance, and the resulting effects are limited only by the deftness and skill of the designer.

Like the accomplished artist or photographer who spends years in developing the ability to appraise and create pleasing compositions, so must the designer of advertising and other kinds of printing expect to devote much practice and study in perfecting his techniques.

The most advisable procedure for the beginner is to start with designs involving formal balance, since it is the simplest. The more complicated informal designs require more skill and can be attempted with greater assurance as proficiency is developed.

PROPORTION

If an advertisement is to be pleasing in design, it must have the proper proportions. Consequently, careful consideration must be given, first of all, to its length and width and to the position of all elements going to make up the design.

Proportion has to do with the relationship of the various sizes, weights, and tonal value of display lines, type masses, illustrations, white space, and other elements, as well as with the shape of the advertisement itself. All should be of such a nature and placed in such a manner that an over-all harmonious effect is achieved. Lack of agreement will result in a faulty design.

The experienced layout man needs no definite formula of proportion to determine such relationship, because he has developed a feeling for the rightness or wrongness of a design. However, the good taste and judgment he exercises are based upon sound principles of proportion which he has learned through long practice, and, although he does not have to use ruler and pen, he subconsciously applies certain rules with which he has become thoroughly familiar. Matters involved in proportion are physical qualities which are measurable, and certain rules have been derived from a study of the work of designers and architects of all periods of artistic development.

The use of equal masses of type, the division of space into equal parts, or the development of equal dimensions, seldom result in a pleasing effect. A variety of shapes and masses is much more desirable to the eye. The work of the designer becomes more interesting and more complicated as he is called upon to fit greater numbers of elements into his design.

Considerable diversity of opinion exists as to the amount of variation necessary in size and shape in order to obtain the most agreeable results. Consequently, several rules have been devised which frequently confuse the beginner. However, analysis and comparison of these rules show that they differ very little in actual practice.

Four ratios, or formulas, are in use among designers of printing: namely, the Printers' Oblong, 1.7321; the Golden Oblong, 1.6181; the Hypotenuse Oblong, 1.4142; and the Regular Oblong, 1.5. In working out a formula, W equals width; L equals length; F equals factor. Proportions are determined as follows:

$$W \times F = L$$
or,
$$L \div F = W$$

Thus, the Printers' Oblong might be found by multiplying the width in picas of a given form by the factor 1.7321. For instance, if a form is to be 10 picas wide, the length desired would be discovered in this way:

$$10 \times 1.7321, \text{ or } 17.32 \text{ picas in length}$$

If either of the other formulas were desired, the length could be found by working out the ratios in a similar manner. The results in each instance closely approximate a ratio of 3 to 5.

A mass of type centered on a line directly in the middle actually would appear to be below center, and the result would be undesirable. The layout man must keep this imaginary line in mind when attempting to determine where to place single lines, groups of type, illustrations, or other display features inside the frame.

Menihan

**Genuine lizard shines
brilliantly in these**

SHOES BY MENIHAN

$17⁹⁵

Lizard shoes like these are the dia-
monds, the rubies, the pearls of the
shoe world .. and the brilliant Menihan styling makes them still more
precious .. in gray or beige lizard

*Other shoes from $6.95 to $28.95—
7th floor*

MAURICE L
ROTHSCHILD

State at Jackson

Figure 47. In this advertisement, great care has been
exercised in selecting types, illustration, and border that
are in close harmony. White space has been used effectively. (Courtesy of the *Chicago Daily Tribune*.)

When more than one group are to be included, the point of balance shifts to the "optical center"—a point slightly above the mathematical center. To be more exact, it is equal to one tenth of the distance between the mathematical center and the top border of the ad. In determining these distances, measurements should be made from the center of a group of type, rather than from the edges.

Although these rules are extremely useful in learning how to work out pleasing proportions, they should not be regarded as absolutely mandatory in all instances. Some deviations often are permissible, but in every design that is to have a pleasing effect on the reader, the sound principles of correct proportion must be followed closely.

HARMONY

The dominating prerequisite of a design in any of the arts is harmony. All other principles are directed toward the attainment of this quality.

Harmony in a design means consistency and fitness to purpose—the unity of all the parts included. Only those elements which result in pleasing effects and contribute to strengthening, or contributing to, the central theme should be used together in a given advertisement.

The size, shape, and tone of every element that goes into the advertisement, and their relationships to one another, are significant. A line of type that is too large and bold; an illustration or type mass of the wrong shape; masses of white space which greatly outweigh the groups of type which they accompany; a border that clashes; or the improper placement of any one of these elements frequently ruins a design that otherwise would be pleasing.

The principles of balance, proportion, and harmony are inseparable. The problems involved are so interrelated that one would be impossible of achievement without the support of the other.

CONTRAST

In an advertisement—where the primary mission is selling—another aspect of design of equal importance is *contrast*. This is accomplished by making one element stand out above the others for the purpose of emphasis. The amount of contrast achieved is dependent upon the degree of variations. Thus, contrast might be regarded as the opposite of harmony. However, it seldom is necessary to sacrifice harmony in order to attain contrast. In fact, a certain amount of variation between elements within an advertisement is highly desirable.

ENSEMBLE
OF GENUINE COBRA
in gray, beige, green and red to
"luxury-note" your spring
wardrobe
BY MENIHAN

THE SHOE
$19⁹⁵
7th floor

THE BAG
$30*
main floor

Cobra is important spring news &
Menihan lifts it to dazzling
fashion heights

MAURICE L ROTHSCHILD
MINNEAPOLIS   State at Jackson—Chicago   ST. PAUL

*Plus Federal Excise Tax

Figure 48. Contrast is obtained in this advertisement by surrounding the rectangular white panel with an area that is gray in tone. By means of this device, the copy which the advertiser wanted to have special emphasis is made to stand out from the rest of the design. (Courtesy of the *Chicago Daily Tribune.*)

Contrast may be obtained in several ways. Variations in size, shape, and tone of type masses and illustrations, and the distribution of white space around or between them, are the most common methods. In layouts where color is used, it also may be effective.

The use together of large and small types, of light and bold type faces, and of type faces that differ widely in design may produce the desired emphasis. Illustrations or type masses that are darker or lighter in tone than others next to them in the advertisement or that are larger in size or of a different shape also are used for the purpose. Ovals, circles, or other irregularly shaped illustrations often result in pleasing contrast.

Color is another excellent medium for producing emphasis, since it seldom fails to attract a reader's attention when employed along with gray masses of type.

The extreme effectiveness of white space must not be overlooked. The addition of a small amount of white space between type masses, around an illustration, or between lines, often will lead to great improvement.

A mistake beginners frequently make is that of failing to separate with white space one group of lines that belong together from other groups. Proper grouping, with the aid of white space, not only is essential for clarity, but also is valuable from the standpoint of contrast in the design. Here again, a certain amount of restraint is necessary, since too much white space might result in a lack of unity, and even spacing between all groups gives a stair-step effect that is not pleasing. Good judgment is of primary importance.

Occasionally, the layout man can be justified in making one line or one illustration out-shout everything else, but in most instances, great variation of elements is not necessary. Sometimes only slight differences are needed to accomplish the best results. Likewise, the tendency to stress too many parts of the advertisement often results in a spotty, checker-board effect that is monotonous and confusing to the reader.

RHYTHM

The experienced designer of advertising knows the importance of *rhythm*. By means of this quality in a layout, he is able to lead the reader from one element to another until the entire advertisement has been read. The ease with which the eye is guided throughout the layout and the direction it takes are dependent upon the skill of the designer.

Figure 49. The principle of rhythm has been employed skillfully in this advertisement. Notice how the reader is carried by an orderly succession of "beats" down through the reading matter. (Courtesy of *Woman's Home Companion* and Johnson-Stephens & Shinkle Shoe Co.)

Rhythm may be obtained by an orderly "beat," or succession of harmonizing tones, shapes, or sizes of parts in an advertisement. This does not mean that all elements necessarily must be the same, but variations must not be so great that the eye has difficulty in adjusting itself to changes which interfere with ease of movement or flow from one element to another.

The aim of the designer should be to lead the reader from one point to another, with sufficient stress at certain intervals to increase interest in those ideas that are to be emphasized, but with not enough to stop him completely until the entire message has been grasped. Interruptions which break continuity set up barriers that often defeat the purpose of the advertisement as a whole.

Rhythm of form consists of an orderly arrangement of the various elements into a definite, unified design, as opposed to a helter-skelter placement of parts within a design.

Linear suggestion is an important part of rhythm. For instance, a row of evenly spaced objects of equal size leads the eye easily and with regular beat across the advertisement. Likewise, the outline or edges of type masses, illustrations, single display lines, or rules, when properly placed, also have linear qualities and assist in directing the eye in its course over the advertisement.

Although, for absolute conformity and harmony, lines should run either vertically or horizontally in an advertisement of rectangular shape, diagonals and curves frequently can be used effectively when the accent is to be on action and life.   These variations of design often present difficulties for the printer, and require considerably more time for setting.   For this reason, many newspapers discourage their use.

CHOOSING TYPES THAT HARMONIZE

One of the first matters requiring the attention of the designer of an advertisement, or any other kind of printing, is the selection of appropriate types for use in conveying the message.   This is not so simple a task as it might seem, but one which requires a thorough understanding of both the possibilities and the limitations of the various faces available.

If pleasing results are to be obtained, the types chosen for a given piece of printing must harmonize in facial design.   Either they must be similar enough to blend together nicely in the printed form, or they should be strikingly different in design so the result will be one of pleasing contrast.

Until one becomes thoroughly acquainted with various faces and, through practice, learns what combinations are desirable, the use of some method for determining problems in type harmony is very beneficial.   A typographical harmony wheel is one of the best of such aids.

Types may be classified according to facial design in much the same way as colors of the spectrum are arranged on a "color wheel."   At one end of the color band is ultra-violet; at the other is infra-red.   In between are the other colors which blend naturally with one another as they occur in an orderly succession of values.

A typographical harmony wheel, comparable to the color wheel, would start at the top with the most decorative designs—the Text types —which would be graded clockwise around from the plainer to the more elaborate designs.

Texts would be followed in order by Scripts and Cursives, Italics, Oldstyle Romans, Mixed Romans, Modern Romans, and finally the Gothics, with the plainest ones falling next to the Square-Serif groups and the more ornate ones being placed next to the least ornate Texts on the type harmony wheel.

In each group, the types should be graded so that they blend gradually with the designs on either side. Thus, fine shadings may be obtained throughout.

ADJACENT HARMONY

The typographical harmony wheel is not difficult to use if the principles of color harmony are remembered. In the case of the color wheel, close harmony is obtained by using together those colors which come next to one another. The same is true of the typographical wheel.

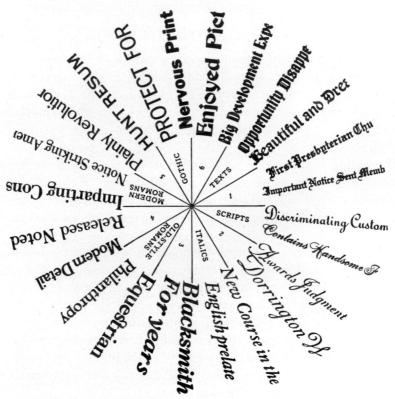

Figure 50. A typographical harmony wheel. Beginning at the top, the Texts, Scripts, Italics, Oldstyle Romans, Modern Romans, and Gothics are arranged clockwise around the wheel. Types having characteristics of two of the major groups are placed in between and numbered as follows: (1) Texts similar to Scripts; (2) Scripts similar to Italics; (3) Italics similar to Oldstyle Romans; (4) Roman types with characteristics of both Oldstyle and Modern Romans; (5) Roman and Gothic types similar to both Modern Romans and Gothics; and (6) Texts that are similar to Gothics. In preparing a typographical wheel for his own use, the student should use extreme care in placing the types so that one group grades off properly into the ones next to it. (Courtesy of Charles L. Allen, *The Journalist's Manual of Printing*. The Ronald Press Company, New York, 1929, page 36.)

For instance, Text types may be used successfully with either Script types or with Gothics—the two groups which adjoin them, one on either side; Scripts, with Texts and Italics; Italics, with Scripts and Oldstyle Romans; Oldstyle Romans, with Italics and Mixed Romans; Mixed Romans, with Oldstyle Romans and Modern Romans; Modern Romans, with Mixed Romans and Square-Serifs; and Square-Serifs, with Modern Romans and Gothics. This kind of harmony is known as *adjacent harmony.* The sweeping conclusion that all the types falling in one group will harmonize well with all members of the groups adjoining it is false. Only those closely similar in design will harmonize best.

Thus, the most decorative Texts will go best with the more elaborate Scripts, which join them on the right; whereas the plainer Texts are the most suitable for use with Gothics, containing slight variations in elements, on the left. The same is true of all other type groups represented on the wheel. In every instance, the choice should be based on a determination of those types most similar in design, and the shape and tone of those selected also must be taken into consideration.

COMPLEMENTARY HARMONY

Another kind of harmony is that known as *complementary harmony,* which is obtained by selecting types that are directly opposite one another on the typographical harmony wheel. In other words, the types having the greatest differences in facial characteristics—those that are the most unlike—may be used successfully together.

If the typographical harmony wheel were separated between the Gothic and Text groups and straightened out into a band similar to the color band, these two types would be at the two extreme ends, just as ultra-violet and infra-red are at opposite ends of the color band. Consequently, according to the principle of complementary harmony, Gothics and Texts can be used together appropriately when extreme contrast is desired.

In choosing companion types from opposite groups on the typographical wheel, great care must be exercised in selecting types that are the most dissimilar in design. Unless this rule is closely observed, the theory of complementary harmony will break down. For instance, although the Oldstyle Roman group lies directly opposite the Text group on the wheel, only the plainest Oldstyle Romans can be used successfully with the most ornate Texts if pleasing contrast is to be obtained, and vice versa.

The typographical harmony wheel should not be regarded as an easy cure-all for the remedy of all typographic problems, but it is extremely helpful to the beginner who needs considerable guidance in the selection of suitable type-combinations.

MONOTYPOGRAPHIC HARMONY

The simplest and most dependable kind of typographical harmony is that referred to as *monotypographic harmony,* which is secured when the members of only one type family are used together. This may be regarded as the closest harmony obtainable, since the types making up a given family all have common characteristics and consequently are very similar in facial design. Thus it follows that any two or more members of the same family of type will harmonize closely when used in the same printing design or layout.

In almost every commonly used type family such variations as *regular, condensed, extra-condensed, boldface,* and the *italic* version are available. Many families contain several other variations. Consequently, by choosing wisely, a wide range of designs and sizes may be selected from the same family, and the results frequently are much more pleasing than when several members of more than one family are used together. In fact, headline schedules of many present-day newspapers are made up of types from the same families, and a similar plan is followed in many high-class, artistic advertisements.

One safe rule of typographical harmony that always should be followed is that simplicity of design is far more desirable and often in much better taste than great diversification of design in which several types of different familial relationships are used. It seldom is advisable to use types from more than two or three families in the same layout, and these should be chosen with careful consideration of typographic harmony.

Too many types in the same design, even though they meet the specifications of type harmony, often result in a more or less cluttered appearance that is not pleasing and that conveys a feeling of restlessness and indecision. The beginner should bear this possibility in mind when planning a piece of printing. The more complicated designs should not be attempted until considerable skill has been developed.

SHAPE HARMONY

In planning an advertisement, careful attention also must be given to *shape harmony.* This means that the shape of the type should conform with the shape of the design itself.

If the advertisement is to be long and narrow, the more condensed varieties of type would be suggested.   In those that are wider than they are long, the wider faces would be more advisable.   The same rule applies to type masses, and to all other elements, including illustrations and border designs, used in a given form.   All these should be of a shape similar to the panel in which they are to be placed.

This rule does not mean necessarily that every type mass or illustration within a rectangular frame must be exactly rectangular in shape, but that all of them which go to make up a major mass within the frame should result in the same general form.   For instance, sometimes a headline consisting of one or two lines is used over a type mass of body matter that is longer than it is wide.   If proper gradation is used so that the headline seems to belong logically to the reading matter, and from the standpoint of design becomes a part of it, the over-all shape is one that would conform to a panel that is longer than it is wide.   On the other hand, a mixture of type masses (including illustrations) of too many varying shapes results in confusion.   Close harmony in shape of types and type masses is just as important as close facial harmony.

Care also must be exercised in selecting types that fit the shape of the mass in which they are to be used.   Some types are very plain in design; others are more decorative.   Likewise, some shapes suggest plainness; others give the feeling of much greater freedom.   A triangular form is suggestive of the latter, whereas a square or rectangle is suggestive of the former.   Thus, a design in which triangular or other irregular shapes are used, or one in which diagonal lines predominate, calls for more ornate types than one in which the reverse is true.

When the design is plain and simple, types such as the Gothics, Square-Serifs, and Modern Romans, in which lines are plainer and the design is more geometric, are the most advisable.   However, in the design containing more variation, Oldstyle Romans, Italics, Scripts, and even Texts might be more desirable.   In other words, the shape of masses which go to make up a given form dictate to some extent the kind of type that should be employed.   This generalization is particularly true in the more modernistic printing where the accent is placed on action and functional design.

TONE HARMONY

When applied to printing of black on white, *tone harmony* refers to the use of elements possessing contrasting colors, or degrees of color, to bring about the general impression of whiteness, blackness, or grayness of a design.

Color means the total absence of color, or white and black with the

Figure 51. This is another example of formal, or symmetrical, balance, in
which men's wear is given formal treatment. An air of exclusiveness is obtained by employing this method of balance, together with an abundance of
white space, and types, illustrations, and border that are in harmonious agreement with the effect desired. (Courtesy of the *New York Herald Tribune*.)

varying shades of gray, when used in this connection. "Tone" refers to the general appearance of the composition as a whole; "color" refers to each part or element used in the design.[1]

If good tone harmony is to be achieved, the various elements used together must not be so widely different in color that they clash with one another; on the contrary, they should result in a balanced, restful effect.

When some elements are much bolder, or "blacker," than other areas, the advertisement has a tendency to take on a spotted appearance that often is not pleasing. If the border is much heavier, or much lighter, in tone than the type matter it surrounds, the result is not pleasing.

In many instances, the fault is not in the choice of suitable types, but the result of too little attention being given to proper gradation from the darker areas to the lighter. A jump from a very bold type mass to a very light one, with nothing of an intermediate tone to bridge the gap, frequently causes pages to have a checker-board effect that is undesirable.

This effect is particularly noticeable in the front pages of many newspapers, especially those which make exclusive use of one-deck boldface heads in their headline schedules, with little variety in sizes. In the case of the more important headlines, three or four lines in 30- or 36-point boldface type frequently are used over a story set in 7- or 8-point body type.

The difference in both size and boldness of the two areas is too great for good tone harmony. A much more pleasing effect could be obtained by using a second deck, set in a smaller size, since it would tend to lessen the jolt on the reader by affording some gradation from the dark to the light tones. The over-all tone of the page also would be more inviting.

The same fault as that mentioned in connection with front pages also may be observed frequently in advertising. Of course, all lines of type or type masses within an advertisement need not be exactly the same weight. Variations in color are necessary to give needed contrast for purposes of emphasis and to add liveliness to the design. If the elements, or parts, used are too nearly alike in shape and color, the design becomes monotonous.

In an advertisement, frequently some area will be much darker or much lighter than another for the purpose of attracting attention. If

---

[1] Charles Laurel Allen, *The Journalist's Manual of Printing*, page 42. New York: The Ronald Press Company, 1929.

the general tone, for instance, is light, the eye will be attracted to the dark elements; if it is dark, light areas may be sought first. Thus, the reader may be directed to the most important message in the advertisement if the designer makes use of the principle of tone and color harmony, either by darkening it to make it stand out from the lighter surroundings or by lightening it so that the contrast with the darker area or areas is striking. However, care should be exercised not to emphasize too many parts of the message by use of great contrast, or the whole ad may lose its effectiveness.

In connection with tone and color harmony, the use of borders and illustrations must not be overlooked. Like every other element within the advertisement, these also should harmonize. A border or an illustration that is darker in tone than other elements in the ad, or vice versa, often ruins an otherwise pleasing design. In choosing them, the color of the type, the distribution and gradation of elements of varying value, and the general tone of the entire design must be taken into consideration.

Likewise, the shape and design of the type employed will help dictate the kind of border that can be used appropriately. For instance, plain Gothic types call for plain borders; Oldstyle Roman types would require a border with some variations, the degree of decorativeness being dependent upon the particular design.

The objective is to select those elements for use together which, because of their similarity in color value, result in a design that is harmonious in tone and therefore pleasing to the reader.

Subject Harmony

Careful thought must be given to the choice of types that will best carry the message of the advertiser to the reader and, at the same time, will harmonize with the subject of the advertisement.

First of all, the designer should attempt to choose types that fit the product involved. For instance, grocery ads will call for type faces that are different from the ones which might be used appropriately in ads dealing with dainty perfumes or fine jewelry. For the former, the sturdier, heavier faces would be indicated; for the latter, they would need to be lighter in tone and more decorative. However, in each instance, the character of the merchandise and the nature of the copy would help to dictate the final selections.

Thus, the job of the designer of an advertisement in choosing types for a given subject has several ramifications. One of the most important prerequisites is that he use good judgment and common sense, based upon a thorough knowledge and appreciation of the types with which he must deal.

This prerequisite involves more than the ability to classify types into races and families according to the various characteristics they possess. Such a mechanical examination, in itself, is not sufficient to determine definitely the uses to which each may be put with the assurance of success.

In the final analysis, the spirit or feeling that a type expresses is the dominant quality that the designer must consider in selecting it for a given piece of printing. Inherently, every type face has certain suggestive qualities all its own. No two of them are alike in every detail —even members of the same family. Each possesses certain individual characteristics which give it an exclusive character and personality. Some types are distinctly feminine in design; others are strongly masculine. In between these two extremes are many that are more neutral and conservative.

A given face may express the feeling of durability, dependability, formality, strength, or rugged individualism. On the other hand, an informal design with many variations may have entirely different connotations. For instance, the Scripts and Cursives and the Italics, which lean to the right, usually are regarded as weaker than the upright Romans and Gothics. Plain, bold designs are stronger than those which are light and decorative. Generally this comparison is true, but it would be wrong to assume that all Scripts and Cursives and Italics are weak and feminine, or that all Romans and Gothics are strong and masculine.

Within each group are members with a wide range of variations, and consequently there is no absolute set of rules to follow which makes it possible quickly to classify a type face into a certain category that does not permit some flexibility. Equally unreliable is the belief that the design of a particular type face dictates unmistakably the uses for which it is most appropriate. Within certain limits, this rule is true, but there are some exceptions.

It would be difficult, indeed, to make a list of only those type faces which express most definitely the feelings of gaiety, sorrow, or pain. Borders, illustrations, white space—and their shape and tone—also must be considered along with the types. Nevertheless, every type face does express a certain feeling which must be regarded with great respect by the layout man.

Figure 52. The types, illustrations, and border used in this advertisement have been carefully adapted to the message to be conveyed. All these elements are light and feminine in tone and result in an over-all effect that is harmonious and pleasing. (Courtesy of the *New York Herald Tribune*.)

READABILITY OF TYPE

As already pointed out, the spirit of the message and the size and shape of the advertisement, as well as the various elements included, must be taken into consideration when the types are selected.

Another factor of equal importance, and one related directly to all the others, is the readability of the types used. The success of any advertisement is largely dependent upon the ease and speed with which the reader is able to grasp the meaning of the message.

If the reader is attracted to an ad in which the types are low in readability, he soon may lose interest because the task is tiring and pass on quickly to something more inviting. Even though he goes through the entire ad, he may emerge with misinformation caused by mistakes resulting from the difficulties involved. In any event, the impressions gained will not be so pleasing as they should have been, and the possibility of the advertisement's producing the desired action as a result will be reduced.

Most people look upon the task of reading as a comparatively simple one, in which the eyes move smoothly from one end of a line to another without much effort and then pass on easily to the next, so long as there is sufficient light. This is a mistaken notion. The problems involved are highly complex.

Aside from the mental aspects, scientific studies reveal that in reading a printed line of type, the eyes move in a series of jumps separated by a series of pauses. A person sees clearly only during the pauses between jumps, and for all practical purposes, he is blind during the interval required for the eyes to jump from one point to another within the line. Photographic reproductions of eye movements in a variety of reading situations indicate that "thought units" are far more important than word units. Thus it follows that scientific typography must not be based merely on observation of type itself.[2] The aim of the typographer should be to select types, and then arrange them in such a manner that a minimum of pauses and also a minimum of retracings will be required in a line.

Several studies tend to show that the variations in readability of the more common body types are slight. For instance, Paterson and Tinker reported that type faces in common use are equally legible and

---

[2] Donald G. Paterson and Miles A. Tinker, *How To Make Type Readable*, pages 3-4. New York: Harper & Brothers, 1940.

concluded that any type face such as Garamond, Antique, Scotch Roman, Bodoni, Old Style, Caslon, and Cheltenham may be used.[3]

However, in another study of the readability of four newspaper headline types, English discovered that they differed considerably in readability.   He found that readers made almost twice as many errors in reading Karnak as they did in reading Bodoni and Tempo, and that subjects read twenty-one per cent fewer words in reading Karnak than in reading Tempo, and eighteen per cent fewer words in reading Karnak than in reading Bodoni.[4]

The types used in the English study were larger in size and the length of lines and style of design were different from those used by Paterson and Tinker.   Tests in the former had to do with headlines; in the latter, with body matter.   Both kinds of composition are used by newspapers, and consequently the findings in each area have special significance for newspaper workers.

Another important study is that of Luckiesh and Moss, which deals with readability and visibility of type.[5]   Many of their findings are based upon results obtained by a *visibility meter* which they developed for use in establishing ratings for various typographic arrangements.

Although there is great need for further extensive exploration of this highly complex problem, much valuable information has been disclosed by investigations which have been undertaken in the field of readability of type.

READER PREFERENCES

Many people spend more time in reading than in eating.   Books, magazines, and newspapers make up the major portion of their fare. As a result, they form certain habits and develop likes and dislikes that are very important from the standpoint of the typographer.

The major part of what one reads is set in capitals and lower-case. In the first primer in kindergarten, type almost invariably is Roman, and the main reading matter encountered as the years pass also is set in Roman types, usually in a regular face.   As a consequence, reader-preference tests usually disclose that most readers believe that caps and lower-case are more legible than matter set in full caps; that Ro-

---

[3] Paterson and Tinker, *How To Make Type Readable,* page 146.

[4] Earl English, "A Study of the Readability of Four Newspaper Headline Types," *Journalism Quarterly,* 21:3 (September, 1944), 217.

[5] Matthew Luckiesh and Frank K. Moss, *Reading as a Visual Task.*   New York: D. Van Nostrand Co., Inc., 1942.

man type is more legible than are other designs; and that regular-face types are more readable than the bolder or lighter versions.

Scientific studies in readability bear out the correctness of the reader's conclusion that type set in caps and lower-case is more legible than lines set in all-capitals. Paterson and Tinker found that all-capital text retards the speed of reading by almost twelve per cent,[6] and English, in his study of headline types, discovered that those set in Cheltenham all-capitals retarded the speed of reading by approximately eighteen per cent, as compared with caps and lower-case of the same design.[7]

Paterson and Tinker also reported that, despite the opinions of publishers and printers, as well as of readers, to the effect that marked differences in legibility will characterize different type faces, their findings indicate that body types in common use are equally legible. They also found that ultra-modern type such as Kabel Light retards readability only slightly, and that material printed in Italics can be read almost as rapidly as that set in ordinary lower-case.[8]

There is not complete agreement as to the comparative readability of ordinary, or regular, lower-case type and matter set in bold-face type, although the conditions prevailing for the tests given were not exactly the same. For instance, Luckiesh and Moss, as a result of typographical studies based upon quantitative appraisals of both visibility and readability, reached the conclusion that "a marked enhancement in the readability of the printed page can be obtained by augmenting the boldness of many types which are now being widely used for body-text."[9]

Paterson and Tinker, on the other hand, stated that ordinary lower-case can be read as rapidly as bold face, and they suggested that the use of bold-face type "should be restricted to occasions when emphasis is desired since reader preferences are definitely against it."[10]

SIZE OF TYPE

In matters of readability, the size of type is so closely interrelated with other factors such as length of line, leading (or white space between lines), type design, and boldness of face, that it would be im-

---

[6] Paterson and Tinker, *How To Make Type Readable*, page 23.

[7] Earl English, "A Study of the Readability of Four Newspaper Headline Types," page 229.

[8] Paterson and Tinker, *How To Make Type Readable*, page 28.

[9] Luckiesh and Moss, *Reading as a Visual Task*, page 177.

[10] Paterson and Tinker, *How to Make Type Readable*, page 28.

possible to state a rule, or rules, that would not break down under certain conditions.

The rule that line lengths should be increased as type sizes are increased seems to be quite universally accepted. However, there is quite general agreement also that maximum and minimum lengths of line exist beyond which a given type face should not be used if high readability is to be maintained. These, of course, will vary according to the design of type employed.

Reader-preference also has to be taken into consideration. Most of the reading matter which people are most accustomed to reading as body text ranges in size from $6\frac{3}{4}$- or 7-point to 12-point. However, there is not complete uniformity in leading in the various publications they see. This lack of uniformity has much to do with readability. The type they read generally is leaded from $\frac{1}{2}$ point to 2 points, and the body faces used in present-day newspapers have been expertly designed in order to promote a high degree of visibility and readability. Consequently, some of them appear to be larger in point-size than they actually are.

In general, the larger a type is the easier it is to see. However, high visibility does not necessarily mean a corresponding high readability factor. The amount of white space within letters, their degree of boldness and closeness of fit, and the over-all design, as well as the actual point-size, have something to do with the readability of a given type face.

An old rule which early printers used for many years to guide them in determining what lengths of line to use for the various sizes of types still seems to be in close agreement with findings based on recent scientific studies. It was to the effect that a line of type should be set at a pica-length one and one-half times the point-size of the type for best results. In other words, if a line were to be in 10-point type, it should be set 15 picas wide for greatest legibility; 12-point type would be set 18 picas wide; 18-point type, 27 picas wide; and so forth.

In the case of body types, typographers have developed a table of minimum and maximum widths of line which will permit ease of reading of the sizes most commonly used for body type in advertising. It is as follows:

8-point	9 to 13 picas
10-point	13 to 16 picas
12-point	14 to 21 picas
14-point	18 to 24 picas
18-point	24 to 30 picas[11]

---

[11] Olson, *Typography and Mechanics of the Newspaper*, page 205.

As a result of their studies on leading, line width, and type size, Paterson and Tinker suggested the following "Safety Zones for Commonly Used Type Sizes":

6 point: 14 picas set solid through 28 picas leaded and 36 picas leaded 2 or more points.

8 point: 14 picas set solid through 28 picas leaded and 36 picas leaded 2 or more points.

10 point: 14 picas 1 or more points leading, to a line width somewhat under 31 picas, with the exception that 2- or 4-point should be used with a 19-pica line width.

11 point: 16 picas leaded to a 34-pica line width leaded 1 or 2 points.

12 point: 17 picas set solid to 33 picas leaded 1 or more points.[12]

These findings may be of value to the designer of advertising or of books who is not confined to line lengths of shorter measure than those recommended, but they are of little help in determining the readability of most of the body matter in newspapers, which goes into columns ranging from 11½ picas to 12 or 13 picas, in most instances. The only conclusion that can be drawn is that type ranging from 6 points to 12 points in size is less legible when presented in these shorter measures than when printed according to the recommended widths of line. Just how great the loss would be at present can only be a matter of speculation.

USE OF WHITE SPACE

The importance of white space in typographic design cannot be over-emphasized. It is needed between lines of body matter to open it up and thus to promote readability. Lines of type that are crowded too close together are hard to read and consequently are uninviting to the reader. On the other hand, too much space between lines also reduces legibility.

There is no general rule to follow in determining how much leading is the most advisable. The amount of leading to be used depends largely upon the character of the type design employed. In some faces, such as Bodoni, a liberal amount of white space is provided in the type design itself by a generous shoulder at the bottom of letters; in others, where descenders are short, much less is provided.

In general, all body matter is made more readable by moderate leading between lines. For many years, 2 points were regarded as the standard amount of leading for all body matter, and with most designs, this usually is sufficient. However, some of the more scientifically de-

---

[12] Paterson and Tinker, *How To Make Type Readable,* page 80.

signed body types have been found to have high readability with less than 2 points between lines.

Generally, the degree of leading required increases as the length of lines is increased, and occasionally generous white space is used for purposes of contrast and display.   The main error to avoid is that of employing so much white space between lines that each line appears to be sufficient in itself rather than a part of the group to which it logically belongs.

White space also is necessary to separate lines of type into proper groupings within an advertisement.   Before effective display can be planned, it is necessary to study the copy carefully to determine what lines belong together.   Then care should be taken to separate the various groups by means of white space.   One common fault in many advertisements is that insufficient attention is given to proper grouping. Another is the "stair-steps" effect obtained by placing almost the same amount of white space between all groups, and frequently between lines within the copy blocks, as well.

The need for a pleasing amount of white space around the various type masses and illustrations, and between type and border, also should be taken into account.   The tendency on the part of advertisers to crowd more type than is advisable into the available space should be discouraged vigorously.   Ample white space between type and border is of the utmost importance if pleasing display is to be achieved.

For purposes of contrast, white space is a powerful agent.   Without its aid, large, bold display lines lose their effectiveness, as do the other elements within the design.   Its potency is demonstrated daily in advertisements in which it is used liberally for emphasis.   The use of a single line of type, or a small type mass, placed in the center of a page and surrounded on all sides by white space is an extreme example; yet this is a device used occasionally by advertisers who want to call the attention of the reader forcibly to some message of special importance.

In direct opposition to this device is the reverse plate, in which white type is surrounded by a solid background of black.   Although high in attention value, because of the novelty of effect, white on black is much less legible than black on white.   In fact, Paterson and Tinker found that black on white can be read 10.5 per cent faster than white on black.[13]   Furthermore, the extreme blackness of the reverse plate makes it difficult to handle along with ordinary type masses which are much lighter in tone.   For these two reasons, the reverse plate should be employed with great care in any printing design.

---

[13] Paterson and Tinker, *How To Make Type Readable*, page 117.

Another place where white space is necessary for increasing readability is at the side of column rules separating the main body matter. The tendency during World War II was to reduce the amount of white space in an effort to conserve space. In place of rules cast on a 6-point body, many newspapers changed to 4-point, and in some cases, to column rules of only a 2-point body size. This permitted such a small amount of white space on either side of the rule that legibility was impaired. Before the paper shortage brought about by the war, at least a 6-point body was regarded as necessary if high legibility was to be retained. Not only does it promote ease in reading, but it also adds to the general tone of the page.

Making the Layout

The printer who is asked to set an advertisement without a suitable layout is like the contractor who attempts to build a house without detailed blueprints. If considerable waste of time and effort is to be avoided and satisfactory results are to be assured, carefully made plans are absolutely necessary.

The advertising man also is at a great disadvantage in his sales efforts if he does not have something tangible to show to a prospective advertiser. Aside from serving as an important aid in selling space, approval of the layout at the start will save much valuable time in meeting deadlines.

The old practice of scribbling some copy down on a piece of wrapping paper and handing it to the printer with instructions to "set it up the best you can" is out-of-date, a relic of the good old horse-and-buggy days. Even in times when newspapers were produced much more leisurely and when competition was far less severe, this practice was not good business. Today it is inexcusable.

Like the architect, the layout man first must decide upon the materials he is going to use. His problem consists of selecting the types, border, and illustrations that will best fit the message at hand and of arranging them into a design which will be both pleasing and effective. Here is where his knowledge of the principles of design and layout must come into play.

His next step is to make several rough sketches, from which he chooses the one which seems to have the best possibilities. These preliminary sketches do not necessarily have to be as large as the finished advertisement, but they should be drawn to scale. Complete specifications can be omitted, since the main purpose is to assist in deciding upon the form that the finished layout will take.

Roughs are extremely useful, however, in that they afford an opportunity to experiment with several possible arrangements, and frequently the best ones are shown to the advertiser who helps make the final choice.

Figure 53. Two "roughs" made before reaching a decision as to the plan to follow in the layout shown in Figure 54.

After selecting the rough sketch that is to be followed, the designer is then ready to make the final layout. A complete layout consists of two, and sometimes three, parts: (1) the skeletonized drawing; (2) the copy sheet, or sheets; and (3) a sheet on which are pasted the proofs of all of the cuts, provided several are to be used. In case there are only two or three cuts (and consequently there is no danger that the printer will be confused), the sheet of proofs is not required. However, frequently it will expedite the work of the printer, unless the proofs are pasted directly on the drawing itself.

THE LAYOUT SHEET

The drawing (or layout, as it is usually called) should be made exactly the same size as the advertisement is to be set. It is an enlargement of the rough sketch selected as the most suitable for the occasion.

Main display lines should be lettered-in directly on the layout. They should resemble as nearly as possible both in size and style the type which will be used by the printer. In order to avoid inaccuracies resulting from guesswork, it is advisable to trace in the lines from a printed type specimen sheet until proficiency is developed.

Illustrations should face into the ad, so that the reader's attention will be directed into the reading matter. The size and nature of an illustration, and its relation to other elements, frequently will suggest its location.   If it is large and to be more dominant than all other display, the head and body types should be subordinated.   On the other hand, if it is less important than these other elements, it should be handled in such a manner that it does not detract from them, but rather so that it will lend support.

Figure 54.   A layout marked with specifications for the printer. In many offices only the markings for display lines are given in the margins; in others more complete specifications are given, including the amount of white space to be allowed between border and type, around cuts, between type masses, etc.   The method followed in giving these specifications also will be found to vary. In the style shown here, the figure above the horizontal line indicates the length of line to be employed; the size and kind of type to be used are given below this line.

If a proof of the illustration, or illustrations, is available, it may be pasted on the layout sheet in proper position.   Otherwise, the picture may be sketched in roughly or its location may be shown by placing the cut on the paper and drawing a pencil mark around it to show the exact amount of space it is to occupy.

The border selected should be of a size and design that will best harmonize with the other elements of display.   If the border is of a special design that does not lend itself to quick reproduction by pencil, a small piece may be cut out and pasted in at one corner at the top, or the design may be indicated at the side by name or number.

Copy for the body matter should not be written inside the limits of the layout.   Instead, the space each group of body matter is to occupy should be shown by lines, preferably boxed-in, drawn to the actual length in each case.   It is not necessary to have exactly the same number of ruled pencil lines as there are to be type lines; however, the amount of space necessary for each group of copy should be figured out, and the exact amount should be shown.

Specifications for all display lines and illustrations and the size of the ad should be written on the layout sheet.   The width of the ad usually is given in columns and the depth in inches.   Thus, a layout sheet for an advertisement to be set two columns wide and six inches deep would have the marking 2×6 placed in the upper left-hand margin.

If a newspaper sells its advertising space by the agate line, the depth often is given first.   For instance, the marking 140×3 would mean that the advertisement is to be 140 agate lines deep by 3 columns in width.

The exact length, size, and type face of all display lines lettered-in on the layout should be given in the margin.   The indication of size should come first, followed by the size and kind of type.   Thus, the marking 15-12 Goudy Bold would mean that a line should be set 15 picas wide in 12-point Goudy Bold type.   In many offices, the figure indicating the length of line is written above and the point size and kind of type below, with a horizontal line separating them, as follows:

$$\frac{15}{12 \text{ pt. Goudy Bold.}}$$

Some newspapers designate each type face with a letter.   For instance, Goudy Bold might be known as "a."   The marking then would be $\frac{15}{10a}$.   The practice followed by a given newspaper will determine the method to be used.

An effort should be made to set as many lines the same length in a given copy block as possible, including the display lines.   This can be done even though in some of the lines the words will not fill the measure completely, since quads can be used at the ends to give the necessary white space on each side.   Such a practice will result in considerable saving of time, since the problem of spacing at the ends of lines in such small areas often is extremely difficult when several lines are set at different lengths.

In each space left for an illustration, the word "Cut" should be written in along with the number, which serves as a key to the cuts shown on the proof sheet. If there are three illustrations, one should be marked "Cut #1"; another, "Cut #2"; and the third one, "Cut #3." Corresponding markings should be placed on the side of each cut to be included so that the printer will have no difficulty in locating them when he is ready to assemble the ad.

In case the name and address of the advertiser are printed from a cut, the space for them should be shown in the same manner as for any other illustration, and the marking "Sig. Cut," along with the name of the firm, should be written in.

Copy blocks shown by the boxed-in lines also should be marked. These are indicated by the letters, "A," "B," "C," "D," and so forth. For instance, if there are two such blocks, the letter "A" should be written near the center of one, and the other should be marked "B."

Some layout men give detailed instructions as to the amount of space to be allowed between lines and around illustrations and groups of body type. However, if all display lines, illustrations, and copy blocks have been located exactly as they are to appear, no other markings than those suggested are necessary in most cases. Experienced compositors usually can be relied upon to set the ad just as it is shown in the layout.

THE COPY SHEET

All copy for the advertisement should be typed out on the copy sheet. Even the display lines already marked and lettered-in on the layout sheet usually are included, since there always is the chance that the layout sheet might be misplaced or destroyed after becoming separated for setting.

In the event that they are typed on the copy sheet, it is not necessary to repeat specifications which were given on the layout. Instead, each line or group of lines not to be cast should be circled with a pencil to indicate that the operator does not need to concern himself with them.

Copy for all blocks shown by boxed-in lines on the layout should be written out in full, in the same general manner as copy for news stories. No attempt to type it the same width as it is to appear in the ad is necessary. In fact, the operator's work generally will be facilitated if it is not handled in this way.

Each group of copy should be labeled with a marking which corre-

sponds to the one used in the layout.   For instance, the copy which is
to go into the space marked "Copy A" in the layout should be headed
with this same marking on the copy sheet.   These headings also should
be circled in pencil before reaching the printer so that he will not mistake them as a part of the actual copy.

After all the copy has been written, specifications as to length of
line and size and kind of type should be written in the left-hand margin
at the top of each group.   Markings for this purpose are the same as
those used to give similar information on the layout sheet, and, like
all other instructions to the printer, should be circled with pencil.

On many newspapers, the job of marking specifications on the layout and copy is left up to the head ad-compositor or to some other
printer in the composing room, because the layout man is not thoroughly
enough acquainted with type faces, printers' terminology, or other
necessary techniques to decide such matters accurately himself.   On
the other hand, it sometimes is felt that greater efficiency is promoted
by centralizing responsibility for this more technical operation.

However, in any case, the layout man should be thoroughly acquainted with the problems involved, so that he can discuss them in-
telligently with the printer, and, if called upon, do the marking-up
himself.

When the completed layout reaches the composing room, it usually
is separated.   The layout, or drawing, is given to the hand compositor,
so that he can begin preparing the border and display lines that are to
be set by hand.   In case some of these lines are to be cast on the Ludlow, the layout may go to the operator of this machine first, and then
to the hand compositor.

The copy sheets go to the Linotype operator, who sets everything
that has been marked to be cast on the machine.   When he has finished, these sheets, along with the type he has cast, are returned to the
hand compositor, who then finishes assembling the ad.   In doing so,
he makes use of the layout sheet, the copy sheets, and also the proof
sheet of illustrations if one has been included.

THE PROOF SHEET

If several illustrations are to be used in the advertisement, a proof
sheet will be necessary.   On this sheet, proofs of all cuts to appear in
the finished ad should be printed or pasted, and each should be marked
according to the indications used on the layout.

For instance, the cut which is to go in the space marked "Cut #1"
on the layout should have the same marking on the proof sheet.   This

same marking also should be placed on the side of the cut that will be furnished the printer.

Value of the Layout

The work of the layout man is highly creative. Aside from possessing the ability to write effective copy, he should have an artistic temperament and the rare ability to visualize and plan typographic designs that will not only be pleasing to the reader but also will result in sales of the merchandise advertised. The more intimately he is acquainted with types, illustrations, the principles of design, and trade practices in general, the better he will be able to perform his duties. His skill as a designer of printing will increase with practice and careful study.

In making layouts, he should always remember that complete clarity and simplicity are of the utmost importance. The layout is the working plan or diagram from which the printer must work, and the fewer the questions left unanswered by the layout man, the greater the efficiency that will be obtained. Whereas the news writer is concerned primarily with keeping readers informed about news happenings as they occur, the advertising man not only must tell them about products and merchandise but also must strive to direct their buying habits into channels that will be of the greatest value to the advertisers.

VI

Copy-Fitting and Estimating

A KNOWLEDGE OF COPY-FITTING IS DESIRABLE for practically every worker on a newspaper. The need is not so great for those in the editorial department, but frequently such information is of considerable value.

For instance, a story may come into the office just a few minutes before deadline, and the editor will ask for "just enough copy to fill five inches on the front page—in a hurry!" Similar requests for two-column leads, editorials, copy for boxes, special notices, bulletins, and so forth are not uncommon around a daily newspaper office. The reporter consequently should know how to determine quickly and accurately the amount of copy needed in such instances.

For the publisher of a small newspaper who depends upon the income from job printing for a part of his income, an understanding of copy-fitting is an absolute necessity, since many of his customers will request an estimate of the cost of a job before it is printed. In figuring the cost of pamphlets, folders, booklets, catalogs, and many other pieces of printing, he must first determine how many printed pages the copy will require. Furthermore, in order to estimate the charges for composition, he needs to know the amount of type that will be necessary. Errors are costly, often meaning the difference between profit and loss. Guesswork is too unreliable to be tolerated.

Likewise, the advertising man is called upon constantly to fit copy and estimate space. In planning an advertisement, he is confronted with many problems of this kind every day. He must be prepared to decide upon the size an advertisement will have to be in order to accommodate the desired copy and be in a position to give advertisers expert advice on this matter and on many others. He must know how to figure out the size of type required to fit a given amount of copy to the space allotted for it in the layout. Again, his problem may be that of finding out how much space will be needed for a specified number of words when set in a given size of type at a certain measure, or the size of type needed for a display line. Consequently, a knowledge of the methods to follow in copy-fitting and estimating are of the utmost importance to the advertising man.

COMMON MEASUREMENTS

Basic to a knowledge of copy-fitting is an understanding of the system of measurement commonly used by the printer. As already mentioned in an earlier chapter, *points, picas, ems,* and *agate lines* are used, rather than inches and feet.

All type sizes, regardless of how the type is cast, are expressed in terms of *points.* Thus, a piece of type which measures 3 picas, or one-half inch, across its body from the extreme top to the bottom of the shoulder is known as 36-point type, since there are 12 points to a pica.

In deciding upon the size of a face of type that has been printed, the measurement should be taken from the bottom of the lowest descender to the top of the highest ascender. When the line is set in all-capitals, or if none of the letters extends below the main line, allowance must still be made for the descenders, since every letter in a given font is cast on the same size body (across from top to bottom) and a shoulder is provided on every piece to take care of those letters which have descenders.

The type in question also might be compared with printed specimen sheets, showing lines of the type in different sizes; or pieces of the type itself might be taken from the case and placed alongside the printed letters in order to determine the size used. However, accurate measurements can be obtained by using a line gauge if the above suggestions are followed.

Since only eleven of the twenty-six lower-case letters in the alphabet have ascenders or descenders, there is usually an appearance of white space between lines, even though the type is set solid (with no additional space between lines)—and this is what generally leads to confusion. Therefore, actual measurement generally is advisable for the beginner.

The length of lines and the depth of type forms are measured in picas by the printer. A pica is 12 points wide, or one-sixth of an inch. Thus, a line 4 inches in length would be 24 picas wide; and a type form that measures 6 inches from top to bottom is said to be 36 picas deep.

The beginner sometimes is confused by the fact that many printers use the terms *pica* and *em* interchangeably in measuring lengths of lines and depths of type forms.   This custom has grown up because the 12-point em is the same width as the pica.   Since the two are identical, the printer often says that a line is so many ems wide.   What he actually means is that it is so many 12-point ems, or pica-ems wide.

An *em* always is the square of the type size.   The em quad in a case of 8-point type is 8 points square; the em in 10-point is 10 points square; and so forth.   Consequently, an em from a given font of type will take up in a line an amount of space equal to the size of type being used.

The amount of space occupied by a given mass of type sometimes is computed in square ems for purposes of copy-fitting and for figuring the cost of composition to be paid for at a certain rate per thousand ems.   The number of ems in any line of type may be found by multiplying its pica-length by 12 (the number of points to a pica) and dividing this by the size of type to be used.

For instance, if the length of line is 15 picas and the size of type to be used is 10-point, the number of ems it would accommodate could be determined in the following manner:

$$
\begin{array}{rl}
15 & \text{(width of line in picas)} \\
\times\ 12 & \text{(points per pica)} \\
\hline
180 & \text{(total points in one line)} \\
\end{array}
$$

$$
\begin{array}{rl}
180 & \text{(total points)} \\
\div\ 10 & \text{(points in a 10-point em)} \\
\hline
18 & \text{(total ems per line)} \\
\end{array}
$$

To find the total number of ems in a given form, the number of lines of type would be multiplied by the number of ems in one line.   If the form were to be 20 lines in depth, set 15 picas wide in 10-point type, the total number of ems would be found by multiplying 20 times 18 (the number of ems in one line), and the answer would be 360 ems.

Another kind of space-measurement used on newspapers is the *agate line*.   An agate line is said to be one-fourteenth of an inch in depth and a column wide.   Actually, Agate type is 5½ points in size, and an inch of space would not be large enough for 14 lines set in type of this size. However, the custom of figuring 14 agate lines to the column inch is firmly established.   This is a common method used by many newspapers and magazines in measuring and selling advertising space.

A space one column wide by two inches deep would be the equivalent of 28 agate lines; a space one column wide by 5 inches deep would hold 70 agate lines; and so forth.

In an advertisement more than one column in width, its depth in agate lines first is computed, and this figure then is multiplied by the number of columns wide the ad is set. For instance, an advertisement three columns wide by ten inches in depth would be figured in the following manner:

$$
\begin{array}{r}
10 \\
\times\ 14 \\
\hline
140 \\
\end{array}
\quad \text{(agate lines deep)}
$$

$$
\begin{array}{r}
140 \\
\times\ 3 \\
\hline
420 \\
\end{array}
\quad
\begin{array}{l}
\text{(columns)} \\
\\
\text{(total agate lines)}
\end{array}
$$

LEADING TYPE MATTER

Type which is set with extra space between lines is said to be *leaded* when the amount used is equivalent to the thickness of a lead. Composition with 2 points of space between lines is said to be "2-point leaded"; that with 1 point of space between lines is "1-point leaded," and so forth.

When type is cast on the Linotype or other slug-casting machines, this space is provided in the slug upon which the type is cast. For instance, an 8-point type face might be cast on a slug that is 8 points in thickness. If cast in this manner, it would be known as "8-point solid." However, if it were cast on a 10-point slug, which allowed an additional 2 points of white space at the bottom of letters, it would be called "8 on 10"—or "8-point, 2-point leaded." If only 1 point of leading is needed between lines, the type would be cast on a 9-point slug and would be referred to as "8 on 9"—or "8-point, 1-point leaded." The same results are accomplished by casting a face on a slug larger than the actual type size as would be obtained if the type were set by hand with a lead placed between lines.

In most instances, some additional space is necessary between lines in order to increase legibility. The degree of leading required will depend upon such things as the size of the type and the style of face being used. For display purposes, much more than 2 points of space frequently is wanted between lines, and if it is impossible to cast the type face selected on slugs large enough to provide the necessary amount, leads or slugs may be inserted by hand to give the desired effect.

In order to understand how to fit copy and estimate space properly, the student must be thoroughly acquainted with the printer's system of measurement, the correct terminology, and how the point, pica, em, and agate line are applied.

There are three common methods of copy-fitting: the word-count method, the character-count method, and the square-inch method. Each will be taken up separately in the following discussion.

THE WORD-COUNT METHOD

As the name implies, the unit of measurement in the *word-count method* of copy-fitting is the word. Three ems of space in a line are regarded as equivalent to that taken up by an average word, when the type is set in 10-point or smaller. In sizes larger than 10-point, $2\frac{1}{2}$ ems are allowed for each word, since the letters are slightly narrower.[1] These figures are applicable only when normal type faces are used. They could not be relied upon in computing space needed for copy set in condensed or extended faces.

Allowances for spaces between words are made in these figures. Furthermore, in every instance, the ems used in computations are of the same size as the type in which the copy is to be set—not pica-ems. Thus, if the copy is to be set in 8-point type, three 8-point ems would be allowed for each word.

When the problem is to determine the area required for a given amount of copy, after the size of type and the length of line have been decided upon, the following steps are followed:

1. Find the total number of words in the copy.

2. Determine the number of words that will fit into one line of type of the specified length, using the size of type decided upon.

3. Figure out the number of lines of type that will be required for all the copy.

4. Find the amount of space down the page necessary for the total number of lines of type.

In determining the number of words in the copy, the number of words in an average line first should be found. This can be done by counting the words in six or eight lines and dividing by the number of lines used. If the copy is typewritten, a pencil line may be drawn vertically down the right-hand side of the page at a point that seems to give an even division of the lines, which will vary slightly in length. In

---

[1] Charles L. Allen, *The Journalist's Manual of Printing*, page 57. New York: The Ronald Press Company, 1929.

this way, the length of the average line can be determined quite accurately, and the number of words contained in one of them can be counted.

Frequently, there will be several pages of copy. If this is the case, the number of words per average line is found in the manner described above. Then the total number of lines in the copy is found by counting the number of lines on an average page and multiplying by the total number of pages. This figure then is multiplied by the number of words to an average line to get the total number of words in the copy.

In figuring the number of lines of copy, those which do not run the full width of the page, such as the ones at the end of paragraphs, are counted as one line. This seeming inaccuracy is taken care of when the type is set, because some of the lines of type do not run full measure either, but must be quadded out at the end.

As an example, let us imagine that we have written a page of copy which is to be set in 8-point leaded type in lines 14 picas wide. Our problem is to find out how many picas of space down the page it will require. Suppose the words in 6 lines of the copy are counted, and we find that altogether there are 90 words. By dividing the 90 by 6 (the number of lines counted), we learn that an average line of copy contains 15 words. Next, the number of lines on the page of copy is counted. Imagine that we find there are 21 lines. By multiplying 21 (number of lines) by 15 (number of words per line), we discover that the copy contains a total of 315 words.

To find the number of words that will fit into one line of type, set in 8-point leaded, 14 picas wide, we must first reduce the length of the line to points by multiplying 14 by 12 (number of points in a pica). This gives us 168 points. The number of ems per line would be the equivalent of 168 divided by 8, since an em in 8-point is 8 points wide—or a total of 21 ems.

An average word set in 8-point type takes up 3 ems of space. Consequently, the number of words each line would hold is equal to 21 divided by 3, or 7 words. By dividing 315 (total number of words in the copy) by 7 (number of words each line of type will hold), we find that the copy will make 45 lines.

Each line of type down the page will occupy a space equal to the type size (8 points) plus the lead (2 points) which comes underneath it—or a total of 10 points. Altogether, the amount of space to be taken up by the total number of lines of type would be equal to 45 (number of lines) × 10 (number of points per line), which gives us a total of 450 points.

To find the number of picas of space required, we would divide 450 (total number of points) by 12 (number of points in a pica) and thus would find that our copy would require a space 37½ picas deep. The total area required for this copy would be a space 14 picas wide by 37½ picas deep.

If calculations to determine the number of lines of type for a given amount of copy result in an answer involving a fraction, such as 50½ lines, the fraction must be counted as one full line and space for 51 lines would be allowed. This provision is necessary since a line of type takes up its full point-size down the page and cannot be cut off for convenience.

Sometimes the layout man will design an advertisement, sketching in the space to be filled with body matter, before the copy has been written. He then has the problem of deciding upon the number of words that will be required to fill the area allowed.

In this case, let us imagine that the space to be filled is 15 picas wide by 21 picas deep, and that the copy is to be set in 12-point, 2-point leaded type. The number of lines of type that will fit into this space can be found by first multiplying 21 (depth in picas) by 12 (number of points in a pica), which results in 252 points. Each line will take up a total of 14 points down the page (12-point type, plus 2 points for leading), so by dividing 252 (depth of space in points) by 14 (points for each line), we find that a total of 18 lines of type can be accommodated.

Next, the number of words that will fit into one line of type is determined in the following manner:

$$
\begin{array}{rl}
15 & \text{(width of line in picas)} \\
\times\ 12 & \text{(points per pica)} \\
\hline
180 & \text{(total points in one line)} \\
\end{array}
$$

$$
\begin{array}{rl}
180 & \text{(total points in one line)} \\
\div\ 12 & \text{(points in a 12-point em)} \\
\hline
15 & \text{(total ems per line)} \\
\end{array}
$$

$$
\begin{array}{rl}
15 & \text{(total ems per line)} \\
\div\ 2.5 & \text{(ems per average word set in 12-point type)} \\
\hline
6 & \text{(words that will fit into one line)} \\
\end{array}
$$

Since one line will hold 6 words and the space will accommodate 18 lines, the total amount of copy needed will be equivalent to 6 $\times$ 18, or

108, which is the number of words that will have to be written to fill the area allotted.

Perhaps the most complicated problem in copy-fitting arises when the number of words in the copy and the size of the space into which it is to be fitted are known, but the size of type has to be decided upon.

For example, suppose we have 180 words of copy which must be fitted into an area 15 picas wide by 18 picas deep. First, it is necessary to estimate the size of type that might conceivably be required. To begin with, we might try 8-point, 2-point leaded type. Our figures would be as follow:

$$
\begin{array}{rl}
18 & \text{(depth of space in picas)} \\
\times\ 12 & \text{(points per pica)} \\
\hline
216 & \text{(total points deep)} \\
\end{array}
$$

$$
\begin{array}{rl}
216 & \text{(total points deep)} \\
\div\ 10 & \text{(points per line)} \\
\hline
\end{array}
$$

21.6, or 21 lines deep (Since each line would take up a full 10 points, only 21 lines could be accommodated.)

$$
\begin{array}{rl}
15 & \\
\times\ 12 & \\
\hline
180 & \text{(points per line)} \\
\end{array}
$$

$$
\begin{array}{rl}
180 & \\
\div\ 8 & \\
\hline
22.5 & \text{(8-point ems per line)} \\
\end{array}
$$

$$
\begin{array}{rl}
22.5 & \\
\div\ 3 & \\
\hline
7.5 & \text{(words one line will hold)} \\
\end{array}
$$

$$
\begin{array}{rl}
21 & \text{(total lines)} \\
\times\ 7.5 & \text{(words per line)} \\
\hline
157.5 & \text{(total words required)} \\
\end{array}
$$

Our answer, in this instance, shows that 22.5 less words than the total number of words in the copy could be fitted into the available space if set in 8-point leaded type, so that particular type would have to be ruled out.

Now, we might see if 8-point solid type would serve our purpose. Our figures would be as follow:

$$216 \quad \text{(depth of space in points)}$$
$$\div \quad 8 \quad \text{(points per line)}$$
$$\overline{}$$
$$27 \quad \text{(number of lines deep)}$$

$$27 \quad \text{(number of lines)}$$
$$\times \quad 7.5 \quad \text{(words per line)}$$
$$\overline{}$$
$$202.5 \quad \text{(total words required)}$$

Thus, we find that the space would require 22.5 more words, if set in 8-point solid, than there are words in the copy.   However, both estimates are close, so we decide to try 8-point type, 1-point leaded (8 on 9).

The problem now is comparatively simple, since we already know that each line when set in 8-point type will hold 7.5 words, and that the total depth of the space is 216 points.   To arrive at our answer, we must use the following figures:

$$216 \quad \text{(depth of space in points)}$$
$$\div \quad 9 \quad \text{(points for each line: 8-point type, plus 1-point leading)}$$
$$\overline{}$$
$$24 \quad \text{(lines required)}$$

$$24 \quad \text{(number of lines)}$$
$$\times \quad 7.5 \quad \text{(words per line)}$$
$$\overline{}$$
$$180 \quad \text{(total words required)}$$

Since this is exactly the same number of words as there are in the copy to be fitted into the allotted space, we should decide upon 8 on 9 type for the purpose.

The word-count method of copy-fitting has several points in its favor.   It is more accurate than the square-inch method, and anyone with a knowledge of simple arithmetic is able to work out problems after the formulas have been learned.   Furthermore, no complicated tables are involved, which would either have to be memorized or kept available, as in the square-inch method.

THE CHARACTER-COUNT METHOD

In most respects, the *character-count method* of copy-fitting is very similar to the word-count method.   The main difference is that in the latter, the word is the unit of measurement, whereas in the former, the unit is a single character.   In other words, instead of determining the number of *words* in the copy, the number of *characters* is figured;

and the number of characters that a line of type will accommodate is calculated, rather than the number of words.

This method results in estimates that are much more accurate, since every character in a standard typewriter takes up exactly the same space in a line, and by counting the number of characters, including the strokes for spaces between words, the exact number of characters in a line of copy can be determined with precision.

Furthermore, the manufacturers of leading type-casting machines have prepared tables giving the average character-count for pica measures, ranging from 1 pica to very wide lengths, in a large variety of type faces and sizes.[2] These averages have been determined by taking into account the length of the alphabet in each instance and the variations of the widths of letters in a given font of type. All such tables are the result of scientific studies aimed toward reducing the chance of errors to a minimum, and they can be relied upon as extremely accurate aids.

Thus, in the character-count method, allowances are made for differences in the length of words in all kinds of copy and also for the variations in the width of characters within an alphabet of a given size and style of type. In the word-count method, every word in the copy is counted as one, regardless of its length. Calculations based on the latter method are not so dependable because of the variation in the length of words.

Whereas computations can be made only for normal type faces by the word-count method, they may be made with equal efficiency for both wider and narrower faces by the character-count method. Consequently, the character-count method of copy-fitting has far greater versatility and is much more dependable.

Basically, the formula to be followed is the same for both the character-count method and the word-count method. The steps in the character-count method are:

1. Find the total number of characters in the copy.

2. Determine the number of characters that will fit into one line of the type decided upon.

---

[2] Several copy-fitting tables are available, some of which can be obtained from the manufacturers of the various type-casting machines. Among them are the following: "A Simple, Accurate Method of Copy-Fitting," by the Mergenthaler Linotype Company; "The Intertype Ready Reckoner," by the Intertype Corporation; and "Monotype Copy-Type Calculator," by the Lanston Monotype Machine Co Another estimating table of value is to be found in *The Journalist's Manual of Printing*, by Charles L. Allen, Appendix III, pages 261-263. New York: The Ronald Press Co., 1929.

3. Figure out the number of lines of type that will be required for all the copy.

4. Find the amount of space down the page necessary for the total number of lines of type.

There are two general kinds of typewriter type: elite, which is the smaller size; and pica, the larger. In elite type, there are exactly 12 characters to the running inch across a line; in pica, there are 10.

In normal typewritten copy, an inch margin usually is allowed on the left-hand side of the page, and approximately the same amount is allowed on the right-hand side. This leaves a space $6\frac{1}{2}$ inches wide for the type.

Consequently, a pencil line is drawn vertically down the page at a point $6\frac{1}{2}$ inches from the left side. All full lines will contain 78 characters of elite type (12×6.5), or 65 characters of pica type (10×6.5). If it appears that the line drawn down the page has defined the length of the average line quite accurately, the total number of characters on the page may be estimated by counting the number of lines of copy and multiplying this figure by 65 if the copy is in pica type, or by 78, if in elite type. If a precise estimate is necessary, each line can be counted as a full line and a correction can be made for those lines which extend beyond the pencil line or do not reach it. This is done by adding the characters which go beyond and subtracting those which fall short. Whatever difference there may be is either added to, or subtracted from, the total, as the case may be.

In order to illustrate how to fit copy by the character-count method, let us imagine that we are planning an advertisement and have one page of typewritten copy which contains a total of 22 lines. The space in the advertising layout into which this copy is to go is 20 picas wide, and our problem is to determine how many picas deep the area will have to be if the type used is 10-point Century Expanded.

The copy has been prepared on a typewriter with pica type, and we find, by following the method previously mentioned, that an average line contains 65 characters. Thus, the entire copy will be equal to 65 (number of characters per average line) $\times$ 22 (number of lines of copy), or a total of 1430 characters.

Next, we find the total number of characters that will fit into one line of Century Expanded type set 20 picas wide. This is done by consulting a character-count table, such as the one shown in Figure 55. According to the table, a line 20 picas long, set in 10-point Century Expanded type, will accommodate 48 characters.

To determine the number of lines of type needed, we then divide 1430 (total number of characters in copy) by 48 (number of characters in line of type), which results in 29+ lines. This means that 30 lines of type will be necessary, since a fraction of a line of characters would require a full line, with the space at the end not occupied by characters being filled in with quads.[3]

Century Bold with Italic

Size	Alphabet	Per Pica	10	11	12	13	14	15	16	17	18	19	20	21	22	23	24	25	26	27	28	29	30
6	95	3.6	36	40	43	47	50	54	58	61	65	68	72	76	79	83	86	90	94	97	101	104	108
8	116	2.94	30	32	35	38	41	44	47	50	53	56	59	62	65	68	71	73	76	79	82	86	89
10	146	2.34	23	26	28	31	33	35	38	40	42	45	47	49	52	54	56	59	61	63	66	68	71
12	168	2.03	20	22	24	26	29	31	33	35	37	39	41	43	45	47	49	51	53	55	57	59	61
14	201	1.7	17	19	20	22	24	25	27	29	31	32	34	36	37	39	41	42	44	46	48	49	51
18	224	1.53	15	17	18	20	21	23	24	26	27	29	30	32	33	35	36	38	39	41	43	44	46
24	310	1.11	11	12	13	14	15	17	18	19	20	21	22	23	24	25	27	28	29	30	31	32	33
30	374	.91	9	10	11	12	13	14	15	15	16	17	18	19	20	21	22	23	24	24	25	26	27
36	444	.76	8	8	9	10	11	12	12	13	14	15	15	16	17	18	18	19	20	21	22	22	23
30 ital	380	.90	9	10	11	12	13	13	14	15	16	17	18	19	20	21	22	22	23	24	25	26	27
36 ital	473	.72	7	8	8	9	10	10	11	12	12	13	14	15	15	16	17	17	18	19	19	20	21

Century Bold Condensed

Size	Alphabet	Per Pica	10	11	12	13	14	15	16	17	18	19	20	21	22	23	24	25	26	27	28	29	30
12	120	2.85	29	31	34	37	40	43	46	49	51	54	57	60	63	66	68	71	74	77	80	83	86
18	177	1.94	19	21	23	25	27	29	31	33	35	37	39	41	43	45	47	49	51	52	54	56	58
24	220	1.56	16	17	19	20	22	23	25	27	28	30	31	33	34	36	37	39	41	42	44	45	47
30	274	1.25	12	14	15	16	17	19	20	21	22	24	25	26	28	29	30	31	32	34	35	36	38
18 ital	223	1.53	15	17	18	20	21	23	25	26	28	29	31	32	34	35	37	38	40	41	43	45	46

Century Expanded with Century Bold

Size	Alphabet	Per Pica	10	11	12	13	14	15	16	17	18	19	20	21	22	23	24	25	26	27	28	29	30
6	95	3.6	36	40	43	47	51	54	58	61	65	68	72	76	79	83	87	90	94	97	101	105	108
7	110	3.1	31	34	37	41	44	47	50	53	56	59	62	65	68	72	75	78	81	84	87	90	94
8	119	2.87	29	32	35	37	40	43	46	49	52	55	57	60	63	66	69	72	75	78	81	83	87
9	133	2.57	26	28	31	34	36	39	41	44	47	49	52	54	57	59	62	64	67	70	72	75	78
10	142	2.41	24	27	29	31	34	36	39	41	43	46	48	51	53	55	58	60	63	65	67	70	73
12	164	2.08	21	23	25	27	29	31	33	35	37	39	42	44	46	48	50	52	54	56	58	60	62
14	194	1.76	18	19	21	23	25	26	28	30	32	33	35	37	39	40	42	44	46	47	49	51	53

Figure 55. Sample character-count tables, from *The Intertype Ready Reckoner*. (Courtesy of Intertype Corporation.)

Since each line of type will occupy 10 points, plus 2 points for leading, the total amount of space necessary for the copy is equivalent to 30 (number of lines of type) × 12 (number of points for each line), or 360 points. Thus, the depth of the area will be 30 picas, because

---

[3] In this instance, the table headed "Century Expanded with Century Bold" was used. The same table would be employed in finding the character-count for lines cast in Century Bold. The reason for this is that the matrices from which this variety of Century Expanded is cast carries two characters—one of them above the other. If the line of matrices is arranged so that the characters at the top are positioned over the opening in the mold, one variety (Century Expanded) is cast; if the lower line of characters comes over the opening, the other variety (Century Bold) is obtained. This arrangement accounts for headings giving the name of more than one variety of a type face over a given table.

360 (total points deep) divided by 12 (number of points per line) equals 30 picas.

This last step actually was unnecessary, since each line was found to require 12 points of space, or the equivalent of one pica. Short cuts such as this should be taken wherever possible. They will be discovered quickly after some practice.

If the problem is to determine the number of words necessary to fill a predetermined area, when the kind and size of type and width of line are known, the same formula as that used in the word-count method would be used, with the exception that the basis for determining the amount of copy required would be characters rather than words. Likewise, in finding the size and kind of type necessary to fit a given amount of copy into a certain known area, the same general plan as that used in the word-count method would be followed.

THE SQUARE-INCH METHOD

The *square-inch method* of copy-fitting is not so accurate as the other two mentioned and consequently is not used so widely. However, it will result in estimates that are sufficiently accurate for preliminary purposes where complete exactness is not absolutely necessary.

When the problem is to determine the number of words that will be required to fill a given space, the first step is to find out how many square inches there are in the area. This is done by multiplying the width by the length in inches.

For instance, the layout man may have planned for a copy block within an advertisement which is 3 inches wide and 5 inches deep. This would make a total of 15 square inches, since 3 × 5 equals 15.

Next, a table showing the number of words that will fit into one square inch of space, when set in a given size, is consulted. The table used generally by printers throughout the trade is as follows:

Size of type	No. words per sq. in. when set solid	No. words per sq. in. when set 2-pt. leaded
6-pt.	47	34
7-pt.	38	27
8-pt.	32	23
9-pt.	27	20
10-pt.	21	16
11-pt.	17	14
12-pt.	14	11

If it is decided that the type is to be set in 10-point leaded, it will be noted that 16 words will fit into one square inch of space. Thus, the total number of words required for the entire space would be 240, since 15 (number of square inches of space) $\times$ 16 (number of words per square inch) equals 240.

In other words, the simple formula to be used in this method is as follows:

$$\text{Square inches of space} \times \text{number of words per square inch} =$$
$$\text{number of words needed}$$

The square-inch method of copy-fitting is useful not only in planning advertisements, but also for many other kinds of composition. It is helpful in estimating the number of pages that will be required to accommodate the copy for a booklet or for some other job which is to consist of several printed pages.

First, a plan for the page size is made, showing the area which is to be taken up by the type. For example, this area might be a space 4 inches wide by 7 inches deep, or a total of 28 square inches.

For purposes of illustration, let us imagine that the copy for this booklet consists of 4800 words, which could be determined by first finding the number of words to an average line and then multiplying the total number of lines in the copy by this figure.

If the type to be used were 12-point, 2-point leaded, the problem would be solved as follows:

$$
\begin{array}{rl}
28 & \text{(number of square inches of space)} \\
\times\ 11 & \text{(number of words of 12-pt. leaded type per square inch)} \\
\hline
308 & \text{(number of words one page would require)} \\
\end{array}
$$

$$
\begin{array}{rl}
4800 & \text{(total number of words in copy)} \\
\div\ 308 & \text{(number of words per page)} \\
\hline
15.58 & \\
\end{array}
$$

This means that 16 pages would have to be allowed for the copy, although the last page would not be completely filled.

In case the type area could not be measured satisfactorily in inches, but could be determined in even picas, the number of square picas contained would be figured first. Then the total would be divided by 36, since there are 36 square picas to one square inch. This would give the number of square inches in the area.

When the problem is that of deciding upon the size of type that would be necessary to fit a certain amount of copy into a given space, it can be solved by first dividing the total number of words in the copy by the number of square inches available to find the number of words required for one square inch of space. Then by consulting the table, it would be possible to determine the type size that could be used most advantageously.

For example, if the space to be filled is 2 inches wide by 5 inches deep, a total of 10 square inches of space would be available. If there were 160 words in the copy, each square inch would have to accommodate 16 words (160 ÷ 10). The table shows that one square inch of type set in 10-point leaded will hold exactly this number of words, so this is the kind of type that should be used.

By making use of the prepared table, computations can be made quickly and easily by the square-inch method, which is satisfactory when fine computations are not required. It is especially useful in planning preliminary sketches for layouts in which some latitude is permissible.

Some Helpful Aids

Most regular news matter is set in one size and kind of type, and the width of column remains the same throughout most of the paper. Consequently, problems of estimating can be reduced to a simple formula by the editorial worker.

It is possible to determine the number of words required for one column-inch of space, either by figuring out the problem by one of the methods already described or by actually counting the words contained in this area. The number of words contained in an average line can be obtained in a similar manner.

If either the word-count or the character-count method is used, it first would be necessary to learn what kind and size of type are being used and the exact column width. The same general method can be followed in working out formulas for matter set for leads two columns or more in width, for editorial matter, and for type commonly used in boxes or for other special display purposes.

This information should be memorized or kept available in written form so that problems in copy-fitting can be solved quickly and efficiently. By following such a plan, the reporter can determine accurately the amount of copy he should write in a given situation. The unnecessary delays and wasted time in the composing room caused when too much copy, or too little, is prepared for a given space on a page can thus be avoided.

Occasionally the layout man wants to use a type face that is not included in the estimating tables available. This is particularly true when types in the larger sizes are desired for display lines in an advertisement. If this problem arises, it is possible to estimate the number of characters that will fit into a line of the desired length by consulting a type-specimen sheet containing the type face in the size wanted. A line-gauge can be placed directly on the sheet, the length measured, and the number of characters counted.

When no samples of the type in the size desired are available, estimates can be obtained by setting up a line of average characters to the required measure and counting them. Using this as a basis, the number of words which the line will accommodate may be computed.

The layout man should have a specimen sheet for each of the types in the composing room which he may have occasion to use. In addition, the number of average characters which will fit into common measures also might be noted on each sheet. These figures may either be taken from tables that are already prepared or may be worked out as suggested above. Furthermore, it is essential that the layout man know what types are available on the machines and the faces that can be obtained from each font of matrices so he will be in a position to plan his work most economically and efficiently.

Without this information, he may make requests that will require time-consuming adjustments on the Linotypes—adjustments which might otherwise have been avoided. Furthermore, he will forestall the possibility of requesting types which are not available in the printing department—an unpardonable error.

VII

Method of Proofreading

THE PURPOSE OF PROOFREADING IS TO MAKE sure that the copy has been reproduced accurately.

After the type has been set, it is placed on a galley and a proof is pulled. This proof then goes to the proofreading department, where it is read carefully by the proofreader, who marks all errors that are to be corrected. On the larger newspapers, he is assisted by a copyholder, who reads the copy aloud line by line, including punctuation marks, paragraphing, and other details, while the proofreader himself marks the proof.

Ideally, the proofreader should be concerned only with mistakes made by the operator or printer in setting the type. However, in most offices he is given authority to change any obvious errors in the copy which may have been overlooked by the writer in his effort to meet a deadline or because of carelessness.

The importance of editing copy accurately before it is delivered to the composing room cannot be overemphasized. Much valuable time and effort can be wasted if the original copy contains errors, or if the writer, as an afterthought, decides that some change should be made after the copy has reached the operator. Every attempt should be made to see that the copy is perfect before it is turned in.

The printer, Linotype operator, or proofreader assumes some risk when he changes the copy in any way. In fact, many newspapers place the responsibility on the writer—where it rightfully belongs—and instruct those who set the type or have anything to do with corrections to "follow copy" without deviation. Advertisers often make the same demand.

Such a practice has one great advantage. It overcomes the habit of "passing the buck" in case errors appear in print, since it is much easier to trace them to their source. On the other hand, the correction by the proofreader of obvious errors, such as misspelled words or improper punctuation, which appear in the copy often saves considerable time that might be wasted in referring the copy back to the writer.

The proofreader holds a place of great responsibility, and he should be selected with care. First of all, he should be alert and dependable, with a sound knowledge of grammar and spelling. In addition, he should be well informed about happenings of the day at home and abroad so that he will be familiar with people and places in the news. Furthermore, a knowledge of printing and the problems involved in producing type by machine and by hand is of great assistance. An understanding of the causes for certain errors makes it easier for him to determine the changes necessary and how the proof corrections can be made with a minimum of recasting by the operator.

Frequently, the intelligent proofreader is able to catch certain errors in spelling or in fact that would get the newspaper into serious difficulty if they were allowed to appear in print. Even the most diligent editor or reporter occasionally makes mistakes, and a good proofreader is of great value to them in their work.

One major requirement is that he be extremely accurate and that he follow copy closely to make sure that it appears in print exactly as it is written. However, in case of doubt, he should not hesitate to refer the copy back to the writer for clarification.

A newspaper that is full of errors reflects unfavorably on the entire staff. The most respected publications are those that can be relied upon for their accuracy, and the proofreader is one of the key men whose business it is to promote confidence and respect on the part of readers.

Need for Good Proofs

The first prerequisite for efficiency in the proofreading department is that the proofs submitted be well printed and easy to read. Great care should be taken to see that the type is properly covered with an ink that is suitable for the paper used, and that the impression is even and of sufficient pressure to insure a good reproduction. Proofs of straight matter usually are pulled on ordinary newsprint, but a better quality of paper often is used for advertisements, editorials, illustrations, and special articles to insure a sharp, clear print.

Dim, gray proofs, or those in which all the lines do not print satisfactorily because some of the type is off its feet or is covered with metal trimmings, are a severe handicap to the proofreader. They are much more difficult to read; errors may be passed over because of poor legibility; and the tendency to guess at the correctness of a portion of the printed matter that is faint often results in errors that otherwise could be avoided.

GALLEY PROOFS

The first proof taken is known as a *galley proof*. This proof is read, and, if no errors are discovered, it is marked "O.K." and returned. However, if any mistakes are marked on the galley proof, it is sent back to the printer or operator, who resets the matter indicated.

The procedure followed in making corrections in hand-set composition has been discussed in a previous chapter. As already mentioned, changes which involve the replacement of letters with others of the same width can be made right in the form. However, where words are to be added or where letters to be replaced are not of the same width, each line containing an error must be placed back in the composing stick, where it can be re-justified after the correction is made. Then it is returned to its place in the form.

Since lines cast on the Linotype are in the form of solid slugs, a new slug must be cast for each line in which an error occurs. When the wording is changed, the operator or printer frequently must recast or reset several lines in order to take care of the correction.

The cautious proofreader will be extremely careful in marking errors of this kind. He must see that the changes are of such a nature that the resetting of several lines will be avoided wherever possible. Sometimes it is possible to alter the wording slightly without changing the meaning, so that the same amount of space in a line will be retained. Such a practice should not be followed except in cases where considerable time will be spent in making the changes, and, if there is any possibility of an objection on the part of the writer, the copy should be referred to him for his approval.

After all the corrections on a proof have been made, the operator wraps up the slugs in the proof and returns them to the bank. Then they are inserted in place of the lines containing errors, and another proof is pulled. This proof is known as a *revise*. If a third proof is required before all errors are taken care of, it is referred to as the *second revise*. Sometimes several revises are necessary, but usually a galley proof and one revise are sufficient for newspaper purposes. In commercial printing plants and publishing houses where books and other larger and more durable works are printed, several other proofs may be taken to insure complete accuracy.[1]

---

[1] For a thorough treatment of the subject, especially as it relates to the production of books, see Joseph Lasky, *Proofreading and Copy-Preparation*. New York: Mentor Press, 1941.

Another proof, known as a *press proof,* is taken of the forms after they have been locked on the press and made ready for printing. This is the final proof, and consequently it is read with great care. Minor corrections can be taken care of by unlocking the forms and making the changes in the forms right on the press. However, any major alterations may make it necessary to remove the form, or forms, involved.

Errors found in a page of a newspaper printed on a rotary press, which uses stereotype plates, are even more serious. In order to correct them, a new plate has to be cast to replace the one containing the mistakes. Since replating is expensive and time-consuming, every effort is made to see that all corrections have been made in the type forms before the original plate is cast.

Page Proofs

Many of these difficulties can be avoided by pulling *page proofs.* As the name implies, these are proofs of pages after they have been put together by the makeup man. They are scrutinized with the utmost care and necessary corrections are made before the plates are cast.

Page proofs are read carefully to see that headlines have been placed over the right stories, that captions and cut lines accompany the cuts they should, that continued lines and jumped stories have been handled properly, and that the date line and page numbers are correct. These, and other details, are checked before the final "O.K." is given.

In the rush of meeting deadlines, the temptation to do without page proofs is great; often time is so limited that they are not taken. As a result, serious errors frequently slip by. Since more time is given to the planning and preparation of Sunday magazine sections, the practice of requiring page proofs is more general. In the production of books, catalogs, booklets, and pamphlets, page proofs always are needed so that a check can be made to see that pages have been made up correctly and assembled in the proper order, according to specifications in the dummies.

Methods of Marking Proof

Every error in the proof requires two marks—one in the margin and another in the text. The mark placed in the margin shows what the correction is to be; the one placed within the text indicates the exact location of the error.

Two methods of marking proofs are in general use on newspapers: (1) *the book system,* and (2) *the guide line system.*

In the book system, marks placed in the margin to indicate errors in a given line are separated by diagonal lines. In the guide line system, the error within the text is either circled or marked with a diagonal stroke and a line is run out to the margin where the correction mark is placed.   Because of the confusion which might be caused by the guide lines crossing one another in the case of several errors close to one another, the book method is much more desirable, especially when only one column of type appears on the proof.

However, guide lines are necessary in marking page proofs containing several columns, since it is then the best method of directing atten-

∧	Make correction indicated in margin.	⌐	Raise to proper position.
Stet	Retain crossed-out word or letter; let it stand.	⌐⌐	Lower to proper position.
		////	Hair space letters.
....	Retain words under which dots appear; write "Stet" in margin.	*W.f.*	Wrong font; change to proper font.
Stet		*Qu?*	Is this right?
✗	Appears battered; examine.	*l.c.*	Put in lower case (small letters).
≡	Straighten lines.	*s.c.*	Put in small capitals.
⋁⋀⋁	Unevenly spaced; correct spacing.	*Caps*	Put in capitals.
//	Line up; i.e., make lines even with other matter.	*C&s.c.*	Put in caps and small caps.
run in	Make no break in the reading; no ¶	*rom.*	Change to Roman.
no ¶	No paragraph; sometimes written "run in."	*ital.*	Change to Italic.
		≡	Under letter or word means caps.
out see copy	Here is an omission; see copy.	⩵	Under letter or word, small caps.
¶	Make a paragraph here.	—	Under letter or word means Italic.
tr	Transpose words or letters as indicated.	∿∿	Under letter or word, bold face.
ℐ	Take out matter indicated; dele.	,/	Insert comma.
ℐ	Take out character indicated and close up.	;/	Insert semicolon.
		:/	Insert colon.
¢	Line drawn through a cap means lower case.	⊙	Insert period.
		/?/	Insert interrogation mark.
☉	Upside down; reverse.	(!)	Insert exclamation mark.
⊃	Close up; no space.	/=/	Insert hyphen.
#	Insert a space here.	⩘	Insert apostrophe.
⊥	Push down this space.	⅋⅋	Insert quotation marks.
⊡	Indent line one em.	ℯ	Insert superior letter or figure.
⌐	Move this to the left.	⌐⌐	Insert inferior letter or figure.
⌐	Move this to the right.	[/]	Insert brackets.
		(/)	Insert parenthesis.
		$\frac{\prime}{m}$	One-em dash.
		$\frac{2}{m}$	Two-em parallel dash.

Figure 56. Proofreaders' marks.

tion to errors inside the page. Furthermore, the number of errors at this point should be kept to a minimum, to reduce the possibility of confusion.

Whichever system is used, the proofreader should place marks in the margin nearest the error, and all marks should be made plainly. A soft lead pencil is best for use in marking errors on proofs taken on soft papers such as newsprint, but pen and ink may be used on coated or harder-finished papers that will not allow the ink to "run" or blur.

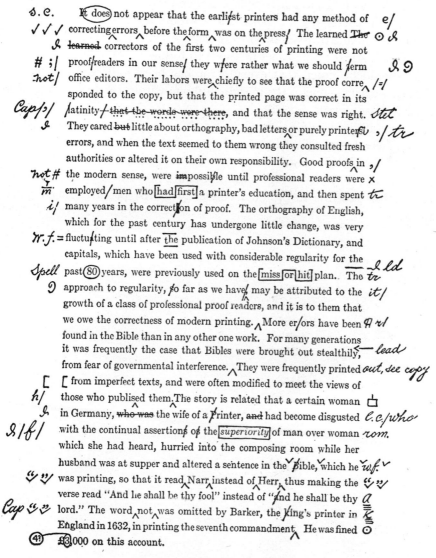

Figure 57. A piece of corrected proof.

One disadvantage in using ink is that it is difficult to erase in case a change is found necessary after a mark has been made.

How Markings Are Used

First of all, the proofreader's marks should be learned. Those shown in Figure 56 are used, with only slight variations, in all newspaper offices and printing establishments, and the student of journalism should become thoroughly familiar with them.

He also should have a complete understanding of how these marks are used in correcting a proof. Most proofs are not so "dirty" as the one used for illustrative purposes in Figure 57. However, the illustration demonstrates the proper methods to follow.

It should be noted that every error has been indicated clearly and that two marks—one in the margin and one within the text—have been used for each error.

Above all, it should be remembered that the proofreader generally is the one who has the final say as to how the type is to appear in the newspaper. Those who read the proofs, therefore, should be chosen carefully, and everyone engaged in producing the newspaper should do everything possible to promote efficiency in the proofreading department.

VIII

Type-Casting Machines

FOR OVER FOUR HUNDRED YEARS FOLLOWING the invention of printing, all type was set by hand. Although many new type faces were introduced and typographical design underwent great changes, no improvements were made in the method of setting type during this period. All books, magazines, newspapers and other kinds of publications were composed in the same manner as the famous Gutenberg Bible, which preceded them.

The need for a faster method was not so great during the colonial days in this country. Our early newspapers were very small and circulations were limited. Many editors not only wrote the news for their papers, but they also set the type and did their own printing by hand.

However, gradual changes in social and economic conditions after the Revolutionary War had far-reaching effects on the printing and publishing industry. The first daily newspapers published by Towne, Claypoole, and Dunlap could be produced satisfactorily with hand-set type, simple hand presses, and ink daubers, since only a few hundred four-page sheets were required to supply their readers. As the population began to grow and expand, a pressing need for greater volume in less time arose.

Some of the problems of mechanical production were solved partially by improvements in the making of paper and other raw materials, and by the introduction of new processes, faster presses, and other printing machinery which made their appearance during the first half of the nineteenth century.

The greatest handicap to any appreciable increase in the size of newspapers and the speed of production was the long delay in discovering a method of composing type that would be superior to the slow and tedious practice of setting all type by hand. Before the invention of a machine which solved this problem, most newspapers were limited in size to four or eight pages. Even the wealthier, big-city dailies were small, despite efforts to meet the growing demands by employment of long rows of hand compositors who worked long hours over their cases. Under the circumstances, the most efficient composing rooms were restricted in the volume of type that could be produced.

The seriousness of this situation was recognized early in the nineteenth century. Inventors went to work on the problem, and many costly experiments were made. By 1880, over forty patents for type-composing and -distributing machines were granted by the government, but none of them proved to be very practical for newspaper use.[1]

The earliest of these were machines designed to set individual letters of type automatically into lines. However, each line had to be justified by hand after the letters were assembled, since no mechanical provision was made for spacing lines to the same length. Moreover, once the individual letters had been called down by the pressure on keys, there was no way of returning and distributing them to their proper boxes except by hand.

Justification of lines and distribution are very time-consuming operations in hand composition, and since they did not solve these two major problems, the value of the machines to newspapers was very limited.

THE UNITYPE MACHINE

The first type-setting machine to solve the distribution problem made its appearance in 1870. Known as the Unitype, it was manufactured by the Wood Nathan Company of New York. It proved to be one of the best of all early type-setting machines.[2]

The Unitype consisted of two cylinders, one located directly above the other. Each had ninety vertical channels, which contained the type. The top cylinder, which rotated over the one below, served as the distributor. Letters were admitted to it by an automatic loader from a galley, where the type to be used was placed.[3]

Each letter contained a different combination of nicks that controlled its passage from its channel in the top cylinder to a corresponding channel in the lower cylinder. As the top rotated, a letter would drop into its proper place when it reached the channel in the lower cylinder which had an opening with the correct combinations.

The bottom cylinder was the magazine, and the keyboard was lo-

---

[1] Alfred M. Lee, *The Daily Newspaper in America*, page 122. New York: The Macmillan Company, 1937.

[2] Kenneth E. Olson, *Typography and Mechanics of the Newspaper*, page 97. New York: D. Appleton and Company, 1930.

[3] Olson, *Typography and Mechanics of the Newspaper*, page 98.

Figure 58. The Unitype. (Courtesy of Mergenthaler Linotype Company.)

cated below it.   The keyboard was so arranged that when a key was pressed, a letter from the corresponding channel in the magazine would drop into place in the line being assembled.   After the line had been set, the operator then had to justify it before it was ready for printing.[4] Although the Unitype failed to meet all the requirements of rapid production, it was capable of doing the work of about four hand compositors.

Besides the Unitype, which was also called the Simplex, or Thorne, type-setter, another machine, called the Paige Compositor, was invented.   However, it did not prove successful, and only two Paige Compositors were built.

OTTMAR MERGENTHALER'S LINOTYPE

Among the inventors who became interested in developing a machine to produce type was a young man named Ottmar Mergenthaler, who was born in the village of Hatchel, in Württemberg, Germany, on May 10, 1854.   At an early age, he was apprenticed to a maker of watches and clocks in Bietigheim, where he worked until 1872.

Like many other young men, Mergenthaler had an urge to see the world; he looked upon America as the land of great opportunity.   Consequently, he arranged for a position with an August Hahl, a son of his employer, who was a maker of electrical instruments in Washington, D.C. Mergenthaler arrived in this country in October, 1872.[5]   His employment placed him in close contact with inventors who were experimenting on instruments for the United States Signal Service.

Mergenthaler's first introduction to the problem of type setting came when he was called upon to make improvements in a typewriting machine which was brought into the Hahl shop by a customer seeking technical assistance.   The machine consisted of a cylinder upon which the characters to be printed were arranged in successive circles.   As the cylinder revolved, letters were printed in lithographic ink upon a strip of paper when the keys were pressed.

This paper then was cut into strips, each containing one line.   The lines were justified by proper separation of words, and then they were transferred to a lithographic stone for printing.

Mergenthaler quickly saw why the machine would not work satisfactorily, and he set about making a model based on his own ideas.

---

[4] Olson, *Typography and Mechanics of the Newspaper,* page 97.

[5] Thomas Dreier, *The Power of Print and Men,* page 21.   Brooklyn, N.Y.: Mergenthaler Linotype Company, 1936.

His plans were approved, and the new machine was completed in 1877.[6] However, it also depended upon lithography and its usefulness was very limited.

His next step was to invent another machine, somewhat similar to the typewriter, which would impress letters one at a time to form lines on a strip of papier-mâché that served as a matrix from which a stereotype plate for use in printing could be cast.   Because of the troubles involved in making suitable casts from the matrices, this machine met with failure.

Convinced that the troublesome features of the papier-mâché method had to be eliminated, he decided that the matrix should be imprinted line by line, instead of one letter at a time.   A new machine embodying this "bar-indenting" principle was built and tested late in 1883.[7] Referred to as the "Mergenthaler of 1883," this was the first machine to bear the name of the inventor.

This was followed the next year by another bar-indenting machine with some added refinements; but since molten metal had to be poured by hand onto the matrices in order to form slugs, production was consequently too slow for the process to compete successfully with hand composition.

Mergenthaler now was convinced that the papier-mâché would have to be discarded entirely.   In its place, he decided to use female metal matrices which could be assembled into a line and justified.   Then a sliding mold was brought against the line and molten metal was forced into the mold against the matrices from a metal pot containing a pump.

The principle of the vertical bars, each bar containing a complete alphabet of letters and blanks for spaces of different widths, was retained.   The main difference was that the characters were indented, rather than raised.   This machine, the true forerunner of the present-day Linotype, was tested before several interested spectators in the early part of 1884.

Up until this time, the work had been sponsored by a group of stenographers, patent attorneys, and some small capitalists.   The driving force was James O. Clephane, a successful stenographer in the law courts in Washington, who was private secretary to Secretary of State Seward during the Civil War period.   Despite many failures and disappointments along the way, Clephane was unwilling to admit defeat. Through his unflinching confidence and the financial backing he always

---

[6] Dreier, *The Power of Print and Men,* page 21.
[7] Dreier, *The Power of Print and Men,* page 25.

managed to arrange, Mergenthaler was able to carry on his costly experiments.

When it became clearly evident that Mergenthaler was meeting with success in his efforts to invent a machine that would compose type faster than the fastest hand compositors or the type-setting machines then in existence, newspaper publishers began to take an active interest in the invention.

In 1885, a syndicate was formed by Whitelaw Reid, of the *New York Tribune;* Stilson Hutchins, of the *Washington Post;* Victor Lawson and Melville Stone, of the *Chicago Daily News;* W. N. Haldeman, of the *Louisville Courier-Journal;* Henry Smith, of the *Chicago Inter Ocean;* and W. H. Rand, of Rand, McNally & Company. They paid a sum of $300,000 for a controlling interest, and a pool was formed of the new syndicate and of all the earlier interests.[8]

Mergenthaler was not satisfied with the type bars. With a new plan in mind, he set out immediately to replace them with circulating brass matrices, each bearing its own finely tooled, individual letter. After being assembled into a line by operation of a keyboard, the slug was cast; then the matrices were returned automatically to the magazine for use again.

This new machine, known as the "Mergenthaler of 1886," was set up and demonstrated in the office of the *New York Tribune* on July 3, 1886. Whitelaw Reid, its famous editor, started the mechanism and christened the new invention the "Linotype." [9]

During the first year in which the Linotype was used in the composing room of the *New York Tribune,* it made a saving of $80,000 for the paper, which demonstrated unmistakably its desirability for newspaper use. In less than two years, about sixty machines were in use in the composing rooms of members of the syndicate.

Nevertheless, publishers outside the syndicate were hesitant to purchase Linotype machines for several years. However, as refinements were made and a satisfactory system of payments was developed to make possible its purchase by smaller publishers, the number of owners gradually increased. Today, practically every newspaper has its own slug-casting machines, and most of the type which appears in our present-day newspapers is produced by type-casting machines which work on principles similar to those used in the Mergenthaler invention of 1886.

---

[8] Dreier, *The Power of Print and Men,* page 30.
[9] Dreier, *The Power of Print and Men,* page 29.

THE INTERTYPE

Another type-casting machine, known as the Intertype, is the principal competitor of the Linotype. Basically, the Intertype works on the same underlying principles, and except for a few mechanical differences, it produces type in the same manner.

The first Intertype did not make its appearance until after some of the original Mergenthaler patents had expired. Development of the first model was begun in 1911 by the International Typesetting Machine Company, of New York, under the leadership of Herman Ridder, who at that time was the executive officer of the Associated Press and the American Newspaper Publishers' Association.[10]

The original idea of the company was to produce three new, but entirely different, type-setting machines. The first machine to be built was a very simple, low-priced machine known as the *Amalgatype:* the second, a line-casting machine called the *Monoline;* and the third, a slug-casting machine which became known as the *Intertype.*[11]

The Amalgatype cast single types and assembled them into lines, which were justified by expanding spacers placed between words. After the line was justified, it then was amalgamated by a secondary casting operation into a line ready for use in printing. The machine was about three feet in height and was very compact, occupying only four square feet of floor space. However, it never was carried beyond the stage of a working model.

Previously developed in Canada and Germany, the Monoline was a line-composing and casting machine which made use of circulating matrices, each of which carried several letters. After the line of matrices was assembled, it was delivered to the casting mechanism, and the matrices then were distributed automatically.

This machine could not cast more than one face of type in the same line, and the plan of the company was to correct this fault so that two or three fonts of type could be used simultaneously. The idea finally was abandoned, and major attention was given over to the development of the Intertype, in which all the most desirable mechanical improvements could be incorporated.

The first model of the Intertype was completed in Brooklyn in October, 1912, and was demonstrated before a group of spectators the fol-

---

[10] *The Development of the Intertype,* page 3. Reprint of a paper read by H. R. Freund, Chief Engineer of Intertype Corporation, before a group of New England publishers and printers in Boston in 1937.

[11] *The Development of the Intertype,* page 3.

lowing month.   The first tool-made Intertype was installed in the *New York Journal of Commerce* in March, 1913.[12]

The plan was to produce a machine simpler in design than existing type-casting machines.   It was to have fewer parts and was to be based on the principle of standardization, which would make possible universal interchangeability, thus permitting a buyer to add extra magazines and other features as he desired.

To begin with, a publisher might purchase a machine with only one magazine; but, as his business expanded, he might convert it into a two- or three-magazine machine by purchasing and installing the additional equipment right in his own plant.   Side magazines and other additional features could be added in the same way as improvements were made and as the owner saw their need.

Another slug-casting machine, known as the Linograph, also was placed on the market by another company to compete with the Linotype and the Intertype.   It was simpler in design, with only one magazine, was more compact, and was much less expensive.   This machine experienced some popularity among owners of smaller newspapers and printing plants for several years, but competition became too strong, and it finally was discontinued.

THE MATRIX

The real heart of the Linotype is the *matrix,* from which the type face is cast.   It is a small, flat piece of brass, varying in thickness according to the width of the letter it carries.   The character, or characters, to be cast from it are stamped on one edge.

In the smaller sizes, each matrix carries two letters, one punched above the other.   One of the characters usually is regular lightface; the other is either the boldface or an Italic version of the same face. Thus, from a single font of matrices, it is possible, in all except the large display faces, to obtain two varieties of type.

For many years only matrices through 14-point were "duplexed" (made to cast two letters), but today many faces through 24-point can be obtained in this manner from two-letter matrices.

The raised printing characters on the face of the slug are cast from the indented characters on the edges of the matrices.   The top of the matrix is cut out into the shape of a "V"; on the inside of the "V" is a series of small notches, forming teeth.   Each character has a different combination of teeth.   This combination controls the matrix's dis-

---

[12] *The Development of the Intertype,* page 5.

tribution back into its proper place in the magazine after a line has been cast. On either side of the matrix, at both top and bottom, are projections known as ears.

THE MAGAZINE

Matrices are stored in a flat container called a *magazine,* located at the top of the machine in an inclined position above the keyboard. It consists of a series of channels, one for each character. Several matrices for each letter are stacked one behind the other up a particular channel. They are held in place by escapement pawls at the bottom of the channels, which keep them from sliding out until the operator is ready to assemble them into a line.

A machine may be equipped with one or more magazines, depending upon its design. Some display models provide for as many as four main magazines and four auxiliary magazines, in which the larger characters and figures are kept. A separate magazine is required for each font of matrices. These magazines are located one above the other and are so constructed mechanically that the font of matrices needed by an operator can either be raised or lowered quickly into position for use by a simple adjustment.

Magazines are detachable and can be removed from the machine and replaced by others when desired. Extra magazines, each containing a different font of matrices, are stored in special racks near the machines. Thus the operator

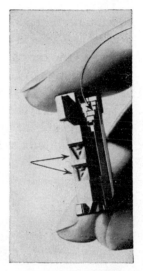

Figure 59. A Linotype matrix. Arrow at top points to matrix combination teeth; the ones at the bottom indicate the casting edge. (Courtesy Mergenthaler Linotype Company.)

may have at his command a wide variety of type faces, all of which can be cast from one machine.

THE KEYBOARD

Directly below the magazine at the front of the machine is the keyboard. Its arrangement is entirely different from that used on the typewriter, with the letters most frequently used grouped closely together.

Each key is connected by a system of rods, cams, and levers with the escapements controlling the release of matrices from one of the channels in the magazine above.

When the key for a given letter is pressed slightly, it sets into motion the mechanism which causes a matrix to drop by gravity out of its channel.   As the operator fingers the keyboard, the desired letters fall one at a time from their respective places in the magazine into the line being assembled.

THE SPACEBAND

The spaceband consists of two thin, wedge-shaped pieces of metal, which taper in opposite directions so that the outside faces always are parallel.   There is a projection on either side at the top, somewhat similar to the ears on the matrix.

The function of the spacebands is twofold: (1) to give space between words, and (2) to justify the line of matrices before casting.

Justification is accomplished when the upper part of the spaceband is held firmly and the lower part is pushed upward, thus causing it to expand and tighten the line of matrices.

Figure 60.   This illustration of a magazine which has been cut away longitudinally shows how all the matrices of one character are retained in a "channel."   (Courtesy of Mergenthaler Linotype Company.)

Spacebands are located in a *spaceband box* directly above the assembling elevator and are dropped into the line automatically when the space-bar—just left of the keyboard—is pressed.

ASSEMBLING THE LINE

The first step in the production of a type-slug is the assembling of the line of matrices. When the keys are pressed, matrices are released from their respective channels in the magazine. They then drop through guides, or chutes, onto a moving assembler belt which carries them down one at a time into the "stick," or assembling elevator. Here the matrices are assembled in an upright position, with the indented edges facing inward. Spacebands are dropped between words.

In the assembling elevator and throughout the entire delivery mechanism there are two rails, or tracks, on which the matrices rest. If matrices are assembled on the top rail, the characters indented on the lower edge of the matrices will be cast; if assembled on the bottom rail, the upper characters will be cast. In other words, if the font of matrices has regular lightface letters at the top and boldface letters at the bottom on its casting edge, either can be obtained by proper adjustment of the rail on which they are assembled.

The assembling elevator serves much the same purpose as the printer's composing stick. When it has been filled

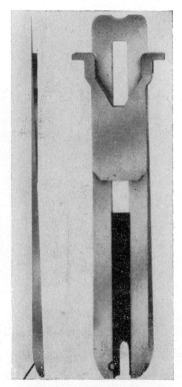

Figure 61. Two views of a Linotype spaceband. It consists of two thin wedge-shaped pieces of metal that taper in opposite directions. (Courtesy of Mergenthaler Linotype Company.)

with matrices, the operator depresses a lever at the right side of the keyboard. This lifts the assembling elevator containing the line up to the delivery slide, which automatically carries the matrices and spacebands to the left. There they are transferred onto a slide called the *first elevator,* which lowers them to a position between the vise jaws directly in front of the mold.

Casting the Line

The second step is accomplished by the casting mechanism. The line itself is cast in an opening, or mold, in a large, revolving wheel known as the *mold disk*. This disk contains either four or six molds, depending upon its design. Each mold is adjustable. By removing two pieces of metal known as liners and substituting them with others,

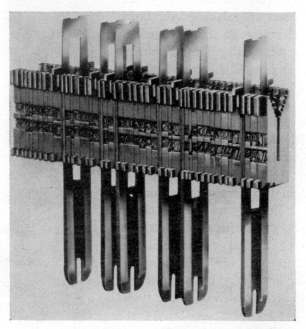

Figure 62. A line of matrices and spacebands assembled together. The bottom parts of the spacebands have been raised, thus causing the line to expand. (Courtesy of Mergenthaler Linotype Company.)

slugs varying in both length and thickness of body may be cast, since the opening into which the molten metal flows is regulated in this manner.

As the first elevator descends, the disk revolves a quarter of a turn to the left, bringing the mold in which the slug is to be cast exactly in front of the line of matrices. After the spacebands have been pushed up from below to justify the line by expanding it to its limit within the vise jaws, the disk moves forward until the mold is tight against the line of matrices, which now are facing in directly over the opening.

Behind the mold disk is a metal pot containing the molten metal.

The metal is forced out by means of a plunger through a series of small holes in a *mouthpiece*. At the proper instant, the mouthpiece is brought forward automatically against the back of the mold, and the plunger descends, sending a stream of molten metal into the mold against the line of indented letters on the matrices. The metal hardens instantly. Thus, a slug, with the faces of the type raised on its surface, is formed.

Then the metal pot recedes, and the disk wheel revolves three-quarters of a turn to its original position, with the hardened slug still in the mold where it was cast. As it does so, a knife at the back of the disk trims the base of the slug.

When the mold comes to a stop, it is in a vertical position in front of other knives, which trim the sides of the slug as it is pushed out by an ejector blade that advances from behind. The finished slug then falls down a chute onto a galley at the left of the operator, where lines are assembled one at a time.

DISTRIBUTION OF MATRICES

The third, and final, step is the distribution of matrices back to their proper channels in the magazine.

As the disk is making its trip back to normal position, the first elevator rises, carrying the line of matrices and spacebands up to the transfer channel. At the same time, an arm, known as the *second elevator,* descends from above. Attached to it is a V-shaped bar with a series of grooves along its surface, into which the nicks on the matrices fit.

When it is seated, a transfer-slide finger pushes the line of matrices into the transfer channel, where the matrix teeth engage the grooves of the second elevator bar. Then the transfer slide moves back, and the second elevator lifts the matrices, leaving the spacebands in the channel, since they have no nicks and consequently cannot be picked up. The spacebands are returned to their box by a transfer lever and are ready to be used over again.

The second elevator lifts the matrices to a point directly in line with the distributor bar, which is also V-shaped, and which contains grooves similar to those on the bar of the second elevator holding the matrices. This distributor bar extends the full length of the magazine at the top of the machine, running directly above the channels into which matrices are kept. It is made so that there is a different combination of grooves ending at the entrance to each channel.

The matrices are pushed off the second elevator bar onto the distributor bar and into a mechanism known as the *distributor box*, where they are lifted one at a time onto moving, auger-like rods called *distributor screws*, which engage the matrices by the ears and carry them along the distributor bar above the magazine.   Each matrix has its own combination of teeth by which it is suspended from the grooves on the distributor bar.   It travels along until it reaches a point where its par-

Figure 63.   Phantom illustration to show each stage of the circulation of matrices through the Linotype.   (Courtesy of Mergenthaler Linotype Company.)

ticular combination of grooves ends, or is cut away, and having nothing to hold onto any longer, it drops off the bar and down a chute into its respective channel in the magazine from which it came.

This ingenious matching of the various teeth combinations of matrix and bar is what permits the various matrices to find their proper channels automatically and makes possible their use over and over again continuously.

Six lines can be assembled, cast, and the matrices distributed by the Linotype machine in the time required to set one line by hand a letter at a time. After the slugs have been used, the type does not have to be distributed, as does type set by hand: it can be remelted and the metal used over again and again in producing lines of type. Thus, new type faces are produced for every issue of the newspaper or for every job in which Linotype slugs are used. This constantly renewed type insures clear, sharp reproduction.

Solid lines of type are much easier to handle than lines consisting of individual letters. Many lines can be picked up at a time with no danger of pi-ing. This is a great advantage to the makeup man who must do his work swiftly in order to meet deadlines. Some of the errors common to hand-set type also are avoided. There is no chance of letters falling out or being pulled out of a line accidentally and no loose spaces or quads work up in a form when it is being printed.

IMPROVEMENTS IN DESIGN

Early slug-casting machines did much to speed up production in the composing room, but they had many limitations. In the beginning, they were able to produce only enough straight matter for the main body of the newspaper, leaving all the larger sizes to be set by hand. Although slugs of different thickness (point-size) could be obtained by changing liners in the mold to regulate the size of the opening into which the molten metal is forced, these machines carried only one magazine. Consequently, one machine might be capable of producing 8-point type, another 10-point, and so forth.

In an effort to meet the growing demands for greater flexibility, faster output, and increased efficiency, both the Mergenthaler Linotype Company and Intertype Corporation have carried on intensive research and experimental programs from the start.

After the first Linotypes were installed, one of the major problems encountered was that of providing a sufficient volume of matrices. At first, the steel punches used in making matrices were cut by hand.

However, it soon became apparent that enough skilled punch cutters could not be secured to meet the demand.

The problem was solved by the invention of a punch-cutting machine by Linn Boyd Benton, of Milwaukee, which was capable of producing punches in quantities, and thus made possible the production of an unlimited number of matrices. Acquisition of the Benton machine by the Linotype Company opened the way for further developments by providing the means for supplying the wide variety of type faces and sizes now available to publishers.

Then provision was made for additional magazines that could be

Figure 64.   The Model 31 Linotype.   (Courtesy of Mergenthaler Linotype Company.)

used interchangeably on a machine. This was followed by multiple-magazine machines, which would accommodate more than one magazine located one above the other.

The addition of auxiliary magazines mounted to the right of the main magazines, of 72-channel main magazines for the larger display matrices, and of disks with either four or six molds to take care of various sizes by simple adjustment have increased greatly the flexibility of production.

A wide selection of models—both Linotype and Intertype—is avail-

Figure 65. The Streamlined Model C4 Intertype with quadding device. (Courtesy of Intertype Corporation.)

able today, ranging from one-magazine machines, designed especially for straight-matter composition, to those carrying as many as four main magazines and four auxiliary magazines, each containing a different font of matrices.

In addition to body type, some of the present-day machines are capable of producing headlines and display matter in sizes up to 36-point and larger.

Many other improvements have been made. Outstanding among them was the introduction of the mixer machines, which make it possible for an operator to draw matrices from more than one magazine, assemble them in the same line, and return them automatically to the proper magazines.

This machine also offers great economies for many types of composition involving quick alteration of faces and sizes. In setting newspaper headlines, which often require decks in different sizes or faces, the operator is able to assemble and cast the different sizes and faces in their proper sequence without having to wait for matrices to distribute before he shifts magazines. The same time-saving possibilities exist in advertising composition which calls for more than one size and kind of face. An added advantage is the fact that the mixing feature is available on machines designed for straight-matter composition as well as on those designed to produce matter for display purposes only.

Present-day machines are vastly superior to the first Linotype invented by Mergenthaler. The many refinements introduced within the space of a lifetime now make it possible for a publisher to obtain a wide variety of type faces and sizes from a single machine. At his command is a type foundry capable of meeting the most exacting typographical demands. No other invention since the discovery of printing itself has done more to revolutionize the industry of printing and publishing. In effect, it was the key that opened the way for a series of other developments that brought about the high-speed production upon which the modern newspaper is dependent.

Need for Basic Understanding

Since the major part of the type used in printing the present-day newspaper is produced by the Linotype or Intertype, an understanding of some of the main problems involved is essential.

In the larger newspaper offices, machines of different styles are departmentalized according to their uses. For instance, there will be one group of machines employed for setting straight matter; another to produce display matter in advertisements; and still another for head-line composition.

On many newspapers with small circulation the pressure for meeting deadlines is not great and the funds for equipment are limited. Here, one or more machines equipped to handle both straight matter and advertising and headline display may be installed. In every instance, machines can be selected to meet the particular needs.

Workers in the editorial and advertising departments should familiarize themselves with the different kinds and sizes of type available on the machines so that the facilities at their disposal can be utilized in the most efficient and economical manner. Furthermore, a knowledge of the types available from each font of matrices is extremely helpful, since composition which requires changes from one magazine to another in order that the type specified may be secured is more time-consuming and consequently more costly. Changes in length of lines and in the point-sizes of slugs also require additional operations, and should be avoided wherever possible.

THE TELETYPESETTER

Invention of the Linotype and its establishment as a necessary adjunct to the composing room did not quiet the demand for still greater output than could be obtained by manual operation. The attention of printers and publishers finally turned to the possibility of developing a mechanical method that would be speedier and more efficient.

Among the men who set to work on the problem was Walter W. Morey, who was engaged in 1925 by Frank E. Gannett, president of the Gannett Newspapers. Morey was to develop a machine that would make possible the casting of type for Gannett's publications from one central plant.

By May, 1926, the first Teletypesetter was ready for its initial test. This test proved satisfactorily that type could be cast automatically. Further simplification and development were carried on with the aid of engineers of the Morkrum-Kleinschmidt Company, of Chicago, and the perfected invention was demonstrated in the plant of the *Rochester-Times Union* on December 6, 1928.[13]

The Teletypesetter is not a type-casting machine, but rather a mechanical unit that can be attached to a Linotype or Intertype to control

---

[13] "Gannett Claims Invention Opens New Era of High Speed Newspaper Production," *Editor & Publisher*, 61:29 (December 8, 1928), 3.

automatically the assembling of matrices and casting of slugs. Mechanical operation of the keyboard is controlled by a perforated tape, which may be prepared locally in the newspaper plant by means of a Teletypesetter Keyboard Perforator.

In effect, the machine is an extension of the automatic printer used by press associations for the transmission and reception of news, in that this tape also can be obtained on an automatic telegraphic reperforator by electrical impulses which translate the copy sent from a distance into code perforations.

Remote control meets the needs of newspaper organizations and publishing concerns with editorial and composing rooms located some distance apart. It is valuable too in those organizations with multiple printing plants which desire simultaneous printing of the same paper or editorial matter in different areas. All the plants can be serviced from a central editorial office.

Although telegraphic, or remote-control, operation is being used to some extent in this country and abroad at present for wire-tape transmission of news reports, the Teletypesetter is more generally employed for local operations to increase the production of line-casting machines and thus to reduce the cost of straight-matter composition within the individual newspaper plant.

The installation consists of two units: the Keyboard Perforator, on which the tape is prepared, and the Operating Unit, which is attached to the composing machine.

The keyboard on the perforating unit resembles that of an ordinary typewriter, and it is possible for the operator to use the touch system. Copy to be set can be transcribed rapidly by the operator into a code-perforated tape, which provides all the controls necessary for line casting, gauges the width of the line of matrices and spacebands within the limits of the justifying mechanism, operates the elevator, and sends the line to be cast.

Figure 66. A roll of tape perforated with Teletypesetter code. (Courtesy of Teletypesetter Corporation.)

After the tape has been prepared, it is fed into the Operating Unit, which is attached to and driven by the line-casting machine. Here the code perforations are translated into lever movements which perform the identical functions normally carried out by the manually operated line-casting machines. This unit will compose any matrices which may be contained in regular 90-channel magazines.

Figure 67. Teletypesetter Operating Unit attached to composing machine. (Courtesy of Teletypesetter Corporation.)

The Teletypesetter offers many advantages over manual operation, aside from the remote-control feature. Since one man can handle as many as four machines equipped with the Operating Units, fewer employees are required. Furthermore, mechanical operation is uniform and continuous, and delays due to distributor stops and other causes are fewer than with manual operation.

When the invention was first announced, predictions were made that eventually all telegraph and cable news, as well as that written locally, would be translated into Linotype slugs as fast as it reached the newspaper office by means of the Teletypesetter. Although that time has not yet arrived, around 200 machines are now in operation in this country, and the number is expected to increase as business conditions continue to improve.

THE LUDLOW TYPOGRAPH

In addition to the Linotype and Intertype, several other line-casting machines have been developed for use in the composing room.   One of them is the Ludlow Typograph, which is designed to enable the hand compositor to produce a greater volume of display and job composition in the form of type slugs.

Brass matrices are kept in cabinets near the Ludlow machine within easy reach of the compositor.   These cabinets require much less space than ordinary type cabinets, since each font consists of only a few matrices for each letter.   The matrices are assembled by hand in a special matrix stick to form a line.   This stick is then placed on the flat surface of the machine and is clamped securely into position over the mold.   Then the operator presses the lever which starts the casting operation.   A plunger forces molten metal from the metal pot into the mold against the line of impressed matrices and a slug is formed. After the line is cast, the stick is removed, and the matrices are distributed back into the case by hand.   Even though only the casting operation is automatic, the Ludlow is capable of producing type much faster than it can be set by hand.

Matrices are made so that they can be placed into the stick quickly, without the necessity of having to watch letters to make sure that the nick and face are in the right position.   Instead of placing one letter at a time in the stick, in all but the largest sizes the compositor can "gather" a group of the flat matrices before putting them into the line.

Figure 68.   Ludlow Casting Machine with matrix cases on either side.   (Courtesy of Ludlow Typograph Company.)

He does not have to work with spaces below the level of the line, and the line does not have to be spaced tightly in order to lift.

For the average line, the total time required for setting and justifying matrices, casting the line, and distributing the matrices is less than is taken just to set a line of individual types, with the distribution still to be done. Another major advantage in makeup and lock-up is that the slugs can be handled much more easily and with greater speed than lines of hand-set type.

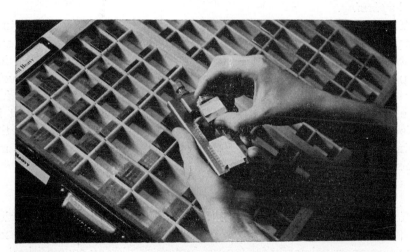

Figure 69. Placing matrices in a Ludlow stick, preparatory to casting a line of type. (Courtesy of Ludlow Typograph Company.)

Since the metal in Ludlow composition is the same as that used for slugs produced on other line-casting machines, the various slugs do not have to be separated when the forms are broken up. Consequently, use of the Ludlow does not disrupt the non-distribution system followed in the modern newspaper plant.

A wide selection of type faces is available on the Ludlow, including popular standard faces and several others designed by the company's expert typographers. Sizes range from 6-point to 84-point for most faces, but special engraved matrices of alphabets and price figures up to 144-point, and larger, can be supplied.

Sloping matrices for the casting of Italic and Cursive type faces were originated by Ludlow. These can be assembled in the stick either by themselves or along with other types by means of an angular space at the beginning and the end of letters in Italic. All letters are given equal support so there is no danger of the kerns breaking off.

Another feature that is particularly advantageous is the speed and accuracy with which rule forms can be cast on this machine.   By means of rule matrices, complicated tabular work can be cast and recast to produce as many lines or forms as desired.

Molds are available in two sizes: one, which will produce a 6-point body, and another, which will produce 12-point.   If the type face is larger than the body size of the slug on which it is cast, the parts of the letters which overhang are supported by low slugs that are placed underneath when the type is made up into a form.   This is known as *underpinning*.

The mold on the Ludlow is 22½ picas in length.   However, if lines longer than this measure are wanted, matrices are set in a long stick and justified, with stops inserted at the proper intervals.   Then the stick is placed on the casting machine and is moved forward progressively for the casting of as many sections as are needed to complete the full line.   Banner headlines and other long display lines can be cast in this way, since the letters overhang from one slug to the next at the point of division and there is no way of telling where the breaks came when the lines are printed.

THE ALL-PURPOSE-LINOTYPE

The All-Purpose-Linotype—or A-P-L—is another machine which casts lines of type from hand-set matrices.   Like the Ludlow, it is used by newspapers primarily for the production of display composition.

A-P-L matrices are available in a wide variety of faces and in sizes ranging from 6-point to 144-point, inclusive.   Sizes smaller than 18-point are supplied in regular Linotype matrices and also are made, on order, in A-P-L matrices to provide universal alignment in the full range of type families.   They are stored in All-Purpose matrix cabinets near the machine.

The A-P-L works on the same basic principle as the casting mechanism of the Linotype.   Matrices are assembled and justified by hand in a special stick, which then is placed in the elevator jaw of the machine.   When all necessary adjustments have been made, the starting lever is pulled and the elevator descends, presenting the line of matrices in front of the mold.   After the line has been cast, the mold disk revolves to normal position and the slug is ejected into a water-cooled pan.

The mold pockets are marked with numerals 1, 2, 3, and 4.   Placed in front of the machine are small cards indicating the mold sizes each pocket carries.   Consequently, the compositor can set the mold without opening the vise to see which one is in position.

Whenever possible, the operator uses a mold of the same size as the type, since this eliminates the need for underpinning. Low slugs are placed under the overhang when a mold of the proper size is not available.

A-P-L molds cast slugs up to 42 picas in length. In composing lines longer than this measure, the matrices are set in a long assembling stick. When the line has been spaced and justified, it is transferred to two or more 42-pica composing sticks, and the remaining space on the right-hand end is quadded out. After the slugs have been cast, the blank ends are cut off, and the slugs are butted together to form the line.

An outstanding feature of the A-P-L is universal alignment. Type families have been divided into two classifications: High alignment, for

Figure 70. The A-P-L (All-Purpose-Linotype). (Courtesy of Mergenthaler Linotype Company.)

types with long descenders; and Low alignment, for those with short descenders. All sizes of faces of High alignment will align perfectly with each other, and all faces of Low alignment likewise will align perfectly. This universal alignment permits the combining of various type families in different sizes, which is very desirable in many kinds of advertising and other types of composition.

Italic and Cursive faces are cast from sloping matrices that are available in three different angle blanks to take care of varying characteristics of the types in this classification. Furniture, rules, borders, and decorative and spacing material also may be cast on this machine.

In order to make the A-P-L equipment self-contained, a slug saw-trimmer is attached to the table of the machine, and a furniture rack is provided for attachment to the under side, so that underpinning for overhanging slugs and other spacing material is within easy reach of the compositor.

Although the A-P-L and the Ludlow ordinarily are used as supplements to the Linotype or Intertype in newspaper offices to produce the larger display faces for headlines and advertisements, the many features available make them adaptable to a wide range of uses in other kinds of printing establishments.

THE MONOTYPE

While Ottmar Mergenthaler was busy perfecting the Linotype during the 1870's, several other inventors were engaged in designing machines that would set type automatically.

Another pioneer in this field was Tolbert Lanston, who received a patent on his first type-setting machine in 1887. Lanston's invention differed from Mergenthaler's in that it made individual pieces of type to form the line, instead of casting a solid slug. His machine consisted of two separate units—a keyboard and a type-making machine.

The keyboard unit was used for making two perforated paper strips. One of these directed the position of the matrix; the other effected line justification. The type-making unit did not cast type, but rather pressed individual letters out of cold metal supplied in long type-high strips, shaved to thickness of the point size of the body desired.[14]

A piece of metal of the required width for a given letter was automatically cut from the metal strip and compressed to correct any irregularities. Then it was held firmly in place while the character was

---

[14] *Monotype Machine Typesetting,* page 8. Philadelphia: Lanston Monotype Machine Company, 1939.

stamped upon its upper end by means of a steel female die. As the pieces of type were completed, they were assembled one at a time into perfectly justified lines.

Lanston christened his new machine the *Monotype,* because it made and set single pieces of type one at a time. It contained all the essential principles of his later machines, with the exception of the method by which the type was made, and it was the direct forerunner of the present-day Monotype.

The Monotype machine in use today consists of two separate me-

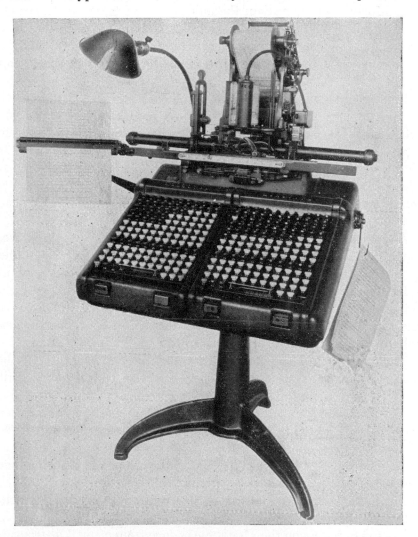

Figure 71. The Monotype keyboard. (Courtesy of Lanston Monotype Machine Company.)

chanical units: the keyboard and the composing machine, or composition caster.

The Monotype keyboard arrangement is the same as that of a standard typewriter, except that there are a greater number of alphabets and no shift keys. Lines may be justified up to 60 picas wide. Width of the capital "M" in points serves as a basis for the set size—or width from side to side—of all other characters in a given font. An 8-point Monotype face, 8-set, means an 8-point face in which the capital "M" is 8 points wide.

In Monotype composition, the unit is one-eighteenth of the capital "M" of the font selected, and all other letters are based on this measurement. For instance, average characters such as the "a" and "g" are 9 units wide, and narrower letters like the "j" and "f" are 6 units wide.

Before starting to strike the keys, the operator must determine the number of units the desired line will hold and set the em scale which will control the length of the line. Then he commences to type his copy. As each key is struck, two holes are punched in the controller paper, which feeds from a roll that revolves slightly at every stroke. These holes later will control the selection of letters made on the type caster, and will also establish the width of the type body on which each character is cast.

An indicator on a scale in front of the operator moves progressively to the right, counting off the units for each letter as it is struck. When he nears the end of the line, a bell sounds to warn that it is almost full.

He then decides whether to finish the final word or to divide it. A pointer on this scale indicates what keys must be touched to justify the line accurately, and he strikes the special keys called for, punching two holes in the paper ribbon at the end of the line to finish it.

This same procedure is repeated for each line until all the copy has been completed. Then the controller paper—or roll of punched ribbon—is ready to be transferred to the composing machine. Here it is fed in backwards, and the holes punched for justifying spaces now come at the beginning of each line, regulating the spaces between words.

The controller paper is the "brains" of the composing machine, since positions of the perforations determine the letter that will be cast, in much the same manner as the holes in a music roll for a player piano determine the notes to be played.

Casting of letters on the Monotype is done from a small matrix case, about the size of a man's hand. For the composition of sizes from 4-

point to 12-point, this case contains 225 matrices which are assembled together in combs, fifteen matrices in a comb, and fifteen combs to the case. Each has a predetermined fixed position in the case.

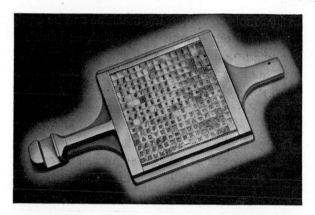

Figure 72. A Monotype matrix case. (Courtesy of Lanston Monotype Machine Company.)

This system makes it possible to include in one arrangement as many as three capital and lower-case alphabets, figures, points, spaces, and special characters for mixed composition in the same job.

The matrix case is placed on the composing machine directly above the mold of the proper point-size, and as the controller paper starts feeding through, the individual matrices are positioned automatically over it one at a time. Movement of the matrix case is controlled by the perforated ribbon, which passes over a mouthpiece containing a row of small openings leading into compressed air tubes.

As the two holes for a given letter in the ribbon pass over their respective openings in the mouthpiece, the air escapes, releasing springs which govern the movement of levers that bring the matrix case into proper position over the mold. At the same time, the machine automatically adjusts the mold to cast the character the right width. Then molten metal is forced out of the metal pot from below into the mold against the individual matrix selected, and the letter is cast. The mold is water-cooled, so that the metal will harden immediately.

When the letters have been cast, they are pushed out one at a time into place in the line. After the line has been completed, it is transferred automatically into position on a galley. Then another one is started. This action goes on continuously and automatically, at a rate of 150 casts per minute.

Corrections of composition set on the Monotype are made in the same manner as in hand-set type, because lines consist of individual letters and spaces. There is no distribution of type or matrices. The type is remelted after the forms have been printed, and the metal is used over again.

The standard Monotype composing machine can be equipped to cast types ranging in size from 4-point to 36-point, and leads, slugs, rules, column rules, and borders. This material can either be supplied in strips or cut to labor-saving measure. Single-column dashes, leads, slugs, and cut-off rules also can be furnished.

In order to meet differing composing-room requirements in the printing and publishing industry, other kinds of Monotype machines have been introduced, including the Material Making Machine and the Giant Caster, which are the most popular for use by newspapers.

The Material Making Machine is a highly specialized machine for

Figure 73.   Monotype Machine Caster.   (Courtesy of Lanston Monotype Machine Company.)

the production of rules, leads, and slugs in continuous strips or cut to labor-saving sizes; column rules and ornamental borders; single-column want-ad rules, braces, and cut-off and decorative end-dashes; and "high" and "low" base for the mounting of cuts.

The Giant Caster, which was brought out in 1926, makes type for use in hand composition in all sizes from 14- to 72-point and strip metal furniture in the same sizes for use in spacing and as base for the mounting of cuts. Types up to 18-point can be cast in justified lines; special matrix cases are used for sizes larger than 12-point.

The Monotype is used primarily by newspapers to supplement the slug-casting machines, which produce the major part of the type needed. It is particularly well adapted to the production of books, catalogs, magazines, and other kinds of composition where quick changes are not necessary.

Among its many advantages is that this machine makes it unnecessary to store large quantities of type, because the perforated ribbon rolls can be filed for future use after being run through once. Furthermore, the type cast is deep-shouldered, clear-cut, true to height, and evenly spaced throughout—features which result in printing of the highest quality.

Although the Monotype could be used satisfactorily to produce all the type necessary for use by newspapers, editors and publishers prefer machines that cast solid lines of type. Furthermore, most type can be produced more rapidly on slug-casting machines, where less time is required for changes from one size and kind of type to another. This is particularly true in the production of headlines and in the setting of other rush copy that comes in just before time for the forms to go to the presses. However, both types of machine possess highly desirable features and can be used together advantageously in the production of newspapers.

THE ELROD CASTER

The Elrod Caster is a simple, easily operated machine used for the casting of strip material—leads, slugs, rule, and base—in sizes ranging from 1-point to 36-points in thickness. It frequently is installed by newspapers as a companion to the Ludlow, which is produced by the same company.

Elrod strip material is not formed compositely of successively cast, individual sections welded together. Rather, a continuous mass of molten metal is progressively cooled and solidified under pressure as it passes through the mold, thus forming a solid, one-piece strip of unlimited length.   The machine also can be set to cut off the strip to a desired measure as it is produced.

Strip material 12 points and upward in thickness can be cast with hollowed body, thus reducing the weight and the amount of metal required.   Material in larger point sizes is used for base under halftones, line cuts, and shell casts for blanking out pages.   It also is used as furniture in imposing and locking up forms for the press.

The Monotype-Thompson Type Caster

The Monotype-Thompson Type Caster is another machine that is used to a limited extent in newspaper offices.   It works on the same basic principles as other Monotype casting units, producing individual types, quads, spaces, ornaments, and borders from 6 points to 48 points in size.

Every type face for which matrices have been made for casting on any Monotype type-casting machine is available for use on the Monotype-Thompson.   Many of these can be cast from matrices rented from the Monotype Matrix Library at a small monthly rental charge.

By making use of this machine, a publisher is able to replenish his type cases at any time with new, clear-cut faces and to add new designs

Figure 74.   The Elrod—lead, slug, rule and base caster.   (Courtesy of Ludlow Typograph Company.)

as they are introduced by the manufacturers of the Monotype. Efficiency in the composing room is promoted, since a practically unlimited supply of new type, quads, spaces, leaders, decorations, and other special characters is available constantly. The machine is especially valuable in commercial printing plants and is being used by type founders in many parts of the world for the casting of type and material to supply the trade.

Cost of Equipment

Composing-room machinery used for the casting of type and material represents one of the major investments of a newspaper. The amount involved naturally depends upon the amount of equipment needed, but even in the smallest plants, the cost is substantial.

Linotypes and Intertypes range in price from $3,500 to $10,000 and higher, depending upon the model and the number of magazines and fonts of matrices included. Ludlow and A-P-L machines, including matrices and cabinets, also vary in price, but the average cost is about $6,000. The Elrod Caster, the Monotype Giant Caster, and the Monotype Material Making Machine range in price from about $3,000 upward, according to the special attachments needed.

In addition, several smaller items, such as saws, mitering machines, and special cabinets and racks for the storage of magazines, matrices, and other material are found in most modern newspaper plants.

The elimination of much of the tedious hand work that was required before the invention and perfection of these labor-saving machines has assisted greatly in promoting efficiency and in speeding up production. Not only the newspapers, but the entire industry of printing and publishing have benefited. Furthermore, much of the progress made in the realm of type design and in newspaper makeup during the past fifty years has been due to the scientific research and costly experimentation carried on by the manufacturers of type-casting machines. These manufacturers have contributed greatly to the changing character of the American newspaper.

IX

Kinds of Printing Plates

THE ART OF TELLING STORIES BY THE USE OF pictures had its origin in prehistoric times. Clumsy carvings in caves and on bones, dating from around 50,000 B.C., serve as the first evidence of man's crude efforts to make and preserve records of his activities.

Ever since that remote period in history, pictures have continued to play an important role in human affairs. Development of the alphabet, early books, and the invention of printing, which opened up new horizons in the field of communication and learning, were an outgrowth of this fundamental means of expression so universal in appeal.

EARLY USE OF PICTURES

The first pictures to appear in books and newspapers were printed from wood blocks, carved by hand. This method of pictorial reproduction continued in use until near the end of the nineteenth century.

Not until sixteen years after the appearance in 1622 of the *Weekly Newes,* England's first regular news tract, were illustrations used to depict current happenings. In the issue of December 20, 1638, this paper carried a news story telling about a "prodigious eruption of fire, which exhaled in the maddest of the ocean sea, over against the Isle of Saint Michael, one of the Terceras, the new island which it hath made." [1] The article was illustrated by a full-page engraving, showing the place where the fire occurred.

Illustrations were used very sparingly by English newspapers until the nineteenth century. Editors in the larger cities discouraged the practice by refusing to accept pictures long after press facilities and engraving processes permitted.

In this country, the first picture to appear in colonial newspapers was printed in an issue of the *Boston News-Letter* for January 19-26,

---

[1] Mason Jackson, *The Pictorial Press*, page 15. London: Hurst & Blackett, 1885.

1707-08. It was a wood-cut reproduction of a new flag being used by the United Kingdom of England and Scotland.[2]

A few years later, small pictures began to find their way into the captions of several colonial newspapers. They were referred to by historians as "devices." The earliest of these headpieces, carved on a wood block, was printed in the *Boston Gazette* in 1719. It consisted of a reproduction of a ship placed on the right, and another of a postman on the left-hand side of the title. Other illustrations used by the *Gazette* as time went on included reproductions of a postman on horseback, a pine tree, and a news carrier holding a copy of the paper in his hand.[3]

The owner of the *New Hampshire Gazette* apparently had the good fortune to obtain a series of cuts made to illustrate an edition of *Aesop's Fables*. He used these to enliven his caption by printing them one after another.[4]

Other attempts included a series of profile portraits, each representing a man wearing a cocked hat, which were either printed from the same cut or were copies from the same original. They were labeled, respectively: Bradley, Governor of Rhode Island, Columbus, Henry Lee, Samuel Adams, and Richard Howell.[5]

About this time, pictures also began finding their way into advertisements. The first ones were small stock cuts of ships, cargoes, and passenger accommodations. A picture of a clock-face identified the watchmaker's advertisement; scythes and sickles announced the hardware dealer; pictures of a hand holding an open book were placed at the head of a bookseller's announcement; and a reproduction of a running Negro accompanied an announcement telling of the escape of a slave.[6]

The first pictures of any real significance came as a result of political and social unrest. Preceding and during the Revolutionary War, they took the form of biting satire, intended to incite feeling either for or against England.

When representatives from the colonies were called for a meeting at Albany in the summer of 1754 in anticipation of the approaching

[2] S. N. D. North, *Newspaper and Periodical Press*, page 81. Washington, D.C.: Government Printing Office, 1884.

[3] North, *Newspaper and Periodical Press*, page 81.

[4] F. Weitenkampt, *American Graphic Art*, page 139. New York: The Macmillan Company, 1912.

[5] Frank Presbrey, *History and Development of Advertising*, page 136. New York: Doubleday, Doran & Company, 1929.

[6] William Murrell, *American Graphic Humor*, Vol. 1, page 11. New York, Whitney Museum of American Art, 1933.

French and Indian War, Benjamin Franklin ran the famous "Join or Die" illustration in his *Pennsylvania Gazette*. This was a picture of a snake divided into eight parts, each of which bore the initials of one of the colonies, along with the legend "Join or Die." [7] The illustration was revived during the agitation against the Stamp Act in 1765, and it again came into prominence during the war.

An event leading up to the Boston Massacre was the occasion for an outburst by the *Boston Gazette and Country Journal*. In the issue of Monday, March 12, 1770, it printed a full-page story telling of the murder of four men. Column rules on the two inside pages were of heavy black border, and directly beneath the story were the pictures—four wood-cut reproductions, shaped like tombstones, lined up soberly side by side across the column. Initials carved on each represented, in order, the names of the men who had been killed.

One of the paragraphs in the story accompanying the pictures read as follows:

Last Thursday, agreeable to a general request of the inhabitants, and by the consent of parents and friends, were carried to their grave in succession the bodies of Samuel Gray, Samuel Maverick, James Caldwell, and Crispus Attucks, the unhappy victims who fell in the bloody Massacre on the Monday evening preceding! [8]

The pictures were small and black and poorly printed, but they were related closely to the news and represented one of the earliest attempts to combine pictures and printed text in the same account.

Scarcity of paper following the Revolutionary War forced practically all pictures out of the newspapers during the first decade of the nineteenth century. First to be revived were the small stock cuts in advertisements, engraved in either wood or metal.

Discovery of the "white line" engraving process by Thomas Bewick in England helped to improve the situation. He found that many of the difficulties of wood-block work could be overcome if an end-grain surface were used. Up to this time, engravers had worked only on side grain. By cutting his blocks across the log, instead of lengthwise, Bewick was able to produce as fine and true a line as the lightest copper-plate engravings. [9] Pictures made by this method began to appear in American newspapers around 1820.

---

[7] Willard G. Bleyer, *The History of American Journalism,* page 79. New York: Houghton Mifflin Company, 1927.

[8] Murrell, *American Graphic Humor,* page 29.

[9] Douglas C. McMurtrie, *The Golden Book,* page 328. Chicago: Pascal Covici, Publisher, 1927.

About this time, the paper shortage was relieved by the invention of the Fourdrinier machine, which produced paper rapidly in an endless sheet. As a consequence, newsprint became plentiful and pictures again started to come back into the newspapers.

America's first "illustrated newspaper," the *New York Mirror,* began publication in July, 1823. Pictures were presented regularly. Volume VIII, 1830-31, of this paper had a list of seven engravings on wood; Volume XV had 21, including one entitled "The Last Arrow," which was an Indian scene previously used in book work.[10]

Coming of Penny Papers

Also in the 1830's, the penny papers made their appearance, and, like the *Mirror,* they made liberal use of pictures. At the same time, attention in England was being given to the possibilities of news pictures, and the famous *Penny Magazine,* founded in London in 1832, gained wide popularity by making a specialty of illustrations.[11]

Spirited rivalry grew up among the large New York dailies in their efforts to outdo competitors in presenting pictured news. On one notable occasion, the *New York Herald* published an eight-page picture annual containing a variety of wood cuts, including scenes of the Mexican War, a cartoon, and pictures of an actor and actress in parts they were taking in a stage production in New York. A year and a half earlier, this paper had scored a beat by printing on May 1, 1835, a two-column picture of a disastrous fire at the Merchants' Exchange, together with a map of the same size, showing the district that was destroyed.[12]

Advertising gradually began to increase in importance in the cheap newspaper, and since only four pages could be printed satisfactorily on the presses then available, pictures were crowded out. As a consequence, emphasis on pictures shifted from the dailies to the weekly newspapers and to magazines, where experimentation continued.

Outstanding among the first illustrated magazines were *Harper's Monthly* and *Gleason's Pictorial,* both of which began publication about 1850 and were highly successful in their field.[13]

One of the leading editors of this period was Frank Leslie, who issued the initial number of his *Frank Leslie's Illustrated Newspaper* in

---

[10] W. J. Linton, *The History of Wood Engraving in America,* page 27. Boston: Estes & Lauriat, 1882.

[11] North, *Newspaper and Periodical Press,* page 125.

[12] Bleyer, *The History of American Journalism,* page 199.

[13] Frederic Hudson, *Journalism in the United States,* page 706. New York: Harper & Brothers, 1873.

December, 1855. Within ten years, his establishment had grown so extensively that seventy wood engravers were required to do the work. In addition to his *Illustrated Newspaper,* he was publishing the *Chimney Corner, Ladies' Journal, Pleasant Hours, Boys' and Girls' Weekly,* and the *Budget of Fun,* a comic newspaper. The aggregate circulation of his weekly and monthly publications averaged more than one million copies.[14] His most serious competition came with the introduction of *Harper's Weekly, A Journal of Civilization,* which began publication on January 3, 1857.

Great improvement had been made in the art of wood engraving, but this method was too slow and costly. In most instances, each picture had to be carved individually on a single block by one engraver, and several days often were required to prepare a large cut. Sometimes the blocks were made simply by gluing pieces of wood together, or by fastening them by means of a long bolt through the entire block in order to make it possible for more than one engraver to work on the cut at the same time.

Many attempts were made to speed up the process, but a more satisfactory method was not discovered until the invention in England of the sectional wood block by Charles Wells in the 1850's.[15]

SECTIONAL WOOD BLOCKS

Wells introduced a system of compounding by which several small blocks could be joined together in a single large one. These little parallelograms could be assorted according to size and fitted together at the back by means of brass bolts and nuts. In this way, blocks of any size could be made.

After the drawing had been sketched on the assembled blocks, the blocks were taken apart and distributed among as many engravers as there were pieces in the block. Thus, the use of larger pictures became more practical.

In an article published in 1856 in his *Illustrated Newspaper,* Frank Leslie gave a graphic account of the steps followed in obtaining and preparing a picture for reproduction. He said, in part:

An Illustrated newspaper, if it fulfills its mission, must have its employees under constant excitement. . . . Information is received that an accident has occurred. . . . Immediately one or more artists are dispatched to the

---

[14] Hudson, *Journalism in the United States,* page 708.
[15] John Clyde Oswald, *A History of Printing,* page 322. New York: D. Appleton and Company, 1928.

point of interest, and by long experience hasty sketches are made that are
to be elaborated when put on the wood, which is the next stage in their advancement. . . .

Innumerable small bits of boxwood are fastened together . . . by screws
on the back of the block. . . . The traveling artist having supplied the subject, other artists again are employed in putting the design on the block. . . .
The hour of publication is near at hand, and here we have a two-page picture
to be engraved. . . . The screws which hold the small parts together are
unloosened, and the block is divided into ten or twenty parts. Upon each there
is but the fragment of the drawing; one has a little bit of sky, another a group
of children cut in two in the middle; another, part of a house; another a
trunk of a tree; another is covered with foliage. . . . Ten or fifteen engravers now seize these fragmentary sketches and work night and day . . .
and finally we have left, carved in relief, the surface which makes the impression on our paper—known as wood engraving.[16]

The new sectional wood block was coming into quite general use on
the larger papers just before the Civil War. Staffs were expanded to
include more artists and wood engravers. The work of a new group
of men known as "artists-on-the-spot" paralleled that of the news cam-
eramen on our modern newspapers. However, instead of taking photographs of an event, they made hasty drawings, which were hurried back
to the newspaper office, where they were transferred to wood blocks
and engraved by hand.

During the Civil War there grew up in this country a famous group
of war artists—or "traveling artists"—who were sent onto the battle-
fields to sketch scenes of the conflict. Frequently, they made their
drawings, under the most adverse conditions, on the front line during
a major encounter. When completed, these drawings were rushed by
native runners through the lines to the waiting editors. Any special
instructions to the office were scribbled on the margin to direct the
home artists in finishing the picture for the wood engraver. One of
the most fascinating stories in the history of American journalism is
that of the work performed by "artists-on-the-spot" and by the "traveling artists" during the trying days of the Civil War.

After the war, the technique of wood engraving improved rapidly.
Eventually, the intricate pencil drawing gave way partially to wash
drawings on the block, which were accomplished by painting in desired
effects on drawings with the brush in order to get more delicate shadings. This led to copying of photographs by the artists and finally to
transferring the photograph directly onto the block for carving.

Early in the nineteenth century, experiments were made with chalk

---

[16] *Frank Leslie's Illustrated Newspaper*, 2:124-25, 1856.

plates, which were formed by coating smooth, flat, steel plates to a depth of about one-sixteenth of an inch with a soft, clay-like substance. The design was sketched on the chalky surface, which was cut through to the plate beneath. Chalk plates did not serve as direct printing plates, but as molds from which metal plates could be cast. Because of its cheapness, the process was popular for many years.

The most important experiments were those dealing with the application of photography to the production of a process that would make possible the reproduction of photographs as well as line drawings. They resulted in the invention of a photo-mechanical process, known as photo-engraving, which had a revolutionary effect on the use of illustrations by newspapers.

Although considerable experimentation in photography had been carried on previously, the first photographs—if permanency is taken as the criterion—were produced by Joseph Nicéphore Niepce about 1827.[17] Dependent upon the action of light for reducing the oil solubility of a preparation of asphalt and lavender oil which was spread upon a plate of silver or glass, his process was the forerunner of all modern photo-mechanical reproduction. Shortly before completing his invention, Niepce formed a partnership with Louis Jacques Mandé Daguerre, who became well-known for the "daguerreotypes" that were popular for many years.

Instead of asphalt and oil, Daguerre polished the silver-coated plate, fumed it with iodine, exposed, developed, and fixed it in a hot brine. The formula was released to the public in 1839 and created great excitement among those people interested in the new art of photography.

However, his announcement was preceded by eight days by the disclosure in London of a process developed by William Henry Fox Talbot, who had discovered a crude method of preservation by bathing the paper in common salt, or potassium iodide, and a way to make any number of positives from the negative by contact.[18] What is believed to be the oldest known lens photograph is a small picture, now in the Science Museum of London, which supposedly was fixed by the Talbot formula.

Talbot continued his experiments and, in 1852, he succeeded in making intaglio photo-engraved plates by means of a sensitized gelatin emulsion spread on copper. When exposed to light through a photographic positive, those areas of gelatin struck by the light became in-

---

[17] J. E. Mack and M. J. Martin, *The Photographic Process,* page 9. New York: McGraw-Hill Book Company, Inc., 1939.

[18] Mack and Martin, *The Photographic Process,* page 11.

soluble, but the rest of the emulsion could be washed away, leaving it bare and susceptible to etching in an acid bath. All photo-mechanical processes in use today are based on this principle.

In 1859, Gillot, a lithographer in Paris, made the first etched blocks by taking impressions in a special ink from designs drawn on lithographic stones, which he transferred to a zinc plate and etched with acid. Gillot's son, who carried on the work after his father's death, discovered that an artist's drawing could be enlarged or reduced in proportion from the original to make the image the desired size, and then might be transferred to a treated metal plate for etching. Photolithography was developed from Gillot's discovery, and illustrations printed by this method began to appear in American newspapers during the 1870's. The first of these appeared in the *New York Daily Graphic* on December 2, 1873.[19]

However, the use of lithography for the reproduction of pictures in newspapers did not gain much headway. Since the illustrations had to be printed separately on special presses designed for the purpose, two press runs were necessary. Only the most prosperous publications could afford the extra cost involved.

Much more important from the standpoint of newspapers was Gillot's introduction of the first relief line plates in 1872. The zinc plate, after being treated chemically, was exposed to light, and then etched in acid, which ate away only those portions that were not to print. Thus, the lines of the image were left standing in relief. Gillot's method was essentially the same as that used today for making zinc etchings.

The *New York Daily Graphic,* the first illustrated daily newspaper in the United States, began publication on March 4, 1873. During the next few years, it carried on costly and important experiments in an effort to improve the photo-mechanical methods of reproducing pictures in newspapers.

THE FIRST HALFTONE

From the start, this paper used line illustrations made by the photoengraving process. Then, on March 4, 1880, the *Daily Graphic* scored its greatest triumph by printing a picture from the first halftone ever used by an American newspaper. Historically known as "Shantytown," it was the work of Stephen H. Horgan, who was head of the paper's photo-mechanical department, at that time the largest on the

---

[19] Oswald, *A History of Printing,* page 320.

North American continent.   One of several men in the United States and abroad who had been working on the idea, he had spent several years perfecting the invention.

A SCENE IN SHANTYTOWN, NEW YORK.
REPRODUCTION DIRECT FROM NATURE.

Figure 75. A section of the "Shantytown" halftone illustration, reproduced same size from the *Daily Graphic*, with the two type lines underneath as they appeared in the original. (Courtesy of *The Inland Printer*, Vol. 72, No. 6 (March, 1924), page 933.)

Although the halftone had been completed several weeks before it appeared in print, "Shantytown" was held for the anniversary number of the *Daily Graphic*. Commenting editorially on the achievement, the paper said:

Today *The Graphic* enters upon the eighth year of its existence. . . .   In the lower left-hand corner is an illustration entitled, "A Scene in Shantytown, New York."   We have dealt heretofore with pictures made from drawings or engravings.   Here we have one direct from nature.   Our photographers made the plate from which this picture has been obtained in the immediate presence of the shanties which are shown in it.   There has been no redrawing of the picture.   The transfer print has been obtained direct from the original negative. . . .   This process has not yet been fully developed.   We are still experimenting with it, and feel confident that our experiments will, in the long run, result in success, and that pictures will eventually be regularly printed in our page direct from photographs without the intervention of drawing.

This prediction was correct. In fact, the halftone proved to be the most revolutionary of all the improvements for the printing of pictures, since it made possible the reproduction of photographs with their infinite gradations of tone.

Of all the modifications made in the typography and makeup of newspapers during the past few decades, none has been greater or more widespread than those occasioned by the growing use of pictures. In striking contrast to the sparsely illustrated newspapers published before 1880 are our present-day editions, carrying a wide variety of pictures, including first-hand, graphic reports from all over the world within a few hours after important happenings have taken place.

Kinds of Photo-Engraved Plates

There are three basic kinds of printing: *relief*, *lithographic* or *planographic*, and *intaglio*.

Relief, or letter-press, printing is accomplished by pressing paper against an inked surface that is raised above the main portion, or body, of a piece of type or printing plate. Ordinary type, Linotype slugs, wood cuts, zinc etchings, halftones, stereotypes, and electrotypes are examples of this method.

Lithographic printing is done from the flat, smooth surface of an inked plate. Consequently, it often is referred to as *surface* printing. In this method, the image to be printed is placed on stone or metal in a greasy ink or pigment, and it is treated in such a way that only the portions that are not to print have a special affinity to water. Thus, when the plate is dampened, the water will adhere just to the areas that are to show white. The image itself remains oily, and, therefore, is the only part of the surface that will attract and hold the ink when it is applied.

When the paper is pressed against the surface of a lithographic plate, the imprint is made from the inked portion, which bears the image. The rest of the plate is covered with a thin film of water that repels the ink.

Where photography is employed, the process is referred to as *photo-lithography*. The first step in preparing a plate by this method is to make an exposure of the copy by means of a camera on a sensitized film, which is developed to form a negative.

The copy may consist of a drawing, a photograph, printed matter, or any combination of the three. For instance, when a newspaper page is to be reproduced, everything, including pictures, ads, and other type matter, is pasted onto a large sheet as it is to appear. The resulting copy may be the exact size desired, or it may be either larger or smaller, since the camera used is capable of reducing or enlarging the original.

After the negative has been made, it is placed over a grained metal plate which is coated with a light-sensitive emulsion. By means of strong light, the image is transferred to the metal plate, and all portions of the emulsion struck by the light passing through the negative are rendered insoluble.

The plate then is rolled up with a special ink and washed in water, which removes all parts of the emulsion that were unaffected by the light. After the plate has been fully treated, only the image will accept ink when it is printed.

Originally, all lithographic printing was done directly from stones that were prepared by hand, and stone presses were developed in which the water and ink were applied by rollers. However, the stone press and true lithography have been replaced largely by offset printing, a process that, in reality, is "indirect lithography," in that the printing is not done from the plate itself.

After the original plate has been prepared, it is fitted onto a cylinder on the press. Directly below it is another cylinder, which is covered with a rubber blanket, and beneath this is a third one, which gives the impression. As the press operates, the plate is inked, and the image is printed on the rubber blanket, which, in turn, "offsets" or transfers this imprint onto the paper as it passes between the two lower cylinders.

The greatest development in lithography and offset printing was the application of photography to the making of plates. Photo-lithographic plates now are used generally. Transfers from them, which are exactly like the original, are prepared by means of the "step and repeat machine."

Although lithographic printing is confined largely to commercial printing plants, a few newspapers in this country today are being printed by this method. During World War II, the armed services made extensive use of offset printing in producing small newspapers in this country and abroad for the troops.

Intaglio, an Italian word that means *engraving,* is a term given to printing that is done from plates in which the image to be reproduced is engraved or etched below the surface. After the plate has been made ready for printing, it is covered with ink.   Then the surface is scraped clean, leaving ink only in the hollows or sunken areas.   When paper is pressed over the plate, it picks the ink out of the crevices, thus forming the image.   Engraved calling cards and the rotogravure sections of newspapers are printed in this manner.

Photogravure and rotogravure are both *intaglio* processes.   The former term refers to flat plates made by the photo-intaglio method; the latter is given to curved plates of a similar kind that are fitted onto cylinders on the press for printing.

Rotogravure had its beginning in England in 1895, but it was not introduced for use by newspapers in this country until 1912, when the *New York Sun* and the *Cleveland Leader* began using the process. The *New York Times* was the first American newspaper to publish continuously a rotogravure section, which started in 1914.[20]

In rotogravure printing, the cylinders holding the etched copper plates revolve in fountains containing a very thin ink, made especially for the purpose.   As the plates pass through the ink trough, the hollows are filled.   When they emerge, a flexible steel plate, called the "doctor blade," scrapes off the surplus ink from the surface.

A continuous web of paper from a large roll passes between the cylinder and a soft rubber roller, which presses the paper against the curved plate.   The pressure of this roller draws the ink from the hollows and deposits it on the surface of the paper.

The first experiments with four-color rotogravure were carried on by the *Chicago Tribune* in its plant in April, 1915.   In 1920 to 1922, this paper began using it for printing its Sunday issue.[21]

The *Tribune* called the process "coloroto."   Each color is printed from a separate intaglio-etched plate as the web of paper passes from one copper cylinder to another.   After the run has been completed, the etched surfaces may be removed from the cylindrical plates by turning them down on a lathe.   They are then ready to be used over again.

Twenty-one special Goss units were installed by the *Tribune* for this process.   The units were capable of producing 12,000 papers an hour, and within the next few years the capacity of such four-color presses had increased to around 40,000 copies an hour.

In rotogravure, the image is not made up of lines and dots, as in letter-press.   Rather, it is composed of an ink film of wide variations in

[20] "Rotogravure Now in Media Limelight," *Editor & Publisher*, 68:21 (October 5, 1935), 5.
[21] Alfred M. Lee, *The Daily Newspaper in America*, page 128.   New York: The Macmillan Company, 1937.

depth. These variations give a rich, artistic quality that adds to the effectiveness.

Because of the heavy expense involved in providing special equipment and departments necessary for rotogravure printing, only a few newspapers have their own plants. The problem is being met for those newspapers without such facilities by the group-printing idea, whereby the service is provided by special commercial plants devoted exclusively to the printing of rotogravure supplements.

Of the three basic kinds of printing, letter-press printing is by far the most common for the production of newspapers. Consequently, each of the printing plates falling under this classification will be treated under a separate heading. However, an understanding of all three processes is essential to the worker in the field of journalism.

At the outset, a distinction should be made between *original* printing plates and *duplicate* printing plates. The former are made directly from the drawing, photograph, or other copy to be reproduced; the latter are not made directly from the original copy, but are reproductions or duplicates of other plates or surfaces used for printing. In effect, they are copies of original printing plates.

THE ZINC ETCHING

The simplest and cheapest kind of original printing plate made by the photo-engraving process is the line cut, or zinc etching—so called because the image usually is etched on a zinc plate rather than on copper.

Zinc etchings are used for the reproduction of line drawings in black and white, or in colors such as red and yellow, which will photograph as black. The copy must consist of lines, black masses, and white areas in which there is considerable contrast, with no shadings or in-between tones. Pen, pencil, or charcoal sketches, and typewritten or printed matter in which strong lines are separated by white space are suitable. Zinc etchings cannot be made direct from photographs, wash drawings, actual objects, or from any other copy in which there is continuous tone, ranging from highlights to deep shadows.

The drawing, or other copy, to be reproduced is placed on a board in front of the camera. Strong light is directed upon the drawing, and it is then photographed on a plate made of glass covered with a sensitized emulsion. This emulsion is similar to that on the film used in ordinary cameras. It contains innumerable particles of silver which are sensitive to light. These particles are changed chemically wherever they are struck by the light, and in this manner pick up a latent (or sleeping) image, which is brought out through a process of development. When the plate is developed, all the areas struck by light turn black, thus forming what is referred to as a negative. The white areas in the copy, which reflected the light and consequently activated the emulsion, now appear dark, and those portions representing the lines of the copy, which reflected no light, are transparent.

Figure 76. Picture printed from a zinc etching. (Courtesy of Pontiac Engraving & Electrotype Company.)

The negative thus formed is stripped off the glass and placed in reverse (or upside-down) on another glass plate so that the picture will not read backwards when it is printed. Then it is placed over a smooth, sensitized zinc plate and exposed under a strong arc light, which causes the transparent image in the negative to be transferred.

The zinc plate containing the "print" now is inked up with a special ink and is placed under running water, which washes away all areas of the emulsion except those that were stuck by light, and, as a result, which were rendered insoluble. The plate then is heated to make the ink "tacky." It is then coated with a red topping powder known as

"Dragon's Blood," which sticks only to the lines of the image which remained visible.

When the plate is cooled, the Dragon's Blood congeals, forming an acid-proof coating over the inked portion. The plate now is bathed in a solution of nitric acid, which attacks and starts to eat away all the portions that are not protected by the Dragon's Blood. The lines of the illustration are left standing in relief on the surface.

After the plate has been in the acid for several seconds, it is removed and again dusted with topping powder to protect the sides of the etched lines. Then it is immersed in the nitric acid bath once more. This action is repeated until a sufficient number of "bites" have been taken to etch the plate to the proper depth.

The plate is cleaned, routed, and mounted on a wood block, or base, and the finished "cut" is ready to be placed in a form for printing.

Illustrations may be printed in colors, as well as in black and white, by the use of zinc etchings. A separate plate is used for each color. Zinc etchings are used widely for the printing of comic strips, cartoons, and hand-drawn illustrations found in advertisements and elsewhere in newspapers and magazines.

THE BEN DAY PROCESS

Ben Day is the name given to a mechanical method of applying line or dot patterns, or tints, to a zinc etching in order to obtain special shaded effects. The process got its name from that of the inventor of the basic idea, Benjamin Day. A wide selection of tints is available, including dots, lines, stippled effects, fabric designs, and some that closely resemble tone gradations in the halftone. In practice, only a few of the available designs are used for the major part of Ben Day work.

The most common method is to apply the design to the zinc plate by means of a Ben Day film before the etching is done. These films are made of a pliable substance resembling thin celluloid. On one side, the screen or tint is embossed, so that the pattern is raised slightly above the surface.

After the illustration has been transferred to the metal plate in the regular way, the sheet of zinc is stained with a weak solution of nitric acid and alum, which causes an outline of the image or design to remain on the surface when the print is washed off. The areas on the plate where the tint is not to appear are first covered, or "stopped out," with a pasty solution of water-soluble gum and gumboge. Then the raised surface of the Ben Day film is inked with a roller and carefully placed over, and in contact with, the plate. When pressure is applied, the inked pattern is transferred to all portions of the metal surface that were not stopped out. Then the plate is washed to carry away the gumboge used in those areas where the design was not wanted.

When this inked pattern is dusted with topping powder and burned in, it also acts as an acid-resist, so that the design it carries is left in relief on the surface, along with the rest of the illustration, when the plate is etched.

Some Ben Day tints may be placed on the negative instead of the plate, but the resulting pattern, when the cut is printed, will be white on

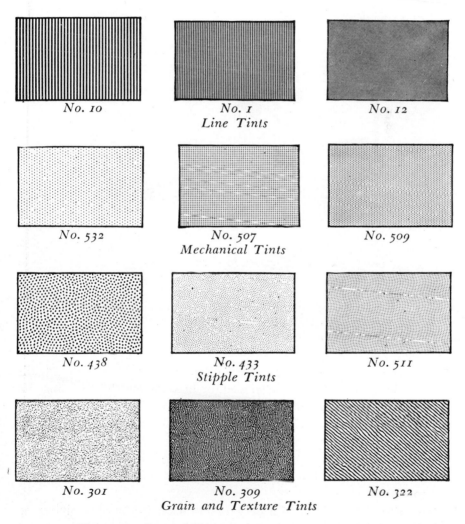

No. 10

No. 1
Line Tints

No. 12

No. 532

No. 507
Mechanical Tints

No. 509

No. 438

No. 433
Stipple Tints

No. 511

No. 301

No. 309
Grain and Texture Tints

No. 322

Figure 77. Some of the commonly used Ben Day tints.

a black ground, since it will be reversed when transferred to the metal plate and etched.   Also, screens can be applied directly to the drawing, or parts of the illustration can be covered with a transparent overlay, carrying a design in either black or white, that is photographed along with the original.

Figure 78.   Picture printed from a zinc etching containing Ben Day patterns.   (Courtesy of Pontiac Engraving & Electrotype Company.)

A special paper containing an invisible Ben Day pattern also is available.   The pattern can be developed, or brought out, by touching the paper with a chemical solution.   By making his drawing on this kind of paper, the artist is able to "paint in" the shadings where he wants them to appear as he prepares the illustration.   However, the main disadvantage is that the design so applied reduces along with the rest of the illustration when the plate is made and, as a result, it often turns out too fine.

The most dependable and widely used practice is that of applying the Ben Day tint to the zinc plate before it is etched.   In this way, no allowances have to be made for any reduction in size of the pattern, and its placement can be controlled accurately.

Ben Day may be used for the printing of colors, as well as for black and white. Screens of more than one primary color are laid upon the same part of an illustration—each screen on a different place in the color set—so that when printed the patterns will blend together to produce the color desired. The screen angle is varied for each color when the Ben Day tints are laid, so that they will come side by side, instead of one on top of the other. Thus the eye "mixes" the primary colors used and produces the desired tone when the plates are printed.

The Halftone

An original printing plate used for the reproduction of all continuous-tone copy, such as photographs, wash drawings, and paintings, is the halftone, also made by the photo-engraving process.

Figure 79. Greatly enlarged section of a halftone screen. (Courtesy of Jahn & Ollier Engraving Company.)

Fundamentally, this type of plate differs from the zinc etching in that it is capable of rendering all variations of tones in a picture, ranging from highlights to deep shadows, whereas the zinc etching can give back only solid lines. This characteristic gives the halftone its name.

The main difference in the photo-engraving process employed is that a screen is used in preparing the negative. This screen consists of two pieces of clear glass, each of which has parallel, ruled lines etched on its surface. These lines have been filled with a special pigment to make them opaque or black.

The two plates are fitted together with a transparent cement so that the lines on one plate run at right angles to those on the other. Although most screens are rectangular in shape, the cross lines are made to run at a forty-five degree angle to the edges in order to reduce the conspicuousness of the screen pattern effect in the resulting halftone.

A halftone screen is rated according to the number of etched lines to the inch. For instance, a screen with 65 parallel lines to the inch is known as a 65-line screen; one with 80 lines to the inch is called an 80-line screen; and so forth. The degree of perfection in the finished reproduction is directly dependent upon the fineness of the screen. However, the quality of the paper upon which the picture is to be printed governs how fine or how coarse the screen may be.

Soft papers, such as newsprint, require the coarser screens. Those in common use by newspapers vary from 50 to 85 lines, but magazines using the harder and smoother grades of paper employ screens of from

50 line   55 line   60 line   65 line

Figure 80. Halftones of four different screens used by newspapers.

100 to 150 lines. When stereotype plates are to be made from the original halftones, with a consequent loss of detail, the coarser screens —usually of 55 to 65 lines—are necessary.

If a cut with too fine a screen is printed, the areas between the dot formations fill up with ink and cause the picture to have a blotched or smudgy appearance that is undesirable. Consequently, care must be taken to order and use halftones that are of the proper screen for the paper on which they are to be used.

The purpose of the screen is to break up the image into an intricate dot formation. Before the copy is photographed, a screen of the proper kind is placed in the camera directly in front of the film. When the exposure is made, the light is reflected into the camera and through the small squares in the screen formed by the cross lines. In this way, the illustration is broken up into a pattern of very fine dots, the size of which in any given area is determined by the strength of the light reflected from it through the lens. The light reflected from the darker portions of the copy—representing the shadows—will be less intense than that from the lighter areas, and the sensitized emulsion on the film consequently will be activated to a lesser degree. Thus, the size of the dots formed on any part of the film's surface will vary according to the tones in the copy from which the light is reflected and, in turn, will control the tones obtained in the printing plate.

When the negative has been developed and flopped, for reversing, it is photographed onto a sensitized zinc or copper plate by powerful arc lamps. The kind of metal used is dependent upon the number of impressions to be taken from the plate and also upon the fineness of the screen. In most newspaper work, zinc is used because it is cheaper and is sufficiently durable with the coarse screen that is used.

When light passes through the negative, it activates the emulsion on the metal plate in all areas that are not covered with the dot formations. Thus, the spaces between and around the dots are rendered insoluble because of the chemical change which takes place. The areas covered by the black dot in the negative remain insoluble, and the gelatin thus protected is removed from the plate when it is washed.

After washing, the plate is treated to make the image impervious to the action of the acid used in etching the plate. Then it is placed in an acid bath which eats away all areas that are not protected, leaving the image that is to print standing in relief.

A nitric acid bath is used for zinc plates; an iron perchloride bath, for copper plates. In some plants, an electric etcher is employed for this purpose. When this method is followed, the plate is placed in a salt solution, and an electric current becomes the mordant, which eats away those portions of the plate that are not protected.

The dots, which appear white when the halftone is printed, range in size from pin-point to very large dimensions. It is through this variation of dot-size and the black areas surrounding them that the fine gradations of tone from highlights to deepest shadows in the photograph can be reproduced with such fidelity.

The number of newspapers operating photo-engraving departments has increased rapidly in recent years. The process no longer is restricted to the large dailies. Inexpensive "one-man" engraving plants began to appear in smaller newspaper offices about 1935, and today many small dailies and weeklies are equipped to furnish their own engravings.

PREPARING PRINTS FOR THE ENGRAVER

The best type of copy for a halftone is a clear, glossy photograph. Since some of the detail is lost despite the greatest of care when the plate is made, it is best to provide prints with good, sharp contrast between the highlights and shadows. Rich shadow areas will reproduce well, but areas that are dull in the original copy will fade out and cause the printed picture to have an over-all gray appearance that is undesirable. Although photographs on some matte papers can be reproduced satisfactorily, any roughness of grain in the surface tends to interfere with proper light reflection, and results in imperfections.

As with zinc etchings, it is possible to reduce or enlarge the copy. However, some detail is lost when the original is "blown up" or enlarged, whereas the image tends to become sharper with reduction. Consequently, the most desirable practice is to furnish prints that are larger than the halftone reproduction will be when printed. Many newspapers require that all prints made by their photographers be 8 × 10 inches in size, or larger.

One method of determining the size of cut a given photograph will make (or scaling) is to use an algebraic formula. For instance, imagine that the photograph is 8 inches wide and 10 inches high, and that it is to occupy a space one column, or two inches, wide.

In this instance, the formula would be $8:2::10:x$. First, the means and the extremes would be multiplied to give the equation, $8x = 20$. Then x (the unknown depth of the cut) would be equal to 20 divided by 8, or $2\frac{1}{2}$ inches.

Another simpler method is to place a piece of transparent paper or celluloid over the photograph and mark off a rectangle equal to the outside dimensions of the picture to be reproduced. Now draw a diagonal line from the upper left-hand corner to the lower right-hand corner. Next, measure across the bottom of the rectangle from the right-hand corner to a point equal to the width of the cut desired. Then, draw a line vertically across the rectangle, parallel to the outside margin, until it intersects the diagonal. The distance from this point to the bottom line of the rectangle will be the depth of the cut.

Special aids for determining the size of cuts usually are provided to picture editors or others who have charge of illustrations. Among the devices frequently used is a circular chart or ruler containing a logarithmic scale of proportions, which is easy to manipulate and gives the answers quickly and accurately.

Lines made with an India pencil on the margin of a print may be used to show the engraver exactly how much of the area of the photograph or drawing is to be reproduced. It is best not to make the marks on the face of the photograph itself since the photo-engraver always has to come inside such lines: the resulting cut may contain less than was intended.

Often special instructions need to be written out. If these notations are made on the back of the print, they should be made lightly in soft pencil so the impression will not show up on the other side and be reproduced along with the picture. A better plan is to write such material on a separate sheet and paste it on the back of the photograph.

When photographs are mailed, they always should be sent in a flat envelope, when possible, and should be protected by heavy corrugated board. If it is imperative that they be rolled, the gelatinized surface should be left on the outside, and they should be inclosed in a sturdy mailing tube for protection.

Four-Color-Process Plates

A separate plate for each color is used in the reproduction of photographs or other continuous-tone copy in full color. In ink pigment, red, yellow, and blue are the primary colors from which all other colors in the spectrum can be obtained by proper mixture.

In four-color-process work, a fourth plate for the printing of black is added to strengthen detail and to give depth to the reproduction by providing the neutral shades of gray that are difficult to secure with the three primaries. Therefore, in preparing a set of four-color-process plates, four halftone negatives are required—one for each of the primary colors and one for the black.

A special kind of plate is required, since the kind used for ordinary black-and-white halftones and line negatives does not have a wide enough range of color sensitivity. Two kinds of plates are used for color: the *orthochromatic dry plate* and the *collodium emulsion,* both of which are made sensitive to color by staining the silver with aniline dyes.

A set of four color-separation negatives is required for the making of the plates from which the various colors are to be printed. The sensitized plate is placed in the camera behind a screen, just as in the ordinary halftone process. However, before each exposure, a filter made of celluloid stained with aniline dye is placed over the lens. A filter is of such a nature that it will transmit, or let through, light rays of its own color, but it will absorb complementary colors.

Consequently, when a negative containing just the blue in the picture is desired, the picture is photographed through an orange filter, which transmits red and yellow, but absorbs all the blue. Even the blue which is combined with other colors to make the green and purple in the original copy is picked out in proper proportions. Thus, when the negative is prepared, all areas in the picture that contained blue will be transparent, and they will constitute the raised surface from which printing will be done after the plate is etched.

In like manner, a negative is prepared for each of the other colors: a green filter is used for the red negative, and a violet filter for the yellow. Since the choice of filter for use in making the black plate is dependent upon the coloring of the copy, it is left up to the expert judgment of the operator.

The plates are made so that the dot formations of the different plates will not print directly over one another but, as far as possible, so that they will appear side by side in the printed picture. The eye of the reader causes the colors to "mix" into secondary and intermediate hues when the reproduction is viewed.

In order to make this arrangement possible, the screen-angle is changed for each plate. Instead of being rectangular, as for black-and-white halftones, the screen used for color halftones is circular in shape so that it can be turned in the holder to the proper position for each color. The common practice is to set the screen-angles for black, red, and blue so that they are 30 degrees apart; the yellow, which is harder to see, is placed between the red and black, 15 degrees from each.

The quality of the full-color reproduction is dependent to a large extent upon the skill of the engraver, who must correct by hand any flaws that show up in the plates during the etching process.

YELLOW   RED

BLUE   BLACK

A SET OF FOUR-COLOR PROCESS PLATES

(*Courtesy of Herman Jaffe and Davis, Delaney, Inc.*)

Figure 81.

1. Yellow

2. Yellow and Red

3. Yellow, Red, Blue

4. Yellow, Red, Blue, Black

OVER-PRINTING OF COLORS PRODUCES THE FINAL IMAGE

Figure 81 (*cont.*).

Three-color halftones are made in the same way as those for four-color, with the exception that no plate is made for the black.   This method has an effect on the strength of ink needed when the printing is done, and, although the colors are purer, results in reproductions that are less sharp in tone and lack the depth provided by the black plate in four-color work.

After the plates have been etched, they are trimmed, routed, and mounted on wood blocks or metal base if the printing is to be done directly from the forms.   The color plates are printed one at a time, so that each registers perfectly with the one preceding it.

The yellow plate usually is printed first, followed in order by the red, blue, and black.   However, no inflexible rule says that they must come in this order.   As the different colors are printed, one plate directly over the other, they merge to give back all the variation of hues in the original copy.

When color is to be printed on the rotary press, a stereotype plate is made for each color.   These plates are clamped on separate cylinders. As the web of paper runs through, it picks up the colors successively, one at a time, and emerges with the reproduction printed in the full four colors.

ELECTROTYPE PLATES

Two kinds of plates are used for the duplication of printing forms. One of these is known as the *electrotype* plate; the other is the *stereotype* plate.

Although superior to the stereotype plate from the standpoint of wear and fine printing quality, the electrotype is more costly and much more time is necessary for its production.   Mainly for these reasons, it has a much more limited use than "stereos" for newspaper work.

The "electro"—as commonly called—is made by depositing particles of metal electrically into molds made of wax, lead, or other suitable substances.   First, the form or printing plate to be reproduced is locked in a special chase.   If a wax mold is to be used, the form is then covered with wax.

When pressure is applied, the wax is forced into every part of the surface to form an almost perfect mold, which is called the *case*.   This case is removed from the type form and is sprayed with graphite (or black lead) so that it will be a conductor of electricity.

Then the case is hung in a bath, generally consisting of copper sulphate and sulphuric acid.   The case is connected to a cathode rod which is hooked up to the negative pole of a dynamo.   Opposite the case are suspended copper bars or plates called anodes. These in turn are connected to the positive terminal of the dynamo. When the current from the dynamo is turned on, the copper anodes are attacked by the electric current and acid and are eaten away. The freed particles of copper are carried across and deposited on the face of the mold, or case. In this way, a thin shell is formed.

The time required usually varies from two to eight hours, depending upon the thickness of the shell desired. When the shell has been built up to the proper thickness, the current is turned off, and the wax case, now containing a thin copper coating over its surface, is taken from the bath. This shell is then removed from the wax mold. The back of the copper shell is covered with a layer of solder similar to tin foil and is filled in with molten metal. After the plate has been "backed up" in this way, it is trimmed, leveled up, and shaved to the proper thickness. Then the blank areas are routed down, and the plate is ready to be beveled, if it is to be used on patent base, or mounted on wood, if it is to be printed as a mounted plate.

If the electrotype is to be used for an extremely long run, it is often plated with nickel instead of copper. Nickel is harder and tougher than copper and also more resistant to the chemical action of color inks.

In producing a nickel, or steel, electrotype, the mold is treated in exactly the same manner as for copper, except that it is placed in an electrolytic bath made up of nickel sulphate and nickel anodes. After the shell has been formed, it is reinforced with copper. From this point on, the plate is treated in the same manner as a copper electrotype.

A lead-molded electrotype is essentially the same as one made from a wax mold. In this instance, the case is made of soft, pure sheet lead. Since lead is a conductor of electricity, it does not need to be graphited, so the lead mold is suspended directly into the depositing bath and then treated the same as all other electrotypes. One of the main advantages of lead molds over wax molds is that the graphiting process is eliminated.

In recent years, another type of mold, known as Tenaplate, has been introduced and is being used widely. It consists of a thin aluminum foil faced with a wax-like material. Plastic molds also have made their appearance. One of the desirable features of the plastic mold is that it does not have to be discarded after being used once, but can be used over and over again.

Electrotype plates are used widely by book publishers, commercial printing plants, and national advertisers because of their extreme durability and the excellence of reproductions obtained. However, improved stereotype plates have replaced much of the work formerly done by the electrotyper because of the saving in both time and cost of production.

STEREOTYPE PLATES

The duplicate plates most widely used by newspapers are *stereotype* plates. Although the stereotype process was discovered early in the eighteenth century, it was not used to any great extent until after the Civil War.

William Ged, a printer in Edinburgh, Scotland, is credited with having invented stereotyping. In 1725, he succeeded in making a plaster of Paris mold of a page of type, into which he poured molten metal to form the printing plate. A few years later, a Frenchman by the name of Gabriel Valleyre discovered that moist clay might be used to make the impression of the original form; when hardened, the clay would serve as a mold from which the cut was cast.[22]

These two methods—the plaster of Paris process and the clay process—were used for almost one hundred years before a more efficient kind of mat was introduced. During this period, stereotyping was not very popular, since the plates did not provide as good a printing surface as the type forms themselves. Furthermore, the molds frequently cracked when the hot metal was poured into them, and the cast would be ruined. Even if the molds did withstand the extreme heat of the metal, they had to be broken in order to remove the finished cut.

Great progress resulted from the invention, in 1829, of the papier-mâché, or wet-mat, method of stereotyping by Claude Gennoux, a French printer.[23] Several other men were working on the idea at the same time, and although the credit generally is given to Gennoux, some doubt still exists as to the rightful claimant.[24]

The matrix for this method was formed by seven layers of paper pasted together with a substance composed of clay, glue made from hides, and oil. The form of type to be reproduced was put on a steam press, or table, and the mat was placed over it. Then an impression

---

[22] Kenneth E. Olson, *Typography and Mechanics of the Newspaper*, page 371. New York: D. Appleton and Company, 1930.

[23] Olson, *Typography and Mechanics of the Newspaper*, page 372.

[24] C. S. Partridge points out that a patent was taken out in 1829 by M. Genoud, of Lyons, which was designed to cover this method of stereotyping, and that Professor Bolas, of the Society of Arts, London, declared that the process was employed by several persons previous to that time. (*Stereotyping, The Papier Mâché Process*, page 10. Chicago: Mize & Stearns Press, 1892.)

was taken by applying pressure and heat at the same time. After the matrix bearing the imprint of the type was dried, molten metal was poured over it to form the printing plate.

This new method was much faster; there was no danger of the molds breaking; and several casts could be made from the same matrix if proper care was exercised. Because of these advantages, interest in stereotyping increased, and several improvements in the wet-mat process were made during the next few years. The use by *La Presse,* a daily newspaper in Paris, of the Gennoux process in 1852 was viewed with considerable interest, and encouraged others to start the practice.

The earliest invention of the curved stereotype plate is thought to be the work of Jacob Warms, of Paris, who obtained a patent for such a process in France, in 1849.[25]

First to introduce the papier-mâché process of stereotyping into this country was Charles Craske, a steel and copper engraver in New York, who started his experiments in 1851. Three years later, in 1854, he made the first curved stereotype plate for a Hoe rotary press in the office of the *New York Herald.* However, the plates did not prove entirely satisfactory and the process was not permanently adopted at that time. But in 1861 Craske made and successfully carried out contracts to stereotype the regular editions of the *Tribune,* the *Times,* the *Sun,* and the *Herald,* and these papers continued to use the process from that time forward.[26]

Also prominent among those who helped to develop the process was James Dellagana, an Italian, who learned about wet-mat stereotyping in France. He later was employed by the *London Times* to experiment with the possibility of duplicating forms which could be utilized for speeding up production.[27]

The semi-cylindrical stereotype plate soon superseded the wedge-shaped columns of type used on the type revolving presses of the period and was directly responsible for the development of the fast rotary presses which appeared toward the end of the nineteenth century.

The wet-mat process eventually was replaced by the dry mat, which was invented by George Eastwood, an Englishman. It was developed to a greater extent in Germany, where Hermann Schimansky introduced a similar process.[28]

---

[25] George A. Kubler, *A New History of Stereotyping,* page 262. New York: J. J. Little & Ives Company, 1941.

[26] Partridge, *Stereotyping, The Papier Mâché Process,* page 11.

[27] Partridge, *Stereotyping, The Papier Mâché Process,* page 10.

[28] Kubler, *A New History of Stereotyping,* page 138.

By 1910, dry mats were being imported to this country from Germany, but the supply was discontinued at the outbreak of World War I. However, in 1917, Henry A. Wise Wood, of New York, began manufacturing dry mats for market in the United States. Seven years later, the Certified Dry Mat Corporation was formed by George Kubler, of Akron, Ohio.[29] Today publishers are supplied by a large number of organizations.

The dry mat is made of a single thickness of heavy, pliable, cardboard-like paper. This paper consists of cellulose pulp, which sometimes is mixed with refined alpha pulps, and which is treated to insure resistance against intense heat.

Figure 82. Dry Matrix Rolling Machine. (Courtesy of The Goss Printing Press Company.)

Dry mats can be bought in large sheets and stored until needed; the time and expense involved in pasting up wet mats are thus eliminated. However, some moisture content is needed in the dry mats so that they will be soft enough to insure a deep, accurate impression of the type form.

Much scientific study was devoted to the problem of storing these mats, and special humidors were invented to keep them moist. However, in 1934, mat manufacturers began furnishing dry mats that were

[29] Kubler, *A New History of Stereotyping*, page 198.

conditioned in the factories. Except in rare instances, mats in use today need no special treatment.

In place of the steam tables, dry-mat rolling machines now are used to take the impression from the type form. The type form to be reproduced is placed on the flat bed of the rolling machine, where it is

Figure 83. The Directomat—a direct pressure molding machine. (Courtesy of Lake Erie Engineering Corporation.)

covered with a blanket made of heavy felt or cork. Then, it is carried forward automatically under a heavy roller that exerts great pressure. Finally, the mat containing the imprint of the page emerges on the other side, ready to be used for casting. Only a few seconds are required, and as many mats as are desired can be made successively from the same form.

The dry-mat process is much faster than the wet-mat method, in which the form had to be heated on the steam table along with the mat.

During the past few years considerable attention has been given to direct-pressure stereotype molding for newspaper work.   The Directo-mat—a machine which operates on this principle—was introduced in 1934 by the Lake Erie Engineering Corporation, a manufacturer of hydraulic equipment.   Today many newspapers are using this kind of press for daily black and white, as well as for color work.

Users of the direct-pressure units claim that they produce deeper, more uniform mats, with less distortion; and that they eliminate stretch and reduce type damage.   Furthermore, the units are said to be faster than the roller, requiring approximately seven seconds for the pressure application and fourteen seconds for the full molding cycle from the time the matrix is placed on the form until it is removed.

Casting the Plate

The simplest type of casting box is that used for making flat stereotype plates.   This type is used extensively by weeklies and small dailies in casting cuts for use where printing is done directly from the type

Figure 84.   Flat casting box for stereotyping.   (Courtesy of The Goss Printing Press Company.)

forms of which stereotype plates are a part.   Most of the larger newspaper offices also have this equipment for the casting of plates to reproduce pictures, cartoons, and other matter which comes to them in mat form from syndicates and various other mat services.

The flat casting box consists of two smooth, heavy, iron plates, hinged together at one end so that the plate at the back can remain upright and the one in front can be lowered to a horizontal position.

First, the mat to be cast is backed up with strips of cardboard in the open spaces. Then the front plate of the casting box is lowered, and the mat is placed face upward on its surface. Three long, steel bars, or gauges, are placed on the edges of the mat—one bar at the bottom and one on each side. The two plates of the casting box are clamped together, leaving an opening at the top for the molten metal to enter, and then they are raised to an upright position.

The metal is melted in a large pot, located near the casting box. It is dipped out with a ladle and poured down over the matrix until the matrix is completely covered. After the metal has hardened, the box is opened, and the metal cut is taken out, trimmed, and made ready for printing.

If the mats are small, frequently more than one can be taped together and cast at the same time. When the metal is hardened, it is taken out and sawed apart to form individual cuts.

The cuts cast in a flat box may be made either thin—about one or two picas in thickness—or type-high, depending upon the height of the bars placed around the sides of the mat to form the mold. If the cuts are to be printed from directly on flat-bed or platen presses, they usually are cast type-high; if they are to go into forms from which semi-cylindrical plates for a rotary press are to be prepared, they can be cast thin and placed on special bases without being fastened down, since the only impressions taken will be those made when the mat is rolled.

In preparing a semi-cylindrical plate for the rotary press, a somewhat different procedure must be followed. After the mat has been prepared, it is backed up with strips of cardboard in the open spaces, as in the flat-cut process. Then it is placed in a device known as a "scorcher," or "former," which roasts or bakes it into the curved shape of the cylinders on the press where it will be placed for printing.

Next, it is taken to the casting machine, which may be either hand-operated, semi-automatic, or entirely automatic. In either instance, the plate is made in essentially the same manner.

Hand-operated casting boxes are much slower than the other types, but they still are being used by some of the smaller newspapers. However, semi-automatic and automatic machines have taken their places in the larger plants, where speed is of great importance.

The hand-operated casting machine consists of a semi-cylindrical casting box and a round, upright core. The casting box, which rests on a metal frame, is supported on either side by protruding rods. These rods serve as hinges so that the box can be raised and lowered from a horizontal to a vertical position.

With the casting box in a horizontal position, the dried mat is placed face upward, with the back against the surface of the mold. Then the box is raised to a vertical position and secured against the core. Hot metal is poured into an opening left at the top until the space around the mat is entirely filled. The metal is allowed to cool for several seconds in order to harden. Now the casting box is released. The plate that has been cast is removed from the mold, trimmed, and made ready for fitting onto the cylinder of the press.

Figure 85. Hand-operated Curved Vacuum Casting Box. (Courtesy of The Goss Printing Press Company.)

The first semi-automatic casting machine, known as the "Citoplate," was produced by C. E. Hopkins and Ferdinand Wesel, of Brooklyn.[30] It was followed by several others of somewhat similar design, including the Hoe, Duplex, Scott, Goss, and Autoplate Junior casting machines.

In 1900, Henry A. Wise Wood, of New York, invented the first successful, entirely automatic casting machine, which was installed in the stereotype foundry of the *New York Herald*.[31] He called this machine the Standard Autoplate Caster. After taking out a patent on the orig-

---

[30] Kubler, *A New History of Stereotyping*, page 264.
[31] Olson, *Typography and Mechanics of the Newspaper*, page 377.

inal machine, the inventor made many improvements. Since then, he has introduced several other stereotype casting machines: the Semi-Autoplate; the Junior Autoplate, single and double; the Senior Auto-plate; and the Automatic Autoplate, which is the most recent.

In these automatic machines, the casting operation is done auto-matically from the time the mat is placed into position until the finished plate is ready to be clamped onto the tubes of the rotary press. Plates can be produced at the rate of four every minute on a single automatic.

In the Standard Autoplate, casting is done against a horizontal core, or cylinder, the face of which is cooled by water. The frame, or "back," holding the mat, can be moved up and down for a distance of about six inches. When in the top position, a semicircular space the thickness of the plate to be cast is left between the mat and the core.

The molten metal is forced into this space by means of a pump. After the metal has hardened, the back falls, taking the mat away for another cast. Then the cylinder turns halfway around, bringing its upper half to the mat for another cast. The first plate is carried with it as it turns. When the plate reaches the top, it is pushed off against two rotating saws which trim its edges. Next it passes under a shaving arch where the interior surface is smoothed to the correct thickness, and water is applied to the back to cool it.

The Junior Autoplate is a semi-automatic machine in which the cast-ing is done against a vertical core, instead of a horizontal core.

Figure 86.   Standard Pony Autoplate.   (Courtesy of Wood Newspaper Machinery Corporation.)

The Automatic Autoplate has a fixed, uniform speed of four casts every minute.   All the operator has to do is to insert the mat, press a button, and remove the plate and tail (excess metal at the end) after the necessary casts have been made.

Figure 87.   The Automatic Autoplate.   (Courtesy of Wood Newspaper Machinery Corporation.)

Several other automatic casting machines have been introduced. Among them are the Multi-Plate, of English manufacture, and the Winkler, built in Switzerland and Germany.

The Winkler contains several new and improved features, including a casting box that connects directly to the metal pot: the stereotype plate is cast by gravity under the head of the whole contents of the metal pot.   The matrix is placed in the machine only once by hand; the operation is started by means of a foot pedal.   All the operator has to do is to place the mat in the machine, start the operation by means of the foot pedal, and remove the finished plate.   Among the advantages claimed for the Winkler are economy of both metal and fuel, low casting temperature, greater output, use of exceptionally hard metal, and need for less floor space.[32]

One important improvement in casting machines is the vacuum box, which is supplied by most manufacturers for both sides or only one side of the box.   Machines can be bought with, or without, this feature. The advantage of the vacuum principle is that air is drawn from under the mat, causing it to hug the curved box more closely and preventing the possibility of its slipping.

Where the finishing operations are done automatically, auxiliary equipment is installed along with the main casting unit.   Such equipment includes a combination saw and trimmer, routers for reducing those areas on the plate which are too high and which consequently might print when the surface is inked, shavers to smooth the inside surface of the plate, and bevelers to provide the beveled edges by which the plates are clamped onto the cylinders of the press.

In many newspaper offices, two or more plates usually are made from each mat.   Thus, more than one unit of the press can be utilized at the same time and the speed of production is increased.   When multiple-unit presses are used, twenty or more plates may be made from each mat for a corresponding number of cylinders on the presses.   In this way, the large metropolitan dailies are able to produce enormous editions in a short period of time.

Ever since the first rubber printing plates made their appearance in 1864, inventors have been carrying on experiments in an effort to discover suitable plastic mats and stereotype plates made of plastic and rubber.   Today several manufacturers in this country are producing such products.   The main stumbling blocks have been the terrific heat necessary for the casting of plates and also the heat that develops on extremely long press runs (such heat causes the rubber plates to swell). However, the new plates are being used successfully by many printing plants throughout the country, and manufacturers are still carrying on experimental work.

GROWTH OF SYNDICATES

The development of stereotyping was a significant aid in the expansion of syndicates and other organizations engaged in supplying news, features, and pictures to newspapers.   The adaptation of stereotyping to these purposes also has had a pronounced effect in popularizing the process generally.

In the beginning, only printed sheets were sent out by the syndicates.

---

[32] Kubler, *A New History of Stereotyping,* page 300.

Later, these sheets were supplemented by making casts of printed matter in a central office and shipping the plates, commonly known as "boiler plate," to newspapers throughout the country.

The idea originated in England about 1850. In 1858, Isaac Hayes and Samuel Harrison, of Sheffield, established a firm in partnership that soon was supplying a large number of newspapers throughout England with single-column, type-high plates.[33]

One of the earliest stereotype companies in the United States to sell prepared cuts was located in Middletown, New York. This company began furnishing type-high, sectional blocks of ready composition in 1872.[34] A branch office was established in Lafayette, Ind., in 1875, as the business expanded. Another pioneer in this field was A. N. Kellogg, a native of Pennsylvania, who was responsible for several important inventions to improve plates and fastenings and for the introduction of a celluloid plate that was distributed throughout the world.[35]

The extreme weight of type-high cuts, which made shipping costs very high, was one of the main obstacles at the start. However, in 1871, B. B. Blackwell, of New York, invented a stereotype plate consisting of a block or base and a thin metal plate, made in such a way that they could be easily separated or assembled. This arrangement permitted newspapers to order a supply of bases which could be kept permanently and used as the necessary plates were delivered.

One of the most important developments came when services began sending out mats which could be used for casting plates in the newspapers' own plants. This service resulted in a great saving in freight charges. The Western Newspaper Union added such a service in 1913 to supplement their daily plate material with picture mats.

Today a great volume of syndicate material almost entirely in mat form is being distributed in this country and abroad by many agencies, including newspaper organizations and the large news-gathering associations, which supplement their daily news services with picture mats.

WIREPHOTO

Great impetus was given to the syndicate business and auxiliary services by the invention of Wirephoto, which was put into practical use by the Associated Press in this country for the first time on January 1,

---

[33] Kubler, *A New History of Stereotyping,* page 317.

[34] Elmo Scott Watson, *A History of Newspaper Syndicates in the United States,* page 34. Chicago: The Publishers' Auxiliary, 1936.

[35] Watson, *A History of Newspaper Syndicates in the United States,* page 35.

1935. Transmitted by electrical impulses, timely news pictures sent by this method are delivered rapidly along with the news that they are to accompany.

Almost from the beginning of telegraphy, experimenters have been working with the idea of transmitting pictures by electrical impulses. American efforts date back to the selenium cell in 1875. However, the first tele-photographic system in this country to gain very widespread attention was inaugurated in 1924 by the American Telephone & Telegraph Company, which had sending stations in New York, Boston, Cleveland, St. Louis, Chicago, Atlanta, San Francisco, and Los Angeles.[36] By this method, a picture could be transmitted in a little over seven minutes. Although the process demonstrated the possibilities that lay ahead, it was discontinued a few years later when it failed to attract extensive commercial use.

The A. T. & T. method was followed by Wirephoto, which started out by servicing fewer than fifty subscribers. Since its inception this picture service of the Associated Press has expanded greatly, and today nearly three hundred newspapers are being furnished Wirephoto print services of varying volume.

The sending unit of Wirephoto consists of a cylinder, around which the photographic print is wrapped. Beginning at one end, the picture is scanned—as the cylinder rotates—by a light beam focused first on a light valve aperture that chops the beam at a frequency of 2,400 cycles, thus passing a pulsating beam that is turned through ninety degrees to focus sharply on the surface of the print. As this beam moves down across the picture, the image is picked up by the light beam and transmitted electrically over the network to the receiving stations.

The receiving unit also contains a cylinder, around which a light-sensitive film is wrapped and enclosed in a light-proof container. Then the film is exposed by a light beam which is focused through an aperture five-thousandths of an inch in diameter. The intensity of this beam varies according to the strength of the current caused by the tones in the picture of the sending machine.

As the impulses are picked up from the picture by the sending unit, they are relayed to the receiving unit. Here the light beam exposes the film on the receiving cylinder. Both units work in perfect synchronization, so that the latent image picked up by the film is an exact reproduction of the original.

At the end of the operation, the receiving machine cuts off auto-

---

[36] Taken from a personal letter, dated November 23, 1935, written to the author by Wilson Hicks, at the time executive assistant of the Associated Press.

matically. Then the cylinder is lifted off and taken into a darkroom, where the negative is removed and developed. From the resulting negative, a print is made which is used as copy in making the plate from which printing will be done.

Figure 88. A view of a cylinder being placed in position on the regular Wirephoto network transmitting unit. The cylinder will accommodate a picture up to 11 x 17 inches in size—half of a newspaper page. (Courtesy of The Associated Press.)

Only a few minutes elapse from the time the ready signal is given at the sending point until the print is finished and ready for the engraver at the other end. When only one finished print is required, the picture may be received directly onto the print paper, thus eliminating the negative photographic process entirely and reducing by several minutes the time required between the completion of a reception and delivery of the print to the engraver.

All member newspapers on a circuit are able to receive a picture simultaneously as it goes out from the central sending station. However, they are permitted to select only the ones they want from the many pictures that are transmitted each day.

Several other organizations entered the field shortly after the initial venture of the Associated Press. Among them were Acme Newspictures, Inc., and International News Photos, two of the largest competing services.   Today millions of illustrations, gathered from all over the world and transmitted by the photo-telegraphic method, are being printed each week in our newspapers.   In 1939, the first colored pictures were sent out by Wirephoto.   During World War II, cable and radio were used for the transmission of pictures from abroad.

This tremendous growth of pictorial journalism was not the result of Wirephoto methods alone.   It was aided greatly by the establishment of picture mat services, the first of which began shortly after the Spanish American War.   Now many leading syndicates and picture organizations, including the Associated Press, which inaugurated a pony Wirephoto service for its members in 1938, are furnishing picture mats to the American press.

After the pictures are received, halftone reproductions are hurriedly prepared.   From these halftones a large number of mats are made. Then the mats are forwarded to subscribing newspapers for the casting of stereotype cuts from which the illustrations are printed.   Thus, both original and duplicate printing plates are utilized for the reproduction of the pictures transmitted.

X

Styles of Printing Presses

The physical development of the news-paper has been closely linked with the invention of machines which have made possible the production of larger pages, an increase in the number of pages, and the printing of complete editions at great speed. Improvement in printing presses has been one of the greatest con-tributing factors to the gradual evolution of the modern newspaper.

The Early Hand Press

John Gutenberg printed his famous Bible on a simple hand-operated machine which resembled the old wine press of his time. His hand press consisted of two tall, upright timbers, held together at the top and bottom with wooden crosspieces. In between were two more cross timbers: one about waist-high, which supported a flat, wooden bed on which the type form was placed for printing, and another somewhat higher, through which passed a wooden screw that rested on the center of a smooth, flat, wooden surface, known as the *platen*. At the top of the wooden screw, a long handle, or lever, was attached. This con-trolled the up-and-down movement of the platen. When turned in one direction, the platen was forced downward against the type form to gain the impression. It was raised by pushing the lever in the op-posite direction.

The form to be printed was put on the bed of the press and inked by means of a ball of leather stuffed with wool. A sheet of dampened paper was placed over the type, and a piece of blanket was spread on the top to soften the impression and to help correct irregularities of the platen. Then the form was pushed under the platen and the lever was pulled, causing the platen to be screwed down tightly against the type. After the impression had been taken, the lever had to be turned in the opposite direction to lift the platen. The blanket was taken off and the printed sheet was removed and hung up to dry. This routine had to be followed for every sheet printed.[1]

---

[1] Robert Hoe, *A Short Story of the Printing Press,* page 6. New York: The Gilliss Press, 1902.

Printing with the hand press was a slow, laborious process. Printers in Gutenberg's time were able to secure around 600 impressions in a day—or 300 sheets printed on both sides.[2] Although some minor changes were made as the years passed, this type of crude, wooden hand press was used for about 150 years.

The first important improvements were introduced around 1620 by William Jensen Blaew, a printer of Amsterdam. He invented a press with a movable bed that could be rolled in under the platen and out again after the impression had been taken. Other changes in his press consisted of a new form of iron hand lever for turning the screw, the spindle of which passed through a square block. The platen was suspended from this block, preventing any twist and insuring a more steady motion of the screw.[3] In this way, a more even impression could be obtained.

The Blaew press was used widely in England and by American colonial printers. In addition to its added convenience, this press was capable of greater production. The number of hand operations was reduced to nine, making it possible for hard-working printers to turn out many more "pulls" per hour.[4]

FIRST IRON PRESSES

As the art of printing spread and developed, the need for a more sturdy press arose. The increase in the size of forms and the printing of more and larger wood cuts called for the exertion of greater pressure, and the wooden press could not stand up satisfactorily under the new demands.

Eventually, it was replaced by a press made entirely of cast iron, including the platen. The first press of this type to be introduced was the Stanhope press, which was built under the direction of the Earl of Stanhope in 1798. In this press, the screw was retained, but its movement was controlled by a combination of levers to afford greater pressure with less exertion. Although heavy and cumbersome, the iron press met with great favor, and many printers who were unable to secure a Stanhope press incorporated the new impression lever principle in their own wooden machines to make them more powerful. However, the additional strain was too great for the wooden structures, and they usually broke down.[5]

---

[2] Alfred M. Lee, *The Daily Newspaper in America*, page 20. New York: The Macmillan Company, 1937.

[3] Hoe, *A Short History of the Printing Press*, page 6.

[4] Kenneth E. Olson, *Typography and Mechanics of the Newspaper,* page 404. New York: D. Appleton and Company, 1930.

[5] Hoe, *A Short History of the Printing Press,* page 7.

Further progress was made in 1816, when George Clymer, of Philadelphia, invented a press in which a new principle for raising and lowering the platen was employed. Instead of the screw, a long, heavy, cast-iron lever was attached to one of the uprights of the frame. The other end was constructed so that it could be lifted and lowered by a combination of smaller levers when the handle was pulled. This arrangement made it possible to gain an impression with greater ease.[6] Clymer's press was named the "Columbian." It afforded a better method of taking the impression, and it was larger and stronger than those which had preceded it. However, it soon was replaced by another press that worked on a somewhat different principle.

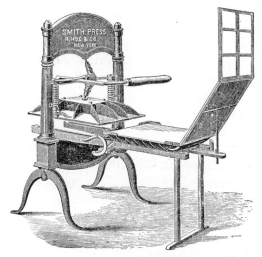

Figure 89. The Peter Smith Hand Press, patented in 1822. (From Robert Hoe's *A Short History of the Printing Press.*)

When it was discovered that cast iron could be used successfully in press construction, several inventors began working on ideas to bring about more efficient operation. Among them was Peter Smith, who was connected with R. Hoe & Company, of New York. In 1822, he devised a press in which the impression was given by means of a toggle joint operated by a single lever. Although a simple change, this development represented the first clear-cut departure from the screw-type press which had been in use since the middle of the fifteenth century.[7]

Employing the same principle, Samuel Rust of New York introduced a machine in 1827 that was greatly superior to the Smith press.[8]

[6] Hoe, *A Short History of the Printing Press*, page 8.
[7] Olson, *Typography and Mechanics of the Newspaper*, page 405.
[8] Hoe, *A Short History of the Printing Press*, page 8.

Known as the "Washington Hand Press," it was used widely by editors and publishers for many years. A few presses of this type still may be found in some newspaper offices as reminders of the "good old days."

Instead of a solid cast-iron frame, the uprights at the side of the Washington Hand Press were hollowed out for the admission of wrought-iron bars that were riveted at the top and bottom of the casting. This feature gave additional strength and reduced the amount of metal needed for the manufacture of the press. The bed moved on a track and could be carried in and out from under the platen by belts attached to a pulley. The pulley was operated by a crank at the side. The impression was obtained by a curved lever acting on a toggle joint. Strong springs—one on either side against the frame—caused the platen to be lifted after the lever had been pulled.

At the outer end of the bed, a tympan frame covered with cloth was attached by hinges so that it could be raised and lowered. Fastened to this frame was another frame, known as the "frisket." The frisket was covered with a sheet of paper in which the parts where the type would print were cut away. This protective covering prevented the chase and furniture surrounding the form from soiling the paper on which the impression was taken. The form was inked automatically by rollers operated by a weight that could be raised by the pressman. When the weight descended, the ink rollers were drawn over the type and were then returned to the inking cylinder.

The Washington Hand Press was capable of printing a maximum of 250 impressions an hour on one side of a sheet, or 125 complete newspapers of small size. Later, R. Hoe & Company, who purchased the patent, improved the machine by replacing the inking system with an apparatus driven by steam power.

APPLYING STEAM TO PRESSES

As conditions began to improve following the Revolutionary War, and as paper became more plentiful, the publishing business began to expand. Since the hand-operated press soon became inadequate to meet the demands of growing circulation and faster production, attention was turned toward the possibility of applying steam power to presses.

Daniel Treadwell, of Boston, was the first to build a press based on this principle. In 1822, he introduced a bed-and-platen type of press in which the bed holding the type forms was raised and lowered by means of a toggle joint controlled by cam action. The impression was taken against an iron platen that was held in a fixed position above the bed by upright iron rods. The rods were attached to a strong cross-piece at the base of the frame.[9]

The ink was held in a fountain at one end of the press, and inking rollers traveled over the form twice while the bed was in its lower position. The sheet of paper was fed in by grippers on the frisket, and the bed was raised for the impression. After being printed, the sheet was taken from the frisket by tapes and carried to a sheet flier that delivered it onto the fly board.

Figure 90. Treadwell's Wooden-Frame Bed and Platen Power Press. (From Robert Hoe's *A Short History of the Printing Press*.)

The most successful machines of this type were developed and patented by Isaac Adams, of Boston, in 1830 and 1836, and by another inventor, named Otis Tufts, of the same city, in 1834. Eventually, in 1858, R. Hoe & Company took over Adams' business and produced over 1,000 machines for use in this country and abroad.

The invention of the Adams press was regarded as a great advancement, since it was capable of producing papers printed on one side at the rate of 1,000 sheets an hour. Moreover, the entire operation was automatic.

FLAT-BED CYLINDER PRESSES

While Clymer, Smith, and Treadwell were busy perfecting the bed-and-platen style of press, other inventors were carrying on experiments

---

[9] Hoe, *A Short History of the Printing Press,* page 12.

with a machine in which the impression could be taken on a revolving cylinder from forms that moved back and forth underneath it on a flat bed.

During the fifteenth century, printing of copper-plate engravings was done on presses made on that same principle. Several attempts to adapt such a press to newspaper and book publishing already had been made.

The first to succeed was Friederich Koenig, a Saxon who went to England in 1806 and obtained the necessary financial backing from a printer in London by the name of Thomas Bensley. Assisted by Andrew Bauer, he produced a machine in 1811 that proved the soundness of his idea.[10]

The type forms in Koenig's machine were placed on a flat bed. The flat bed then was carried under a cylinder which stopped three times during a complete revolution. Sheets were fed in one at a time from a board at the top of the cylinder.

On the first one-third turn of the cylinder, the sheet was secured on the tympan by the frisket; on the second, the impression was taken against the cylinder and the sheet was removed by hand; on the third movement, the empty tympan was returned to its original position ready to receive another sheet. As the cylinder revolved, the bed holding the type moved forward underneath to give the impression. Then it was inked and returned to its starting point as the printed sheet was delivered.

Koenig's first press was followed in 1814 by another, in which the cylinder revolved continuously and gave one impression on every complete revolution. A part of the surface of the cylinder was slightly reduced in diameter, so that the bed holding the form could move back under it without giving an impression after the sheet had been printed.

He also developed a press containing two cylinders which would print only one side of the paper, but which doubled the press's production capacity; and another two-cylinder press for the printing of both sides of the sheet during one operation. The latter press contained a long bed, which accommodated one form at each end. After the sheet was printed on one side by one of the cylinders, it was moved by tapes over a registering roller to the other cylinder, where it was printed on the other side. Because the form printed on one side was located directly over the one on the other side, it was called a *perfecting press*.

In 1814, the *London Times* installed two steam-driven, two-cylinder

---

[10] John Clyde Oswald, *A History of Printing,* page 339. New York: D. Appleton and Company, 1928.

presses, designed by Koenig, which were capable of producing 1,100 copies an hour.[11]   As a result, the time necessary for the press run was reduced to three hours.   Thus the *London Times* was responsible for two outstanding achievements: it became the first newspaper ever to be printed on a cylinder press, and also the first to use steam power for the printing of a newspaper.

Several other inventors introduced cylinder presses during the first part of the nineteenth century.   The most important of these presses was a two-revolution cylinder press, patented between 1828 and 1830 by D. Napier, an English press manufacturer.[12]

Figure 91.   A single-revolution, or drum, cylinder press.   (Courtesy of Babcock Printing Press Corporation.)

This machine was speedier than the one-revolution, or drum, press which preceded it.   Although it worked on the same basic principle, the cylinder was smaller and made two complete revolutions for each sheet printed.   On the first revolution, the impression was given; on the second, the cylinder was raised by toggle joints in order to permit the return of the bed.

Napier also introduced grippers, or fingers, for grasping the sheet as it was fed in, carrying it around the cylinder for the impression, and delivering it after the printing was complete.

The first flat-bed cylinder press to be made in America was built by

[11] Olson, *Typography and Mechanics of the Newspaper*, page 408.
[12] Hoe, *A Short History of the Printing Press*, page 17.

R. Hoe & Company about 1830.[13]   Known as the "Single Large Cylinder," it was similar to the Koenig invention in that an impression was
obtained from only a portion of the surface of the cylinder, which made
one complete revolution for the printing of each sheet.   The rest of
its circumference was turned down sufficiently to permit the type forms
on the bed to move back under it without touching.

After learning about the Napier press, Robert Hoe sent Sereno New-
ton, who later became his partner, to England to study this machine.
As a result, R. Hoe & Company constructed improved presses known
as the "Single Small Cylinder," the "Double Small Cylinder," and the
"Large Cylinder Perfecting."

The single-cylinder press was capable of producing 2,000 impressions an hour.   To meet the demand for still greater output, the double-cylinder press was developed.   The use of two cylinders instead of
one made it possible for two men to feed in sheets on separate cylinders
at the same time; thus the capacity was doubled to a total of 4,000 impressions an hour.

In some offices, several of the faster presses were installed.   For instance, in 1845, the *New York Herald,* edited by James Gordon Bennett, was making use of four double-cylinder presses, operated by four
men to a press, to print its 12,000 copies—the largest aggregate circulation in the world at that time.[14]

Several improvements have been made in flat-bed presses since their
introduction, including automatic inking by composition rollers, fliers
and tapes for delivering the sheets after printing, and devices to facilitate the drying of ink as the sheet comes off the impression cylinder.
Auxiliary equipment such as folders and automatic feeders, which can be
attached to the press, also have been invented.   These and other refinements have replaced many of the manual operations necessary on
the early cylinder presses.

Many present-day weekly and semi-weekly newspapers, and a few
small dailies, are being printed on flat-bed cylinder presses, which also
are used widely in commercial printing plants.   The hand-fed, two-
revolution press is the most common.   However, the one-revolution,
or drum, press still is being used to some extent by newspapers in the
rural areas.

The two-revolution presses are capable of approximately 2,000 impressions an hour.   They are particularly well adapted to weeklies
where the two runs can be scheduled on separate days.

---

[13] Oswald, *A History of Printing,* page 343.
[14] Olson, *Typography and Mechanics of the Newspaper,* page 409.

The bed of the press is large enough to accommodate four pages of ordinary size. Thus the forms for four pages are locked onto the press and printed on one side of a large sheet. Then these forms are taken off and replaced by forms for the other four pages. The sheets bearing the first impression are turned over, returned to the feed board, and run through a second time for printing, or "backing-up," on the reverse side.

Figure 92. A two-revolution flat-bed cylinder press. (Courtesy of Miehle Printing Press & Manufacturing Company.)

On the second run, the folder is attached to the press, and each sheet is folded and trimmed as it comes off the press. Since each complete paper requires two press runs, approximately 1,000 eight-page papers an hour can be produced—exclusive of the time necessary for makeready. If the paper is to be only four pages in size, all four pages can be locked onto the press in such a manner that, by turning the sheets endwise before they are run through the second time, pages one and four will be backed by pages two and three. In this way, two complete papers are printed on a single sheet which is slit down the middle and folded into two separate units.

If a special edition of sixteen pages is desired, two sheets containing eight pages each must be printed. Such a printing requires twice as much time as that needed for a paper of eight pages.

THE FLAT-BED, WEB-PERFECTING PRESS

Another kind of flat-bed press, designed for daily newspapers of small circulation, is the web-perfecting press, which was introduced late in the nineteenth century. In this press, the type forms are placed on flat beds and the impression is taken from cylinders. However, except for these two features, the principles of operation are strikingly different from those employed on the other flat-bed machines already mentioned.

In the first place, there are two stationary beds, one located directly above the other, onto which the forms are locked. Each is large enough to accommodate four forms of regulation newspaper size. Over each bed is an impression cylinder. These cylinders revolve back and forth in unison over the beds as the press operates.

The paper is fed onto the cylinders from a large roll at the back of the press. The web of paper is threaded in over rollers which guide it under the lower cylinder, where the first four pages are printed on one side of the paper. Then the web is carried around to the upper cylinder, where the other four pages are printed on the reverse side directly over the first impression—the perfecting feature of the press. The paper web then passes on to the back of the press, where it is automatically cut into sheets that are trimmed and folded into completed newspapers ready for distribution or mailing.

The slack which otherwise would accumulate in the web is taken up by equalizing rollers—one at the bottom and another at the top—which rise and fall at the proper instant. Their movement is so timed that the web is fed in and drawn out of the press at an even speed, allowing the paper to stop long enough for one impression before it is carried on through for the next.

In the first web-perfecting presses, the paper was printed on one stroke; then the cylinder was raised sufficiently to clear the type on the

Figure 93. The Duplex Model "E" Two-Way Flat-Bed Web-Perfecting Press. (Courtesy of The Duplex Printing Press Company.)

other. The Goss "Cox-O-Type" and the Duplex Model A, both of which work on this principle, are capable of printing from 3,000 to 3,500 complete newspapers an hour.

The Duplex Model E is the most recent and the fastest type of flat-bed, web-perfecting press. It gives an impression on both the forward and return strokes, printing and delivering two complete papers for each revolution of the drive wheels. Consequently, production speed is stepped up to 6,000 copies an hour, which is almost twice the output of the others.

Many web-perfecting presses of both types are being used for the printing of small dailies with circulation under 10,000, and for the larger weeklies and semi-weeklies. They are especially well suited for the production of four- or eight-page newspapers of ordinary size or sixteen-page tabloid-sized editions.

For publications in the lower circulation bracket of more than eight pages, two independent presses may be installed side by side and operated as a synchronized unit by one motor-drive to deliver a ten-, twelve-, fourteen-, or sixteen-page edition. Although few newspapers make use of the unit combination, the "twinning" of two separate presses in this manner is one method of taking care of circulations beyond the capacity of a single press.

One major advantage of the flat-bed, web-perfecting press over the hand-fed, flat-bed, cylinder press is its ability to produce newspapers completely printed on both sides, folded and ready for distribution, at a much greater speed. Furthermore, this style of press is much less expensive than the rotary press, and yet it is fast enough to serve effi-

Figure 94. The Goss Double-Unit 16-Page Cox-O-Type Flat-Bed Web-Perfecting Press. (Courtesy of The Goss Printing Press Company.)

ciently and economically the publishers of newspapers with modest circulation.

After it was perfected, this press became very popular. However, it was preceded by other machines which were invented in an effort to keep pace with ever-growing demands for speedier production, and some of the improvements introduced earlier were embodied in it. One of the earlier machines was the type-revolving press.

THE TYPE-REVOLVING PRESS

The first type-revolving press was constructed by R. Hoe & Company and installed in the office of the *Philadelphia Public Ledger* in 1846. Known as the Hoe Type Revolving Machine, it was based on an entirely new principle. Instead of the type forms being locked onto flat beds, they were fastened onto a large central cylinder placed in a horizontal position. On the surface of this cylinder, slightly curved, cast-iron beds were constructed—one for each page of the newspaper.

The forms were locked into place with V-shaped rules, which tapered toward the feet of the type, causing the surface of the type to form a true circle. When properly secured to the beds, the cylinder could be revolved at high speed without great danger of the type flying off.[15]

From four to ten impression cylinders, according to the output desired, were grouped at intervals around this central cylinder. Sheets were stacked on feed boards and fed onto cylinders where automatic grippers, or fingers, grasped them and carried them around against the revolving forms on the central cylinder. After each sheet was printed, it was led out underneath the feed board by means of tapes to the sheet fliers. The fliers then delivered it to a table where the printed papers were piled.

The first type-revolving press had only four impression cylinders, requiring four boys on platforms to feed in the sheets. Running speed was approximately 2,000 sheets an hour for each feeder, giving a total output of 8,000 sheets printed on one side every hour. As demands for presses with still greater speed persisted, type-revolving presses with more than four impression cylinders were constructed.

The New York newspapers were quick to recognize the importance of the new invention. Three years after the initial installation in Philadelphia, the *New York Herald* began using a machine with six impression cylinders that was able to produce as many as 12,000 sheets an hour. Other publishers purchased presses of similar design. Eventually, as many as ten impression cylinders were grouped around the cen-

---

[15] Hoe, *A Short History of the Printing Press*, page 12.

tral cylinder, which contained a corresponding number of beds. The hourly output was raised to around 20,000 papers printed on one side of the sheet.

The first type-revolving press to be adopted by a European country was installed in *La Patrie* in Paris in 1848. Eight years later, *Lloyd's Weekly Newspaper,* in London, ordered the first press of this type to be used in England. The *London Times* immediately placed an order

TEN CYLINDER ROTARY TYPE-REVOLVING PRESS

Figure 95. A Ten Cylinder Rotary Type-Revolving Press. (From Robert Hoe's *A Short History of the Printing Press.*)

for two ten-cylinder presses to replace the ones then in use, which were the invention of an Englishman by the name of Applegath, who, with the aid of a machinist named Cowper, had constructed them for the *Times* in 1848.[16]

These new presses were type-revolving, but the cylinders were arranged vertically, instead of horizontally, as on the Hoe press. The type was placed on a large, upright, central cylinder, but the surface was not in the form of a complete circle. Instead, each column presented a flat surface, so that the forms themselves were polygonal. Sheets were fed into the vertical impression cylinders grouped around the central cylinder by means of a system of tapes that carried them sideways between the impression cylinders and the type cylinder to give impressions on one side. Still in vertical position, the sheets were delivered into the hands of boys who caught them as they emerged and

---

[16] Hoe, *A Short History of the Printing Press,* page 16.

placed them in piles.   At best, this press could produce only 8,000 impressions an hour on one side of the sheet.

The Applegath presses made for the *London Times* were the only ones ever constructed, since the Hoe type-revolving presses were found to be far superior.

Although the type-revolving presses continued to be used by newspapers in this country until after the Civil War, they placed rigid limitations on the kind of type display that could be employed.   Since the V-shaped column rules could not be broken to admit lines more than one column in width, newspapers were forced to use vertical display. Otherwise, there was great danger of the type flying off the beds.   Even after presses which would permit horizontal display had been invented, many years elapsed before American newspapers forsook the practice.

The adaptation of curved stereotype plates to newspaper presses, which eventually brought about the change, was not the outcome of a desire on the part of editors for a new typographical design, but rather for a machine that would print at a greater speed.

James Dellagana was among the first to replace forms of type on the type-revolving press with curved stereotype plates made from papier-mâché matrices.   A leading stereotyper in London, he made curved column plates for the presses of the *London Times*.

In America, Charles Craske began producing curved stereotype plates of entire pages for the type-revolving presses of the *New York Herald* in 1854, and soon other newspapers adopted the new method. By casting duplicate plates of the type pages, it was possible to increase the output greatly by employing several presses at the same time. Shortly before the outbreak of the Civil War, the *Herald,* an outstanding pioneer in this development, was using five type-revolving presses that printed from duplicate plates made by the stereotyping process.[17]

Type-revolving presses using curved stereotype plates could attain speeds greater than any of the machines which preceded them, but they had one main disadvantage which had to be overcome before any significant increase in output could be obtained.   This was their inability to print on both sides of the paper in one operation.   The rotary press soon was to solve this problem.

The First Rotary Web-Perfecting Presses

The adaptation of stereotype plates to newspaper presses was an outstanding achievement.   Another that proved to be of equal importance was the development of the Fourdrinier paper-making machine during

---

[17] Olson, *Typography and Mechanics of the Newspaper,* page 413.

the first part of the nineteenth century. This machine fabricated paper from pulp in an endless sheet, which was cut up into smaller sheets for use on the presses. However, not until the 1860's did paper manufacturers begin furnishing their product in continuous rolls as well as in cut sheets. This new development was an important factor in the changes in press design that were to follow.

William Bullock, of Philadelphia, was the first to introduce a press that would print both sides of the sheet at the same time. In his machine the paper was fed into the cylinders from a continuous roll, or web.[18]

Bullock's press consisted of two pairs of cylinders. Each pair was made up of an impression cylinder and a cylinder on which the stereotype plates were fastened. The paper was fed from a roll and cut into sheets by serrated knives in the cylinders before the impression was given. After the sheets had been cut, they were carried through the press by means of tapes and grippers, and emerged from the second pair of cylinders printed on both sides.

Because of the difficulties involved in accurately cutting off the sheets at high speed, and because of the unreliability of the delivery of sheets, this press was abandoned by many of the first newspapers that installed it. As improvements were made, however, it gained in popularity.

Meanwhile, the *London Times* was experimenting with a similar idea. In 1868 it began construction of the first successful rotary perfecting press. Known as the Walter press, it closely resembled the Bullock invention.

It contained a few differences, however. All cylinders were made the same size and were placed one above the other. The sheets were cut after the web had been printed instead of before. Then they were conducted by tapes to a sheet flier that moved back and forth, "flirting" them alternately into the hands of two boys sitting opposite one another beside the sheet flier. These boys did the final operation of folding the papers by hand.

Three years later, in 1871, a greatly improved rotary press that was fed from a roll of paper was produced in America by R. Hoe & Company. This machine contained an automatic cutting and folding attachment which did away with handwork in the final step and delivered completed papers at much greater speed. It was capable of 18,000 copies an hour, but the average speed maintained in most newspaper offices was between 12,000 and 14,000.[19]

---

[18] Oswald, *A History of Printing,* page 342.
[19] Hoe, *A Short History of the Printing Press,* page 47.

The initial Hoe rotary press was placed in the office of *Lloyd's Weekly Newspaper,* in London.   The first one in the United States was installed by the *New York Tribune.*   As the machine was adopted by most of the large newspapers in the United States and Great Britain, it eventually displaced the Walter press.

The greatest advancement came with the introduction by R. Hoe & Company of the Double Supplement Rotary Press, so called because it was able to print from two rolls of paper simultaneously and thus produce a supplement that could be folded right along with a regular eight-page edition.

The first press of this type was built for James Gordon Bennett's *New York Herald* in 1882.[20]   It consisted of two units, set at right angles to one another, one of which was twice as long as the other. One or both units could be employed, depending upon the size of the edition to be produced.   In case a newspaper of only eight pages was to be printed, the first unit would be used; but a supplement could be added whenever desired by means of the second unit.   The press was capable of turning out four-, six-, eight-, ten-, or twelve-page papers at the rate of 24,000 copies an hour.

The paper was fed in from a large roll to the first unit, where it passed first between one set of cylinders and then on to another.   Each set consisted of an impression cylinder, which pressed the paper against a printing cylinder onto which four curved stereotype plates were clamped—two on a side.   The four pages printed on one side of the web by the first set of cylinders were backed up by those on the other.

At the same time, paper from another roll was fed through the second unit, in which the cylinders were smaller, and was printed two pages on each side of the sheet.

As the two broad webs, or ribbons, emerged, they were brought together, laid evenly over one another by turning bars, and pasted together.   Then they were carried down upon a triangular former, which folded them along the center margin, and on over a cylinder containing a revolving blade that cut the sheets apart into sections as it gave the final fold.

The discovery that two units, instead of one, could be used together successfully demonstrated the possibility of multiplying the output of a rotary press indefinitely by the employment of additional units and suitable cutting and folding attachments.

---

[20] Olson, *Typography and Mechanics of the Newspaper,* page 415.

MULTIPLE ROTARY PRESSES

The next significant advance came with the installation of a machine known as the Hoe Quadruple Newspaper Press in the office of the *New York World* in 1887. This new press, which worked on the same principle as the Double Supplement, surpassed all previous records in speed. It was capable of producing ten-, twelve-, fourteen-, or sixteen-page papers at the rate of 24,000 copies an hour, or 48,000 eight-page papers an hour.[21]

The Quadruple Press was regarded as a marvelous engineering feat, but in 1889 R. Hoe & Company began building another of still greater capacity for the *New York Herald*. This was the Sextuple Press, consisting of six sets of cylinders, each of which carried eight stereotype plates. It was capable of producing 72,000 eight-page papers, 36,000 sixteen-page, or 24,000 twenty-four-page papers an hour.[22]

A new feature was employed in that the units were placed parallel to one another, instead of at right angles, and paper was fed in from three rolls—one from each end and another from the center. Improved folding and cutting devices were so constructed that they could be adapted to the maximum size of paper or to other combinations, as desired.

Then, in 1895, new records were set with the introduction of the Octuple Perfecting Press, which had a running hourly speed of 96,000 four-, six-, or eight-page papers; 72,000 ten-page papers; 60,000 twelve-page papers; 48,000 fourteen- or sixteen-page papers; 42,000 eighteen-page papers; 36,000 twenty-page papers; or 24,000 twenty-four-page papers.

In order to meet the demands of the larger newspapers, presses with even greater capacity soon were introduced. First came the Decuple, consisting of a sextuple and quadruple set end to end which fed into common folders located in the center. It was followed by a machine known as the Improved Octuple and Color Press, which was able to provide four-page papers in colors, in addition to the regular octuple edition printed in black. Then a Double-Sextuple was constructed for the *New York Journal* that eclipsed all the others. It had twelve eight-page printing cylinders, making possible the production of 96,000 twelve-page papers in black, or 48,000 sixteen-page papers in color, every hour.[23]

---

[21] Olson, *Typography and Mechanics of the Newspaper,* page 416.
[22] Olson, *Typography and Mechanics of the Newspaper,* page 416.
[23] Olson, *Typography and Mechanics of the Newspaper,* page 417.

Constantly climbing circulations have led to the building of presses that reached even greater heights.   Our great metropolitan newspapers of the present day have very costly installations taking up space equal to almost a block in length.   Some of these installations are several decks high.   Papers are printed, folded, counted, and delivered by conveyors at almost unbelievable speeds.

One of the largest is the press used by the *Chicago Daily Tribune*. It consists of ninety-five Goss units and is capable of producing over two million twenty-page papers or one million forty-page papers an hour.   This mammoth installation represents an investment of well over $5,000,000.

Such tremendous output has been made possible by the engineering skill of inventors and manufacturers who adapted the idea of using stereotype plates on cylinders in place of type forms that had to be clamped onto the earlier type-revolving presses by means of V-shaped bars.

Although R. Hoe & Company was a leading pioneer, other manufacturers began to enter the field of newspaper press construction as the number of newspapers increased and circulations continued to expand.

Figure 96.   A view of a section of the *Chicago Daily Tribune's* pressroom.   (Courtesy of The Goss Printing Press Company.)

Among them was the Goss Printing Press Company, organized in Chicago in 1885, which began producing rotary presses the output of which varied according to the number of printing cylinders employed.

Unit Rotary Presses

In 1911, the Goss Printing Press Company produced its first machine built on the unit plan. Each unit consisted of two pairs of cylinders, or couples. Each pair was made up of one cylinder onto which the stereotype plates were fastened and another which gave the impression. The press was made in such a way that a publisher could set up the number of units necessary to take care of his anticipated needs, but he might add one or more units to the original installation as his requirements grew.

The first Goss unit-type press was placed in the office of the *Holyoke* (Massachusetts) *Transcript*. It consisted of three units and was capable of producing 30,000 forty-eight-page papers an hour. During the same year, Walter Scott & Company installed its first low unit-type press in the plant of the *Worcester* (Massachusetts) *Telegram*.[24]

Figure 97. The Goss Headliner Rotary Press. (Courtesy of The Goss Printing Press Company.)

Because of its extreme versatility, the unit-rotary press has become highly popular among newspaper publishers, who are able to place the printing units end to end or stack them above one another, depending on the pressroom space available. Furthermore, the necessity of having to invest in an entire new press in order to meet growing demands is avoided.

---

[24] Olson, *Typography and Mechanics of the Newspaper,* page 419.

THE TUBULAR PRESS

The most recent development is the Tubular Press, designed for use by daily newspapers with moderate circulations. As the name indicates, the printing cylinder is only large enough in circumference to accommodate one plate, instead of two as in the rotaries using semi-cylindrical plates. The plates are made tubular in shape to fit onto cylinders that are considerably smaller and consequently rotate at a higher speed.

A tubular press of four units is capable of producing sixteen-page newspapers, but additional units and folders may be added at any time when more pages are required. Any, or all, of the units and folders may be operated or left idle in any desired combination up to the capacity of the press. The running speed of the tubular press ranges from 30,000 to a maximum of around 45,000 papers an hour—in multiples of two pages. The size of the edition depends upon the number of units employed.

The tubular press is much less expensive than the large rotaries printing from semi-cylindrical plates, and it is particularly well adapted to newspapers with circulations ranging from around 6,000 to 25,000.

IMPROVEMENTS IN PRESS DESIGN

Since 1900, many improvements have been made in fast printing presses. Devices for the control of web-tension have been invented to overcome delays caused by breakage of the paper and to assure more perfect register. Folding and cutting equipment has undergone steady improvement to keep pace with the ever-increasing speeds and the larger editions.

Much experimentation has been conducted on methods to improve inking facilities in order to assure more even color on all pages pro-

Figure 98. The Duplex 16-Page Standard Tubular Press. (Courtesy of The Duplex Printing Press Company.)

duced at high speed. Among the more recent developments is a Goss continuous ink-feed system, involving an entirely new principle. Ink is taken from the fountain roller by a helical-ribbed roller which transfers it in a continuous overlapping pattern to the transfer roller. Uniform color is maintained throughout the ranges of press speed; ink feed is regulated in direct proportion to press speed. No pulsating or oscillating motions develop and the entire system is continuous.

Another advanced feature is the new tension plate lockup available on Goss presses. Plates are held circumferentially under constant tension, preventing any relative movements or working of the plates on the cylinders and overcoming the possibility of their working loose on long runs at extreme speeds. Tests have shown that printing quality is improved, the life of blankets on impression cylinders is lengthened, and a great many web breaks are eliminated.

These and other improvements have resulted in less mechanical troubles, reduced power requirements, better lubrication, and greater protection of pressmen from injuries.

PROVISION FOR COLOR

Serious attention also has been given to the development of presses that will provide color in regular editions of the newspaper.

The *Chicago Daily Tribune,* one of the leading pioneers in the use of color, printed its first four-page, four-color section on news presses in 1901. Other large newspapers, including the *New York Journal,* the *New York World,* the *New York Herald,* and the *Boston Post,* began experiments at about the same time. However, most of the outstanding achievements have come in recent years.

The following record of the use of color by the *Tribune* shows the progress made by that paper and indicates what the general trend has been:

1926—First use of two-color, double-page advertisement on news presses.
1929—First use of a two-color page by a retail advertiser.
1931—First editorial use of two colors in a Sunday fashion section.
1932—First use of a three-color page for retail advertiser.
1936—First use of four colors—in a fashion section.
1939—Use of three- and four-color news pictures; also first four-color map printed on news presses.

Since 1939, and throughout World War II, the *Tribune* made extensive use of maps, cartoons, and pictures printed in color.

Several other newspapers in this country have been employing color in recent years, and although the practice is not general, interest is increasing in R.O.P. (run-of-paper) color. As a consequence, press manufacturers have given careful study to the problem, and the latest improvements in press design have included provision for color.

The printing of color is more involved than the printing of ordinary black and white. As pointed out in the discussion on printing plates, four separate plates are required for a full-color reproduction—one for each primary color and another for the black, to add richness. Four separate impressions are required in the printing operation.

When such an illustration is printed on a flat-bed cylinder press, the sheet of paper must be fed through four times, and the ink must be changed for each run. In the rotary press, the web must pass through four separate couples, each of which prints a different color. Various combinations are provided to permit such arrangements.

Color cylinders, together with their companion impression cylinders, may be installed at the top of regular units, or color may be obtained on any or all webs by reversing cylinders within a unit. A combination of these two methods also may be used. Special installations are obtainable in which the color cylinder is placed above a unit in such a manner that it prints from the same impression cylinder used in the couple to which it is attached. Another arrangement consists of two sets of cylinders for color—one is placed at each side over the two couples below, which make up the regular printing unit.

Within certain limits, newspaper publishers are able to select the number of colors they want and to place them on the pages desired by making use of the various combinations in press design now obtainable from leading manufacturers of presses.

To further facilitate the use of color, special portable, color ink fountains that are detachable may be obtained. These are attached over the regular fountains (carrying black ink) on any printing cylinder to give the color required. After the run is completed, the color ink fountain can be taken off and moved to any other unit on the press.

One of the most difficult problems in color printing has been the development of suitable inks for use on fast presses printing on soft news print. However, great progress has been made in the adaptation of ink and paper, and with the remarkable advancement in press design, color undoubtedly will play an increasingly important role in newspapers of the future. Such a trend is evident in the recent announcement by a leading manufacturer of printing presses that over ninety per cent of the orders now on hand, which have accumulated since the start of World War II from newspapers throughout the country, call for the inclusion of color equipment.

THE OFFSET PRESS

Most of the newspapers in this country today are being printed on flat-bed cylinder or rotary presses. However, a few of the smaller publications make use of the offset press.

This type of press works on an entirely different principle, since printing is done from lithographic plates which require special treatment.

The press consists of three main cylinders, located one above the other. The printing plate is fastened to the top cylinder and prints onto the surface of the middle cylinder, which is covered with a rubber blanket.

The paper passes between the middle cylinder and an impression cylinder at the bottom to gain the impression, which is "offset" from the rubber blanket, instead of being printed directly from the plate.

Sheets are fed into the press by an automatic feeder attached at one end. After being printed, they are carried around between the impression cylinder and a delivery cylinder that deposits them in a pile at the other end of the machine. Two runs are required to print the sheet on both sides.

A leading manufacturer of offset presses in this country is the Harris-Seybold Company. However, several other manufacturers produce presses of this kind. The ATF-Webendorfer press, distributed by American Type Founders Sales Corporation, is found in many commercial plants.

ATF-Webendorfer sheet-fed offset presses are available in three sizes: $13\frac{1}{2} \times 19$ inches, 17×22 inches, and 22×28 inches. Because of size limitations, newspapers printed on these presses are small and consequently they are well adapted only to tabloid editions.

With the 17×22 inch press, two 11×17 inch pages might be printed on one side of the sheet, which then would be backed up by two more pages, giving a completed sheet containing four pages. Thus, two sheets printed on both sides would be needed for an eight-page edition and four press runs would be required.

Rotary web presses for offset also are available. They can operate with two rolls of paper, printing one color on each side of the web and delivering an eight-page standard-size newspaper at speeds ranging from 10,000 up to 40,000 cylinder revolutions an hour.

Although offset presses are used mainly in commercial printing plants, interest on the part of publishers of small newspapers has increased in recent years as improvements in design have been made.

THE PLATEN PRESS

Many newspapers have job-printing departments in which commercial work such as letterheads, business forms, wedding announcements, and other smaller jobs are produced. In many communities, these departments are lucrative adjuncts to regular newspaper publishing. For much of this kind of work, the platen press is used.

The platen press was invented early in the nineteenth century. The first American patent was taken out by Daniel Treadwell, of Boston, in 1826.[25] The earliest machines were operated by foot power. Later, Samuel Ruggles, of Boston, introduced a similar press with some desirable changes, but neither the Treadwell nor Ruggles machine was very popular.

However, in 1850, George P. Gordon, of New York, produced a greatly improved platen press that soon came into general use. So universal was the acceptance of his press, that the name "Gordon" eventually became a common designation applied to job presses generally. In Gordon's press, the form is locked in a vertical bed, and the paper is fed onto a flat surface, called the platen, either by hand or automatically. The impression is gained when the platen rocks up against the bed holding the form, which is inked by rollers that pass up and down over the type as the press operates. The platen and bed are hinged together at the bottom, and, because of the action involved as the two come together, all machines operating on this principle are referred to as "clamshell" presses.

Another type of platen press, in which platen and bed are brought into position parallel to one another before being drawn together for the impression, was invented several years later by Merritt Gally, of New York. Known as the Universal or Colt's Armory, this press is heavier and stronger than the Gordon, but somewhat slower.

Both the "clamshell" and "parallel motion" types of platen presses are in general use today. The two most common sizes are the 10 × 15 inch and the 12 × 18 inch, either of which is too small to be practical for newspaper production. In both presses, the platen is covered with packing, consisting of pressboard and hard-finished paper, over which a heavy manila drawsheet is clamped by means of bales at top and

---

[25] Oswald, *A History of Printing*, page 342.

bottom. Gauge pins are fixed on top of the drawsheet to hold the sheets of paper in proper position. After makeready has been completed, the sheets are fed, one at a time, onto the platen against the gauge pins as the press operates.

Automatic feeders have been invented which fit onto the front of the press and which feed sheets onto the platen and remove them after

Figure 99. The Chandler & Price Craftsman Automatic Platen Press. (Courtesy of American Type Founders Sales Corporation.)

printing by suction control. Several other kinds of presses have been designed for job work and commercial printing, but the platen press is by far the most common in newspaper plants.

PRESENT-DAY ADVANTAGES

R. Hoe & Company, Inc., Goss Printing Press Company, Walter Scott & Company, Duplex Printing Press Company, Wood Newspaper Machinery Corporation, Miehle Printing Press Company, and several other manufacturers are engaged in furnishing presses to American newspapers.

As a result, newspaper publishers are in a very favorable position. They may make their selections of printing equipment from a wide range of precision-built machines, designed to meet individual needs. Some presses are made especially for newspapers with small circulation; others for moderate-sized dailies; and the immense rotary installations for the great metropolitan editions. This desirable situation has been made possible by the engineering genius of press manufacturers, who have been alert to changing needs and have been willing to carry on expensive scientific research in building machines of a high order.

XI

Headlines and Headline Schedules

EARLY COLONIAL NEWSPAPERS WOULD APPEAR dull and uninteresting to the modern reader. They were very small, and the headlines placed over the stories were mere captions, or one-line labels, seldom exceeding 14 points in size.

The one issue of this country's first newspaper, *Publick Occurrences,* in 1690, consisted of four pages, with printed material on only three of them. Pages were approximately $7\frac{1}{4} \times 11\frac{1}{4}$ inches in size. There were only two columns to the page and the body type was about 12-point.

As newsprint became more plentiful and as more satisfactory presses were invented, the page-size of newspapers gradually increased, and so did the number of columns to the page. With plenty of cheap paper at their disposal, several editors in the 1830's began producing the famous "blanket sheets," some of which became so large that they were unwieldy.

The high point was reached when an issue of the *Illuminated Quadruple Constellation,* published by George Roberts, of Boston, appeared on July 4, 1859, with pages that measured 35×50 inches in size. Each page consisted of thirteen columns about $13\frac{1}{2}$ picas wide.[1] However, these mammoth sheets were too cumbersome for easy reading, and the fad died out. Little change in headlines took place during this time.

With the outbreak of the Civil War, headline display took on somewhat greater importance. Larger types were used over important stories; more lines were employed to summarize the news; and the meaningless labels were replaced by lines containing action verbs that said something.

In order to provide a complete summary, the number of decks in a

---

[1] John E. Allen, *Newspaper Makeup,* page 17. New York: Harper & Brothers, 1936.

headline over big news was increased until it often occupied a half column in depth.   Cross-line and inverted pyramid forms were used alternately.

The need to say more than could be accommodated in two lines led to further experimentation.   First, pyramids of two lines or more were used.   Then, a new style of headline known as the hanging indention made its appearance.   It consisted of one line at the top set flush on both sides, with two or more lines underneath indented on the left-hand side.   More emphasis was placed on providing headlines that would attract greater attention and give a better summary of the news.

DEVELOPMENT OF HORIZONTAL DISPLAY

To the three styles of headlines mentioned—the cross-line, the inverted pyramid, and the hanging indention—another was added in the 1880's.   The newcomer was called the drop-line, or step, headline.   It consisted of two or three lines, each of which was indented progressively to the right, allowing better display in the top deck of a headline.

Until the latter part of the nineteenth century, practically all American newspapers used single-column headlines exclusively and a style of makeup known as vertical display.   The large dailies were printed on type-revolving presses, which necessitated the locking of type onto the printing cylinders by means of wedge-shaped rules, making impossible the use of lines longer than the width of one column.   Although the smaller newspapers using flat-bed presses could have printed material wider than one column successfully, for the most part they followed the lead of the big dailies.

The introduction of the rotary press overcame this problem, since the type might be set in any manner desired.   A stereotype plate then could be made for use on the printing cylinders, without danger of its flying off as high speeds were attained.   However, not until William Randolph Hearst's *New York Journal* and Joseph Pulitzer's *New York World* began their great battle for supremacy in the 1890's did headlines of more than one column in width appear to any great extent.[2] Both editors recognized the possible value of larger headlines and prominent display.

The outbreak of the Spanish-American War gave rise to important news that lent itself admirably to such treatment, and the two papers exploited to the utmost the possibilities presented by horizontal display. Large banners, spreads, and a generous use of the other styles of head-

---

[2] Kenneth E. Olson, *Typography and Mechanics of the Newspaper*, page 214. New York: D. Appleton and Company, 1930.

line forms, together with large illustrations, ushered in the famous period of "yellow journalism" that was to have a lasting influence on the physical appearance of American newspapers.

Although the extremes to which the *Journal* and the *World* frequently resorted were looked upon with disfavor by many publishers, they proved conclusively that headlines and front-page display could be used effectively to advertise and sell newspapers, as well as merely to bulletin the news. The banner and spread headline eventually became well established in the American newspaper.

After the war, headline display became much more conservative, and newspapers in general reverted to page-designs that were gray and uninteresting. This trend lasted until the next great crisis in American history, World War I.

Events leading up to World War I again brought forth large headlines in great volume, and during the conflict, most American newspapers made generous use of banners and spreads. Readers became accustomed to more prominent horizontal display, and street sales were greatly influenced by the kind of headlines and makeup employed.

The tendency to "play up" the news with large headlines was not completely abandoned after the war. Especially in areas where newspaper competition was particularly strong, banners and spreads were retained to promote sales, even though the news which they accompanied often did not warrant such prominent display.

The Modern Treatment

Again, headlines were toned down after World War I, and there was a definite trend toward more conservative makeup. The industrial depression, which reached its lowest point in the 1930's, also had its effect.

In their search for ways of reducing costs, editors turned their attention to headline schedules as one place where economies might be effected. One outcome was the development of a new style of headline that could be written more rapidly and set with greater speed. Known as the flush-left headline, it received wide acceptance and was a great aid in giving a streamlined appearance to newspapers.

Editors throughout the country began to break away from the traditional headlines of several decks and commenced experimenting with a more modern treatment. Their experiments resulted in the adoption of one-, two-, and three-deck heads and far greater freedom in the technique of makeup.

New emphasis on pictures, which began to appear in greater numbers after the introduction of Wirephoto transmission in 1935, added to the possibilities of new makeup techniques. Pictures gradually won a place on the front pages of even the most conservative newspapers, and daily picture pages were added by many newspapers.

World War II gave new impetus to the necessity of doing away with nonessentials. Restrictions on the supply of paper resulted in further trimming of headlines and in the careful scrutiny of all other elements of page-design and makeup. Although banners, spreads, and illustrations were used freely during the war period, the number of decks was cut still further. Many editors resorted to complete schedules built with headlines of one or two decks.

The full-cap headlines in many newspapers that held sway for so many years were replaced gradually by caps and lower-case, which permitted more letters to be set in a line and aided greatly in readability. Some newspapers continue to use full-cap banners, but the major trend in the headline schedules of modern newspapers is toward caps and lower-case.

As a result of these and other changes, American newspapers emerging from the war period were simpler and more compact in design, with many of the traditional characteristics common to those of earlier periods missing or greatly revised.

Many of the gains already made have been based on scientific research and careful planning. Great emphasis has been placed on the value of simplicity in design of headlines and makeup.

Forms of Headlines

A headline may consist of one or more parts, or units, each of which deals with different facts drawn from the news story it accompanies. All the units used go to make up the complete headline. Each of the individual parts, consisting of one or more lines and separated either by a dash or by white space, is known as a *deck*.

Sometimes only one deck is used as a complete headline, but when more than one part are employed, the first, or top, deck deals with the most important fact to be announced. Consequently, it should be larger or bolder than the other units accompanying it, which are referred to as *subordinate decks*.

One of the first steps necessary in planning headlines is deciding upon the form, or forms, that are to be used together. In addition to the banner headline, which consists of a single line extending all the way across the top of the page, there are several styles from which to choose.

1. *The Cross-Line.* This is the simplest form available. It consists of a single line and may be one or more columns in width. The type

may run flush on both sides or the words may be centered in the measure.

Plans Yule Party

EXAMPLE 1.

Many newspapers use the one-column cross-line over less important stories, but because of the limitations placed on the number of words permitted, this practice is not regarded with favor. Two or more lines afford the headline writer an opportunity to write more than a mere label and consequently are much more satisfactory.

In headlines consisting of more than one deck, the cross-line sometimes is employed to give variety. It also is used quite widely on editorial pages to promote a more formal treatment. However, many newspapers have discarded the cross-line entirely.

2. *The Drop-Line.* This form of headline also is referred to as a "step-line" or "step-head," since the lines are indented and step down progressively from the left. It usually consists of either two or three lines.

Truman Lifts
Import Duties
From Lumber

EXAMPLE 2.

In a two-part drop-line form, the first line is set flush to the right, and the second line, which runs flush to the right, is indented on the left-hand side. The three-part drop-line consists of one line set flush to the left at the top, the second line centered in the measure, and the third line running flush to the right, with indention on the left end.

The drop-line form is used to some extent as a complete headline, but more extensively as the top deck of a headline of two or more decks.

3. *The Inverted Pyramid.* The inverted pyramid form usually is employed as a subordinate deck in a headline. It generally consists of three lines, with the one at the top extending all the way across the column. The two succeeding lines are each set shorter than the one above, with words centered in the measure.

Because of its descending order in the length of lines, this is the most difficult form of headline to write and takes more of the operator's time in setting.   As a result, it has been replaced by simpler forms on many

Growing Demand for Russ
to Curtail Use of
Veto

EXAMPLE 3.

newspapers.   However, it still is used quite widely in combination with other forms in headlines of two or more decks.

4. *The Hanging Indention.*   The hanging indention is an outgrowth of the desire to get more words into the headlines.   Like the inverted pyramid form, it is used mainly as a subordinate deck.   The first line is set flush on both sides; all those which follow are indented an even amount of space on the left.

Morrison Tells Commons
Purpose Is Solely for
Efficiency and Economy

EXAMPLE 4.

5. *The Flush-Left.*   This is the most modern headline form.   It is simpler in design and allows much more freedom for the headline writer.

Fatal Blast
On North Side
Still Mystery

EXAMPLE 5.

The flush-left form may consist of one or more lines.   Lines always are set flush to the left-hand side of the column, and each line is shorter than full-column width.   There is no standing rule which says that any one of the lines used shall be the longest; however, for the most pleasing results, a uniform style should be followed throughout the schedule.

Many modern newspapers make exclusive use of the flush-left form in their headline schedules, using it not only for the top decks but for subordinate decks as well.   A common practice is to run all lines flush-left in these subordinate decks, but to indent them one or more ems on the left-hand side.   Such indention provides white space to balance the space allowed at the right side of lines in the top deck.   When treated in this manner, the resulting form sometimes is referred to as a *modified flush-left* or *square-indention*.   In all flush-left headlines consisting of more than one deck, the subordinate decks should be indented.   (See sample headline schedule in Fig. 101.)

Although the flush-left form had been used previously for display purposes in advertising and for headlines in magazines, it did not gain much headway in newspaper headline schedules until the 1930's.   The first paper to introduce the principle for this purpose was the *New York Morning Telegraph*, which began using flush-left headlines during 1928.

The Linotype News began campaigning for the new idea early in 1929, and has been a leading pioneer of flush-left design.   The *Cleveland News* adopted a flush-left head-dress in 1934; the *Seattle Star,* in 1935; and the *Los Angeles Times,* in 1936.   Since then, scores of American newspapers, both large and small, have begun using this simpler and more modern style of headline.

The flush-left headline has gained wide popularity for several reasons.   In the first place, it is much easier to write because of the flexibility allowed in unit count.   Furthermore, it can be set much more easily and rapidly by the Linotype operator, and the provision for white space at the end of lines gives a greater feeling of airiness and freedom to the page.

6. *The Spread*.   A headline or deck which extends over two or more columns is known as a *spread*.   The most common forms used in this manner are the flush-left, the drop-line, and the cross-line.

Full Agreement on Trieste
Reached by Big 4 Ministers

By Walter Kerr.

NEW YORK, Nov. 27.—The Big Four Council of Foreign Ministers completed successfully tonight their long effort to reach agreement on the problem of Trieste.

EXAMPLE 6.

Other Less Common Forms

The Flush-Line. In effect, this style of headline is the flush-left form carried to its greatest extreme. Since the unit count must be exact in order to avoid an undesirable amount of white space between words or letters, great care is required in writing it.

Continued Rise
Of Farm Prices
Into 1947 Seen

EXAMPLE 7.

The flush-line always consists of two or more lines, each of which is set flush on both sides of the column. Thus, the amount of white space is reduced to a minimum, and the headline appears crowded and uninviting. However, to overcome this fault, a subordinate deck—usually of the flush-left variety—is used with it. Because of its greater simplicity, the flush-left form is much more popular and has replaced the older flush-line form in most newspapers.

The Astonisher. One of the most recent innovations is the use of a single line set in smaller type above the main deck. In some instances, it consists of a striking statement aimed toward gaining the attention of the reader; at other times, it gives additional facts concerning the story and thus serves the same function as other decks. Occasionally, it reads into the deck over which it is placed, and consequently sometimes is referred to as a *read-in* headline. It also is called an *overline* or *whip-lash.*

GOOD FOR MORALE

Visit of U.S. Ships
Still Topic in Turkey

EXAMPLE 8.

The Rocket. This is the most unorthodox form of headline. It is so called because of the "streamlined" principle involved. In the rocket style, the lead itself begins with the headline, which carries the reader directly into the story. Making use of the flush-left form, the first word is capitalized and all others are handled just as they would appear in ordinary composition.

Great trouble
has developed
in View county

over the naming of
new officers who are
to handle distribution

of funds collected for use in feeding and clothing victims of the recent storms and floods which swept over the area two weeks ago.

EXAMPLE 9.

The rocket form was introduced by the *Alamosa* (Colorado) *Courier*, and at the start received considerable attention. However, the problems involved in training reporters to write leads that would be adaptable to this kind of treatment and the necessity of rewriting leads on most wire stories made its use impractical, and it was discontinued.

The Jump Head. Ideally, every story on the front page should be given in complete form. However, long articles often make such an arrangement impossible if all the important stories are to be given some "play" and if pleasing page-design is to be maintained. Some newspapers make a practice of carrying material from several stories over to other pages in order to pull the reader inside the paper, but the general practice is to edit copy in such a way that the number of breaks will be kept to a minimum.

When part of the story is continued to another page, it is accompanied by what is known as a *jump head* to assist the reader in finding the material carried over. Frequently, the full headline is repeated for this purpose. Other variations are used, but in every instance, an effort is made to use one or more words from the original headline so the connection will be unmistakable to the reader.

Some newspapers make the jump head strikingly different. A common method is repeating one important word from the original headline, set in large type as a cross-line, with the continued line given underneath. Another is the use of a single deck, set in the same form as that employed on the front page. Again, it may be in the form of a

US to Keep
Navy Bases

(Continued from Page One.)

Mead

(Continued from page one)

Number 5

EXAMPLE 10.

number, keyed to that part of the story carried on the front page. Occasionally, the jump head is placed inside a border (boxed), but since more time is required to set this type of headline, it is far less popular than the simpler designs.

Boxed Heads. When borders or rules are placed around a headline to give it prominence, it is called a *boxed head*. Although the boxed head was popular for many years, it gradually is being forced out of the

Between the Lines
by BILL BROWN

Porch Railing
Gives Way, Aged
Woman Injured

Grid Yanks
Sign Smith

WALTER WINCHELL
On Broadway

EXAMPLE 11.

more modern headline schedules, which are placing great stress on simplicity in design. However, many newspapers still make some use of this style of headline.

In a fully boxed head, the rule or border is placed on all four sides. Sometimes a headline consisting of more than one deck is boxed, but as a general rule only one deck is used.

When the headline is not surrounded on all four sides by rules, it is referred to as a *modified box-head*. Three general plans are followed in designing the partially boxed head. One method is to use rules on both sides and at the top; another is to place them on the left-hand side and at the top; and a still simpler treatment is to use a rule above and below the type lines. Regardless of the design chosen, enough white space should be allowed around the type line or lines so that the headline will not appear crowded.

Placing of rules around a headline or story sets it off as a separate unit on the page. Too many of such individualized groups can be very detrimental to the over-all design of a page, in which unity and close harmony are essential for pleasing effects.

Folo Heads. The folo head is used on news which relates to the main story and which is run in the same column under the main head-

---

George E. Brunner of Camden, CIO-PAC backed Democrat, said shortly before that on the basis of unofficial returns he conceded Smith's election.

WEST VIRGINIA

Charleston, W. Va., Nov. 5 (*P*)—United States Sen. Kilgore, whose bid for reëlection was the subject of a vigorous campaign fight by the national Democratic administration, was engaged in a close battle with Republican Thomas B. Sweeney with almost two-thirds of the West Virginia election ballots reported tonight.

pipe lines is for transportation of oil, not natural gas.

Bauer voiced the view that the best operation of the lines would be by the government itself, but said the co-operative he proposed would be the nearest thing to government operation.

ATOMICS TO RIVAL COAL.

Compton Says Only Politics Can Interfere With Development.

PARIS, Dec. 2.(AP)—Atomic power may become a serious competitor to coal in the United States by about 1955 "if political difficulties do not seriously intervene," Dr. Arthur H. Compton said today.

The atomic scientist, who is chancellor of Washington university at

EXAMPLE 12.

---

line. For instance, following a local story telling of a "polio" epidemic, a report from other cities may be run under a folo head.

The same plan often is followed to bring together different angles of a story within a given area, all of which are run under the same date line. Similar heads sometimes are used over information which comes into the office after the main story has been sent to the operator.   All such related material later is brought together under the main head-line to give a complete roundup of the news.

Several styles are used.   Some newspapers employ a cross-line head; others use two lines in smaller type sizes, set flush-left or in the style used in regular headlines; and a few employ boxed heads for this pur-pose.

The Sub-Head.   In order to break up long columns of gray body-matter, a sub-head is used at intervals of about every two or three para-graphs in longer stories to let light into the type mass, and make it more inviting.

The most common style of sub-head is a single line in the bold-face version of the body type being used, set centered in the measure in caps

lumber products available for U.S. housing.   Practically no other lumber is imported from abroad.

Industry Pessimistic.

A Washington spokesman for the lumber industry declared the presidential order would be "of no real help in relieving the housing shortage" because, he said, the kind of lumber imported from Canada is not in short supply here.

man at a mid-town hotel (Wal-dorf-Astoria) in the evening cli-maxes the day's program.

Glad Hand Offered

New York officially was holding out the glad hand in the grand manner. It would like, officially, to have the United Nations settle down on the rolling green acres at the Flushing fair grounds. The permanent site problem, however,

"We always knew it was a fire-trap," he said, "but we had no place else to go."

* * *

CRANES AND pneumatic drills were used to break up and re-move the rubbish to reach the victims. Thousands of spectators and friends and relatives of those in the tenement were held behind fire lines.

Co., and John Doherty of 2337 Commonwealth av., international representative of the United Steel Workers of America.

EX-SCHOOL SUPERVISOR.

Bachrach was educational di-rector of the Chicago Technical College and a teacher and super-visor in Chicago schools from 1901-27. He was vice president of the Dearborn Company. furni-

EXAMPLE 13.

and lower-case.   Newspapers following a flush-left style of makeup, frequently use a line of this kind set flush-left.   However, since white space is provided on only the right end of the line, the main purpose of the sub-head is not so fully achieved as when the line is centered.

Variations include the use of full-caps in place of caps and lower-case for single-line sub-heads, and the employment of two lines set flush-left in either caps and lower-case or full-caps.   Occasionally, sub-heads are set in a different style or size of type from that used for the text, but this practice is very limited because of the extra time and cost involved.

An innovation, planned as a substitution for the sub-head, is the setting of the first two or three words in a paragraph in full-caps at intervals down the column.

Selecting Type for Headlines

Several considerations enter into the selection of types for use in headlines. The types chosen must be attractive, easy to read, and sturdy enough to withstand the terrific pressure of stereotyping and the wear of long runs at high speeds. Above all, they should be well fitted to the purpose for which headlines are intended: namely, that of announcing, or advertising the news and summarizing it in such a manner that hurried readers can grasp the meaning quickly with a minimum of effort.

There are many excellent type families from which to choose, and personal taste has much to do with the selections for a given paper. However, if satisfactory results are to be obtained, certain fundamental principles of design must be followed.

In the first place, the types selected must harmonize with one another if pleasing effects are to be obtained. Monotypographic harmony is the simplest and easiest to attain in headline building as well as in all other kinds of printing. Although such harmony involves the use of type from only one family, very effective schedules can be made by employing the many variations in size, weight, and width of faces that are available. The closest possible facial harmony is thus assured.

The *Milwaukee Journal,* which makes skillful use of the Cheltenham family, and several other outstanding newspapers that have won frequent awards for typographical excellence, follow the plan of using only one type family.

A more common practice, however, is that of using one good type to carry the major part of the load, supplemented by one or more other type families to provide greater contrast and variety. The use together of two or more families of type which are very similar in design and fall next to one another on the type harmony wheel results in adjacent harmony.

For instance, an Oldstyle Roman might be used with a Modern Roman; Modern Roman with a Square-Serif design; and a Square-Serif with a member of the Gothic race. Mixed Romans usually will go well with either Oldstyle Romans or Modern Romans, since they carry characteristics of both. In every instance, close attention must be given to the selection of type families that possess common characteristics, since the degree of harmony will depend directly upon similarities in design.

Some examples of companion faces which result in good adjacent harmony when printed together are: Caslon and Century, Century and Bodoni, Bodoni and Tempo, Memphis and Metro, and Metro and Erbar.   These are only a few of the many possible combinations that would meet the requirements of adjacent harmony.

Greatest contrast can be obtained by employing types that result in complementary harmony, which is attained by using together members of families which lie opposite one another on the type harmony wheel.

For example, complementary harmony might be attained by using a very plain Gothic design together with one of the more decorative Old-style Romans, such as Caslon, Goudy, or Garamond.   Many other suitable combinations will suggest themselves.

Of the three kinds of harmony discussed, monotypographic harmony is the simplest and safest.   Once the family to be used has been decided upon, any member can be used with complete assurance that no serious conflict in facial design will develop.

When either adjacent harmony or complementary harmony is desired, great care must be exercised in selecting types that are to be used together, since conflicting elements of design will result in undesirable effects.   The greatest pitfall of all is the use of too many families of type in the same headline schedule.

The employment of several designs or families—even though they meet the specifications of harmonious relationship—frequently defeats the purpose of attractive headline dress.   Such a practice conveys an unfavorable impression to the reader who unconsciously may be bothered by the resulting confusion, although he may not be able to analyze the exact cause.

Excellent results can be obtained by using one or two families of type in the headline schedule.   When more than two are employed, great care should be exercised in selecting types that harmonize closely, since every addition of a type family multiplies the problems involved and complicates the work of the designer.

Although Oldstyle Roman types were used almost exclusively for many years in headlines, present-day editors are making extensive use also of the Modern Roman, Gothic, and Square-Serif types in their schedules.   Of these, perhaps the greatest care has to be taken with Square-Serif designs, since they are plain and blocky, and the bolder versions give a very heavy effect that often is undesirable.   However, very pleasing results can be obtained with the medium and light Square-Serif designs.

LEGIBILITY OF HEADLINE TYPES

The nature of headline composition places certain limitations on those types that can be employed successfully. The largest number of headlines used in a given edition are one column in width, and the measure consequently seldom exceeds twelve or thirteen picas. Despite this restriction, the types must be large enough and bold enough to command attention and to direct the reader into the story which they accompany if the headline is to fulfill its proper function.

At the same time, the headline writer must be provided with a type that will allow him enough letters—or units—in a line to express his ideas adequately. This often means that the type used either must be in condensed form or that the design must be one in which the letters fit closely together.

For several decades, American newspapers attempted to overcome this problem by using very condensed faces in their headlines, usually set in full-caps. Many fonts of the old Title-Line types, which should be discarded in favor of more legible faces, still may be found in many present-day offices.

Numerous tests on readability of type have shown that condensed faces are much more difficult to read than regular widths and that they greatly retard the speed of reading. Accordingly, many editors have replaced them entirely with more legible faces, but others continue to use condensed varieties.

As a result of scientific investigations on readability and legibility, leading type-founders and manufacturers of type-casting machines have introduced new condensed type faces especially designed for headline usage. They are more open and much easier to read than the old Title-Line faces. Nevertheless, the employment of condensed types should be held to an absolute minimum.

Setting headlines in full-caps is poor practice. Lines in caps and lower-case can be read much more rapidly and with greater ease. Furthermore, the major portion of printed material which a person reads during his lifetime is set in caps and lower-case. Even though he may not know the results of tests on the subject of legibility, he much prefers those kinds of types with which he is most familiar. Consequently, if full-caps are to be used at all, they should be limited to those occasions where special emphasis or unusual effects are desired. Ample spacing between words should be used in order to keep them from "running together."

Although some newspapers continue to set banners and top decks of headlines in all-caps, there has been a definite trend in recent years toward complete headline schedules set in caps and lower-case exclusively.

JUDGE TO OFFER OWN EVIDENCE IN COURT TODAY

Rent Squeeze Under Way, Tenants Say

CHURCHILL ASSAILS RED BALKAN POLICY

Normal Meat Supply Expected Here Soon

Figure 100. Examples of headlines set in all-caps and in caps and lower-case. Notice how much easier it is to read the ones in caps and lower-case. In the all-cap headlines, there is a tendency for words to run together unless ample space—at least an en quad—is used between them.

Douglas C. McMurtrie, who was one of the leading pioneers of caps and lower-case for purposes of display, gave the following advice to members of the Inland Daily Press Association at one of their annual meetings in an address on the typography of newspapers:

I deplore the fact that most streamers are set in caps. . . . If you must use streamers, set them in the most readable alphabet which is at your disposal. Streamers in upper and lower case, even though not exceedingly large, are more vivid and easier to read, and more interesting.[3]

Another fact to remember in connection with legibility of type is that sufficient spacing should be used between words in a line and between the lines of a headline. Crowding of words and of lines together in the headline greatly retards the speed of reading and leads to frequent mistakes.

FITTING TYPES TO HEADLINE FORMS

The belief that selection of a good type family is all that is necessary to assure a successful headline schedule is erroneous. Another phase of headline design of equal importance is fitting the types chosen to the form, or forms, to which they are best adapted.

There are four basic forms of headlines to be considered: namely, the flush-left, the hanging indention, the drop-line, and the inverted pyramid.

The plainest and most modern is the flush-left. Consequently, it lends itself best to the plain and more modern type designs. Gothic and Square-Serif types are particularly well adapted to flush-left treatment because of their extreme plainness. Bodoni, with its geometric design, thin, straight-line serifs, and clean-cut, chiseled appearance also is extremely well fitted for this form. The flush-left style also is acceptable for Century and Cheltenham, both of which are members of the Mixed Roman group and are closely related to the Modern Romans in facial design. Likewise, these same types may be used satisfactorily in the hanging-indention form, since it also is a plain design in which straight-line effects predominate.

The more decorative types, including Oldstyle Romans, which contain curved and slanting serifs, off-balance shadings, and other variations of design, are not as suitable for the plainer headline forms because they do not have enough common characteristics. They should be used in the forms that contain the most variations—the drop-line or inverted pyramid.

Goudy, Garamond, Caslon, and the more decorative Scripts and Cursives fall naturally into this category. Century and Cheltenham also can be used safely in these forms, because of their mixture of Modern and Oldstyle Roman characteristics.

---

[3] Douglas C. McMurtrie, "Papers Must Modernize!" *Editor & Publisher*, 74:10 (March 8, 1941), 40.

In other words, the choice of headline forms should be regulated by the nature of the design of the types that are to be used in the headline schedule. The plain, modern types should be placed in forms having similar characteristics; the more decorative designs should be used in forms that possess a wider range of variations.

The width of a given type design also has much to do with its adaptability. For instance, Caslon in the regular variety is a rather wide face and consequently cannot be used very successfully in headlines that are one column in width, since not enough letters can be admitted to a line. However, it is a very good choice for headlines of two or more columns in width. On the other hand, letters in Bodoni are close-fitting and somewhat smaller, thus permitting the use of more characters in a line. This is one of the reasons it has gained such wide popularity as a headline type.

Combining the Headline Forms

Although some editors make use of one-deck headlines exclusively throughout their newspapers, a more common practice is to include some headlines that consist of more than one part in order to permit greater variety. If such headlines are used, another problem in design is involved: that of selecting headline forms that will conform from the standpoint of shape and tone harmony when they are used together.

If we regard the words and lines making up a deck as a unit, we are concerned with three basic shapes: a rectangular form, a parallelogram, and a triangle, representing, in order, the flush-left, the drop-line, and the inverted pyramid. The hanging-indention form resembles the rectangle more closely than it does the other two.

The most desirable plan is to limit the number of differing forms combined in a given headline to not more than two, since too many shapes used in such a small design result in conspicuous lack of unity.

If the first deck of a headline is set flush-left, the closest harmony can be obtained by using other flush-left forms in subordinate decks. The second deck of a two-part headline of this kind should be indented from one to one and one-half ems to provide white space on the left-hand side. The white space thus allowed tends to balance that at the right-hand ends of the lines in the first deck, and a pleasing design results.

The hanging indention, because of its close similarity to the flush-left form in shape and structure, is a form that can be combined very satisfactorily with the flush-left. It also is plain, with straight-line effects predominating.

Next to the flush-left, the drop-line is the most popular form being used for the first deck in present-day headlines.   It usually is combined with the inverted pyramid.

Of the three shapes, the rectangle and the parallelogram are the strongest designs and consequently are rightly chosen for the main decks in headlines.   The inadvisability of using flush-left, drop-line, hanging-indention, and inverted-pyramid forms together in the same headline is readily apparent when shape harmony and simplicity of design are considered.

In addition to fitting together forms that harmonize from the standpoint of shape, the problem of tone, or color, harmony also must receive careful attention.   The main objective should be to combine groups of type that will result in pleasing gradation of tone from the darker areas downward into the mass of body-type of the news story, which is the lightest.

The tone of a headline form is determined mainly by the size and weight of the type face employed and the number of lines included. The amount of white space used between lines and at the sides also has much to do with the design.

One objection to a schedule made up entirely of one-deck headlines is that the transition from the larger headline forms to the gray text directly below is too abrupt.   Contrast in some instances is so pronounced that the reader subconsciously is jolted as his eyes pass from the very dark headline area into the light reading matter.   The visual adjustment required is much greater than would be necessary if another deck of intermediate tone led the reader's eye down the columns in a more gradual, orderly fashion.   Furthermore, the page takes on a spotted effect in those portions where the contrast is too great.   This spottiness is injurious to the over-all design.

Another device used in obtaining pleasing gradation is setting the first few lines of the story in a slightly larger size than the main body-type.   Sometimes these lead paragraphs are set in boldface in order to give more gradual gradation.

On main stories employing two-column headlines, the practice of starting off the story in a two-column measure is followed by many newspapers.   The type is either in a larger size than the body-type or is more heavily leaded.   The main purpose, of course, is to give better display to the first part of the story; but also the practice often aids in providing pleasing gradation of tone.

UNIT COUNT IN HEADLINES

The headline writer must work rapidly and produce copy that can be set by the operator without delay once it reaches the type-casting machines. Each line in all headlines must contain the right number of letters and the proper spacing if the headlines are to be uniform and readable.

In order to meet these requirements, the headline writer must be provided with a reliable guide by which to work. Although no single system can be applied without modification to all type faces, a general plan has been devised by printers and copy editors to serve as a basis for the "counting in" of headlines. This plan can be adapted readily to the various headline forms and type faces in a given schedule.

The formula is based upon the assumption that most characters are of practically the same width and consequently may be considered as one unit. Those that are wider or narrower are given values proportionate to their variance from the letters of average width.

The system consists of two parts: one applies to headlines set in caps and lower-case letters, and the other to those set in all-capitals.

The count for caps and lower-case headlines is as follows:

$$
\begin{array}{lr}
\text{Lower-case letters i, f, l, j, and t} \dots\dots\dots\dots & \tfrac{1}{2}\ \text{unit} \\
\text{Lower-case letters m and w} \dots\dots\dots\dots\dots & 1\tfrac{1}{2}\ \text{units} \\
\text{All other lower-case letters} \dots\dots\dots\dots\dots & 1\ \ \text{unit} \\
\text{Capital I} \dots\dots\dots\dots\dots\dots\dots\dots\dots & 1\ \ \text{unit} \\
\text{Capitals M and W} \dots\dots\dots\dots\dots\dots\dots & 2\ \ \text{units} \\
\text{All other capital letters} \dots\dots\dots\dots\dots\dots & 1\tfrac{1}{2}\ \text{units} \\
\text{Punctuation marks} \dots\dots\dots\dots\dots\dots\dots & \tfrac{1}{2}\ \text{unit} \\
\text{Figure 1} \dots\dots\dots\dots\dots\dots\dots\dots\dots & \tfrac{1}{2}\ \text{unit} \\
\text{All other figures} \dots\dots\dots\dots\dots\dots\dots & 1\ \ \text{unit} \\
\text{Spaces between words} \dots\dots\dots\dots\dots\dots & 1\ \ \text{unit} \\
\end{array}
$$

Application of this system to a typical flush-left headline would be made in the following manner:

EXAMPLE 14.

A different count is necessary for headlines set in all-caps. The method generally followed is:

Capital I............................ $\frac{1}{2}$ unit
Capitals M and W..................... $1\frac{1}{2}$ units
All other letters....................... 1 unit
Punctuation marks.................... $\frac{1}{2}$ unit
Figure 1............................. $\frac{1}{2}$ unit
All other figures...................... 1 unit
Spaces between words................. $\frac{1}{2}$ unit

A flush-left headline set in all-caps would be counted thus:

OFFICIAL SEES 11½

CONTROLS OFF 11½

FOOD TONIGHT 11

EXAMPLE 15.

In the drop-line and inverted-pyramid forms, extreme care in counting is necessary if symmetrical design is to be maintained. Much more freedom is provided in flush-left headlines and in the hanging-indention form.

When the count for a headline has been established, great care should be exercised to stay within the limits indicated. Each form requires individual treatment.

In a three-line drop-line deck, the spaces left at the end of the first line and at the beginning of the third line should be equal, and the second line should be centered in the measure with just enough white space on either end so that a diagonal line is established on each side of the form. If the center line is too short or if either of the other lines is longer than the specified count, the desired symmetrical effect will be destroyed.

Occasionally, an extra half unit may be crowded in by reducing the amount of space between words, but every effort should be made to allow adequate spacing. Otherwise, legibility will be sacrificed.

Writing copy for the inverted-pyramid headline also requires close attention. Unless each line is of the proper length, the design suffers. Enough words should be provided so that normal spacing can be utilized, and the white space allowed at the ends of the second and third lines should be distributed in such a manner that the pyramid is as nearly perfect as possible. If the third line is too short or too long, the effect is not pleasing.

The number of units in lines of a flush-left head does not have to be so exact, since this form lends itself to a more informal treatment. Provision is ordinarily made for a more or less ragged appearance on the right-hand side. However, if too much white space is allowed at the end of lines, the headline will appear to be chopped off, and the page will take on a spotted appearance. Crowding of lines also should be avoided. The only safe plan is to follow religiously the unit-counts established for each headline on the schedule. Violations almost invariably cause trouble.

If the headline copy sent to an operator contains lines that are too long, they must be rewritten. Rewriting causes delays and slows down production. Sometimes the operator will omit a letter because the head will not "fit," and will depend upon the proofreader to catch the error and provide new copy. However, often the mistake is not detected, and the faulty headline appears in the newspaper.

Every headline writer should realize that type cannot be stretched or shrunk to accommodate his whims or deficiencies and that the responsibility for pleasing design rests largely on his ability to prepare copy that conforms to the adopted system of unit-count. The importance of accuracy cannot be overemphasized.

THE HEADLINE SCHEDULE

A collection, or a showing, of all the headlines used by a newspaper is known as a *headline schedule*. It ordinarily consists of examples of every style of headline, printed on one large sheet or in booklet form for convenience in handling. Sometimes the unit-counts for all headlines are included.

Every style of headline is given a separate number, letter, or some other designation, so that complete specifications as to the type employed, its size, and the column-width do not have to be furnished when the headline is written. The operator merely has to glance at the headline-number written on the copy in order to determine the exact style to be followed in setting it.

Copies are furnished to the headline writers on the copy desk, to the makeup editors, to the machine operators, and to all other staff members who have anything to do with the typography and makeup of the newspaper.

Such a system is very valuable. Work in every department involved is thus simplified and coordinated; chance for errors is minimized; and considerable time which otherwise might be wasted in passing along the proper instructions is saved.

The importance of becoming thoroughly acquainted with the headline schedule followed by a newspaper cannot be overemphasized. Everyone having a part in the work should know all the headline styles, the kind and the size of types employed, the problems involved in headline production, and all the other essential technical matters concerning the use of headlines.

In an effort to preserve individuality, an editor usually attempts to build a headline schedule that differs from those followed by other newspapers in his own territory. Consequently, no standard formula can be set down. Some offices follow headline schedules that are exceptionally simple, with only one type family, one basic headline form, and a small number of headlines; in others, the selection of styles and the number of headlines provided are much greater.

Whatever plan is decided upon—and that decision is largely a matter of individual taste—the desirability of simplicity of design, the harmony of the elements selected, and the resulting legibility and readability should not be overlooked.

Although the nature of headline schedules varies greatly, newspapers follow much the same pattern in many respects, since the purposes are fundamentally the same regardless of the styles employed.

Headlines included in any schedule may be classified according to the uses for which they are intended and the kind of job that they have to perform. In general, they fall into the following groupings: (1) large headlines, including *banners* and *spreads,* which are used for heavy display purposes on the biggest news of the day; (2) *top heads,* the most prominent one-column designs that accompany main stories at the top of the page; (3) *secondary heads,* for use over stories that are not important enough for top position but are entitled to more prominence than other stories on the page; (4) *subordinate heads,* consisting of the smaller one-column structures set in sizes of around 18 points, or smaller in a single deck; (5) *contrast heads,* which are set one or more columns in width for use with feature stories and regular news, and which frequently are employed between main heads, below the fold, or elsewhere on the page in order to obtain pleasing balance and contrast and to give stronger and more unusual display than could be obtained with subordinate headlines; and (6) *special feature* or *departmental heads,* which are used over special columns on the editorial page or in other departments of the newspaper where a more unusual treatment is desired.

1—1 30-pt. Bodoni Bold Condensed
14-pt. Bodoni Bold

Seventeen Men Leap 196 Yards In Four Jumps

Then They Turn Back And Turn Cartwheels Quickly Out of Town

1—2 30-pt. Bodoni Bold Condensed
14-pt. Bodoni Bold

Seventeen Men Leap 196 Yards

Then They Turn Back And Turn Cartwheels Quickly Out of Town

1—3 24-pt. Bodoni Bold Condensed
14-pt. Bodoni Bold

Fifty-Four Youths Prance 2,237 Yards

Then They Turn Back And Turn Cartwheels

1—4 24-pt. Bodoni Bold Condensed

Fifty-Four Youths Prance 2,237 Yards

1—5 18-pt. Bodoni Bold

Seven Young Girls Enter Golf Contest

1—6 18-pt. Bodoni Bold Italic

Seven Young Girls Enter Golf Contest

1—7 18-pt. Bodoni Bold

Seven Young Girls

1—8 18-pt. Bodoni Bold Italic

Enter Golf Contest

1—9 14-pt. Bodoni Bold

Seventeen Local Women Enter Two Golf Matches

1—10 14-pt. Bodoni Bold Italic

Seventeen Local Women Enter Two Golf Matches

Figure 101. The headline schedule on this and the succeeding three pages was prepared from samples furnished by the Mergenthaler Linotype Company. Six fonts of matrices would be required to produce these twenty-two headlines, in which only nine faces—all from the Bodoni family—are employed. The decks in 30-point Bodoni Bold Condensed, 24-point Bodoni Bold Condensed, and 30-point Bodoni Bold would be obtainable from one-letter display matrices; the 18-

2—1 30-pt. Bodoni Bold
14-pt. Bodoni Bold

Seventy-seven Young Men Run From Here to There And Quickly Return Again

**Then They Turn Round and Turn Cartwheels
And Street Corners Rapidly Out of This Town
And Toward Many Other Fine Large Cities**

2—2 30-pt. Bodoni Bold
14-pt. Bodoni Bold

Seventy-seven Young Men Run From Here to There And Quickly Return Again

**Then They Turn Back
And Turn Cartwheels
And Street Corners
Rapidly Out of Town**

2—3 30-pt. Bodoni Bold
14-pt. Bodoni Bold

Seventy-seven Young Men Run From Here to There

**Then They Turn Round and Turn Cartwheels
And Street Corners Rapidly Out of This Town**

Figure 101 (*Continued*).

point Bodoni Bold and Bodoni Bold Italic, and the 14-point Bodoni Bold and the
14-point Bodoni Bold Italic would come from two-letter matrices.

2—4 30-pt. Bodoni Bold
14-pt. Bodoni Bold

Seventy-seven Young Men
Run From Here to There

Then They Turn Back
And Turn Cartwheels
Quickly Out of Town

2—5 30-pt. Bodoni Bold

Seventy-seven Young Men
Run From Here to There

2—6 24-pt. Bodoni Bold
14-pt. Bodoni Bold

Seventy-nine Lively Kangaroos
Leap From Home to Breakfast

Then They Turn Round and Turn Cartwheels
And Street Corners Rapidly Out of This Town

2—7 24-pt. Bodoni Bold
14-pt. Bodoni Bold

Seventy-nine Lively Kangaroos
Leap From Home to Breakfast

Then They Turn Back
And Turn Cartwheels
Quickly Out of Town

Figure 101 (*Continued*).

2—8 24-pt. Bodoni Bold

Seventy-nine Lively Kangaroos Leap From Home to Breakfast

2—9 24-pt. Bodoni Bold Italic
14-pt. Bodoni Bold Italic

Seventy-nine Lively Kangaroos Leap From Home to Breakfast

Then They Turn Round and Turn Cartwheels And Street Corners Rapidly Out of This Town

2—10 24-pt. Bodoni Bold Italic
14-pt. Bodoni Bold Italic

Seventy-nine Lively Kangaroos Leap From Home to Breakfast

Then They Turn Back And Turn Cartwheels Quickly Out of Town

2—11 24-pt. Bodoni Bold Italic

Seventy-nine Lively Kangaroos Leap From Home to Breakfast

2—12 18-pt. Bodoni Bold

All Factories Humming, Workers Also, As Humming Birds Besiege This City

Figure 101 (*Concluded*).

No uniform method of numbering the headlines included in the schedule is followed. However, a common practice is to call the largest one-column headline number *1;* the next in size, number *2;* and so forth. The number assigned increases or decreases according to the relative size and importance of the particular headline involved.

In order to prevent confusion, often the complete designation includes a number indicating that the headline is to be set one column wide. Thus, the most important one-column headline might be known as *1-1;* the next, *1-2;* and so forth.

The same general plan also is employed for headlines of more than one column in width. In order of importance, the two-column headlines would be called *2-1, 2-2,* and so forth; and headlines wider than two columns would be handled in a similar manner.

Banners and long spreads usually are given special designations, which often include a number to indicate the size of the type to be employed. For instance, if the banner is to be set in 96-point regular boldface type, it might be known as the *96-A;* if set in 96-point Italic bold, *96-B;* and so forth. Many newspapers include one number in every designation to indicate the size of type to be used.

The main objective is to devise a method that is simple and easy to follow, so that the possibilities of confusion and error will be overcome.

Using Banner Headlines

When the strongest possible display at the top of the page is desired, the banner headline is used, since it extends all the way across the page and can be set in very large, bold type. The size of the type employed ordinarily is determined by the importance of the story. The range of sizes employed usually is from 72-point to 120-point, or even larger on certain occasions. However, few stories warrant greater play than this, and when they do, a common practice is to use more than one banner headline. The top one is usually set in a boldface Roman or Gothic type, and the one underneath in an Italic version of the same face or in a face that harmonizes satisfactorily.

Whenever a banner is used, close attention must be given to the choice of type. Excellent results can be obtained by setting it in a type face from the same family as that used for the rest of the headline schedule—or for the major part of it. For instance, banners set in Bodoni Bold and Bodoni Bold Italic would be fine selections for inclusion in a schedule composed entirely of headlines set in Bodoni. This combination would give the closest harmony obtainable.

On the other hand, a good Gothic face, such as Tempo, or Spartan, would go exceptionally well in a schedule in which Bodoni types predominate. Railroad Gothic, which is more formal and contains fewer variations, might be used, but it would be less suitable than the more lively varieties.

Since the banner holds top position on the page, it should be strong and masculine. Any suggestion of weakness is undesirable. Consequently, when a single banner is used, it should not be set in an Italic face. However, if two banners are employed, the second one might be in Italic to provide contrast.

The question of caps and lower-case vs. all-caps also must be considered. As already pointed out, lines set in caps and lower-case are more legible and, for this reason, the most desirable from the standpoint of the reader. However, some newspapers run all-cap banners regularly, apparently with the belief that the larger line will have more "pull" on readers and that what is lost in legibility will be made up in the added attention-getting value of the larger faces.

When two banner lines are used on the same page, both of them

Figure 102. Typical banner headlines being employed by newspapers. In the double banner using Bodoni, the second line is set in Italic to afford pleasing contrast. When Gothic faces are used for both lines, the first often is set in all-caps and the second in caps and lower-case. A better plan would be to use regular caps and lower-case in the first line and Italic in the second, since readability would be better.

should never be set in all-caps.   The more acceptable practice is to set the one at the top in caps and the other in caps and lower-case.   If more contrast is desired, the second line can be set in this manner in an Italic face.   Newspapers using caps and lower-case throughout their entire headline schedules frequently set the second line in Italics—and often in a smaller size than the first line—in order to gain more pleasing effects.

A common practice is to have the banner read out into the last or "turn" column, where it is followed by one or more decks which carry the reader on down into the story.   Sometimes a deck of two or more columns in width is used for this purpose; or the first deck may be two columns wide, followed by another only one column in width.   Thus the decks are graded down more gradually into the news.   A study of newspapers will reveal that varying methods are followed in planning decks that are employed along with the banner line.

If two banners are used, the second line usually is made to drop into the first, or inside, column.   However, there are no established rules to govern where the story accompanying the banner shall be placed on the page.   Frequently it is shifted to some other column on the page, depending upon the problems involved in makeup.   Naturally, a regular system on which the reader can depend from day to day is the most desirable.

Some newspapers use only white space to separate one banner from another; others employ a long dash or cut-off rule.   When the latter plan is followed, care should be taken to select a rule that harmonizes with the type.   The device should be as simple as possible so that it will not detract the attention of the reader from the headline.

A cut-off rule always should be used below a banner or spread to separate it from the stories below to which it does not refer.   The rule also helps direct the reader into the column where the story that the headline accompanies is run.

Spread Heads

Next to banners, spread heads are the most suitable for heavy display purposes.   In recent years, they have taken the place of banners in many newspapers, which employ the latter only on stories that require exceptionally big play.

The spread heads most frequently found in a schedule are of the two- and three-column variety.   They may consist of one or more decks, depending on the importance of the story or the effect desired, and the decks may vary in column-width.

In the two-column head, the first deck ordinarily consists of 24-, 30-, or 36-point type. The second deck, if two columns wide, usually is set in 14-point, which provides good gradation down into the smaller body-type of the story which follows. If the second deck is only one column in width, it should be of such a size that the drop from the first deck to the text is not too great. Here again, 14-point type is a common choice.

Another style of spread that is used extensively consists of a single line that extends over several columns and is placed directly under the banner. If the banner breaks into column eight, the spread usually reads out into column one. The headline decks which accompany it may vary in width and in number, just as with the banner.

When heavy display is desired, a two- or three-part spread may be set in 48-point, or larger, type three or more columns wide, with subordinate decks in smaller type and narrower in width.

Frequently, the spread form is used in a combination headline over two or more closely related stories calling for prominent treatment. When this arrangement is used, the first deck often is set three columns

Figure 103. Good display often can be obtained by the use of spreads in combination with other decks or headlines. The above examples show some of the possible effects available.

wide, followed by a one-column deck on either side below it.   A feature head is placed in between the one-column decks for purposes of contrast.

Many other interesting combinations which make use of the spread head are possible because of its adaptability to innumerable situations which require special treatment.   Since it is so extremely versatile, some newspapers make the mistake of mixing too many forms with it in one complete headline, which result in needless confusion and a design that is not pleasing.

There are several arguments in favor of the spread head.   In the first place, it reduces the necessity of running large banners every day. Consequently, prominent display can be given to more than one story, and a more even play can be awarded to the important news stories of the day.

Furthermore, the size of spreads can be controlled by reducing or increasing their column-width and the number of lines to the deck, so that a lead story can be given more nearly the kind of treatment it deserves.

Only when the story is exceptionally important is it necessary to "shout" with 10-line (120-point) type.   By utilizing spreads, news can be displayed in a more modulated manner, and strong emphasis can be obtained as the occasion demands.   When a really big story does break and the editor wants to give it "both barrels," he has the banners in reserve for a stronger blast.

In those cities where newspapers for display on news-stands are folded twice, leaving only the upper right-hand quarter of page one visible, the spread headline becomes a valuable aid in helping to sell papers. When the main news is displayed in this manner, the prospective customer is able to read the entire spread headline quickly and easily; whereas if a banner is employed, he cannot see the entire headline, since it will be cut in two by the fold and much of the sales value will be lost. For this reason, many large dailies in the cities prefer to use spread headlines in place of the banner.

In smaller communities where newspapers are home-delivered and news-stand competition is not a problem, there is no need to use large banners except when the news is so outstanding that it needs smashing display.   In most instances, good spread headlines over the lead stories are sufficient and much more appropriate, since they make it possible to "play" the news according to its importance.   Furthermore, by reducing the amount of space that otherwise would be given over to banners, more is left for the presentation of interesting news.

The advisability of using banner headlines every day, regardless of the prominence of the news involved, is very questionable, except in cases where street-sales competition is severe. Even then, properly used spreads often prove more effective in the long run.

TOP HEADS

As already pointed out, the headlines in the schedule that are next in importance to banners and spreads from the standpoint of display are those known as *top heads,* so called because they are used at the top of the page over some of the biggest stories of the day.

There is no uniformity among newspapers as to the number of decks employed or the styles of the forms combined in these top heads. However, three different varieties are in most common use today: namely, the multiple-deck headline; the two-deck; and the single-deck.

In newspapers using multiple-deck top heads, the number of forms combined together seldom exceeds four. In this style of head, the top

DECISION ON RIGHT OF LEWIS TO END KRUG PACT PUT OFF

Both Sides Agree to Delay Case Till After Supreme Court Rules on Fines

LATTER LIKELY BY JAN. 28

Action Stays Union Moves to Dismiss Declaratory Judgment and Injunction

N. A. M. Asks Labor Curb to Rebuild U. S.

1,800 Industry Leaders Hear Coal Strike Cited as 'Sell-Out' to Unions

Wason Against Any Yielding to Lewis

Harriman Asserts Next Congress Must 'Clarify' the Rights of Labor

Figure 104. The top heads of the *New York Times* (left) and the *New York Herald Tribune* (right) consist of four decks. The *Times* uses a dropline in the first deck, an inverted pyramid in the second, a cross-line in the third, and an inverted pyramid in the fourth deck. The first and third decks in the *Herald Tribune* top heads are flush-left, and the second and fourth decks are hanging indentions.

deck usually consists of three, or sometimes four, lines set in 30- or
36-point boldface type.   In the second deck, 14-point boldface type is
the usual choice, and this size often is repeated in the fourth deck.
The third deck ordinarily is set in larger type than that in the second
and fourth decks, with 18-point a popular selection.

Although the percentage of editors still employing top heads of the
multiple-deck variety is small, several outstanding newspapers continue
to follow this practice.   Among them are the *New York Herald Tribune* and the *New York Times,* both of which have been consistent winners in newspaper typographical contests for several years.

Many editors have turned to the two-deck headline for use on top
stories.   It takes up less space down the column, and, at the same time,
provides for enough words to give a good summary of the news.   Furthermore, by selecting types of the proper weight, sufficient tone gradation is permitted.

Where two-deck headlines are used, the first deck may consist of
three lines in 30-point, or larger, type, and a second deck in perhaps
14-point.   Here again, the combination employed depends largely on
the type family and the kinds of faces included in the schedule.

Before its change-over to tabloid size, the *Chicago Sun* used a top
head of two decks, with 42-point Erbar Medium in the first deck
and 14-point Metro Medium in the second.   Both decks are set flush-
left, and the second is indented on the left-hand side.

Wyatt Acts
On Tucker's
Bribe Charge
Clark Asked to
Probe Lawyer's
Reported Offer

Bevin Urges
Great Powers
Adopt Give,
Take Policy
Britain Will Insist
Potsdam Formula
Be Accepted in
Full or Rewritten

Figure 105.   The top heads of both the *Chicago Sun* (left) and the *Washington Post* (right) are of the flush-left variety, with the second deck indented on
the right-hand side to promote readability and to create a more pleasing design.

In an effort to conserve space during World War II, several editors did away with all headlines containing more than one deck. In newspapers adopting this plan, the top heads consist of a single deck, usually set in 30-point type, or larger. This arrangement results in great contrast on the page, since the jump in size and boldness from the headline to the body-type is large and no intermediate deck is provided to give tone gradation down toward the reading matter.

SECONDARY HEADS

In addition to the stories that are considered worthy of top position on the page, there always are others that deserve prominent display. Headlines used on stories of this kind, which are placed above the fold, are referred to as secondary heads.

Most newspapers include one or two secondary headlines in their schedules; some have as many as three or four. This makes it possible to give a story the degree of play it rightfully deserves because of its prominence in the news, and also allows the makeup editors considerable freedom in selecting headlines that will assure good design on the upper half of the page.

Usually, the same general style as that employed in the top heads is used in the secondary heads. For instance, if the top deck of the No. 1 headline contains three lines, the No. 2 top deck may have only two lines. The second decks of both may have the same number of lines. The same size and kind of type usually are employed; the only difference is in the number of lines in the top deck.

MINERS START COAL FLOWING FROM PITS

Virtually All Expected Back at Work Today—Clash Over Hat Style Keeps 600 Idle

Bid for French Presidency Is Lost by Thorez

Communist Lacks 51 Votes Despite Socialist Support; New Coalition Is Sought

Figure 106. The *New York Times* (left) has only two decks in its secondary headline. The first deck consists of two lines, set in the same kind of type and the same style of form as that used in its top head; and the three-line inverted pyramid in the second deck is the same as the second deck of its top head. The *New York Herald Tribune's* secondary headline (right) consists of decks similar to the first two in the top head, but the type is somewhat smaller.

If two secondary heads are included, the No. 3 headline—as the second one might be called—could also have two decks, each consisting of two lines, with the first deck set in 24-point type, and the second in 12- or 14-point.

A third secondary head, which would be known as the No. 4, might consist of a single deck set in the same size as the top deck of the No. 3. (See Headline Schedule, Fig. 101.)

Thus, the tone of each of the headlines would be reduced slightly or graded downward in order of importance.   The differences would appear mainly in the size of type, the number of lines, and the number of decks.   Accordingly, the amount of emphasis given to a story can be regulated closely by the style of secondary headline chosen.

Meyer Resigns
As President
Of World Bank

**Work of Launching
Institution Is Now
Completed, He Says**

Estonians Sure
Of Stay in U.S.

Figure 107.   The first deck of the *Washington Post's* secondary headline (left) contains three lines in the same size type as that in its top head, and the second deck also is one line shorter.   However, the *Chicago Sun* (right) uses only one deck of two lines in its secondary headline, set flush-left in a smaller size of type.

Secondary headlines have a definite place in any schedule since they afford the means of brightening up the center area of a page.   When the drop from strong head display to smaller structures is too abrupt, this section of the page often appears gray and weak.   Use of good secondary headlines assists greatly in overcoming this fault.   Furthermore, secondary headlines are of great value in inside-page makeup. Here they ordinarily are used in place of the top heads, which frequently are reserved for front-page use only.   They also are used for other main stories on these pages.

It is well to have two or three secondary headlines from which to select.   In the interest of good design and makeup, at least one good secondary headline should be provided—and more, if appropriate sizes and styles of type are available.

SUBORDINATE HEADS

For the smaller, less important stories, headlines in type sizes ranging from 18-point downward to 12-point (and sometimes as small as 8-point) are used. These are known as subordinate heads.

In most newspapers, subordinate heads consist of one deck, which is made up of either two or three lines. The flush-left or drop-line forms ordinarily are used, and both regular boldface and boldface Italic types are employed.

Two-deck subordinate heads sometimes are found in schedules where top heads and secondary heads contain several decks. One style calls for a cross-line in the first deck set in 12- or 14-point type, and a second deck of two lines in an inverted-pyramid form. If the flush-left style is followed, both decks may be flush-left.

A single cross-line set in 12- or 14-point type sometimes is used. However, this style of subordinate head is not advisable because it is too small to admit a sufficient number of words and is lacking in good tone value.

Chinese Block
Reds' Retreat

Railmen Complain
Of Station Smoke

Dies After Fall

Income Tax Forms
Being Prepared for
Mailing on Tuesday

Has 75 Units Under Way

**About 30 Near Completion in
Bergen Co. Development**

Figure 108. Some styles of subordinate headlines.

The tendency in recent years has been toward subordinate heads in sizes no smaller than 12-point, and many newspapers restrict the smallest heads to 14-point type sizes. Use of these larger sizes insures greater attention-value and sufficient tone to break up the gray mass of body-type in a column.

Although every schedule should include several subordinate heads, they should not be used indiscriminately. If they are, the bottom half of the page, where most of them normally are placed, will not have sufficient strength to balance the upper portion.

Some newspapers—primarily in the weekly field—use more subordinate heads in their makeup than any other style. Even though such an arrangement may permit a larger number of stories on the page and a much smaller investment in types, such a practice is a great mistake. The resulting page-designs are gray, dull, and uninteresting because no appreciable differentiation is made between the more important stories and those of lesser value.

Contrast Heads

Headlines in the schedule which are used to add variety and liveliness to the page are referred to as *feature* or *contrast heads*.

One common use for this type of head is to prevent "tomb-stones" —a condition brought about by placing two headlines of the same kind side by side in adjoining columns. The reader has difficulty in pre-

Haswell
Digs Up Facts
On Miners

They Live in a Car
2 Children
Put Problem
Up to Santa

FUTURE HAIRCUT
Barbers Plan
To Educate
Customers

Jimmy O'Brien
Dies, but Not
On Clark St.

Photos of Sun
Taken with
Aid of Rocket

Summary
Of Coal Crisis

Figure 109. Different styles of one-column contrast headlines.

Britain Dumps Two Socialist Principles

Policy Confuses Anew as Draft Is Endorsed, Free Speech Curbed

South Side Group Demands Crackdown on 200 Taverns

Grand Crossing-Chatham Ministers Seek Sunday Closing and Strict Supervision

CONCILIATORS OPTIMISTIC

Glimmer of Hope Seen In 27-Day Bus Strike

Canada Cautious on Combining With U. S. on Northern Defense

But Concrete Action Has Begun, Troops of Both Nations Will Test Gear at Manitoba; Truman, Mackenzie King May Have Discussed Issue

Jailers Silent On Details Of Plans to Hang 11 Nazis

Figure 110. Two-column headlines, such as the ones shown above, are used for contrast.

venting his eyes from moving across the column-rule from lines in the headline on the left to those in the one placed next to it on the right.

Furthermore, the two heads arranged in this manner tend to make up a single unit as far as tone value is concerned. Greater contrast will make the resulting effect less monotonous and more interesting.

Contrast heads usually are set in Italics or in some other style of face that is strikingly different from types used in the main head-dress. Two or three lines are set one column in width, or wider, depending on the effect desired. In many schedules, boxed or partially boxed heads are included for use as contrast heads.

It also is advisable to have several two- and three-column headlines set in regular boldface and boldface Italics in varying sizes for use over feature stories and larger news stories. These headlines may be of both the one-deck and two-deck variety, so that selections can be made according to the importance of stories involved. Common sizes used in headlines of this kind are 18-point, 24-point, and 30-point. If three-column heads are employed, somewhat larger types can be used.

A recent innovation that is gaining in popularity is the two-column headline in which an overline, or "astonisher," is placed directly above the first deck and usually set flush-left. This line sometimes is under-lined with a rule to give added variety.

Care should be taken not to allow too much white space at the end of the overline, since this often destroys pleasing symmetry in the design. The astonisher type of headline should not be overworked. It should be saved for use in those areas on the page where unusual treatment is needed to gain attention and to give added variety.

Special Feature and Department Heads

Almost every modern newspaper runs regular features prepared by columnists or regular staff writers which appear in approximately the same place in the newspaper day after day. In order to give unusual display to this type of news, special feature heads usually are provided in the schedule.

Boxed heads often are used for this purpose. Another common practice is that of combining types that are strikingly different in design. Type and line drawings or photographs also are used together in order to gain unusual effects.

Frequently electrotypes are made of these "standing heads," so called because they are not torn down and distributed, but left standing, after a run has been completed. They can be left standing because the metal used in such plates is much more durable than ordinary

ALL ABOUT THE TOWN

with Dale Harrison

Gracie Allen Says:

Between the *Lines*

—By Tex Reynolds—

A LINE O' TYPE OR TWO

*Hew to the Line, let the
quips fall where they may.*

Reg. U. S.
Pat. Office

Matter of Fact

By Joseph and Stewart Alsop

ON THE AISLE

On the Oblique Approach in Temperamental
Matters, and Some Other Things

By Claudia Cassidy

Figure 111. These six special feature and department headlines are well-planned and attractive. Close attention has been given to the choice of types, illustrations, and borders that harmonize.

type metal.   Consequently the plates will last much longer before having to be replaced.

Although standing heads may serve a useful purpose, they should be used with caution.   After a reader has seen them a few times, they grow monotonous and tend to become mere labels.   Generally, good live news, or feature heads giving some pertinent facts about the accompanying news are much more inviting and interesting from the reader's standpoint.

If the name of the writer or the department label seems important, it may well be carried in an overline above the first line of the headline.   Then the headline would serve a double purpose, in that it would not only direct the reader to a column or story of special interest, but it also would give the reader a summary of the news.   Furthermore, the headline writer and the makeup man would be afforded more freedom in planning pages with greater variety of design.

Although special feature heads are used extensively, many newspapers have replaced them with regular feature and news headlines, in the belief that the space taken up by illustrations and short, catchy lines can be used to better advantage by providing forms in which more words are allowed to give some significant facts about the accompanying news.   The trend in this direction is growing among present-day editors, and it is commendable.

For several years, there has been a growing practice on the part of editors to departmentalize some of the news.   In addition to placing editorials on a separate page—a tradition of long standing—many newspapers have special pages for society and women's interests, sports, financial news, features, and pictures.

To give the right kind of atmosphere and individuality to these pages, headline types other than those used in the main schedule frequently are employed.   For instance, on women's pages, the more feminine varieties—such as Garamond, Goudy, Caslon, and the lighter versions of the Gothic and Square-Serif types—are common choices.

Sports call for strong, masculine types, including the bolder faces. Where headlines in the regular schedule are Modern Roman or Oldstyle Roman, the sports page may make use of Gothic or Square-Serif faces, which denote greater sturdiness and vigor.

In addition, special column headlines planned to carry out the general feeling on these pages frequently are employed on regular features. Headline forms also may change with the introduction of different type faces in a given department, and properly so.   As already pointed out, a form that is most desirable with the plain Gothics, Square-Serifs, and Modern Romans is not so suitable with the more decorative type families.

When different types are used on special pages, they should be analyzed and evaluated in accordance with the basic principles governing headline design, and the selection of types should be directed toward pleasing harmony among all of the elements going to make up the page.

Occasionally a newspaper will select a different type face for the main heads on a special page, but will make use of subordinate heads from the regular schedule. Distinctiveness is thus attained, and at the same time similarity to the headline scheme in the rest of the paper is maintained.

CUTLINES

Since the types which accompany pictures, like headlines, are used to display and advertise the news as well as to enlarge upon it, they logically should be considered along with the headline schedule.

The lines used to help tell the news involved in an illustration (or cut) are known as *cutlines*. The line which is placed above the picture is referred to as an *overline,* or *caption;* and the lines of type that appear beneath the picture are called *underlines*.

When an overline is used, it should be set in the same kind of type as that used in the regular schedule, or in a face that harmonizes. Usually, boldface type is used, either in regular or Italic faces. The former is a stronger design and generally is preferred, unless more contrast is desired.

The most common style of overline is the cross-line centered in the measure. However, newspapers following the flush-left plan frequently run the overline flush-left. When this is done, enough words should be included to keep the line from running too short; otherwise, too much white space is left at the right end of the line, and the resulting design is not pleasing. Equal distribution of white space, as permitted in the cross-line style, generally is more desirable.

Many newspapers following the more modern flush-left style of makeup use no overlines. Instead, the title is set as a cross-line directly over the underlines below the picture. Another plan is to use the first few words in the first line of the underlines as the title. These words usually are set in capitals or in a type face that is different from the remaining cutlines.

Sometimes when unusual effects are desired, the cut is mortised to allow the cutlines to be inserted within the limits of the picture itself, but this device usually is reserved for special occasions.

The size of type used in overlines varies according to the width of the picture and the style of type employed. Ordinarily, 14- or 18-point type is used over pictures one column in width, and 18-point or 24-point are the most common sizes for use with two-column cuts. Pictures that run more than two columns in width may require proportionately larger types. However, in every instance, good judgment must be exercised in selecting types that are not so large that they attract too much attention and injure the design of the picture unit.

Although boxes still are used around overlines to some extent, this is not a common practice in present-day newspapers. When rules or borders are used, they should harmonize with the types and not be so prominent that they detract attention from the title itself or from the picture. A better plan is to dispense with boxing of the overline entirely, since there is less chance of its appearing to have been set off into a separate unit.

Some newspapers set their underlines in regular body type; others use the boldface version of the body type. Another growing practice is that of setting the underlines in Gothic type or in Italics in order to provide contrast with the Roman type used for the text. Occasionally, the underlines are printed in a slightly larger size than the body-type. Whatever plan is followed, the types used should be in close harmony in size, weight, and style, and the variations should not be so great that they detract from the design of the page as a whole.

When cuts are from one to three columns in width, the underlines usually are run the full length of the printed picture. If the illustrations are four columns or more in width, the accompanying underlines should be set in two or more columns, depending upon the size of the picture. Lines that are longer than three columns are hard to read, and consequently it is desirable to break the type mass up into columns, with either white space or a column-rule to separate them.

Since the portion of the cut that prints is slightly narrower than the column-width, because of the space at the sides allowed for fastening the plate to its base, underlines should be set slightly narrower than the column, or columns, that the cut occupies. To be correct typographically, the underlines should be the same width as the printed picture, or slightly narrower.

The amount of indention allowed on either side usually ranges from 6 to 12 points, but it will depend upon the method followed by a given

Oregon Tot Set for Jap Winter

Randa Henry, 4, daughter of Lt. Col. and Mrs. Elmer T. Henry, Portland, selects a new snow suit and shows it to an M. P. guard aboard the 8th army exchange train, novel department store on wheels which serves U. S. army families in isolated outposts of Japan. The Henrys are stationed in northern Japan. (United States army signal corps photo)

Examine Fish from Bikini

[Associated Press Wirephoto]

A. D. Welander (left) holds a puffer, a fish from atom bomb test area at Bikini, in gloved hand as he shows it to L. R. Donaldson at the University of Washington, Seattle. The fish is still radioactive.

A TEMPORARY PROBLEM FOR OPA
Patrolman Ben Szech with James J. Bradley, 13-month-old boy left with the OPA by its mother, Mrs. Charles Bradley, 7240 University av., as a protest. Later she reclaimed the child. SUN PHOTO.

WRIGHT HEADS GREEK RELIEF—Howell Murray (left), retiring chairman, presents gavel to Warren Wright, new Chicago head of the Greek War Relief Association, seeking million-dollar quota of 12 million national figure.

Figure 112. In the picture unit at the upper left both caption and cutlines are set in a medium-weight Square-Serif type. Caption and cutlines, both Gothic, are placed below the picture at the upper right. Some newspapers prefer to box the caption over the picture like the one at the lower left; others let the first few words of the cutline serve as the caption and give them added emphasis by setting them either in capitals or bold-face. For the best effect the cutlines should not extend beyond the edges of the cuts.

newspaper in preparing cuts. Thus, if the printing surface of a picture to be run in a 12-pica column is only 11 picas wide, the underlines would be indented the equivalent of 6 points on either end of the line. The same amount of indention would be allowed for cuts more than one column in width if uniformity is to be maintained.

Copy for Headlines

Copy for headlines ordinarily is written by hand in soft lead pencil so that corrections or changes can be made quickly and easily. It should be neat, legible, and marked correctly so that no time will be lost once it reaches the composing room.

Most offices follow the same general methods. First, the designation calling for the style of head desired, together with the guideline, is written in the upper left-hand corner of the sheet and encircled to show that these instructions are not to be set.

Underneath these instructions, the headline is written word for word and line for line as it is to appear in print. Lines then are drawn at the sides of each deck to indicate clearly the style to be followed so that the operator can tell at a glance the kind of forms desired.

Most headlines are set on display machines, whereas the body-type of the story is cast on straight-matter machines. Consequently, when the complete copy for a story reaches the composing room, it is separated: the headline sheet goes to one machine and all the rest of the copy goes to another. After the type has been set, it is brought together and assembled properly before it is placed in the forms.

Consequently, copy for practically all headlines must be written on separate sheets. However, if the head is of such a nature that it can be cast on the same machine as the body-type, it may be written above the story on the first page. Obviously no guideline is then required, but the style to be followed must be clearly indicated. Any special instructions to the operators should be written clearly in the margin and encircled.

Work for Improvement

Many changes have been made in headline styles during recent years, and today no standard practice is followed. Almost every year brings some new ideas that are aimed toward betterment, and alert newspapermen are constantly striving to improve their methods.

First of all, an understanding of the principles of design upon which good practices are based and a thorough acquaintance with the headline schedule are essential for any person who has anything to do with the typography and makeup of a newspaper. He should make a constant study of what other newspapers are doing, especially those which have been recognized as outstanding for their typography and design, and he should be willing to experiment and to accept changes directed toward improvement.

XII

Front-Page Makeup

IN OUR COLONIAL NEWSPAPERS, THE NEED FOR concern about headlines and their placement on the page was not pressing. With only two or four small pages at their disposal, editors were interested primarily in filling their columns with as much interesting reading matter as possible.

People were able to read the entire paper thoroughly in much less time than is required to merely skim through the pages of a present-day newspaper. Readers undoubtedly would have raised serious objections if space had been wasted on typographical display. No devices were necessary to tempt them or to direct them in their search through the meager offerings. Headlines and display were held to a minimum, and consequently the problem of makeup was very simple.

However, as newsprint became more plentiful and more efficient presses were invented, the size of newspapers gradually increased. Although the first penny papers of the 1830's began as small editions, they were forced to increase in size soon after their establishment in order to accommodate the growing volume of news and advertising. For instance, Benjamin Day's *New York Sun* started out with only four pages, each measuring approximately $8 \times 10\frac{1}{2}$ inches, but within two years, the *Sun's* pages had grown to 14×20 inches.[1]

The introduction of advertising had a profound effect upon the physical appearance of newspapers. Those printed in New York were especially successful in attracting advertisers and frequently had to enlarge their issues to six or eight pages by adding special inserts. The page-size also was gradually expanded to permit longer columns and more of them to the page.

Until the Civil War, most newspapers devoted the greater part of their front and back pages to advertising. The pages printed first usu-

---

[1] Kenneth E. Olson, *Typography and Mechanics of the Newspaper*, page 289. New York: D. Appleton and Company, 1930.

ally were blurred when the sheet was turned over for the second run, and consequently the editorials and important news were placed inside. The momentous news growing out of the Civil War changed this situation, and advertisements on the front page finally were replaced by big stories of the day.

Longer, action headlines, in place of the one-line labels, also became popular, and new forms gradually were introduced. Sub-heads made their appearance to open up the gray masses of reading matter and to permit more white space, and column-widths went through a period of experimentation, with variations running from 10 picas to 20 picas, and back again. Eventually, the page-size settled down to a standard of about 20 inches in length by five or six columns in width.[2]

Because of the mechanical limitations mentioned in an earlier chapter, vertical display was used until near the end of the nineteenth century. Not until the invention of stereotyping and its adaptation to rotary presses was it possible for the big dailies to break column rules for headlines or advertisements of more than one column in width.

Horizontal display was introduced in the 1890's and the *World* and the *Journal* in New York exploited the newly discovered technique to the limit. Large banners, spreads, and illustrations were used to shout the news in a sensational orgy that lasted until after the Spanish-American War.

Although the practices followed by Pulitzer and Hearst were branded as "yellow journalism" and condemned by many of their contemporaries, several of the methods introduced by their newspapers have had a lasting effect on the American press. Banners and spreads have been retained for heavier display purposes by many newspapers, and the idea of using pictures has been adopted in varying degrees.

Another outcome was the change to a page approximately 21 inches in length by seven 13-pica columns in width. Later, the column-width was reduced to $12\frac{1}{2}$ picas in order to allow eight columns and more advertising to the page; and finally, to 12 picas. Today, most daily newspapers contain eight columns to the page, and the column-width is generally 12 picas. Many weeklies use a similar form. A few newspapers reduced column-widths to $11\frac{1}{2}$ picas during World War II in an effort to conserve newsprint, but the change was not general.

Since the introduction of Wirephoto in 1935, there has been a marked increase in the number of pictures used by our newspapers. Added pictures present new problems for the makeup editor.

---

[2] Olson, *Typography and Mechanics of the Newspaper*, page 290.

In recent years, more serious attention has been given to matters of typography and makeup than ever before. Much experimentation has been made in the direction of simpler and more attractive headlines and the building of newspapers that are more pleasing and more effective in the presentation of news and advertising. Many of the customs and traditions that shackled editors for so many years have been replaced by practices that permit far greater freedom and designs that are more pleasing and readable.

IMPRESSION ON READERS

When a new reader picks up a newspaper for the first time and begins to turn through its pages, he immediately begins to gain certain impressions regarding it and regarding the persons responsible for its publication. And these first impressions often are lasting ones.

If the display is quiet and reserved, he classifies the paper as conservative; if the headlines shout their wares in types that are heavy in tone, he forms an entirely different opinion.

Carefully planned makeup, orderliness on editorial and other special pages, attractive advertising, and pleasing design all have a desirable effect. If pages are poorly printed, or if the body-type and headlines are hard to read, he draws conclusions that are not so favorable. Even the texture of the paper, which may stand up crisply, or fall limply in his hands, helps to shape this new reader's likes and dislikes. Another consideration that enters sharply into his reactions is the similarity of this newspaper to others with which he is familiar.

Alert makeup editors and others responsible for the design of a newspaper know these things. They also are aware that a sudden change from one style of makeup to another style strikingly different, even though the new methods are based upon sound principles of design, might be resented seriously by readers who have been accustomed to practices followed for many years. Habits of long-standing are not easily broken.

Many readers of the *Kansas City Star,* famous for its quiet, conservative makeup and display, undoubtedly would raise their voices in protest if that paper should change overnight to the style of makeup followed by the *Chicago Herald-American* or the *New York Herald Tribune.* On the other hand, readers of these papers in Chicago and New York probably would find the design and makeup of the *Kansas City Star* stodgy and uninteresting.

However, editors in many communities could greatly enhance the appearance and readability of their newspapers by redesigning their headline schedules. In some instances, only a few changes would be necessary to attain the high standards of typographical excellence to which readers are entitled; in others, a complete replacement of type faces and headline styles might be required.

A plan followed successfully by several editors who decided on the latter plan has been that of preparing readers ahead of time by telling them about the proposed changes and the benefits they could expect as a result. By selling them on the idea that the paper would be more legible and more attractive with the new headline schedule, they found that there was little resistance and that readers soon got accustomed to the new typographical dress.

Effects of Editorial Policy

Although the actual work of setting the type and assembling it into forms is done in the composing room, the editorial department is responsible for preparing the copy and for determining the style of makeup.

On weeklies and small dailies, the planning of pages generally is supervised by the editor himself, who frequently leaves up to the printer the actual placement of all except the more important stories. The number of stories is small and the problems involved in fitting type into only a few pages are simple.

Problems increase in complexity as the size of the paper grows, and the editor must delegate responsibility for page planning to one or more members of the staff on the larger dailies. Sometimes the city editor, the telegraph editor, or the news editor is given the assignment as a part of his regular work, but on the larger dailies, the man selected has to devote all his time to direction of the work. He is given the title of *makeup editor* or *news editor*.

The makeup editor has an important position on any newspaper. His duties include not only the planning of every page in the paper but also the supervision of the placement of type in the page forms by the makeup men in the composing room. The makeup editor is called upon to coordinate the ideas and activities of every department in building pages that will be acceptable and attractive.

On most newspapers, he is given considerable freedom; on others, he is forced to follow a standard pattern that can vary little from day to day. Editorial policies often have a strong influence on certain phases of design and makeup, and the makeup editor himself may have some part in shaping them.

Some editors require that a large banner headline be run in every issue, regardless of the importance of the news it accompanies; that the number of stories on the front page must never exceed—or, perhaps, fall below—a certain limit; and that only a specified number of stories can be allowed to break over to other pages.

Figure 113. Front page of the *Christian Science Monitor*. This newspaper won Second Honorable Mention in the Sixteenth Annual Exhibition of Newspaper Typography, conducted by N. W. Ayer & Son, Inc. It now follows the "no-break" principle, which calls for jumping no stories to inside pages.

Again, the editors may demand that no stories be continued to other pages. Several newspapers are following this plan, including the *Christian Science Monitor,* which is one of the most recent to adopt a "no-break" front page.

There are several arguments in favor of this treatment. In the first place, completion of all stories on page one makes it unnecessary for the reader to have to turn inside in order to complete them. Furthermore, the practice forces reporters to condense their stories, including only the most important facts.

On the other hand, those who oppose the new trend contend that many readers want much more detail than can be included in the briefer accounts and do not object to having to turn to the inside for more complete information. By placing "jumped" stories on regular pages every day inside the paper and by using simplified, readable jump heads, they believe the situation is solved more adequately, since more of the important stories can be brought to the reader's attention on the front page where adequate display is the most effective.

One method followed by some newspapers in handling extremely long stories is that of employing the "flipped" story technique. Under this plan, the story running the full length of the column is placed in column eight, on the right-hand side of page one, and is continued—or "flipped"—to the first, or left-hand, column on the second page. This arrangement avoids the necessity of having to use a jump head, but it also reduces makeup possibilities on both page one and page two, and frequently when the page is turned, light coming through the newsprint reduces legibility.

The use of pictures or cartoons frequently is controlled by editorial edicts, which sometimes call for illustrations above the fold only; or they may ask that illustrations be used both top and bottom for purposes of balance and to add liveliness to the page. The maximum or minimum size and number of pictures to be employed likewise may be specified.

Many papers contain one or more special columns on the front page, and a few regularly place the leading editorial of the day on this page. Other editorial "musts" may include: summaries, bulletins, indices to direct readers to material on the inside of the paper, and promotional material (often in boxed form). The makeup editor must be thoroughly acquainted with the editorial policies affecting his work, since they frequently figure prominently in the kind of design he will be able to plan.

The number of rules set down for the makeup editor to follow should be held to a minimum.   The more freedom he is allowed to exercise, the more the newspapers and readers stand to benefit from his ingenuity and skill.

Mechanical Limitations

In addition to restrictions resulting from editorial policies, several mechanical limitations also must be considered.   The most important of these are the size of the page, the number of columns to the page, and the margins allowed.

As already pointed out, the majority of daily newspapers in this country have adopted pages that are eight columns in width, with 12 picas as the standard column-width.   Many weeklies also have changed to a column of this width, and most large national advertisers, using both daily and weekly newspapers, plan their advertising on this basis.

The reduction to this narrow measure has necessitated a reappraisal of body-type and the manufacture of new faces designed especially for maximum legibility in slightly smaller sizes.

The fact that column-widths in general are uniform does not mean that all page-sizes are likewise standard.   On the contrary, considerable variation exists.   About the only regular feature is that all newspaper pages are rectangular in shape, and longer than they are wide. To be in keeping with the principles governing pleasing proportion, a page should be about one-third longer than it is wide.

Margins also have much to do with the resulting design.   Here again, there is no uniformity.   Exceptionally wide margins which would require increasing pages to a size that would be awkward to handle are not advisable; and, on the other hand, too great a reduction in margin-width does not permit enough "breathing space," causing the page to appear cramped and overcrowded.

John E. Allen, former editor of the *Linotype News,* had this to recommend:[3]

. . . Newspaper pages with side margins much more than 4 picas wide, top margins much more than 4 picas deep, and bottom margins much more than 5 picas deep, suggest carelessness, rather than artistry.

During World War II, page-sizes were trimmed by newspapers in order to stretch newsprint allotments as far as possible; consequently, a series of reductions in the width of margins resulted.

---

[3] John E. Allen, *Newspaper Makeup,* page 28.   New York: Harper & Brothers, 1936.

Newspaper Personality

The front page of a newspaper frequently is referred to as the "show window." It is the one the reader sees first, and consequently the editor who disregards this fact would be forfeiting his best opportunity to build confidence and readership.

Here he has a chance to display the most important stories and pictures of the day and to set the stage for the rest of the paper typographically. The treatment used on the front page will have much to do with influencing a reader to turn to the inside, and careful attention should be given to building a design that is both pleasing and interesting.

The first requirement is that all elements going to make up the page should harmonize and be placed in proper relationship with one another, as well as with the news they accompany. Although headlines form the major part of the front-page design, several other significant elements also are included. The appropriateness of each of these elements should be determined, since their combinations into a unified pattern are what establishes a newspaper's character and personality.

Nameplate and Ears

One of the typographical units on the front page that has persisted from the time of the earliest newspapers is the *nameplate,* so called because it gives the name of the publication and usually is printed from a durable metal plate.

The nameplate serves much the same purpose as the title printed on the cover of a book or at the beginning of an article: it identifies the newspaper and gives some significant facts about the publication.

Many newspapers include small masses of type, or illustrations, on each side, or sometimes on only one side, of the title to give additional facts about the paper or the news it contains. At other times, such devices are used strictly for decorative purposes. They are known as *ears.*

Our earliest colonial newspapers ran nameplates either in Roman capitals or capitals and lower-case, usually in the same style of type as that used for the body-matter. Some of them made use of small illustrations printed from wood cuts to add more variety.

Growing competition led many influential newspapers in the 1670's to change from Roman to Old English (or Text), which at that time was the boldest variety of type available in many offices.[4] However, after

---

[4] Allen, *Newspaper Makeup,* page 83.

using this style of type for several years, some editors shifted back to Roman.

The types employed by colonial editors were imported originally from England, and the nameplates produced with them necessarily bore close resemblances to those employed on newspapers published in the British Isles. The basic pattern established at that time has been followed with some variations ever since. The main changes have been in the size and structure of ears, and in the use by some editors of more modern types as they made their appearance.

In some newspapers, where one or more columns run high at the side, the nameplate is designed so that it will take up the remaining space across the top of the paper, which may be seven columns or less, depending upon the style followed. This practice is of rather recent origin and is not very widespread.

Once a certain style of nameplate has been adopted, an editor is very reluctant to change to another, since readers over the years learn to regard it as the paper's trademark and often look for it first when buying from the news-stand. Thus, it becomes a symbol of identification and often is a newspaper's best selling agent.

The influence of tradition on the nameplate in American newspapers has been very strong. Many of our oldest publications have not changed the style used since their origin several decades ago. This practice has proved very desirable where headline types and other typographical elements on the page have been chosen with close attention to matters of type harmony and design. However, the retention of outdated headlines and headline forms merely to justify continued use of a traditional style of nameplate is an unsound policy.

One of the main prerequisites is that the type used in the nameplate should be strong and dignified, since it announces the name of the newspaper to all who will observe. Its voice should be firm and confident if it is to command due respect and represent the owners and staff in a suitable manner. No note of apology or weakness should be apparent in the approach. Consequently, Italic and Script types, which are the weakest styles of all, should be used with extreme caution. A certain amount of strength can be obtained by employing the bolder versions of these types, but their use sometimes results in effects that appear forced and out of place. Romans (both Oldstyle and Modern), Gothics, and Texts are much better adapted to the purpose. Hand-tooled versions sometimes are employed to add variety, and often the type used is designed especially for a newspaper.

Another requirement is that the type in the nameplate should harmonize with that used elsewhere in the head-dress. Here, as in the headline schedule, the rules of typographic harmony must be applied for pleasing results.

The simplest and the quietest harmony is obtained by using the same style of type in the nameplate as that employed in the headline schedule. Such use results in monotypographic harmony. Among the many newspapers following this plan is the *Rutland Daily Herald,* which uses Garamond Bold exclusively for display purposes in its make-up. To add variety, a cut also is employed.

Adjacent harmony can be obtained by selecting a type for the nameplate that is closely related in design to that in the headline schedule. The *Milwaukee Journal,* using Century Bold in its nameplate along with Cheltenham in the headlines, is a good example.

When the headline schedule is entirely in Gothic, pleasing effects can be had by using Roman type in the nameplate. For instance, the

A   B

Figure 114. (A) The *Rutland* (Vermont) *Daily Herald,* which employs Garamond in its nameplate and throughout its headline schedule, won Third Honorable Mention in the Sixteenth Annual Exhibition of Newspaper Typography, conducted by N. W. Ayer & Son, Inc. Although the display is quiet in tone, it has a clean, dignified, attractive appearance. (B) Winner of the F. Wayland Ayer Cup in the Sixteenth Annual Exhibition of Newspaper Typography for its excellent typography, the *Rochester* (Minnesota) *Post-Bulletin* creates a pleasing effect on the front page by using Caslon Bold in the nameplate, along with a head-dress in Gothic faces. The *Post-Bulletin* also won first place in its class in the Seventh Annual Typography Contest of the Inland Daily Press Association.

Rochester Post-Bulletin has selected Caslon Bold as a companion for the Gothic faces in the headline schedule. Even greater contrast would result from using a bold Text type in the nameplate, and Gothics for the headlines.

The greatest contrast can be afforded by choosing a type for the nameplate that is widely different in design from the headline types. More newspapers employ complementary harmony of this kind than either of the other styles mentioned.

A large number of newspapers, like the *New York Times,* the *Chi-*

Figure 115. Each of the newspapers represented here used good judgment in selecting type for the nameplate that harmonizes pleasingly with the headdress.

cago Daily Tribune, and the *New York Herald Tribune,* use a bold Text type along with contrasting faces in the headline schedule. Others prefer a hand-tooled Text type, such as that employed by the *Salt Lake Tribune* and the *Oregonian,* which somewhat reduces the heaviness of tone but adds variety.

If the most satisfactory results are to be obtained, the type used in the ears, as well as that used in the headlines, also must harmonize with that in the nameplate. Furthermore, the ears should not be so large and bold that they detract from the title itself, which is the most important part of the design.

When ears are boxed, the rules or borders employed should be in conformity with the type-design. For instance, Gothic type in an ear would call for a plain, single-line border, the weight of which should be determined by the tone of the type mass it surrounds and the over-all tone of the nameplate; whereas a more decorative border might be used with Roman type, with the degree of variation depending upon the style of type it accompanies. If illustrations are included in the nameplate, they should be of a tone and size that are in harmony with the rest of the design. No element included should be allowed to outshout the title if a harmonious effect is to be maintained.

Since the nameplate and ears are printed regularly, day after day, they should be replaced before they are worn so badly that they are battered and broken. Otherwise, the printing in this important place on the page will appear ragged and ill-kept, instead of bright and clear-cut.

The Date-Line

In addition to the nameplate and the headlines, several other elements must come under close scrutiny. One of these is the type-line placed directly under the nameplate, containing information such as the volume number, place and date of publication, edition, and sales price, which is known as the *date-line.*

Since this element is a definite part of the head-dress of the newspaper, the most desirable plan is to set the main line of the date-line in a face from the same type family or from one of the families used in the headline schedule.

The sizes used most commonly range from 10-point up to 14-point, depending upon the style of type selected. The use of types larger than these usually is not advisable, because they would require more space than is necessary and would give more prominence than is warranted.

Although rules were not used in some of our earliest publications, the practice of placing one above and another below the date-line finally was begun.   Today most newspapers in the country use such rules.

For many years light, parallel rules were used to add interest to pages that usually contained few, if any, display lines to break up the grayness of tone.   However, when attention was turned to heavier headlines and more contrast in makeup, the parallel rules were replaced by other styles that were more fitting for use with the changing styles.

Many present-day newspapers use single one- or two-point rules. These rules are exceptionally well adapted for use with type in which there is little contrast between light and heavy elements, and, because of their simplicity, they can also be used appropriately with types containing considerable variations.   Gothic faces demand these simple rules, and Modern Romans also harmonize satisfactorily with the single-line rule.

Another common style is the oxford rule.   When this is employed, it should be of a weight that conforms in tone to the strokes of the type it surrounds.   It is best adapted to type faces in which considerable contrast exists between elements.

The oxford rule is a desirable choice for use with Modern Romans, such as Bodoni; with Mixed Romans, such as Century and Cheltenham; and with several of the Oldstyle Romans.   It is more appropriate on pages which use the drop-line and inverted-pyramid headline forms.   Such pages contain considerably more variety than where the simple, modern, flush-left forms are used.   Selections should be governed by the style of type these rules accompany in the date-line and head-dress, and also by the general headline forms employed.

The amount and distribution of white space between rules and the type-line which they surround have much to do with the attractiveness of the date-line.   To be correct, the type should appear to be centered between the rules, an arrangement which calls for slightly more leading above than below the line because of the white space provided by the shoulder of the type.   An allowance of approximately four points of space above and below, including the shoulder, usually results in a pleasing appearance.

When oxford rules are used, the heavy line of the upper rule should be at the top, and it should be at the bottom on the lower one, so that the design will be symmetrical.

Rules that are too heavy or too light in color for the type they accompany result in elements that are not in keeping with the principles of good design and create an unpleasant area on the page.

BODY-TYPE

From the standpoint of readability, as well as that of creating pleasing page-designs, the body-type which usually makes up the major part of the page must be legible and inviting to the reader.

The width of the column places limitations on the style of type selected. Of necessity, it must be small in order to allow sufficient words, with proper spacing between them, in a line. Letters must fit closely together and yet be open enough in design to be easily read, and sturdy enough to withstand the terrific pressure of stereotyping.

The character of the type, its size, and the amount of leading (pronounced "ledding") between lines are what determine the tone and readability of these important masses. The type used in one-column measures should be adaptable to the longer measures that are called for throughout the paper.

Although the size of body-type used by newspapers varies, the tendency of dailies is to set their news matter in 7-, $7\frac{1}{2}$-, and 8-point faces, with the amount of leading ranging from $\frac{1}{2}$ point to 2 points.

Several important studies have been made on the readability of body-types for newspapers. One of the most recent was an investigation conducted by Miles A. Tinker and Donald G. Patterson. Their purpose was to determine the effects of varying line-widths and leading upon the readability of 8-point newspaper type.

In a survey of printing practices for newspaper body-type, they found that Excelsior was more than holding its own over a period of years; that the use of 8-point type was rapidly increasing; that a 12-pica line-width was almost universal on front pages of newspapers, although line-widths up to $25\frac{1}{2}$-picas were employed on editorial pages; and that set solid, $\frac{1}{2}$-point, 1-point, and 2-point leading were the most common.[5]

The results of their study revealed that leading had no effect on readability when 8-point type was set in a 12-pica line; that leading had no consistent effect on lines set 24 picas wide, although such a width was read more slowly than the standard; that 2-point leading improved the readability of material set in a 30- and 36-pica line; and that even with 2-point leading the text was read no faster than standard. An 18-pica line-width with 1- or 2-point leading was found to produce the most readable text.

---

[5] Miles A. Tinker and Donald G. Patterson, "Effect of Line Width and Leading on Readability of Newspaper Type," *Journalism Quarterly*, 23:3 (September, 1946), 307.

The data collected in this study indicated that textual materials with a rather wide range of line-widths and leading were equally legible. It was pointed out that readers judged text with the larger amounts of leading to be more pleasing for each length of line considered. Consequently, it was recommended that when a 12-pica line-width is used for 8-point type, 1 or 2 points of leading should be used, even though the leading does not increase readability, if reader opinions are considered important.

These findings were extremely significant, coming at a time when many newspapers were debating whether to return to more leading between lines after having reduced it to save space during World War II.

THE COLUMN-RULE

The thin line used between columns on the page is known as a *column-rule*. Before World War II, practically every newspaper printed in this country made use of a hairline rule, centered on a 6-point body, and a majority of present-day newspapers still employ this style.

However, in order to cut down on the width of the sheet and thereby make a saving in newsprint, many newspapers during World War II commenced casting column-rules on a body narrower than 6 points. In doing so, they reduced the amount of white space provided by the shoulder between type and rule, causing the page to appear more crowded and reducing legibility.

The amount of white space allowed by the beveled shoulder of the column rule cast on a 6-point body is not too generous. In fact, slightly more white space would reduce the tendency of the eye to move from one column over into the adjoining one, and at the same time would let more light into the over-all design. Both of these results would be desirable.

When the column-rules are pieced together to provide desired lengths, care should be taken to see that no white breaks or gaps are left, and battered and nicked rules should be discarded. Although these faults cannot always be entirely avoided in the rush of meeting frequent deadlines, they should be held to a minimum.

A small number of newspapers, including the *Cincinnati Enquirer* and the *Gazette and Daily*, of York, Pennsylvania, make use of white space between columns instead of the column-rule. Enough space must be employed in this practice to separate the columns of type adequately, or readability will be impaired. An allowance of only 6 points is not sufficient; a minimum of 12 points of white space is necessary, and 18 points would be still better from the standpoint of legibility and page-design.

Since the front page more or less establishes the pattern for the rest of the paper, the style followed there should be carried out through a majority of the pages in order to provide uniformity. Too many separate page-designs prevent the orderliness that readers expect and lead to a feeling of confusion. However, a different kind of treatment might well be adopted for the editorial page, the woman's page, and for other special pages where the news carried adapts itself to a more tailor-made design.

Figure 116. The *Cincinnati Enquirer* uses white space instead of column rules on its front page. It also adds variety by running column two wide.

THE CUT-OFF RULE

Another kind of rule used by most newspapers is the *cut-off rule*. The most common and the most adaptable type is the light, single-line rule. However, several other varieties are employed, including the wavy rule, the parallel rule, and the oxford rule.

Cut-off rules are used to separate (or cut off) units which go to make up the over-all design. They are employed below headlines of more than one column in width to separate the heads from other reading matter that is not related to them and to help direct the reader to the column, or columns, into which the headlines "read out"; to even off the bottoms of stories printed in two or more adjoining columns that are followed by other stories; to separate advertisements from one another and from reading matter that may come above or below the ads; above continued lines; under jump heads; to separate elements in a headline; and sometimes to separate single-column stories from headlines of the same measure that appear underneath.

Since the cut-off rule extends all the way across a column, or columns, and is intended to slow down or stop the reader rather than carry his attention on, it should be used only in those places where clear-cut sep-

aration of one unit from another is needed.   Furthermore, the style of
the cut-off rules selected should conform in design with the types they
accompany.

The weight of the cut-off rule should be determined largely by the
manner in which it is to be used.   For ordinary purposes, the single
rule should be light in weight—either 1 point or hairline face—but single lines coming below heavy banners or spreads ordinarily need to be
of 2 or even 3 points in order to harmonize properly with these darker
elements.

Tone harmony also must be considered carefully when styles other
than the single-line variety are used.   In the case of oxford rules and
parallel rules, the problem is somewhat more complicated, since these
designs are inherently heavier than the single-line and contain more
variations.

If consistency is to be maintained, only one style should be used
throughout the paper.   The mixture of single-line, oxford rule, parallel
rule, and wavy-line varieties—or a combination of these designs—
should be avoided, except in cases where special effects are desired on
the page.

Small ornaments sometimes are used to join column-rules and cut-
off rules where they come together, in order to provide a more finished
and decorative appearance.   However, the trend in recent years has
been away from this practice.   In the first place, more time is required
of the makeup man who has to match and fit the rules together on the
page.   Furthermore, the modern treatment permits much more freedom in such matters than the more formal styles of makeup which were
in vogue several years ago.   The percentage of newspapers outstanding
for typographical excellence which today make use of these devices is
very small.

The most popular style employed by newspapers that still follow this
practice is the simple diamond-shaped ornament: an outlined diamond
for newspapers with medium- or light-toned head-dress, and a black
diamond for those of heavier tone.   Here again, the kind of ornament
chosen should be in harmony with the style and weight of type in the
headline schedule.

"30" Dashes and Jim Dashes

There are two kinds of dashes in common use: the *"30,"* or *finish,
dash;* and the *jim dash.*

Several kinds of "30" dashes are available, but the plain, single-line
variety is the most popular and the safest to use.   The more ornamen-

tal dashes can be employed if they harmonize in design with the type faces they accompany, but they never should be so unusual that they attract undue attention. Whatever style is used, it should be of a weight that conforms with the weight of the types.

For use in 12-, 12½- or 13-pica columns, the "30" dash should not run much more than 8 picas wide or much less than 7 picas. About the same proportions of the measure should be taken up with the dash in columns wider than 13 picas, but less than two regular columns in width. When employed in columns wider than two columns, the dash should be somewhat less than two-thirds of the column so that it will not be too pronounced in tone.[6]

The jim dash is a short line used to separate decks in a headline, to set off a headline from the story, and to separate items within a story or special column.

Several kinds of jim dashes, including both ornamental and plain varieties, are available, but the plain, single-line dash is the simplest and safest. Like the "30" dash, the jim dash should harmonize both in weight and design with the types. Since it is used to separate units or items rather than to indicate the end of an article, it should be surrounded, above and below, by equal amounts of white space.

If jim dashes for use in regular columns are less than 5 picas in width, they are not effective; and if they are wider than 5 picas, they may be mistaken for "30" dashes.

Two Firemen Smoke Victims

$2,500 Blaze Destroys Attic; Tenants Escape, but Tardily

Two firemen were overcome by smoke early Monday in a fire which destroyed the attic of a two story frame house at 1721-23 N. 4th st. The firemen, William Horsch, 28, of 613 N. 31st st., and George Janczewski, 29, of 1508 S. 6th st., were in good condition in the county emergency hospital. Both are members of hook and ladder company No. 2.

Mrs. Ernest Matthews, one of the five Negroes living in the upper flat, first learned of the fire when an unidentified man rapped at her door and said, "Your house is burning, ma'am." She said she thought he was joking and refused to believe him. After he left, she went to Mrs. Robert Jones, also living in the upper section of the flat, and told her about the caller.

"He was fooling you," Mrs. Jones said, as the fire engines stopped in front of the house. The women escaped without injury.

The fire of undetermined origin was confined mostly to the attic. Firemen fought the blaze for more than an hour. Damage was estimated at $2,500.

Figure 117. The two decks in the headline over this story are separated by a jim dash. A finish, or "30," dash is used at the end to indicate that the story is finished and to separate it from the headline that would appear underneath.

---

[6] Allen, *Newspaper Makeup*, page 105.

For use in columns over 13 picas, but less than two columns in width, the jim dash should be about one-third the width of the column; but in columns wider than two regular columns, it should be slightly less than one-third the width of the wider column.[7]

Between decks of a headline, the amount of leading used around the first dash should be followed throughout the rest of the headline to insure uniformity and attractiveness. Although some newspapers still use the jim dash to separate decks, especially in multiple-deck headlines, the practice is being discontinued by many others, which are making use of white space instead.

Use of Boxes

Although boxes are not used so widely as they were several years ago, many newspapers still employ them for purposes of display. Since rules or borders around a mass of type serve as a frame to set it off as a separate typographical unit on the page, a boxed element usually has high attention value.

The earlier practice of using very decorative and unusual borders, including stars, dashes, flowered effects, dots, and other highly ornamental devices, has been displaced, for the most part, with designs that are much saner. The plain, single-line rule, in either 1 point or 2 points, is the most widely used today. However, the oxford rule and parallel rule are employed by many newspapers, and a few still employ more decorative designs.

Whatever kind of border or rule is selected, it should harmonize with the types, and the same style should be used throughout the paper in order to maintain uniformity. Too many designs, even though they are harmonious, lead to confusion.

The placing of a headline over reading matter inside the box is advisable, and the headline styles employed naturally should conform with those used elsewhere in the head-dress. Judicious use of white space inside the borders also is necessary. Approximately 6 points of space should be allowed on each side, and enough at the top and bottom to afford pleasing balance within the frame. White space likewise should be provided between the headline and the reading matter, and the body-type itself should have enough leading to avoid a crowded appearance. For most pleasing results, boxes should conform in shape with the page: that is, they should be longer than they are wide.

Poorly joined corners are an indication of careless workmanship. Borders for use in boxes should be properly mitered, if mitering is

---

[7] Allen, *Newspaper Makeup,* page 107.

necessary to make them fit together, and they should be checked to see that they "pull" together before they are locked in the page.

The modern trend is away from complete boxes and toward rules or borders just at the top and bottom of the type mass. The boxed effect is obtained by setting the type from 12 to 18 points narrower than the column-width, which permits a good distribution of white space at the sides. Headlines should be set the same measure as the body-matter, or centered in this measure, in order to preserve uniformity. The simplest treatment, and a very satisfactory one, is to let the column-rules serve as the side rules, with a plain-line rule placed across the column at top and bottom.

Boxes and boxed effects are used for a variety of purposes. Prin-

Contest Winners Now on Display

Winning newspapers in the 8th annual Typography Contest of Inland Daily Press Association now are being displayed on the main floor corridor of Fayerweather Hall.

Awards were made at the February meeting by the Northwestern chapter of Sigma Delta Chi, national professional journalism fraternity which sponsors the contest each year.

One hundred twenty-five newspapers throughout the mid-west, representing over one-fourth of the Inland membership, participated this year. Entrants were divided into five classes, according to circulation, and five awards were given in each class.

Anyone interested in studying examples of newspaper design and makeup of a high order is invited to this exhibit.

Contest Winners Now on Display

Winning newspapers in the 8th annual Typography Contest of Inland Daily Press Association now are being displayed on the main floor corridor of Fayerweather Hall.

Awards were made at the February meeting by the Northwestern chapter of Sigma Delta Chi, national professional journalism fraternity, which sponsors the contest each year.

One hundred twenty-five newspapers throughout the mid-west, representing over one-fourth of the Inland membership participated this year. Entrants were divided into five classes, according to circulation, and first, second, third, and two honorable mentions were awarded in each of these classes.

Anyone interested in studying examples of newspaper design and makeup of a high order is invited to see this exhibit.

Figure 118. Oxford rule has been used for a border in the boxed story on the left. This harmonizes well with the Bodoni Bold type of the headline. The 2-point border used in the boxed story at the right also is in good taste, since it is plain like the Gothic type in the headline and of approximately the same weight.

cipally, they are employed to give special display to unusual stories, news summaries, bulletins, indices, weather reports, and special inserts within longer stories which present late developments or additional sidelights.

For the most part, boxes and boxed effects should be used sparingly, since each represents an individualized unit in itself. Too many of them cause the page to appear spotted and "over-done."

By-Line and Credit-Line

Most newspapers give the name of the writer in a special line over some of the more important stories of the day. This line is known as a *by-line*.

BILL TO SET UP LABOR COURTS FILED IN SENATE

BY PHILIP DODD
[Chicago Tribune Press Service]
Washington, D. C., March 19—
Legislation which would set up a special court system to settle labor disputes and interpret existing labor laws was introduced in the senate

Figure 119. The by-line over this story is set in all-caps, with the credit-line set smaller, below it, in bold caps and lower-case.

Also, it is customary to print the name of the service or organization furnishing certain stories or pictures not produced by members of the newspaper's own staff. In some cases, certain departments or individuals working on the newspaper are credited in this manner for the work they do. The lines of type used for this purpose are referred to as *credit-lines*.

By-lines ordinarily are set in the same type face as that used for the body-matter, or in one that harmonizes closely. Boldface capitals in the same point size or boldface capitals and lower-case in a slightly larger size also are used widely. Some newspapers using Roman body-type set these lines in Gothic to obtain complementary harmony.

The credit-line follows the by-line when the two are used together over a story. The credit-line usually is set in somewhat smaller type than the body-type and often is in Italics to provide contrast with the type used in the by-line. Neither of these two special lines should be so large and bold that it detracts the attention of the reader from the story.

Initial Letters

Some newspapers make use of initial letters at the beginnings of groups of text matter in an effort to dress up an article or a page. The-

oretically, the purpose of the initial is to call attention to where the
reading matter begins, and the practice of using a series of them—one
every few paragraphs—down a column is fundamentally wrong.

Fitness implies a consistency between the initial and text matter.
The letter selected should be in harmony with the body-type both in design and in weight.   It should appear to have been made for the particular style of lettering in the type it accompanies.   Thus, monotypographic facial harmony is highly desirable.

As the initial is the first letter of the first word in a paragraph, uniformity can be preserved by setting the rest of the letters of the word
in capitals.   This scheme serves to tie in the initial with the body-type.
When the first word consists of only two or three letters, the second
word also should be set in capitals, as shown in the following example:

> IN HIS radio interview reporting on the Paris
> conference, Senator VANDENBURG pointed to the
> fact that the five treaties dealt with there were only
> on the rim of the problem of the peace.   "The Ger-
> man and Austrian treaties," he said, "will be the
> key to postwar Europe."

The initial should align with the text, both at the top and bottom, and
the amounts of white space between it and the type at the sides and
bottom should appear to be equal.

Because of the problems involved in setting and handling initials,
most newspapers never use them.   Another well-founded reason for
their unpopularity is the belief that they cause the areas in which they
are employed to appear spotted.   They are better adapted to special
inside pages where a more bookish or tailored effect is desired than to
the front page.

COMING OF PICTURES

Editors of our earliest newspapers did not have to concern themselves
with the fitting of pictures into their patterns of makeup and design.
In the beginning, pictures were incidental.   First illustrations to appear had no connection with the news.   They came first in advertisements, and publishers used the first thumb nail cuts reluctantly.

During the Revolutionary War, political cartoons were employed
voluntarily by a few editors.   At no time, however, even during that
stormy period, were pictures used in large numbers; and shortly after
the conflict, illustrations practically vanished for a while.

They were revived again by the penny papers, some of which used them quite freely; and during the Civil War, a few of the larger papers made laudable attempts to furnish pictures to their readers. However, the number employed by newspapers in general until near the end of the nineteenth century was very meager in comparison with the number used in present-day pictorial journalism.

The real birth of pictorial journalism as we know it today came with the invention of the halftone in the 1880's and its adaptation to the curved stereotype plates on fast rotary presses. The first halftone ever to be printed in a newspaper on a web-perfecting press employing stereotype plates appeared in the *New York Tribune* on January 21, 1897.[8] It was the reproduction of a portrait of Senator Thomas C. Platt, of New York, and was prepared by Stephen H. Horgan, who invented the initial halftone that had appeared in the *New York Daily Graphic* seventeen years earlier.

Although lacking the refinements of present-day photo-engravings, these early efforts set the stage for more generous use of illustrations by newspapers. Pulitzer and Hearst demonstrated the pulling power of pictures in their newspapers during the period of "yellow journalism." Shortly after Pulitzer's *New York World* began using them during the 1890's, the managing editor remarked that the circulation had commenced rising like "a thermometer on a hot summer day." Nevertheless, most editors did not share his enthusiasm, and the acceptance of pictures in any great quantities by newspapers was slow.

However, illustrations gradually found their way into more and more newspapers as World War I approached, and before hostilities had ceased, many editors had become convinced that pictures in the news were here to stay. Then, in 1919, America's first tabloid—the *New York Daily News*—made its appearance, exemplifying the faith its publishers placed in pictured news. Growing circulation figures from the start indicated the wisdom of their decision to tell the news of the day by means of pictures as well as by the printed word.

Although not so prosperous as their mighty rival, the *New York Daily Mirror* and several other tabloids soon were established. Operating on the theory that pictures tell a story just as adequately, or more so, than an equal amount of text, these smaller picture papers set a new style in American journalism. Their success has been dependent upon generous use of illustrations.

Tabloids led to a growing consciousness of pictures on the part of editors. This was strengthened still further by the introduction of

---

[8] Allen, *Newspaper Makeup*, page 158.

Wirephoto in 1935, which opened the way for the use of spot pictures alongside spot news coming from distant places. The cinema and picture magazines also had pronounced effects on the use of pictures by newspapers.

In contrast to the occasional cuts in early publications, hundreds of pictures surge over the desks in metropolitan newspaper offices every day, and even the smaller papers are furnished a good supply from which to choose.

For many years, only the wealthy newspapers in large cities were able to afford the equipment and staff necessary for picture coverage. However, as engraving and photographic techniques improved, and operating costs were reduced, more and more editors began to use pictures. An aid to the smaller newspapers was the introduction of the one-man engraving plant. This unit was within the reach of many papers that formerly were not financially able to compete with the larger papers. Leading schools of journalism have established courses in photography and picture editing in order to provide training in this important phase of journalism.

Many reader-interest studies have demonstrated the soundness of picturing the news. In addition to much research in this field carried on by individual newspapers, several organizations have conducted significant surveys. A summary of the first twenty-four studies in the *Continuing Study of Newspaper Reading,* sponsored by the American Newspaper Publishers Association, included much valuable information.

For instance, it was shown that the most-read news picture, exclusive of the picture page, was seen by a median of 87 per cent of the men and 90 per cent of the women; whereas only 65 per cent men and 63 per cent women read the best-read news story, and 58 per cent men and 32 per cent women read the story accompanying the banner headline on the same day. The picture page itself drew an even higher percentage of attention from both men and women.[9]

Pictures cannot be handled in exactly the same way as news stories, since each of them is a distinct unit and must be treated in such a way that it blends harmoniously into the over-all design of the page. At the same time, the size and importance of a picture have much to do with its placement on the page as well as with the nature of the typographical elements which accompany it.

[9] Norman J. Radder and John E. Stempel, *Newspaper Editing, Make-up and Headlines,* page 348. New York: McGraw-Hill Book Company, Inc., 1942.

Makeup with Pictures

Theoretically, the amount of space given over to a picture should be determined by weighing its news value against that of a written story which might occupy the same area on the page.   Naturally, the human element enters strongly into the decisions made, and the play given to the same picture received on any day will vary widely from one newspaper to another.

Few newspapers follow a set policy as to the number of pictures to be presented on the front page.   The number is regulated by the importance of the illustrations available on a given day and their significance in the news.

Except on those days when pictures are exceptionally newsworthy, many newspapers, such as the *New York Herald Tribune,* follow the practice of running only one picture at the top of the front page next to the outside column.   It usually ranges in size from one column to as many as four columns wide, depending upon its importance in the news, and it is tied in with the main story of the day.   (See Figure 129.)

The *Kansas City Star,* a newspaper which was extremely reluctant in adopting front-page picture display, places a good-sized picture in the center at the top of the page when only one illustration is employed. Another plan calls for the placement of a two- or three-column picture at the top of the page and a one-column cut next to the outside column at the bottom, for purposes of balance.   These illustrations assist greatly in brightening up a page that otherwise is very gray typographically.

When picture usage is restricted to the top half of the page, as in many newspapers, some good two-column news or feature headlines are needed at the bottom to keep the page symmetrical; otherwise, the page looks top-heavy and badly out of proportion.

A more desirable plan is to use pictures in both the top and bottom areas of the page, since both need brightening.   The placement of illustrations in only one of the areas usually causes the other to appear drab and uninteresting by comparison.

Another group of papers, of which the *Des Moines Register-Tribune* is a good example, follows a very flexible policy in front-page makeup in which pictures play an extremely important part.   As a general rule, several illustrations are used in every issue, and when the news is "big" or unusual, the amount of space devoted to pictures may reach, or even exceed, 50 per cent of the printed page.   The *Register-Tribune* also

makes frequent use of an arrow to direct the reader's attention from the
text to the picture accompanying it. The same device is employed by
a number of other newspapers.

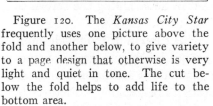

Figure 120. The *Kansas City Star*
frequently uses one picture above the
fold and another below, to give variety
to a page design that otherwise is very
light and quiet in tone. The cut below the fold helps to add life to the
bottom area.

Figure 121. The front page of the
Des Moines Tribune usually carries several pictures, some of which frequently
are very large. An arrow often is used,
as on this page, to direct the reader's
attention to the picture relating to a
given news story.

This plan of using pictures above and below the fold is observed by
a growing number of newspapers. For instance, the *Louisville Courier-
Journal* follows quite a consistent pattern which calls for one large cut
at the upper left-hand side of the page, and another—generally somewhat smaller—at the bottom in the center or shifted to the right-hand
side, depending upon the size and placement of other elements on the
page. (See Figure 128.)

Although many newspapers try to follow a regular pattern, most of
them allow enough latitude to take care of the more important news
breaks. Consequently, it would be impossible to classify the styles followed into any well-defined categories. The makeup on practically all
newspapers using pictures on their front pages varies slightly from day
to day.

Rules to Observe

Picture editors will agree that the attention-value of a picture generally is directly dependent upon its size. The larger the picture, the more readers it is likely to stop. On the other hand, its ability to hold attention and to cause readers to recall what they have seen is regulated by several other factors as well.

The picture must tell its story clearly and quickly. Just as in the news story, the unessential "facts" should be cropped out if it is to accomplish its purpose adequately and efficiently.

The way a picture is printed will have much to do with its effectiveness. The first requirement is that the print from which the halftone is to be made must be clear and sharp, with sufficient contrast to insure that all important detail will be brought out distinctly in the engraving.

The screen used will depend upon the quality of newsprint upon which the picture is to be printed. The most commonly used halftones in present-day newspapers are of 50-, 55-, 60-, and 65-line screens. The relative coarseness of the halftones is unavoidable because of the softness of the paper on which they are reproduced. Some newspapers using paper of better quality make use of an 85-line screen. In every instance, great care should be exercised in determining the screen that will give the best results.

Good presswork is also necessary. Not enough or too much impression, failure to build up cuts to the proper height by means of underlays, flaws in stereotype plates, and insufficient inking or too great a flow of ink are some of the common faults to be avoided. Pictures that are smudgy, too faint, or otherwise poorly reproduced often are more of a detriment than an aid in the production of pleasing pages.

Few pictures are capable of "standing alone." Usually they must be accompanied by explanatory lines if they are to tell their stories most adequately. Even the picture magazines, which in the beginning contained only illustrations, with little, if any, written explanatory matter, have learned this lesson. Today they still are experimenting along with newspapers in an attempt to discover the most effective formula.

Overlines and underlines are used to explain the pictures. The style of type and its arrangement should be planned in such a way that the entire unit—including the picture and the accompanying printed matter—is harmonious and pleasing.

A rule followed by old-time printers required that pictures never should be placed in an outside column on a page, but that at least one column of reading matter should hem them in on the outside. Although this rule has been discarded by most present-day newspapers, it has some definite merit. If the outside edges of a picture have a tendency to fade out or are very light, the rule still would be safe to follow. Cuts used in an outside column always should have good tonal quality around the edges or they should be moved to the inside of the page.

A picture always should be placed next to or near the story which it is to accompany, if there is one. The most common practice is to run the picture at the side of the story or above it. Sometimes it is inserted within the text itself. In no event should it be removed so far that the reader has difficulty in connecting picture and story.

When a picture of a person is printed, it always should be placed so that the person is facing toward the inside of the page or directly forward. If he faces toward the outside, there is a tendency on the part of the reader to be led off the page and away from the story. Also, placement of pictures on the fold should be carefully avoided.

Most pictures appearing in newspapers are one column or more in width. However, the small halftone cut is used to some extent, especially for the purpose of reproducing pictures of people in the news. These are sometimes referred to as "thumb-nail" cuts. They are not so easy to handle as cuts of full-column width, since type lines coming at the sides must be set in shorter measure to provide the "run-around," and run-arounds require more time on the part of the compositor.

For the most satisfactory results, the small cuts are made six picas wide by about nine picas deep. The sides are trimmed flush, with shoulders allowed only at top and bottom for tacking the plate to its base. This kind of cut is sometimes used in feature heads to reproduce the picture of the writer. The thumb-nail cut should be used sparingly. Careful attention must be given to its placement in relation to other accompanying elements, since too many small cuts scattered around the page result in an undesirable spotted effect.

THE EDITORIAL CARTOON

Another kind of illustration sometimes employed on the front page is the editorial cartoon. The *Chicago Daily Tribune,* the *Milwaukee Journal,* and several other important newspapers carry editorial cartoons as a regular daily feature. The cut used by these two newspapers generally is three columns in width, and it always is placed in the center, or near center, at the top of the page. The *Tribune's* cartoon is printed in four colors every day of the week, except Sunday, to increase its attention-value.

Used in this manner, the cartoon becomes an effective editorial device for bringing to the attention of readers, and driving home, opinions regarding important issues of the day. It also is an effective means of adding liveliness to the page.

PLANNING THE FRONT PAGE

The makeup editor, or anyone else having charge of makeup, must be thoroughly acquainted with the tools with which he is to work and with the editorial policies of his newspaper. He also must know what stories and pictures are to be provided for each page.

The method of handling copy and writing headlines is not the same on all newspapers. In some offices, one desk handles all the various kinds of copy that are to appear. Usually the desk itself is semicircular, or "horseshoe," in shape; the chief sits in the interior, which is known as the "slot." On the outside "rim," facing him, are his assistants. Since telegraph news, local news, sports news, and all other news is taken care of on this kind of desk, it is known as the *universal desk*.

Another kind is called the *departmentalized desk*. Here copyreaders deal with only one type of news, such as sports, or financial news, and each department has its own specialized staff.

On most large newspapers, a *semi-universal* desk is employed, with a separate man or staff handling sports, financial news, and so forth. Since the size of the staff is limited on the small newspaper, with frequently only two or three men on the editorial side, each reporter often is expected to write his own headlines. The editor himself has the final word.

Regardless of the kind of desk employed, someone must decide on the style of headline that is to be used with a given story. In many offices, this decision is made by the desk editor. He indicates on the copy the style of head to be used and then turns it over to a man on the "rim," who makes the necessary revisions in the copy and writes the headline according to the specifications. Then it is ready to be sent to the operators.

Throughout the day, a record is kept of all stories sent to the composing room and of all pictures ordered from the engraving department. This record gives information as to the style of headline prepared for each story and the approximate amount of space required. The makeup editor then knows exactly what he will have to work with in planning his pages.

A common practice is to withhold decision on the kind of headlines to be used on the major stories until shortly before edition deadline.

However, these stories are read as they come to the copy desk, marked "HTK" (head to come), and sent on to the composing room, so that the type for all except the headlines can be set by the operators ahead of time.

Shortly before edition deadline, the makeup editor generally has an informal conference with the other news executives to discuss the major stories and pictures of the day so that they can determine together the treatment to be employed. When these decisions have been made, the copy desk is given its instructions to prepare the headlines selected, and the headline copy then is rushed to the composing room.

After agreement has been reached regarding the "play" to be given the main stories, the makeup editor is ready to prepare a layout for the page. The procedure followed in planning the front page differs somewhat from that used for inside pages, since inside pages contain advertising. (Procedures for planning inside pages will be discussed in a later chapter.)

The page layouts are made on sheets of paper known as *dummy sheets*. They usually are about $8\frac{1}{2} \times 11$ inches in size and are ruled off into the number of columns on the full-sized page. Number of inches often is indicated by scales along the side.

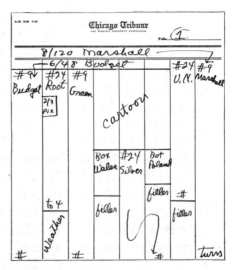

Figure 122. This front-page dummy of the *Chicago Daily Tribune* is typical of the practice followed in many newspaper offices.

Beginning at the top of the dummy sheet, the makeup editor writes in the slug-lines for the various stories and pictures that are to appear on the page. If there is to be a banner, he writes in the slug-line and draws a line to show where it will "read out." This slug-line corresponds to the marking placed on the story and the headline copy when they were sent to the composing room. Thus it serves as a key to the makeup man when he is ready to place the type into the form.

Then the makeup editor writes in the slug-lines for the top heads to show where they are to appear and indicates the placement of pictures by means of rectangular boxes with crossed diagonal lines sometimes drawn through the allotted space. Inside this area, he usually writes a guide-line or brief description to tell what picture is to run in the space. If an overline, or underlines, are to accompany the picture, they also may be indicated.

A line, sometimes with an arrow at the end, generally is drawn down the column following each slug-line to show approximately how much space will be required for the story. If another story is to follow, a horizontal line may be drawn across the column, and the slug-line for the next story is written underneath.

Some newspapers indicate only the main stories, leaving the makeup of the rest of the page to the *makeup man*—the printer who makes up the page after the type has been set and assembled into galleys. He should not be confused with the *makeup editor,* since their duties are entirely different and separate. Although the makeup man is a careful workman and usually can be depended upon to produce a page that is well designed typographically, he is not closely enough in touch with the news to evaluate it as well as those who had a hand in its preparation. Consequently, he needs more complete instructions.

Often the makeup editor or some other editorial executive stands at his side to tell him where to place the rest of the stories required, but even this plan is less efficient and more time-consuming than that of providing him with a detailed dummy. The dummy serves the same purpose for the makeup man as the blueprint does for engineers building a bridge. The more complete the dummy is, the surer the makeup editor can be that the results will meet with the approval of his associates and the less chance he runs of being blamed if the finished product is not as pleasing as that visualized by them.

The front page—as well as every other page in the newspaper—should be considered as a unit, and it should be planned as such. The bottom of the page should be given as serious consideration as the top, and the center area also should not be neglected if the over-all design is to be attractive and well-balanced.

After the top heads have been indicated, the slug-lines for the stories at the bottom should be marked in. This bottom area probably will need some two-column headlines and perhaps a picture to afford pleasing balance with the heavy display at the top. All these major elements should be indicated, since they will serve as the main skeleton around which all the other less important stories with smaller headlines will be placed.

Generally, it is impossible to show in exact detail all the stories and headlines that eventually will be included, since it is extremely difficult to write and plan stories and pictures ahead of time that are tailor-made for the space the designer might want them to occupy.   As headlines and stories are placed in their respective places in the form, it becomes necessary in most instances to omit a paragraph here and there to make them fit properly into the pattern; and short items of live news, known as *filler* often must be slipped in when stories run shorter than expected.

However, the dummy should be prepared as completely as possible so that the makeup editor can better visualize the page as it will appear in printed form, and so that the makeup man will have a careful plan from which to work.   Frequently, the makeup editor will want to shift some of the elements around to different positions after he has made his original draft in order to get the desired effects.   By making use of the dummy sheets, he is able to experiment until he is satisfied with the design.

When the dummy sheet has been completed, it is sent to the makeup man in the composing room.   Since the front page is considered the most important page in the paper by many editors, the makeup editor— and possibly the managing editor himself— accompany the dummy sheet so they will be on hand to select the smaller stories needed to fill up space and to decide on any changes that may have to be made at the last minute.

Starting at the top of the chase, with the dummy sheet as his guide, the makeup man begins placing all headlines, stories, pictures, boxes, and other elements into the form until every column has been filled. After the form has been completed, he locks it up by means of quoins at the side and bottom, and it is then ready to be sent to the stereotypers, who make the plates which are fitted onto the cylinders of the rotary press.   If a flat-bed cylinder press is used for printing the paper, the form is sent directly to the pressroom, where it is locked with others onto the bed of the press and made ready for printing.

Building the Design

The makeup editor must have an understanding of the basic principles of good design and the ability to apply them skillfully in arranging typographical elements on the page.   In the final analysis, his job is to fit together masses of gray tones, varying in shape, onto a rectangular white background in such a way that the over-all pattern is interesting and pleasing to the eye.

If a newspaper page is held away at a distance and viewed with the eyes partly closed, the manner in which the units of gray contribute to the building of the whole page-design is easily discernible.   Also apparent will be the inappropriateness of some of these elements if they happen to be of the wrong shape, or too dark or too light in tone, to harmonize properly with surrounding elements.

In order to visualize the effects he can obtain, the makeup editor must be thoroughly acquainted with every headline in the schedule— its size, shape, and the degree of color it will lend to the page when printed. Not until he is familiar with such intimate details will he be able to handle them with the dispatch and skill required for a job that by its very nature is highly specialized and exacting.

Every part of the page should be considered in terms of its suitability to the unified design and of the individual treatment necessary to adapt it to the desired pattern. One of the primary considerations should be that of permitting enough "light" between and around elements to provide pleasing contrast. If the masses are crowded too closely together, the page will be uninviting and hard to read.

Sufficient leading should be placed under the nameplate to set it off attractively from the date-line. There should be a generous amount of white space between the bottom rule under the date-line and the top heads; the decks within every headline should be separated clearly; and enough light should be admitted around all other units to relieve grayness and add life to the page.

This need for white space should be kept in mind when the headline schedule is prepared for the newspaper. The schedule should include enough headlines of varying size and structure so that the makeup editor will be able to obtain the proper gradation of tones throughout the page and at the same time to vary the amount of emphasis by display required for the different stories he must handle.

If he has only a few headlines from which to choose, all of which are of approximately the same size and weight, the resulting design will suffer. Sometimes a newspaper will overwork one or two styles of headlines, either because of a lack of sufficient type faces or improper use of those on hand. In such a situation, and when the types chosen are too bold, the resulting page will be spotted, often presenting a checker-board effect that is unpleasant and difficult to read. On the other hand, when all headlines are almost as light in tone as the body-matter, the design becomes gray and uninteresting. Variations of sizes and weights of headlines and their relationship to one another throughout the entire page must be considered carefully.

The tendency on some newspapers is to grade the heads down in size and weight from the heavier forms at the top to lighter ones in the bottom area. However, care must be taken not to allow too great a difference in the tones of the upper and lower parts of the page or it will appear top-heavy.

A much more desirable plan, and one that is constantly gaining favor, is that of bolstering up the bottom of the page with two- and three-column headlines and pictures, thereby overcoming the feeling of top-heaviness and at the same time permitting the use of more important

Figure 123. This front page lacks variety very badly. The design also is greatly damaged by the use of advertisements, which should be kept off the front page. Furthermore, lines in several headlines are too short, which results in too much white space on the right-hand side.

Figure 124. The headlines used on this front page are too bold and as a result cause it to appear "spotted." The use of so many headlines of the same kind is monotonous; and the all-cap headlines in small type are ineffective and extremely hard to read.

stories in this area. This plan accomplishes two purposes: it results in a more pleasing over-all design, and it leads the reader over the entire page instead of stopping him at the top and letting him shift for himself from that point on. There is no good reason for allowing the most valuable page in the paper to fade out into a gray, uninteresting expanse of small, unimportant headlines when enough good news is available to warrant stronger and more attractive display.

The middle area of the page also should be given attention. One of the main faults with many front pages is that they are "weak in the middle." Such a situation can be remedied by closer editing of long stories, or jumping them to inside pages, to permit the use of headlines in this area above and below the fold.

Stories in outside columns, or anywhere else on the page, which are allowed to run almost the full length of the page seriously limit the possibilities of pleasant makeup by reducing the number of columns available for display. The narrow expanses of gray body-type are injurious to the over-all design. If the entire page is to be considered as a single unit, as it should be, a story should be permitted to run the full length of the column only when it is of such unusual importance that it overshadows all other considerations.

"Rivers" of white space running through the page should be avoided. They are caused by allowing too much white space at the ends of headlines that are placed too close to one another down or across the page. Headlines should be positioned far enough apart and in such a way that the white area in one does not appear to connect with that in another that is nearby, thus breaking up the page into misshapen and unattractive patterns.

Several other "don'ts" which the makeup editor should keep in mind are summarized below:

1. Don't use too many type families in the headline schedule. One or two harmonious designs are sufficient for pleasing results.

2. Don't employ too many headline forms of differing styles together. Be sure that whatever forms are used are properly fitted to the type styles selected. Keep headlines simple and easy to read by limiting the number of forms and decks.

3. Don't use tomb-stones, as a general rule, since they tend to reduce legibility. Weigh this fact carefully against others when such combinations are considered primarily for typographical effects to gain balance on the page.

4. Don't place headlines on the fold. The fold cuts them in two, unless the paper is held entirely open. The reader must waste valuable time in straightening out the paper or turning it back and forth to see the entire headline and to get the meaning. Thus, reading time is slowed down, which is in complete opposition to the main purposes of good headline display and makeup.

5. Don't use too many boxes, since each is a typographical unit in itself, and an oversupply of these separate elements breaks up the page into a patchwork of patterns that is detrimental to the over-all design.

6. Don't place advertisements on the front page. Readers have a right to expect *news* on the most accessible page in their newspaper. News is the commodity in which they are most interested, and it should not be crowded out by material of less importance to the majority of readers. Even the advisability of running promotional ads for the newspaper itself is questionable when tested on this basis. If they are used, they should be kept small and made to fit into the rest of the design of the page without attracting the reader's attention away from the main news of the day.

7. Don't be guilty of "over-ornamentation." A page filled with decorative types, boxes, dashes, cut-off rules, and other unusual elements, even though they are basically harmonious, is as lacking in good taste as the person who overdresses merely for the purpose of "making an impression." The result usually is more freakish than pleasing.

8. Don't be afraid to experiment. Too much "sameness" day after day becomes monotonous. Creativeness is just as valuable in front-page design as in any other kind of art. So long as sound principles of design are followed, experimentation in makeup is a healthy sign.

9. Don't cut the page in two with a long headline that slices across several columns below the fold. Such a headline has the effect of dividing the page into two separate parts and consequently is ruinous to an over-all, unified design.

10. Don't forget the value of pictures in building interesting and attractive pages. The use of local pictures, as well as those coming in from the outside, rate very high in reader-interest. In addition, they can be used very advantageously in providing balance and liveliness on the page.

These are some of the more important considerations the makeup editor should observe in planning the page that is to serve as the "show window" for the rest of the paper. However, no standard formula can be followed successfully day after day without interruption. At best, many of the rules must be somewhat general in nature, allowing enough flexibility for the makeup editor to adapt his materials and techniques to the flow of news that changes constantly.

Styles of Front-Page Makeup

The need for fitting headlines and display to changing news situations accounts in large measure for the wide variations of methods followed throughout the country. Likes and dislikes on the part of editors and the capabilities of those in charge of makeup also strongly affect the practices employed by any newspaper.

Despite these and other variables, over the years several styles of front-page makeup have grown up into which present-day newspapers can be classified. Although the terminology used to identify the patterns differs slightly, they will be referred to in this discussion as follows: (1) Balanced Makeup; (2) Contrast-and-Balance Makeup; (3) Brace, or Focused, Makeup; (4) Broken-Page, or Circus, Makeup; and (5) Streamlined, or Unconventional, Makeup.

In studying these various styles of makeup, it should be remembered that a newspaper sometimes will shift from one method to another, and occasionally it will make use of a combination of two styles that overlap in its efforts to provide suitable display for the various situations that arise. However, for the most part, a newspaper will attempt to follow one pattern regularly so that readers will learn to recognize the newspaper by the style employed.

BALANCED MAKEUP

This style of makeup is more strongly based on traditional practices than any of the others. For many years it was the leading favorite, and many present-day newspapers, both dailies and weeklies, still are using the plan. No great departure has developed from the techniques employed by our earliest editors at a time when news was much scarcer and production of pictures by means of halftones was unknown.

Balanced makeup gets its name from the fact that elements on the page are carefully balanced, one against another. With the optical center of the page serving as a fulcrum, the headlines are planned and placed in such a manner that perfect balance is obtained. Some newspapers following this plan position all their heavier display at the top of the page, allowing the bottom area to run gray. However, a more general practice today is that of introducing two- and three-column headlines in the lower half of the page to provide a more symmetrical over-all design.

Front pages of the *New York Times* are excellent examples of this formal style of makeup. Although this paper occasionally varies its techniques slightly, the pages shown in Figures 125 and 126 demonstrate the two most common methods employed.

In one of these pages, the three-column spread on the right is balanced by another of exactly the same kind placed on the left-hand side, and the two secondary, two-column headlines, which come underneath in columns two and three and six and seven, also are identical in form.

In order to add strength and size to units, the *Times* makes use of tomb-stones, always consisting of two similar one-column headlines placed side by side. Such a combination is employed at the top of the page to separate the two spreads. Near the center of the page, the tomb-stone unit in columns two and three balances perfectly with a similar arrangement in columns six and seven. Even the two-line classified advertisement at the bottom of column one is balanced by another of corresponding weight in column eight.

When news is regarded to be of less vital importance, one-column headlines are used in the two outside columns, with the two-column secondary headlines placed next to them on either side at the top of the page. In the two center columns, the tomb-stone effect is employed.

Two-column structures, reading out into two-column lead paragraphs, are balanced across the page near the center, and these are followed by one-column heads placed directly opposite one another—one in column two and the other in column seven. Thus, perfect balance is maintained in the center area as well as at the bottom of the page.

The ears at the sides of the nameplate likewise are of the same size and design. The Text type in the title carries out the formality and traditional conservatism of the makeup of the page.

Although many newspapers employ balanced makeup, none of them attains greater bisymmetrical perfection than the *New York Times,* which always has been noted for its quiet, dignified formality.

The general tendency of most editors following this scheme of makeup is to produce pages that are rather gray in tone. Pictures, cartoons, and other more modern features are reserved for the inside pages. However, pictures can be used in this style of design, provided they are balanced in tone and in placement on the page.

The use of balanced makeup also results in pages that have a "bookish" appearance which seems best adapted to a select group of readers who are interested enough in the news not to object to long stories and display that lacks the more modern approach.

One of the main objections to perfectly balanced pages is that they often appear to have been planned meticulously with ruler and pen.

Figure 125. This front page of the *New York Times* is an excellent example of Balanced Makeup. Tombstones are used deliberately to carry out desired typographical effects.

Figure 126. Another kind of Balanced Makeup used by the *New York Times* is shown above. Here one-column headlines are employed in the outside column on each side of the page.

Also, in order to obtain typographical niceties and mechanical exactness, sacrifices in readability often must be made. Furthermore, the use of the same scheme day after day, with little change, results in monotony.

CONTRAST-AND-BALANCE MAKEUP

Another style of makeup is that referred to as *contrast-and-balance*. It is more difficult to secure than bisymmetrical, or formal, balance, which can be judged precisely, but it allows much more freedom. The type of balance sought is what the artist calls "occult," or informal, balance. It is an adaptation of the methods used by the designer of advertising in obtaining non-bisymmetrical balance in his layouts.[10]

Informality is achieved by balancing masses against one another diagonally from top to bottom, as well as across the page. Using the optical center of the page as a fulcrum, masses of unequal weight are brought into harmony by moving them uneven distances from the central point.

This style of makeup does away with the necessity of cutting so many stories and of placing headlines in exact positions to make them fit into a preconceived pattern. It allows the makeup editor and headline writers much greater freedom in "playing" stories according to their importance. The makeup editor may vary the size and weight of headlines used according to the value of the news and place them in irregular positions on the page so long as they contribute to an over-all design that is inviting and pleasing to the reader.

In addition to a more flexible headline schedule, a wider selection of other elements usually is provided in contrast-and-balance makeup, including pictures and cartoons. As a result, the possibilities for variety and interest are multiplied, and the resulting pages may differ in character from day to day.

One of the leading adherents of contrast-and-balance makeup is the *Milwaukee Journal,* which has won numerous awards for its excellent typography. This paper builds its front page around an editorial cartoon three columns in width that always is located at the top of the page. Its position is dependent upon the top heads used on any given day.

When a banner headline is employed in the *Journal,* it generally appears in columns three, four, and five; but if the banner is replaced by a spread headline on the right-hand side at the top of the page, the cartoon is shifted one column farther to the right. (See Figure 127.)

---

[10] Olson, *Typography and Mechanics of the Newspaper,* page 309.

Other headlines are placed in irregular positions down and across the page.

The front page in Figure 127 makes use of a five-column, two-line spread for the major display. By using a two-column spread in the two outside columns on the left-hand side at the top and another of the same weight adjacent to the cartoon farther down on the same side of the page, and by placing two pictures under a two-column feature headline near the bottom, pleasing contrast and balance are obtained.

The half-column cut just below the fold in column five helps to brighten the center area, and the boxed effect slightly below the fold in the long story in column eight assists in breaking up the gray expanse of body-type and balances with the "Milwaukee" column-headline on the other side of the page.

The *Louisville Courier-Journal,* another newspaper which follows the

Figure 127. The *Milwaukee Journal* uses a Contrast-and-Balance style of makeup on its front page. A cartoon is carried at the top. When a spread headline is used over the main story, as in this example, the cartoon appears in columns four, five, and six. However, it is run in columns three, four, and five when a banner headline is employed. Frequently pictures are run in the bottom area of the page in order to brighten it and to afford pleasing balance.

Figure 128. The *Courier-Journal* of Louisville, Kentucky, which won First Honorable Mention in the Sixteenth Annual Exhibition of Newspaper Typography, conducted by N. W. Ayer & Son, Inc., also follows the Contrast-and-Balance style of makeup. This paper regularly uses large pictures—one above the fold and one below—to add interest to the design. All headlines are from the Bodoni family of type, which is widely used by newspapers.

contrast-and-balance plan of makeup, is much more liberal in its use of pictures on the front page. The example shown in Figure 128 is typical of the scheme used by this newspaper.

Most issues contain two large illustrations on the front page, one of which is placed in the upper left-hand corner at the top. It always is balanced by another of almost equal size that is positioned below the fold. The illustrations always are large and well printed.

The hand-tooled Text type in the nameplate of the *Courier-Journal* is an excellent choice as a companion face for the Bodoni, carrying out the contrast features of the page. Other more modern characteristics include the use of white space in place of column-rules in some areas; the doubling-up of long stories into rectangular units under long headlines; the exclusive use of flush-left forms in headlines, none of which contains more than two decks; the placement of captions underneath pictures instead of in the traditional location at the top; and the employment of partially boxed inserts to help break up long columns of reading matter. All these features, combined with skillful placement on the page, result in a bright, effective design that cannot fail to attract and interest readers.

Brace, or Focused, Makeup

The *brace,* or *focused,* style of makeup places major stress on the one main story of the day. This emphasis is accomplished by running the story under the strongest headline on the page and by arranging other elements in such a way that they assist in focusing the attention of the reader on this prominent area. The *New York Herald Tribune* makes use of this technique regularly on its front page. The example shown in Figure 129 shows the pattern followed by this newspaper.

Positioned in the upper right-hand corner, the spread is a flush-left form four columns in width, followed by three one-column decks in column eight. A large picture, three columns by approximately five inches in depth, that ties in closely with the news, is placed directly under the spread, adjacent to column eight, in which the story is run.

No other area on the page is as heavy in tone, and consequently the reader's attention is focused on this corner the moment he sees the page. Furthermore, all other headlines, except those at the extreme top, are arranged in a diagonal line that assists in leading the eye into the heavier area. Thus, these elements appear to be braced against the picture and the spread headline at the top of the page. This feature is what caused makeup editors to label it the "brace" style of makeup.

From the standpoint of newspapers which have to depend upon news-stand sales for much of their revenue, the brace style of makeup offers one great advantage: the major display is located in that part of the page which comes on top when the paper is folded twice. In New York City, where many newspapers are displayed together on the same stand, this is a very important consideration. However, many editors in less congested areas also follow this plan of makeup, and others using the balanced page frequently shift to the brace style when a big story breaks that they want to give more prominent display than could be obtained with the more formal treatment.

The main fault with brace makeup usually is the tendency for most pages to be very top-heavy. Unless fairly strong two- and three-column headlines are used below the fold and elsewhere on the page, the design is greatly out of balance. On the other hand, the strengthening of headlines in other areas on the page reduces the pulling power of the heavy display in the upper right-hand corner. Such a reduction tends to defeat the main purpose of the brace style of makeup.

Figure 129. This front page of the *New York Herald Tribune* is an excellent example of the Brace, or Focused, style of makeup. The *Tribune* was a runner-up in its class in the Sixteenth Annual Exhibition of Newspaper Typography, conducted by N. W. Ayer & Son, Inc., and previously had won many honors for its excellent typography and makeup.

Attractive pages can be designed by the makeup editor who is willing to compromise by distributing some elements throughout the page that are strong enough in tone to add interest but not so heavy that they detract seriously from the major display.

BROKEN-PAGE MAKEUP

Some newspapers seem to be opposed to any kind of balance on the front page—at least, to any styles presenting balanced effects that give an over-all feeling of unity.

Instead, every story, with its accompanying display, is handled as a separate unit. Indices, summaries, and other masses also are treated in this way. Much less attention is given to the symmetry and orderliness of the entire design than to the individual treatment of the individual elements. By making use of single-column headlines alternated with wider structures, an attempt is made to break up all the columns on the page. Such a style is referred to as *broken-page*, or *circus, makeup*.

Large banners, spreads, pictures, boxes, a nameplate that may be changed in width and position from day to day, and great contrast between heavy and light areas are among the foremost devices employed. Several editors follow the practice of printing one or more of the major headlines and other units in color for increased attention-value, and a few print the front page on colored paper. In general, less attention is given to close harmony in the types and headline forms used together in the design.

Figure 130. The front page of the *Chicago Herald-American* is an example of Broken-Page, or Circus, makeup. On this page, the five-column spread at the top of the page under the banner, and the sports results at the bottom of columns one and two were printed in red to attract attention.

The front page of the *Chicago Herald-American* shown in Figure 130 is a typical example of broken-page makeup. On this page, not a single column has been allowed to finish without a break. Even the outside columns have been broken.

In addition to the banner and the spread under it, which was printed in red, several other heavy headlines have been used on the page. Poster Bodoni, a very bold face, has been used in the five two-column headlines in columns three and four. The one-column headline in column five near the bottom and another at the top of column seven also were set in this type. As a result, there are several dark-toned areas on the page which stand out in strong contrast to the lighter areas.

The "National League and Late Race Results" headlines, like the six-column spread, were printed in red, which tends to attract special attention to this area.

Three headline forms are used: the inverted pyramid, the flush-left, and the drop-line. In the first, a plain Gothic type is used, which would be more suitable for a form with less variation. Several other rules of good design are purposely broken in order to arouse excitement and to secure a maximum of attention. The total result is a broken design in which several elements, by their heavy tone and unusual treatment, clamor for attention, and many of the principles of pleasing design and makeup are violated.

Readers who are unaccustomed to this "shouting" style of makeup find it confusing, distasteful, and hard to read. However, the makeup editor has succeeded in achieving a feeling of sensationalism—a technique that has been employed for many years by this newspaper and others that make their appeal to the masses and depend upon newsstand sales for a large part of their circulation. Only on this ground could broken-page makeup be defended, since it breaks too many rules governing attractive and orderly design.

UNCONVENTIONAL PAGE MAKEUP

The four styles of makeup already discussed have been followed for several decades by American newspapers. However, in recent years, several innovations in front-page design have been introduced which differ in many respects from the traditional styles. For convenience, papers not using one of the four traditional styles will be referred to in this discussion as following *unconventional*, or *streamlined*, page makeup.

Unconventional makeup is the outcome of a desire on the part of editors to create front pages that are more functional. Stress is placed on obtaining greater readability, more definite direction of readers to important stories, the provision of summaries and indices, and the departmentalization of news.

Flush-left headlines with fewer decks, elimination of column-rules in favor of white space, wider columns, "skyline" banners, use of white space instead of dashes, and smaller nameplates that can be shifted from one position to another are some of the more modern features employed in varying degrees by newspapers following this plan. The main feature is the willingness of makeup editors to experiment freely in an effort to obtain the most effective combinations. As a result, the character of the front page changes with almost every issue in order to keep in harmony with the constant shifts in the flow of news.

The *Oregonian,* of Portland (Figs. 131 and 132), is an excellent example of newspapers making use of the modern approach. In this paper, all headlines except the main top head contain only one deck, and they are flush-left exclusively. The type used is a Square-Serif variety, which has been used sparingly in front-page display by most newspapers. However, by employing a condensed variety in medium weight for all but the banners, this paper succeeds in obtaining pleasing results. The nameplate is in a hand-tooled Text type that harmonizes

Figure 131. The *Oregonian,* of Portland, Oregon, follows the Unconventional, or Streamlined, style of makeup. The four pages printed here show some of the various techniques used to give variety to readers.

well with the rest of the head-dress. Pictures also are employed, and considerable space is devoted to them when the occasion demands.

All these features contribute to a more modern-looking page, but the manner in which the various elements are handled in makeup is what sets off unconventional makeup distinctly from the other four styles.

Although the *Oregonian* sometimes appears using the conventional contrast-and-balance design, with the nameplate in its traditional place at the top of the page, its general tendency is to employ techniques that are in opposition to many of the accustomed practices.

The pages shown in Figures 131 and 132 demonstrate some of the unconventional methods used.

The display given to main stories at the top of the page undergoes the major changes from day to day. The page in Figure 132 shows perhaps the greatest departure from conventional styles, in that the nameplate has been dropped far down into the page to allow the use of an important story above it, which is topped by an eight-column banner. This arrangement has the effect of cutting the page into two separate units. It is not good practice from the standpoint of correct design, but it accomplishes the purpose of forcibly directing the reader's attention to the featured news of the day. The makeup editor was

Figure 132. Sometimes the *Oregonian* prints a story above the nameplate and under a banner headline in order to create an unusual page-design. This arrangement tends to cut the page into two separate segments.

willing to sacrifice typographical niceties in order to give outstanding news an unusual treatment that would not fail to emphasize its importance. In doing so, he observed one of the main purposes of unconventional makeup: that of making the page more functional. At the same time, the area below the nameplate was carefully planned to form a contrast-and-balance design, and the page as a whole has an orderly appearance.

Top-of-the-page display in the examples in Figure 131 differs with each issue. In one of these pages, the banner is placed high above the nameplate, and instead of reading out into the accompanying story, it is followed by a long cut-off rule, at the end of which are printed the words telling readers where to look for the story. A banner of this kind, which comes at the extreme top of the page, frequently is referred to as a "skyline banner" because of its high position.

The other examples make use of the skyline banner idea, but the treatment of display is different in each. In one page, the nameplate is seven columns wide, and the line reads out into two single-column decks that lead the reader down into the story; in the other, the nameplate is compressed into five columns, and the banner is followed by a three-column deck that reads out into twin decks—one placed on either side of a two-line feature headline which separates them. Thus, the banner is made to tie in with two closely related stories, one of which gives the local angle, and the other, the national.

Although no banner is used in the other example, a three-line spread is run high in the two outside columns to emphasize the story's importance, and the nameplate is reduced to six colur s in length.

Sometimes one or more columns are run high on the left-hand side of the page, and various other combinations are used by this paper in its efforts to provide interesting and varied makeup.

The *Cincinnati Enquirer* and several other newspapers are experimenting with another variation in design which they refer to as *streamlined makeup*. Editors of the *Enquirer* began their experiments on August 8, 1945, when they "streamlined" the daily and Sunday editorial pages. Later, they extended the method to other sections of the newspaper, and on June 23, 1946, they began using a new seven-column format on page one of the news section.

Two of the main features of streamlined makeup are the omission of column-rules in favor of a pica or more of white space, and the employment of column-widths that do not conform with the standard 12-pica column.

Both of these characteristics are apparent in the *Enquirer's* front page. It consists of seven columns 11½ picas wide and another one 19 picas in width; column rules have been replaced with white space. (See Figure 116.)

Also, some of the headlines are constructed differently from the conventional styles. Instead of presenting different angles of the story in each deck, the words in one deck may be part of an idea that is carried on and expanded in those that follow.

Another departure is placing longer stories in two-column units, in which the type may be set two columns wide or in single-column measure, with white space separating the columns. As a result, much more white space is admitted, and the page has a less crowded appearance and is lighter in tone than most ordinary pages using column-rules.

Many newspapers have discontinued the traditional practice of running long stories down a single column, an arrangement which results in a gray, uninteresting, vertical unit that often is detrimental to the over-all design of the page. Instead, these stories are placed in horizontal, rectangular units, under headlines that are two or more columns in width, depending on the length of the stories involved and the type of makeup required to produce pleasing effects on the page.

The result generally is much more satisfactory from the standpoint of the reader, who has a tendency to shy away from extensive masses of gray reading matter. Although the same amount of body-type may be handled in the horizontal unit, it is shorter in depth and contains some white space between columns, which makes it appear more inviting.

The use of horizontal units is highly desirable not only as an aid in increasing readership of important stories, but also as a device for breaking up the long columns of gray reading matter into units that are more adaptable to interesting makeup.

In recent years, some newspapers have shown a growing tendency to write news stories more concisely and to classify them under department headings. The first newspapers in America to fully departmentalize their pages were the *Daytona Beach Morning Journal* and the *Palm Beach Times,* which began the practice in 1936.[11] Since then, several others have experimented with the idea.

Attention was called to the necessity for change by some experimental pages designed and produced under the direction of Herbert Brucker, formerly an associate professor in the Graduate School of Journalism, Columbia University, who presented his views in a book entitled *The Changing American Newspaper,* published in 1937 by the Columbia University Press.

Using the news on the front page of the *New York Herald Tribune* for March 3, 1937, as a basis, the front page of his experimental newspaper, called *Gist,* was very unorthodox. It was 14 × 20½ inches in size and contained five columns 15-picas in width. Except for a three-column spread in Bodoni Bold on the left-hand side at the top of the page, all other headlines were single-line labels set in Poster Bodoni and Poster Bodoni Italic.

Short summaries of most of the stories carried under top headlines

---

[11] Herbert Brucker, *The Changing American Newspaper,* page 64. New York: Columbia University Press, 1937.

throughout the issue of the *Herald Tribune* were run under the departmental crossline headlines, and summations of leading stories that were run elsewhere in the paper were printed in a two-column box under the heading "Today's Headlines." The nameplate of simple design occupied three columns of space across the top of the page, and two single-column pictures, placed side by side, were positioned at the

Figure 133A. The news carried on this front page of the *New York Herald Tribune* was used in designing the front page of *Gist*, shown in Figure 133B. (Reproduced by permission from Herbert Brucker, *The Changing American Newspaper*. New York: Columbia University Press, 1937.)

top of columns four and five. No other major display was used on the page.

Commenting on the new design, Mr. Brucker had this to say:

A first page of the kind outlined . . . with the usual front-page stories on the inside, will have the advantage of not giving on the front page the details

Late City Edition of the 3 Cents

Gist
of Today's News

Vol. 96 No. 32,980   Copyright 1937   Wednesday, March 3, 1937
Graduate School of Journalism, Columbia University

Lewis Wins U. S. Steel Recognition, 40-Hour Week and $5 Minimum Pay

THEY NEGOTIATED the steel agreement: John L. Lewis (left), head of the Committee for Industrial Organization, and Myron C. Taylor, chairman of the board, U. S. Steel Corporation.

Labor

ORGANIZED LABOR has won formal recognition from the chief unit of the United States Steel Corporation. This epochal step was quietly announced in Pittsburgh last night by Philip Murray, chairman of the Steel Workers' Organizing Committee and chief lieutenant of John L. Lewis in the Committee for Industrial Organization.

Today's Headline

Roosevelt comes out for new wage-and-hour laws this session; sends Congress N.R.A. post-mortem urging new regulation of business be more flexible. *Labor, page 2*

Steel's 40-hour week hailed in Washington by Administration leaders; Navy Department holds it clears way for immediate ship construction. *Labor, page 2*

Sit-down strikes close two major parts plants in Detroit serving Ford Motor Co., which is revealed as early C.I.O. objective. One strike settled. *Labor, page 2*

Vandenberg backs Wheeler-Bone Amendment in radio speech attacking Roosevelt's court plan. Sumners implores justices to quit. *National News, page 3*

James Roosevelt may attend coronation of George VI as secretary of American delegation; President says idea is news to him. *Foreign News, page 3*

Niagara Falls Power Co. defies order of state commission to cut use of river water to one-fourth. *Business, page 14*

Mysterious death of four-year-old Queens girl caused by attack in "most brutal murder in 27 years!" *Crime, page 2*

S.E.C. charges Germany has secret debt of 2 billion dollars; cautions investors in new bond issue. *Foreign News, page 8*

New York City

THIS YEAR'S summer city hall will be Chisholm Manor in College Point Park, Queens, Mayor LaGuardia announced yesterday. Page 9.

The State

HUGE CAKES of ice rumbled down Niagara Falls last night, jamming the river and threatening the Maid of the Mist steamers. Page 7.

Business

THE New York State Water Power and Control Commission has ordered the Niagara Falls Power Co. to cut the amount of water it takes from the Niagara River from 20,000 to 4800 cubic feet a second.

National News

SENATOR Arthur H. Vandenberg of Michigan endorsed the Wheeler-Bone amendment as a substitute for the President's Supreme Court plan in a nationally-broadcast radio speech last night.

Foreign News

THE Securities and Exchange Commission in Washington yesterday in effect charged the German Government with maintaining a secret debt of about $2000 million.

Crime

JOAN MORVAN, a four-year-old Queens girl who died Monday, was murdered. Death followed peritonitis caused by a criminal attack, Dr. Howard W. Neail said after an autopsy yesterday.

Entertainment

Personal

Weather: Fair and slightly colder today. Tomorrow, mostly cloudy and warmer.

Figure 133B. The front page of *Gist*, experimental newspaper designed under the direction of Herbert Brucker. (Reproduced by permission from Herbert Brucker, *The Changing American Newspaper*. New York: Columbia University Press, 1937.)

of eight or nine leading stories. But it will more than atone for this by making possible quick and easy absorption of the complicated news of this complicated world. It will banish that newspaper reader's constant annoyance, the page-one story jumped, just when he is getting interested, to some unknown spot in the acreage within. . . .

. . . The success of the entire plan suggested . . . will depend considerably upon the understanding and skill with which both page one and the inside are put together. If the reader really feels that, having read the first page, he gets the essence of all the day's news, he will be satisfied with it. And if he finds the information, background, interpretation, and entertainment he seeks inside, he will buy and read again tomorrow.[12]

Several barriers stand in the way of adoption of the kind of format and treatment suggested. In the first place, national advertisers have standardized on the 12-pica column, and the 15-pica measure provided in the experimental newspaper is not easily adaptable to pages carrying advertising. Furthermore, editors are extremely hesitant about changing from styles of makeup that have served them well for many years to one that is new and radically different. However, many editors during the last few years have introduced special columns devoted to digests of the news, front-page summaries, and indices—trends that are similar to some of the proposals forwarded by *Gist* in 1937. Some newspapers, like the *Cincinnati Enquirer*, also have replaced column-rules with white space and have reduced the number of columns to the page.

Front Pages of Tabloids

Our first tabloids were highly sensational, making their appeal to the masses by means of screaming headlines, many pictures, and stories featuring sex, crime, and divorce scandals. Pages were small in size so that they could be handled easily on crowded trains, subways, and busses.

During the years that have elapsed since the *New York Daily News* was introduced in 1919, many newspapers using smaller format have made their appearance. Some of them still possess characteristics similar to their boisterous predecessors, but the general trend has been toward saner presentation of news and more dignified makeup.

Because of smaller page-size and fewer columns, the possibilities of display are not as great as on standard-size newspapers. In general, front pages are of two varieties: those that make use of large headlines and pictures to the exclusion of news stories, all of which are placed on

---

[12] Brucker, *The Changing American Newspaper*, pages 26-27.

the inside; and those that closely resemble the larger newspapers in typography and design.

Of the former group, the *Chicago Daily Times* and the *New York Daily Mirror* front pages, shown in Figure 134, are typical examples. The page is approximately 12 × 15 inches in size, providing space for five 12-pica columns. However, except for cutlines accompanying the large illustrations used, all news stories are placed on the inside.

The headline employed always is in extremely large, bold type and relates to the main story of the day, carried on page two. Sometimes more than one "banner" appear on this page, which also announce the stories on the inside. The number of pictures likewise may vary, but they are always large and dramatic. Thus, such tabloids attempt to draw readers by large headlines and illustrations instead of by actual news stories accompanied by quieter display.

Another group of tabloids follows a plan similar to that used by the *Gazette and Daily*, of York, Pennsylvania. Although the page is only approximately 12 × 17 inches in size, this paper employs contrast-and-balance makeup and looks much like larger papers using the same style.

However, it has several modern features that are not common to many newspapers in this classification. All headlines are flush-left; white space is used in place of column-rules; and second decks, if they

Figure 134. Typical examples of the style of front-page makeup being followed by many tabloid newspapers. They are characterized by large headlines and pictures, and small page size.

can be regarded as such, are summaries in 10-point Bodoni Bold type. Simple boxes and pictures are used to add variety to the page.

Because of its very interesting and attractive design, the *Gazette and Daily* was awarded "Honorable Mention for Tabloids, regardless of circulation," in the Sixteenth Annual Exhibition of Newspaper Typography, conducted by N. W. Ayer & Son, Inc.

EXPERIMENTS IN MAKEUP

The person who aspires to become a skillful expert in makeup must make a careful study of the subject. He should constantly seek new ways of improving the design of the pages for which he is responsible. One of the best ways to improve techniques is to spend considerable time experimenting with new ideas which might result in better designs. This experimenting can be done by preparing a set of tools made expressly for the purpose.

Figure 135. The *Gazette and Daily,* of York, Pennsylvania, employs a type of makeup that is somewhat similar to that followed by many standard-size newspapers. This paper was chosen as the most outstanding tabloid entered in the Sixteenth Annual Exhibition of Newspaper Typography, conducted by N. W. Ayer & Son, Inc.

Several samples of each headline in the schedule, together with pictures of varying sizes and other typographical elements used on the front page, should be collected. They may be pasted on cardboard backings to facilitate handling. Sheets of paper the exact size of the page, ruled off into columns, with the nameplate printed, or pasted, at the top, also will be needed.

With the aid of these materials, different treatments may be tested by placing the elements desired on this skeletonized page and shifting them around in an effort to obtain the most pleasing results. Sometimes experimentation may be wanted in only certain areas or sections of the page; at other times, the whole page may be remodeled.

To make the resulting designs as realistic as possible, columns of body-type may be pasted onto the page or prepared on cardboard strips in the same manner as headlines and other elements.

By making use of this simple technique, it is possible to try out new

Figure 136. All four of the newspapers represented above won awards in the Sixteenth Annual Exhibition of Newspaper Typography, conducted by N. W. Ayer & Son, Inc. In the class of standard-size papers of less than 10,000 circulation, the *Owensboro* (Kentucky) *Inquirer* was awarded First Honorable Mention; the *Antigo* (Wisconsin) *Daily Journal,* Second Honorable Mention; and the *Santa Fe New Mexican,* Third Honorable Mention. The *Reading Eagle,* of Reading, Pennsylvania, won Second Honorable Mention in the class of standard-size papers of from 10,000 to 50,000 circulation.

methods before applying them to the front page proper; and when new headlines for the schedule are contemplated, they may be tested beforehand. In addition to providing the makeup editor with a method of experimentation that is simple and effective, it is a great aid in developing the ability to visualize and create designs that are more pleasing and attractive.

Experimentation should be supplemented by careful study of the practices followed by other newspapers, especially those that are noted for their outstanding achievements in typography and makeup.

WINNERS IN TYPOGRAPHY CONTESTS

Several state and regional press associations and other organizations interested in newspapers sponsor contests in efforts to promote greater interest in good newspaper typography and makeup. A growing consciousness among editors of the need is reflected in constantly rising participation in these competitions, which have increased greatly in popularity since their origin a few years ago.

One of the largest is the Annual Exhibition of Newspaper Typography, which was started in 1931 by N. W. Ayer & Son, Inc., a national

Figure 137. The newspapers represented here also won awards in the Sixteenth Annual Exhibition of Newspaper Typography, conducted by N. W. Ayer & Son, Inc. The *Durham* (North Carolina) *Morning Herald* won First Honorable Mention in the class of standard-size newspapers of from 10,000 to 50,000 circulation; and the *Richmond* (Virginia) *Times-Dispatch* won Second Honorable Mention in the class of standard-size papers of more than 50,000 circulation.

advertising agency, for the purpose of stimulating interest among newspapers in better typography and better printing.

A large trophy, known as the F. Wayland Ayer Cup, is presented each year to the newspaper selected by a jury of judges as the most outstanding, and "Honorable Mentions" are awarded to newspapers selected as the best in each of four circulation groups. Awards are made on the basis of excellence in typography, makeup, and presswork. The additional factor of paper-saving uses of type and format also was considered during World War II.

All English-language daily newspapers in the United States are eligible to participate in this exhibition by sending in copies of issues published on those dates selected by the sponsoring organization. In 1946, more than 1,200 newspapers entered the Sixteenth Annual Contest.

In 1946, the Ayer Cup went to the *Rochester* (Minnesota) *Post-Bulletin*. In addition, "Honorable Mentions" were awarded to papers in the following circulation and format groups: standard-size papers of more than 50,000 circulation—First Honorable Mention, the *Courier-Journal*, Louisville, Kentucky; Second Honorable Mention, the *Richmond* (Virginia) *Times Dispatch;* Third Honorable Mention, the *Christian Science Monitor*, Boston, Massachusetts. In this classification, the *New York Herald Tribune*, the *Los Angeles Times*, and the *Philadelphia Inquirer* were selected as runners-up by the judges.

Standard-size papers of from 10,000 to 50,000 circulation—First Honorable Mention, the *Durham* (North Carolina) *Morning Herald;* Second Honorable Mention, the *Reading* (Pennsylvania) *Eagle;* Third Honorable Mention, the *Rutland* (Vermont) *Herald.*

Standard-size papers of less than 10,000 circulation—First Honorable Mention, the *Owensboro* (Kentucky) *Inquirer;* Second Honorable Mention, the *Antigo* (Wisconsin) *Daily Journal;* Third Honorable Mention, the *Santa Fe* (New Mexico) *New Mexican.* In this classification, also, the judges chose a runner-up, the *Rhinelander* (Wisconsin) *Daily News.*

Tabloids, regardless of circulation—the *Gazette and Daily*, York, Pennsylvania.

In commenting on the results of the judging, H. A. Batten, president of N. W. Ayer & Son, Inc., pointed out that the selection of the winner points up the fact that newspapers in every category—the small town publication as well as the metropolitan daily—are earnestly striving to reach and maintain high standards of typography and makeup.

Another organization which has been sponsoring a similar contest on a somewhat smaller scale for several years is the Inland Daily Press

Association, whose membership is made up of over 400 dailies throughout the Midwest. Newspapers are entered in the following classifications: Class A—inland dailies up to 5,000 circulation; Class B—from 5,000 to 10,000 circulation; Class C—from 10,000 to 25,000 circulation; Class D—from 25,000 to 75,000 circulation; and Class E—over 75,000 circulation.

Winners in the 7th Annual Typography Contest, conducted for this

Figure 138. These newspapers were first-place winners in their respective classes in the Seventh Annual Typography Contest of The Inland Daily Press Association.

association in 1946, were as follow: Class A—First Place, the *Rhinelander* (Wisconsin) *Daily News;* Second Place, the *Columbia* (Missouri) *Missourian;* Third Place, the *Daily Illini* (Champaign-Urbana, Illinois); Honorable Mentions, the *Daily Times Herald* (Carroll, Iowa), and the *New Ulm* (Minnesota) *Daily Journal.*

Class B—First Place, the *Boulder* (Colorado) *Daily Camera;* Second Place, the *Marinette* (Wisconsin) *Eagle-Star;* Third Place, the *Waukesha* (Wisconsin) *Daily Freeman;* Honorable Mentions, the *Fremont* (Nebraska) *Guide and Tribune* and the *Daily Mining Gazette* (Houghton, Michigan).

Class C—First Place, the *Rochester* (Minnesota) *Post-Bulletin;* Second Place, the *Appleton* (Wisconsin) *Post-Crescent;* Third Place, the *Palladium-Item* (Richmond, Indiana); Honorable Mentions, the *Kenosha* (Wisconsin) *Evening News* and the *Warren* (Ohio) *Tribune Chronicle.*

Class D—First Place, the *Green Bay* (Wisconsin) *Press-Gazette;* Second Place, the *Daily Pantagraph* (Bloomington, Illinois); Third Place, the *Decatur* (Illinois) *Herald;* Honorable Mentions, the *Wisconsin State Journal* (Madison, Wisconsin) and the *Cedar Rapids* (Iowa) *Gazette.*

Class E—First Place, the *Chicago* (Illinois) *Sun;* Second Place, the *Salt Lake* (Utah) *Tribune;* Third Place, the *Milwaukee* (Wisconsin) *Journal;* Honorable Mentions, the *Minneapolis* (Minnesota) *Star-Journal* and the *St. Joseph* (Missouri) *News-Press.*

It will be noted that some newspapers were given awards in both of these contests.

Many of the examples used in connection with this discussion are sample front pages from newspapers which won recognition in the two contests in 1946. Front pages of the *New York Herald Tribune,* six times winner of the F. Wayland Ayer Cup, and the *New York Times,* which won this award four times in previous years, also have been included. All these pages have been brought together for the express purpose of providing readers an opportunity to study and compare the front pages of newspapers that have been adjudged the most outstanding for their excellence of typography and makeup.

By following the results of these and other typography contests conducted each year throughout the country and by seriously studying the winning papers, editors and students can benefit greatly.

Newspapers that never have entered such competitions might well consider the advantages afforded for the encouragement of better design and makeup that would appeal not only to readers but also to others interested in determining the most effective advertising media.

XIII

Inside-Page Makeup

THE FRONT PAGE REQUIRES SPECIAL ATTENTION because it is the "show window" of the newspaper. The desire of readers to turn to the inside generally is conditioned by the attractiveness and effectiveness of the treatment used on page one.

Inside pages also must be designed with equal care if interest is to be maintained throughout the entire paper. The editor who fails to accept this important fact and to plan accordingly is not making the most of his opportunities. He not only penalizes the reader but also himself, since advertisers today generally place their business with those newspapers which seem to offer the best assurance of good reader-traffic. Pleasing design and makeup rate high in their estimation of a newspaper's worth as an advertising medium.

In our earliest newspapers, which consisted of only two or four pages, there was little advertising, and the problem of makeup was very simple. When ads did appear, they ordinarily were run on the front page, which was regarded more as a front cover or wrapper to protect the inside pages that carried the bulk of the news. Consequently, advertising space on this page was much cheaper.

Some newspapers, including the *Boston Post* and others in the New England states and elsewhere, still follow this traditional practice, which, in turn, is a carry-over from the practices in England during colonial times. However, the majority of present-day editors in this country carefully avoid placing advertisements on the important front page.

Advertising typography was greatly limited for many years because of mechanical restrictions. Not until the invention of stereotyping and its adaptation to rotary presses was it possible to break column-rules on the larger papers that made use of type-revolving presses. When measures wider than one column were desired, the ads had to be planned in such a way that the material in one column would carry over the column-rule into the next. This arrangement was very unsatisfactory from both the standpoint of design and readability.

Wood cuts were the main media available for the reproduction of pictures until the invention of photo-engraving near the end of the nineteenth century. Consequently, the use of illustrations was held to a minimum by most editors. Even after the mechanical difficulties were overcome, many newspapers were slow to accept changes.

Eventually, the importance of using the front page as the "show window" for displaying important news was recognized, and advertising gradually was moved to the inside. However, for many years little attention was given to careful planning of inside pages, which seemed to be regarded more as a convenient dumping ground for less important news and haphazardly arranged advertising.

As advertising increased in volume and took on great significance as a source of revenue, editors and advertisers alike commenced to take keener interest in the improvement of makeup and design of inside pages. Research departments were established by many large newspapers and advertising agencies to test the effectiveness of various techniques. The investigations proved conclusively that well-designed advertising placed in orderly, attractive arrangements on inside pages had decided advantages over the hit-or-miss system that had prevailed for so long. As a result of scientific study and encouragement provided by typographical contests, great strides have been made in recent years toward the production of newspapers that are interesting and attractive throughout.

However, many present-day newspapers are not giving sufficient attention to inside pages. Frequently the front page will be exceptionally well done, but the rest of the paper will be completely lacking in orderliness and attractiveness.

Just as much thought should be given to the planning of interesting inside pages as to the front page, since it is here that both advertising and news are placed. The value of advertising is dependent, like news, upon readership, and without this source of income, few newspapers would be able to exist.

Consequently, it is of primary importance from the standpoint of the reader, the advertiser, and the publisher that inside pages should be designed in such a way that they will be inviting and thus encourage readers to go through every page in the paper. By making use of interesting news and pictures properly displayed along with well-planned advertising, it is possible to obtain high readership on these pages. Every inside page should be planned with extreme care.

Limiting Factors

Although the same general principles of design and makeup are applicable to both front pages and inside pages, the inclusion of advertising multiplies the problems involved and calls for different techniques.

The nature and amount of advertising which is to appear in a given edition strongly affect the kind of treatment that can be used most effectively. The number of pages is determined by the quantity of advertising scheduled, and the number of column inches of advertising allotted to a given page reduces proportionately the space left for news and its accompanying display. Thus, every inside page usually requires individual attention.

There is no standard rule regulating the percentage-wise distribution of advertising and news. Most publishers feel that they should carry approximately 60 per cent advertising and 40 per cent news if they are to succeed financially. Some run a higher percentage of advertising, but such a policy often leads to the dissatisfaction of readers.

However these same percentages will not be used on every page, since generally no advertising is run on page one, and it also may be kept off other special pages, or greatly reduced. Furthermore, the size and character of the ads themselves may make it advisable to devote less space to news on some pages than on others.

The main objective of the makeup editor should be to allow enough space for news on every page to insure effective display and to create sufficient interest on the part of readers to attract and hold their attention. He should not lose sight of the fact that the newspaper's primary function is to print the news; but he also should remember that it has the additional duty of informing readers about needed merchandise and of directing them to desirable markets once the policy of running advertising has been adopted. Advertising has become an important part of the economic structure, and, as one of its leading media, the newspaper should attempt to serve readers and advertisers in the best possible manner.

Planning Inside Pages

Before the makeup editor can plan the display of news and pictures for inside pages, he must know how much advertising is to appear and the manner in which it is to be distributed throughout the paper. This information is furnished to him by someone in the advertising department whose duty it is to prepare two dummies for every page. One of these goes to the composing room to guide the makeup man in placing advertisements in the form ahead of the news matter. It shows clearly the position, size of space, and the name of firm for each advertisement to appear on the page. On the other, only the space to be taken up by the advertising is indicated. This is given to the makeup editor, who fills in the rest of the page with news and its accompanying display.

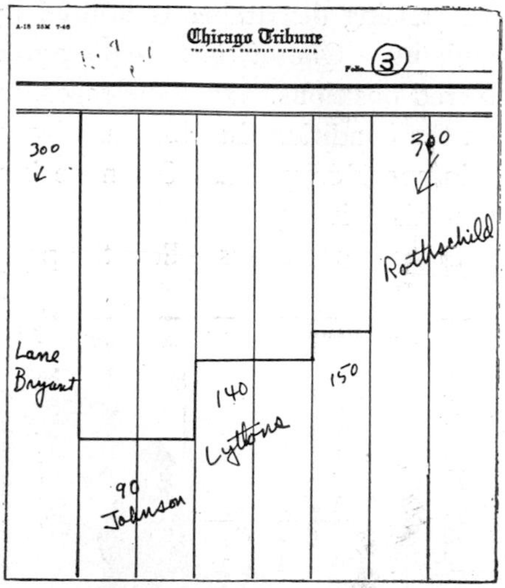

Figure 139. Dummy sheet of an inside page to show the placement of ads and the space they will take on the page. The figures "300," "90," etc. written in spaces given to ads indicate the column depth in agate lines each will occupy.

Planning the placement of advertising for inside pages is handled by the advertising manager on smaller papers, but on the large dailies, this work generally is in charge of a special executive known as the *advertising dispatcher*.

As each page is planned, certain rules must be observed. In the first place, enough space must be left to permit a good supply of news so that the reader will be attracted to the page as he goes through the paper. The space provided should be sufficiently large and of such a nature that the news can be displayed effectively. Pages that are overcrowded with advertising are not pleasing to readers; consequently, the advertising should not be crammed into only a few pages, but spread out as much as possible through the entire paper, with enough space for news on every page to make it interesting and inviting.

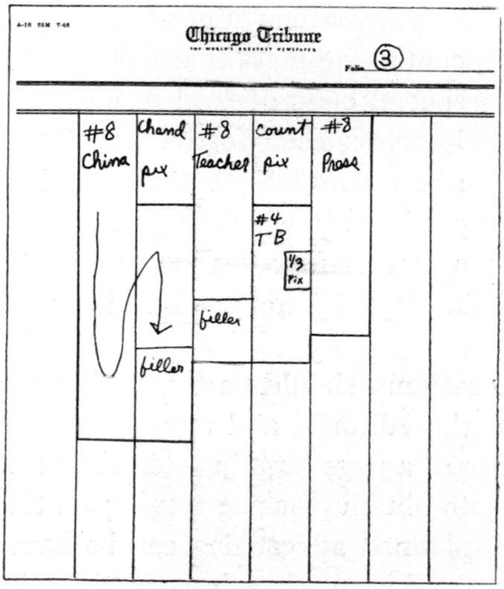

Figure 140. Dummy sheet of an inside page to show where stories are to be placed on the page. The space to be taken up by ads is left blank.

Like the makeup editor, the

advertising dispatcher is limited by certain policies that must not be violated. One of these is the agreement to give some advertisers preferred positions. In some cases, an advertiser may contract for space on the condition that his ads always be run in a given position on certain specified pages. Often he is willing to pay an additional charge for this privilege.

Some newspapers follow the practice of placing advertising on pages

Figure 141. Half-pyramid style of placing advertising.

carrying news of a related nature. For instance, ads dealing with sporting goods, tobacco, and liquor may be scheduled to appear on the sports page; bank and investment house ads, on the financial page; woman's apparel ads, on the woman's page; and theater and amusement ads, on pages carrying news about entertainment. Sometimes higher rates are charged for these positions. Many newspapers reserve the right to distribute advertising according to their own discretion.

The placement of ads on pages containing news that will draw a special class of readers not only increases the effectiveness of the ads themselves, but also assists readers in locating information about products in which they are likely to be interested. Furthermore, such a plan contributes to the over-all unity of the newspaper and aids in the departmentalization of advertising along with the news.

Those responsible for inside-page makeup should be thoroughly acquainted with the problems of both the editorial and advertising departments. The advertising structure of a page largely determines the kind of editorial treatment necessary to obtain pleasing results; on the other hand, the effectiveness of well-planned advertising can be hampered by improper display of the news. Harmonious interrelationship between news and ads must exist if inside-page makeup is to accomplish the most satisfactory results. Close cooperation between the advertising dispatcher and the makeup editor is highly essential.

METHODS OF PLACING ADVERTISING

Several methods are followed in the placement of advertising on the inside pages. One of the most common is the *half-pyramid,* in which the ads are stepped up gradually in a diagonal line from the bottom of the page at the left-hand side. The height of the pyramid depends upon the amount of advertising to appear. (See Fig. 141.)

Sometimes the ads extend all the way to the top, limiting the number of columns available for news in this area. When they do not reach entirely to the top, all eight columns in the upper portion of the page are left free, and because of this feature, the half-pyramid method is more desirable than any of the others. It allows the makeup editor to plan an interesting and attractive page; furthermore, advertisements can be positioned in such a way that each is touched by reading matter, which is an important consideration from the standpoint of the advertiser in that it increases the possibility of readership.

Figure 142. Double-pyramid style of placing advertising.

When several small ads are to be placed on a page, the *double-pyramid* method frequently is used in an effort to avoid "burying" some of them. Starting at the base of each pyramid at, or near, the center of the page at the bottom, the ads are stepped up diagonally on each side of the page.

This arrangement usually permits the running of reading matter next to all the ads, and leaves the columns at the top of the page open for news display. Care should be taken not to allow the pyramid thus formed on the left-hand side to run too high, since it is important that a sufficient amount of this area be left free to permit the display of news and the use of a good starter head.

Sometimes the nature of the advertising to be included calls for the use of the *rectangle-and-pyramid* method. In this kind of design, one or more advertisements of the same width extend the full length of one

Figure 143. Pyramid-and-rectangle style of placing advertising.

side of the page in the form of a rectangle, and the rest are placed in the form of a pyramid extending up the opposite side of the page. This plan limits the amount of space for the display of news, but often it cannot be avoided because of the volume, size, and shape of the advertisements scheduled for the page.

One of the least desirable methods is the *double-rectangle,* which results in what is referred to as the "well" style of makeup. Ads of the same width are stacked, one directly above the other, in two rectangular forms —one on either side of the page— leaving only the center columns open for reading matter.

The number of columns left free for news is dependent upon the width of the two rectangles. In every instance, the makeup possibilities are limited, since the area that remains is reduced to a long, narrow "well" that makes attractive display of news almost impossible. For this reason, the *double-rectangle* method is carefully avoided by most newspapers.

The most objectionable is the *hit-or-miss* method, so called because the advertisements are thrown onto the page in a helter-skelter fashion, with no apparent attention being given to the principles governing pleasing display. Such a practice results in pages that are confusing and completely lacking in orderly design.

Few newspapers are able to follow only one method of advertising placement. Those papers which make a

Figure 144. Double-rectangle style of placing advertising.

strong effort to abide by the half-pyramid style frequently are forced by circumstances to shift to another method on some pages in order to accommodate the advertising scheduled in the number of pages allotted, and at the same time to preserve high readability and pleasing design.

By combining the most acceptable methods—the pyramid, the double-pyramid, and the rectangle-and-pyramid—it is possible to maintain an appearance of unified design throughout the paper and to provide a maximum of space for the display of news.

When a combination of methods is used, an attempt should be made whenever possible to treat matching pages which fall opposite one another in the same general manner. For instance, if the pyramid-and-rectangle method is employed on page two, it also should be used on

Figure 145. Hit-or-miss style of placing advertising.

page three so that the feeling of consistent agreement will be heightened when the reader opens up the pages.

Typographical Standards

Few present-day publishers have complete control over the design of all advertisements that appear in their newspapers since many are furnished by outside agencies in the form of stereotype mats or printing plates ready for use. The desires of local advertisers who have certain preferences also must be respected. However, by setting up certain standards which cannot be violated and by stressing the importance of skilled craftsmanship, excellent results can be obtained.

Many newspapers have established certain rules in an effort to avoid over-display brought about by the use of heavy rules, black type, and other discordant elements which are ruinous to good page-design. Such bargain-sale practices tend to give a feeling of cheapness and gaudiness.

These regulations generally control the size and boldness of the types and cuts that may be employed. When the elements desired are to exceed certain specified limits, they must be toned down by means of outline and shaded effects and the use of Ben Day screens. Such rules also apply particularly to extremely large types containing broad, black lines, and to reverse cuts. The very dark areas would give a spotted effect to the page that would be detrimental to the tonal quality and over-all attractiveness of the design.

Another desirable practice is attempting to place advertisements of approximately the same tone quality on the same page, and of keeping the headline- and picture-display of news in consistent agreement. When one or more elements on a page greatly outshouts all the others, the entire design is damaged. A much better plan is to distribute the very strong elements in such a manner throughout the paper that every page is as harmonious and pleasing as possible. Some pages will be heavier or lighter in tone than others, but the newspaper as a whole will be far more attractive and readable.

Advertising Typography

The principles of good design and layout which already have been mentioned in a previous chapter should be followed in planning advertisements. Since every ad is an individual problem, methods of treatment vary greatly. However, certain rules may be applied to all of them.

The types, illustrations, borders, and all other elements going into every design should be selected with careful attention to the character of the message to be conveyed and their suitability from the standpoint of harmonious agreement. Although the practice of using the same types as those employed in the head-dress is satisfactory, type faces from other families and races should be included to add variety and liveliness to the pages.

Companion faces selected for use together in advertisements should be of designs that harmonize well with those used in headlines, and the number employed should be limited in the interest of good taste. The practice of including many novelty faces just because of their unusual qualities is not sound. There is much to be said for simplicity and straightforwardness in the presentation of advertising messages, just as in the presentation of news.

When borders are used, they should be in harmony with the type designs employed. If the types are plain and geometric, with straight lines predominating, highly decorative designs should be avoided; in no event should borders be so black or unusual that they detract the attention of the reader from the headlines and text. On the other hand, if borders are to accomplish their purpose, they must increase the attractiveness of the over-all design and contribute to the effectiveness of the message presented.

The manner in which borders are handled by the compositor also is highly important. Care should be taken to see that they fit perfectly together at the corners and that those used are not nicked or worn. Special attention should be given to the standing ads that are run in several consecutive issues of the paper. Frequently, the borders as well as the type become worn and battered and must be replaced.

Another fault that should be avoided is that of overcrowding an advertisement with reading matter and headline display. Judicious use of white space is just as important in increasing interest and readability in advertisements as in the news. Solid gray masses have a tendency to discourage readers. In addition to making the advertisements more appealing typographically, a pleasing use of white space contributes greatly to the over-all attractiveness of the page-design.

In recent years, several newspapers have begun the practice of using no borders around advertisements. They feel that in many instances the column-rules at the sides and the cut-off rules at the top and bottom are sufficient, and that the employment of any additional rules or borders is unnecessary and wasteful. This plan was adopted by many newspapers during World War II as a means of conserving newsprint. Frequently, such a method works out very effectively, especially when the ads are inside the page and when enough white space is provided around the outside elements.

However, difficulties arise when ads employing no borders are placed in outside columns on the page, since the gray masses next to the margin usually are not even and consequently present a jagged, uneven effect, with nothing to hold them together and to provide a feeling of unity. As a result, the white area extends from these outside elements to the extreme edge of the page. Generally, the amount of white space thus allowed is greater than that provided on the other side of the ad next

Figure 146. Page containing ads without borders.

to the news column, and the design appears to be out of balance. Even though the two white areas are balanced, the ad as a whole is thrown out of line with those ads above or below it which use borders, and the over-all design suffers.

The use of cut-off rules between advertisements is a practice of long-standing. However, the pressure brought about by insufficient news-print during World War II led many editors to discard them. Instead, a small amount of white space is employed to separate advertisements on the page. This device contributes to greater simplicity, and generally is more desirable, since it requires less time on the part of the compositor and adds to the attractiveness of the page by dispensing with an element that usually served no useful purpose in the over-all design.

Another practice of rather recent origin is the use of color in news-paper advertising. The experimentation and close cooperation of press manufacturers have made it possible to equip newspapers to print with color in regular editions. The value of color in attracting attention to an advertisement is great, and, in addition to its tremendous pulling power, it aids materially in brightening up the page. Advertisers recognize its potential advantages over ads printed entirely in ordinary black and white, and many are willing to pay a much higher rate in order to be given the exclusive use of color on a page.

PLANNING DISPLAY OF NEWS

After the location of advertisements has been determined and the dummies have been received, the makeup editor is ready to plan the display of news for each page. The amount of space with which he must deal is much smaller—and of a different shape—than that of the front page, on which no ads are carried. Consequently, he must employ somewhat different techniques for those pages on which advertising is to be printed.

Beginning at the top of the page, the first thing to be considered is the *running head*. This is the line giving the page number and the date and place of publication. Many newspapers still follow the traditional practice of running this line across the full width of the page, with a headrule eight columns wide placed directly underneath to separate it from the top headlines. The same style of type as that used in the date line on page one ordinarily is used, and the words generally are set in full-capitals. The type selected should harmonize closely, both in design and weight, with the rest of the head-dress, and it should be in a size small enough so that it does not attract undue attention.

During World War II, several newspapers reduced the width of the running head in an effort to save space. In some instances, it was trimmed down to one column in width and run in the outside column of the page; in others, it was made to occupy the two outside columns. Some of the tabloids removed it from the top of the page and placed it vertically along the outside edge, with the letters centered one below the other. Several column inches of space were conserved, and most of the newspapers that made the change continued the practice after the war ended.

Many editors insist on a carefully planned front page, but they give little or no attention to the inside, allowing the makeup man to place the news according to his own discretion. As a consequence, the inside pages often lack orderliness, and compared with the front page are dull and uninteresting. Such a practice is a great mistake, since the manner in which the news is displayed on the inside pages has a great effect on readership. Aside from offering news in a much more satisfactory and functional manner, appropriate display is a great asset to advertisers in that it is the best available method of leading readers onto the pages where the ads are located.

Following the same plan as that used on page one, the most important stories should be placed at the top of inside pages. Every page should contain interesting news, accompanied by at least one good "starter" headline, in order to direct the reader to the biggest news and to hold up the page design. If enough space is left at the top of the page, more than one of the stronger headlines can be used advantageously. Secondary and two- or three-column feature headlines usually are employed for this purpose. The smaller subordinate headlines in types of 18 points or smaller should not be assigned to this top position, since they are too weak and ineffective to impress the reader.

Contrary to the plan followed on page one, the main head on an inside page generally is placed in the outside column, or columns, on the left-hand side. This is the most desirable position, since readers normally enter a printed page from the left side, and they have been conditioned to expect the main news to appear in this area on inside pages.

Sometimes a banner line is used as a starter at the top of the page to hold up the design and to give strong emphasis to the main story. It ordinarily is followed by a cut-off rule underneath and reads out into a secondary headline or second deck placed above the text in column one. On the other hand, it may be accompanied by a two-column spread if more strength is desired.

Occasionally, a newspaper will use an eight-column line, in large

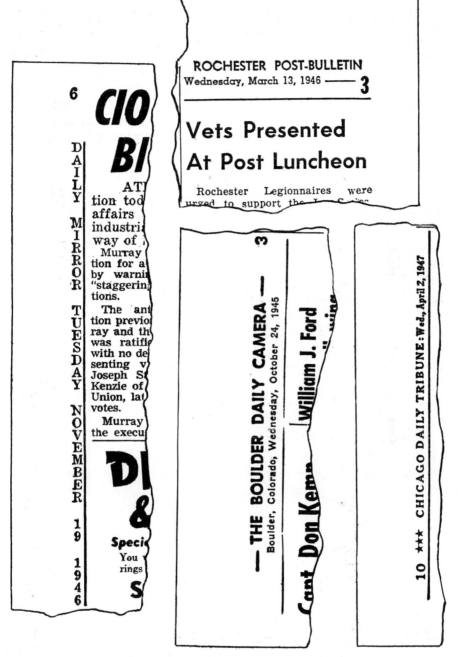

Figure 147. Shown above are some of the styles of running heads being used by present-day newspapers. In addition to these, many papers employ a running head that extends all the way across the top of the page.

type, which does not tie in with any one story on the page. The headline then serves the purpose of a "label," often pointing out the character of the news to be found on the page. Again, it may serve as a department headline on one or more of the special inside pages. In addition to attracting the attention of readers and guiding them in their search for news, the line is an aid in adding strength in this important area on the page. Although the banner line can be made to serve a useful purpose on inside pages, if it is overworked it will lose its effectiveness and result in monotony.

Careful attention should be given to the middle and bottom areas of these pages. Headlines and other elements should be placed in such a manner that pleasing gradation and balance are maintained. Top-heaviness is just as objectionable on inside pages as on the front page.

When space is available, good feature headlines and pictures should be used along with subordinate headlines in the area below the fold, as well as at the top of the page. An effort should be made to make the entire area left for news as interesting and lively as possible. Furthermore, the weight and over-all tone of the advertising on the page should be taken into consideration when headlines and other news dis-

Figure 148. Many newspapers, like the *Reading Eagle,* use a banner-line at the top of an inside page to accompany one of the most important stories.

Figure 149. In some papers, a banner-line is employed to serve the purpose of a page-label, as shown in this page from the *Muncie Star.*

play are being planned. The closer the agreement, the more harmonious and attractive the entire page-design will be.

Boxes frequently can be used advantageously for purposes of contrast and variety; however, too many individualized units are detrimental to the over-all effect, since they have a tendency to break up the page and give it a spotted appearance. The use of boxed labels over country correspondence and special columns does not accomplish the purpose of good display so efficiently as regular news and feature headlines that are well planned. Good news or feature heads are much more effective, since they permit the headline writer to tell readers something about the news included. By incorporating the name of the town or the writer in the headline, or using it as a by-line, a far more satisfactory summary of the news can be provided; at the same time, the design will contribute to the unity and attractiveness of the page as a whole. Boxed elements should always be used sparingly.

Pictures are a great aid in adding interest and liveliness to inside-page makeup. If the illustrations are of striking news value, they frequently can be used effectively in the outside columns at the left-hand side of the page at the top, where the reader will see them first. They also serve a very useful purpose in other areas on the page to provide balance with the heavier top display, or to bolster the display elsewhere in an effort to carry readers throughout the entire page.

In order to avoid giving readers the impression that a news picture is a part of an advertisement, most makeup editors avoid placing cuts in adjoining columns, but separate the picture from the advertising by at least one column of reading matter. However, when little chance of confusion exists, pictures frequently are run next to the advertisement. Good judgment, rather than an inflexible rule, should dictate the most desirable procedure.

Another practice to be avoided is that of using tomb-stones. The same rule should apply to their employment on inside pages as that followed in the makeup of the front page.

It is essential that enough light be admitted to the news areas on the inside pages to make them inviting to the reader. Spacing between decks and around them and other elements on the page should be ample enough to insure a maximum of readability. Subheads should be used throughout the text of long stories to break up the long expanses of grayness.

The possibilities for pleasing display naturally are greater on those pages in which all the columns at the top and a generous amount of space elsewhere on the page are left free for headlines and accompanying news stories. As the number of available columns is reduced, the problem becomes increasingly more difficult, and the ingenuity of the makeup editor is put to greater tests in his efforts to create interesting and attractive pages.

STYLES OF INSIDE PAGE MAKEUP

One of the most common styles of makeup for inside pages is *balanced makeup*. This may be achieved in several ways. Strong one-

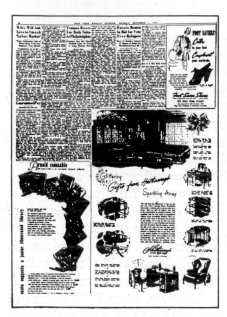

Figure 150. An example of balanced inside-page makeup, in which all top heads are one column in width. Contrast heads would be better than dead ends to separate main heads.

Figure 151. An example of balanced inside-page makeup, in which two similar two-column spread headlines are used along with a picture placed between them.

column headlines of the same design may be used in alternate columns across the top of the page, with dead ends of stories or contrast headlines separating them. One-column pictures or boxes also are employed between the main heads to afford pleasing contrast and to add interest.

Sometimes a two-column headline is placed on the left-hand side at the top of the page to balance another of the same kind on the right. Newspapers using pictures frequently place a cut in between the two heads to take up the rest of the space.

The inside page of the *New York Herald Tribune* shows how balance may be obtained by the use of one-column headlines; that of the *Chicago Sun,* in which the same number of top columns is utilized, illustrates the kind of interesting display that results from the use of two-column headlines and illustrations. (See Figs. 150-151.)

When all eight columns are left open at the top of the page for news display, another variation may be obtained by placing one of the main headlines in column one and another of the same kind in column eight. The other headlines on each side descend in order of size as they approach the center, where a two-column headline or picture is placed.

In the balanced style of makeup,

Figure 152. An example of descending inside-page makeup.

a careful attempt always is made to combine headlines, pictures, and other elements in such a way that the top of the page will appear carefully balanced. The technique employed naturally will depend upon the number of columns available and the importance of the news to be displayed.

Another style of makeup is that referred to as *descending order.* It is obtained by placing a strong starter headline in column one. Headlines in other columns grow successively smaller as the right side of the page is approached.

The makeup editor finds descending order a useful method to employ when the space for news stories is limited and when all stories must grow progressively shorter across the page to the right-hand side, since it gives him

Figure 153. An example of focused inside-page makeup.

an opportunity to use up several stories of lesser importance for which he sometimes has difficulty in finding suitable places. The descending order style of makeup also has a tendency to lead the eyes of the reader gradually across the page by providing news that is displayed according to its importance in a quiet and attractive manner.

A third style is one which may be referred to as *focused makeup,* since it is designed to claim the first attention of the reader when he enters a page. A common device is to run a large picture that is much heavier in tone and larger than any other element on the page in the upper left-hand columns. This picture frequently is followed by a large headline and story to which it is related (See Fig. 153). By using other strong headlines throughout the news space, this paper has created a page that looks highly interesting and attractive.

Although the strongest element ordinarily is placed at the top on the left-hand side of the page, it may be shifted to the inside columns in order to allow the pleasing display of other important stories. However, the picture and headlines used in this manner always dominate the page and form the main center of interest.

READERSHIP OF INSIDE PAGES

Since the number of readers attracted to inside pages is of great concern to a newspaper, many studies have been conducted in an effort to obtain some reliable guides. One of the most important of these is *The Continuing Study,* carried on by The Advertising Research Foundation. Investigations to determine what material people read disclosed a sustained level of reading of 96 per cent or better for the inside pages of both Section One and Section Two, for men and also for women. A breakdown of the findings is given in the table on page 401.[1]

A study of these figures indicates that people read carefully the inside pages as well as page one, but that the percentages differ greatly according to the type of news carried. For instance, only 37 per cent of the men and 21 per cent of the women read the editorial page, whereas 90 per cent of the men and 89 per cent of the women read the picture page.

LEFT-HAND VS. RIGHT-HAND PAGES

Contrary to the belief of many people, this study also revealed that left-hand newspaper pages have a slightly higher readership than right-

---

[1] *The Newspaper As An Advertising Medium,* page 109.   New York: The Bureau of Advertising, The American Newspaper Publishers' Association, 1940.

hand pages. The tabulation given for 107 left-hand pages and 105 right-hand pages indicated that 75 per cent of the women read right-hand pages and 77 per cent read left-hand pages. Sixty-five per cent of the men showed a preference for right-hand pages, against 69 per cent for left-hand pages.[2]

Part of Paper	Median Reading*	
	Men	Women
The front page	98%	98%
Section I	99%	100%
Inside pages, Section I	96%	99%
Section II	99%	99%
Inside pages, Section II	98%	99%
Editorials	37%	21%
The editorial page	81%	80%
Comics	82%	79%
Financial news	29%	10%
Radio listings and news	36%	44%
Society news and pictures	45%	87%
Sports news and pictures	78%	46%
Picture page	90%	89%

* (Percentages are for people reading anything in part of paper indicated.)

The scientific data provided by *The Continuing Study* should be of great value as a guide to editors seeking information regarding the most effective placement of advertising and other material on the inside pages of their newspapers.

TREATMENT OF SPECIAL PAGES

Although much of the news which is to appear on inside pages can be handled in a more or less routine manner, most newspapers provide special pages that are planned to have outstanding appeal to the various classes of readers.

The number of special pages carried varies considerably. On the smaller newspapers, where the number of pages is limited, there may be only one or two, whereas the dailies in metropolitan centers generally have several, often with more than one page devoted to a particular kind of news. However, practically every daily newspaper has an editorial page, a sports page, and a society or woman's page on which stories and pictures are segregated for special treatment.

Since the typography and makeup of these special pages generally differ in some respects from other inside pages, they will be discussed separately in the following chapters.

[2] *The Newspaper As An Advertising Medium*, page 109.

XIV

The Editorial Page

ALTHOUGH THE NUMBER OF SPECIAL PAGES RUN by various newspapers differs greatly, practically every publisher provides an editorial page which is given special treatment. From the time of our earliest newspapers, editors have been following this practice. Some of the most outstanding figures in American journalism achieved their fame through the editorial page. During the era of personal journalism, Dana, Greeley, Watterson, Raymond, and Bowles were able to wield tremendous influence by vigorous writing carried on the editorial pages for readers who looked to them for information and guidance.

However, as newspapers continued to increase in size and the amount and cost of equipment mounted, one-man ownership was replaced in many places by corporations in which several individuals were interested. As a result, the character of the editorial page, along with the rest of the paper, underwent some changes. One of the most significant has been the substitution of the writings of several men for those of a single individual—the editor-owner—who used to dominate the page.

Naturally, there have been some exceptions. One of the most notable was that of the *Emporia Gazette,* a small daily newspaper in Kansas, owned by the late William Allen White, who built a nationwide reputation by his brilliant writings and powerful editorials.

In addition to leading editorials expressing the newspaper's views on important issues of the day, most present-day editorial pages contain interpretative articles, feature stories, cartoons, and other material of special interest to readers; but in many communities, the strong personal touch that characterized the editorial page a century ago has disappeared. Its passing has been accompanied by a marked decline in readership, which is explained in part by the fact that modern readers have less time to devote to their newspapers and have developed the habit of hurriedly scanning headlines and news. Another reason is the failure of many editors to give proper display to the material which they place on this important page.

Despite the knowledge that has been gained by readership studies regarding the value of appropriate display and pleasing design, some newspapers persist in producing dull, gray editorial pages that are more of an invitation to turn on to something interesting than to stop and read what is on the editorial page.

There is no reason why this special page should not be one of the brightest and most attractive parts of the paper, and many editors have succeeded in accomplishing excellent results by using great care in selecting the material that appears and then giving it the kind of typographical treatment that will attract and hold readers.

Variation in Widths of Columns

In general, newspapers do not follow a standard pattern in designing the editorial page. In fact, probably less uniformity exists here than in front-page makeup.

Several devices are used in an effort to give the page individuality and to set it off by distinctive treatment from all other pages in the newspaper. One of the most common of these devices is using columns of different widths to provide variety and to increase readability. For many years, all newspapers employed columns of the same width and number on the editorial page as on all other pages, and some are still following this scheme. Aside from helping to add distinctiveness to the editorial page, the use of wider columns permits the employment of a somewhat larger body-type with more white space between lines than that employed in regular news columns. Consequently, greater ease of reading and a more interesting appearance result.

Furthermore, when type is set in the longer measures, the articles take up less space down the column, and the long, narrow-column expanses of gray reading matter common to the old traditional style of makeup are avoided. Articles appear shorter and less forbidding to the reader, and consequently more inviting. Reader-interest surveys have shown that pages employing the older style of narrow column have a lower readership than those in which wider columns with larger type and more white space between lines are used.

Many newspapers have broken away from the traditional plan by changing the width of at least some of the columns on the page to provide a more distinctive and interesting makeup. Some of them, like the *Rutland Daily Herald,* have increased slightly the width of columns, all of which are set the same measure, and have reduced to seven the number of columns on the page. The change is not great, but it lets in more light and results in more attractive pages.

The *Salt Lake Tribune* and the *Washington Post* also employ seven columns on the editorial page, but each gives the page a somewhat different treatment. In the *Salt Lake Tribune,* the first two columns take up the space of three ordinary columns, and the last five columns are narrow, whereas the *Washington Post* runs the first three columns wide.

Figure 154.   Editorial page of the *Rutland Daily Herald.*

Sometimes the wide column is placed in the center of the page and three regular-width columns are run on either side.

Another group of papers uses only six columns. For example, the *Christian Science Monitor* follows this plan, with all columns set the same width; but the *Chicago Sun*—also with six columns on the page—runs columns one and six in wider measures.[1]

Figure 155. Editorial page of the *Salt Lake Tribune*.

---

[1] Throughout this book, all references to the *Chicago Sun* relate to practices that were followed before it changed to tabloid size on September 28, 1947. Sample pages of the *Sun* used for illustrative purposes likewise were taken from the standard-size editions.

This great variation in the style of makeup indicates the desire on the part of some editors to make the page distinctive.

Column Rules vs. White Space

Most of the pages already mentioned have provided more white space between columns than is used on regular news pages. This has been accomplished in several ways.

Figure 156. Editorial page of the *Washington Post*.

In order to let more light into the page, the *Washington Post,* the *Salt Lake Tribune,* and the *Christian Science Monitor* have used column-rules cast on a wider than ordinary body, which allow more shoulder on either side. The *Rutland Daily Herald* and the *Chicago Sun* have dispensed with column-rules entirely, using instead approximately one pica of white space to separate columns. This results in a more open design and one that is more modern in approach.

The *Salt Lake Tribune* makes use of both of these plans on its edi-

Figure 157. Editorial page of the *Christian Science Monitor.*

torial page. No column-rule is used to separate the leading editorials in columns one and two, but rules cast on a wide body are placed between all other reading matter on the page.

A liberal amount of white space between columns helps to prevent the eye from jumping across from one column to another; it also results in breaking up gray masses into designs that are more pleasing and more inviting.

Figure 158. Editorial page of the *Chicago Sun* of December 12, 1946.

SIZE OF BODY TYPE

When the width of columns is increased, care must be given to the selection of a size of body-type that is most legible in the longer measures. Frequently, the same type as that employed in the regular news columns can be used successfully, provided that the length of line is not too great; and the reading matter generally can be made more inviting by the use of more leading between lines. However, a slightly larger size of type usually is advisable. Especially, those newspapers using body-type that is less than 8 points in size for regular news columns should carefully consider the advantages of employing a larger size on this page. Ten- or 12-point body-type, with at least 2-point leading, results in higher legibility and in a page that is more inviting to the reader.

In the wider columns, including those in which the leading editorials are carried, the type ordinarily should be somewhat larger than in columns of regular width. Furthermore, the most advisable plan is to provide type of sufficient size and with enough leading in each column to assure that an over-all evenness of tone will be maintained throughout.

Sometimes a page will take on a spotted or streaked effect in certain areas where type masses containing a minimum of leading are placed beside others that have been opened up with white space. In the interest of good page-design, this effect should be avoided. On the editorial page, as on all others, one of the primary aims should be to provide reading matter that is easy to read, pleasing in tone, and inviting to the reader. A study of the accompanying examples of editorial pages will show that most of them have observed this rule closely. In some, the same size of type has been used throughout where columns are of the same width; in almost every instance where the width of columns varies, the size of type in the wider columns is larger than that used elsewhere on the page. In general, type masses have been given generous leading in all columns in the interest of high readability.

PLACEMENT OF MASTHEAD

To many readers, the masthead has become a symbol that tells them when they have reached the editorial page as they turn through the paper. For many years, it always was placed at the top of column one on the left-hand side of the page, and many present-day newspapers follow the same practice. Among those using the traditional plan are the *New York Times,* the *Washington Post,* the *Milwaukee Journal,* and the *St. Louis Post-Dispatch.* In some papers, several column inches are taken up; in others, the material has been condensed so that only a small amount of space is required.

Another slightly different plan calls for setting the masthead two columns in width and placing it at the top of the two outside columns on the left-hand side of the page. The editorial pages of the *Rutland*

Figure 159.   Editorial page of the *Courier-Journal.*

Daily Herald, the *Salt Lake Tribune,* and the *Courier-Journal* show the effects gained by using this style. Here again, the space devoted to the masthead depends upon the amount of reading matter included and the kind of display employed.

A few newspapers place the masthead copy at the extreme top of the page above the headrule. For instance, the *Chicago Sun* uses a small nameplate, similar in design to that used on the front page, which is centered above the headrule. The names of the publisher and editor

Figure 160. Editorial page of the *St. Paul Dispatch.*

are run in small type underneath it.   The place of publication is given in two lines at the extreme left-hand side.   These lines are balanced by the mailing privilege, which is printed in the same manner on the extreme right.   The page number and date of publication are given on either side of the nameplate.   To carry out the label effect on the page, the word "Editorial" is printed directly above the headline used over the main editorial in the first column.   Thus the *Sun* has succeeded in freeing the top of the first column for its leading editorial. Furthermore, this treatment lends distinctiveness to the page and results in a very pleasing design.

The *Christian Science Monitor* follows a somewhat similar plan in its top-of-the-page design.   However, it repeats most of the material carried above the headrule in a lengthy masthead following the traditional pattern, which is placed at the bottom of the outside column on the right-hand side of the page.   The word "Editorial" is printed in large type at the top of column one and is made to balance with a similar headline structure located at the top of the outside column on the other side of the page.

A growing number of newspapers bury the entire masthead in one of the columns at the bottom of the page.   The *St. Paul Dispatch* places its masthead at the bottom of column eight.   The column chosen for its location differs in the newspapers following this plan.   Some of them, like the *Dispatch,* head column one with the word "Editorials"; others use no label of this kind whatsoever.

Great merit lies in the plan of freeing the top area on the left-hand side of the page for interesting reading matter, since this has been found to be the most important spot on the entire page, and it is here that the leading editorial of the day logically should be placed.   The masthead has the lowest readership of any item of similar size on the page; in fact, most studies have shown that very few readers ever look at it. Furthermore, editorial pages that have rated highest in readership studies have dropped the masthead from its traditional position at the top of the page.

When the masthead is placed above the headrule, it still may serve the function of labeling the page as the one containing editorials.   In fact, the individualized treatment usually given this page ordinarily should be sufficient to guide the reader, and undoubtedly some justification exists for the belief on the part of some editors that the use of any space in the editorial columns for the masthead is unjustified.

When tested on the basis of readership value, the masthead is not entitled to the prominent play given to it by many editors.   If it is to be retained on the editorial page, it should be treated in such a way that it adds dignity and effectiveness to the over-all design and serves some useful purpose for the reader.

Styles of Editorial Headlines

To be in keeping with the purpose and content of the editorial page, the types selected should denote dependability and dignity. If the suggestion of weakness is to be avoided, the use of Scripts and other decorative varieties should be held to a minimum. As on other pages, several styles of headlines should be provided, including some Italic varieties and faces of different weights and sizes so that pleasing variety and contrast may be achieved.

The styles of type chosen should be adapted to the character of the material. They should be clear, attractive, and legible, and should harmonize well with one another. The most common plan is to use only one type family, thus giving a design of monotypographic harmony. Many papers use the same family as that used in the rest of the headline schedule.

The *Milwaukee Journal* follows this plan, making skillful use of the Cheltenham family in the lighter varieties. The *Rutland Daily Herald* produces a clean, highly attractive page with the light versions of Garamond. The *Courier-Journal,* the *Salt Lake Tribune,* and others that use Bodoni in their regular schedules employ the same type family for headlines on the editorial page.

Many newspapers seem to be satisfied with small, hard-to-read label headlines over most articles on the editorial page. This kind of head has little value either from the standpoint of attention-value or reader-interest. Instead of stressing the importance of what they have to say with good substantial headlines, these papers make use of insignificant, one-line labels that they would scorn to use on anything but the most unimportant stories in the regular news columns. Obviously, this practice is a great mistake. Readers are penalized, and the page takes on a gray, uninteresting appearance. It is just as necessary to employ attractive and interesting headlines over editorials as on other important news in the paper.

On this page as on all others headlines should be of sufficient size and length to permit the use of enough words to give adequate summaries of the articles they accompany.

If one-line label headlines are employed, they should be used only in the wider columns, and the style and size of type should be adapted to the message to be conveyed to the reader. Some of the sample editorial pages, including the *Christian Science Monitor,* make skillful use of the label headline. Although some sacrifice in clearness of meaning results at times, the type used is large enough to give good display, and the over-all design of the page is orderly, dignified, and attractive.

A more adequate summary is possible in the two-line style of headline used by the *Courier-Journal* and the *Salt Lake Tribune* over their main editorials. The readers, as a result, are given a much more complete understanding of the content of the accompanying articles. Both of these pages offer excellent examples of strong, well-planned display that not only gives the reader a good understanding of the news involved but also is interesting and inviting.

Value of Good Display

The value of adequate typographical display on the editorial page should not be underestimated. In a study of thirty editorial pages included in *The Continuing Study of Newspaper Reading* (conducted by the Advertising Research Foundation), Robert R. Rand, a graduate student at the Medill School of Journalism in 1941, made some significant findings.

He discovered that 10.1 per cent more readers of the papers investigated were attracted to the editorials using larger, more modern headlines, wider columns, and larger body-type than to those employing small, one-line label headlines and the same body-type and column-width as used throughout the rest of the paper. Highest reader-interest scores, in every instance, went to those newspapers giving special attention to good typographical display. Rand concluded that "editors can do more to increase reader interest in their editorials through typography than in any other single way." [2]

In the final analysis, the value of an editorial, regardless of its content, is directly dependent upon the number of people who read it. Adequate typographical display is a valuable aid available to all editors who are interested in gaining the highest possible readership.

Feature and Column Headlines

In addition to editorials prepared by members of the staff, most newspapers carry special columns, letters to the editor, feature articles, and other kinds of news on this page.

The editorials ordinarily occupy only one or two columns, usually on

[2] Robert R. Rand, *A Study of Reader Interest in Thirty Editorial Pages,* page 59. Evanston, Ill.: The Medill School of Journalism, Northwestern University (Thesis), 1941.

the left-hand side, and the rest of the page is devoted to the other material. Headlines used in this area of the page ordinarily are different in
structure or size than those employed over the editorials, and properly
so.

The main objective should be to select headlines that will harmonize
attractively with those used in the editorial section, and, at the same
time, that will give the articles the kind of display that will attract and
interest readers. Every part of the page should be given careful consideration if the space is to be properly utilized.

Many newspapers follow the plan of using boxed headlines over regular special articles written by columnists. When boxes are used, care
should be taken to see that the borders harmonize with the type employed and that they are replaced before they become battered and
worn.

One of the main objections to the boxed head as commonly used by
many newspapers is that it often contains a single one-line label, which
is of little value in giving the reader an understanding about the content of the article it accompanies on a given day. Frequently, only the
name of the writer is centered inside the borders. Sometimes this is
given in small type underneath the title of the column. Again, the
title of the column may be used by itself. In any of these cases, the
main value of the headline is that of directing the reader to a column;
he is forced to read the article in order to learn the gist of the news.

For many readers who always are highly interested in the comments
of a favorite writer, an uninformative heading may be sufficient. However, others are unwilling to stop every day in their search for news
without something more informative to attract their interest.

Also, some tendency exists to allow too much white space at the ends
of lines and around them in this style of box in order to give them re-
spectable size. Consequently, light areas often develop on the page,
and the use of too many boxes of this kind causes spotted effects that
are detrimental to the over-all design.

Since every box, regardless of its perfection, is an individualized
typographical unit, the employment of several boxes together on a page
is not advisable. Those that are used should be planned carefully so
that they will give pleasing contrast and harmonize with other elements
which they accompany. If handled properly, a judicious use of boxes
can add to the appearance of the page. However, if too many boxed,
standing heads are used on the editorial page, it becomes dull, gray, and
uninteresting. Only a few should be used. In most instances, attractive headlines that "say something" and offer more variety from day to

day are far more desirable from the reader's standpoint, and they are much more serviceable in building attractive and interesting pages.

Many newspapers with editorial pages of the more modern design follow the plan of using good one- and two-column headlines over special columns and feature articles. When these are used, the name of the writer or the title of the column frequently is given in an overline in type smaller than that used in the main headline. The *Chicago Sun* and the *Courier-Journal* make effective use of this type of headline. Sometimes the name of the writer as well as the title of the column is given in a line underneath the headline.

This arrangement makes possible far stronger display and gives the headline writer an opportunity to summarize the news more effectively. Furthermore, he has more strong typographical units with which to work, and less chance arises that certain areas on the page will appear gray and uninteresting, since he is not so handicapped in his efforts to obtain pleasing effects below the fold to get effective balance throughout the page.

One-line label headlines in the portion of the page not occupied by editorials should be used with caution. Unless the column is wider than regular news columns and unless the size of type is sufficiently large, they fail to fulfill a useful purpose. Label headlines are much less effective than the larger headline structures, which give better tonal quality and provide for more adequate summaries. Furthermore, less danger exists of obtaining gray, uninviting areas on the page.

Robert R. Rand's study of thirty editorial pages revealed that the position of articles on the page and the typographical appearance of the display of special columns had a significant effect on reader-interest. Correlations indicated that columns on the left side of the page above the fold attracted 22.1 per cent of the readers; left side of the page below the fold, 23.1 per cent; right side of the page above the fold, 18.2 per cent; and right side of the page below the fold, 16.2 per cent.[3]

Rand discovered that typographical treatment of material in these areas was much more important than its position on the page. Columns with simple label headlines that contained body-type of the same size as used in regular news columns stopped only 16.2 per cent of the readers; whereas the articles displayed with larger, more modern headlines and with larger body-type stopped 19.9 per cent of the readers.

These findings emphasize the great importance of placing stronger display below the fold and of providing considerably more concentration on the bottom of the right-hand side of the page. The employment of

[3] Rand, *A Study of Reader Interest in Thirty Editorial Pages*, page 75.

good feature headlines over articles and the opening up of body-type in these areas would do much to add liveliness and to increase reader-interest in many newspapers.

On the other hand, the use of headlines that are too large and too bold should be avoided. Need for pleasing gradation from the headline down into the reading matter should be remembered. When the

Figure 161. This editorial page could be improved by the employment of somewhat smaller headlines, in order to keep the jump in size from the headlines to body-type from being so great. This change also would reduce the "spotted" effect in the page-design. However, it is neat and orderly.

jump in size or in tone is too great, readability is lessened and the resulting high contrast causes the page design to be spotted and lacking in unity. Furthermore, much valuable space is taken up by headlines that might be used to much better advantage for additional interesting news.

The placement and design of headlines used on the editorial page will be dictated to a large extent by the styles used over the editorials. Every effort should be made to select headlines that harmonize well with one another and to place them in such a way throughout the entire page that the over-all design is pleasing and inviting to the reader.

Letters to the Editor

Many newspapers devote a portion of the editorial page to "letters to the editor," a feature that usually rates high in readership. In fact, Rand found that this type of news attracted 9.1 per cent more readers than the editorials themselves.[4] One of the reasons for this undoubtedly is that people want to see what other people in the community think about certain issues in which they are interested, and they particularly like to have articles written by themselves appear in the newspaper. Furthermore, there is a flavor of neighborliness and friendliness to this type of news that makes it appealing to many readers.

In themselves, these characteristics are not enough to draw some readers to the "letters to the editor" department; however, appropriate headlines and attractive display play an important part, and many editors could increase readership on this page by giving more careful attention to the typographical treatment used in "letters to the editor."

Some editors fail to make the most of their opportunity by placing the letters under small label headlines; no effort is given to make them appear interesting and inviting. Since this material is important to the reader, it should be given the kind of treatment that is more in keeping with its news value.

If a standing head, "Letters to the Editor," or something of a similar nature, is used over the columns, it should be of sufficient size and displayed in such a way that it will attract readers. A few brief facts about the more important letters might well be incorporated.

Furthermore, if an item is important enough to be run in the column, it deserves a headline that will tell the reader something about its contents. The editor who is satisfied with small, one-line, label headlines throughout and no other devices to "dress up" these letters to the editor is bypassing an opportunity to build readership on the editorial page.

[4] Rand, *A Study of Reader Interest in Thirty Editorial Pages*, page 90.

Rand discovered in his study that in newspapers using interesting display on these columns, the reader-interest was as much as 10 per cent higher than in those where small headlines, regular news-column widths, and ordinary body-type were employed.

For instance, "Letters to the Editor" in the *Courier-Journal* (see Figure 159) stopped 51 per cent of the men and 45 per cent of the women; whereas in another paper, which gave no special treatment to this type of news, only 12 per cent of the men and 9 per cent of the women read the material.[5]

Use of Illustrations

The most common type of illustration used on the editorial page is the cartoon. A high percentage of Amercan newspapers are employing this type of picture to brighten and to add interest to the page. When only one cartoon is used, it generally is placed at the top of the page. Its location is determined somewhat by the width and the arrangement of columns on the page. Many newspapers run it in, or near, the center, as does the *Rutland Daily Herald;* others place it in the outside columns on the right-hand side of the page.

The size of the cartoon carried at the top of the page also varies. In some papers, it completely dominates the page. In others, it is small.

The *Courier-Journal* and the *Chicago Sun* carry two cartoons regularly on the editorial page. In these papers, the one at the top is considerably larger. The cartoon at the bottom of the page is placed in the right-hand area and is a great aid in attracting attention to that portion of the page that has been found to be the lowest in reader-interest in most papers.

In every instance, the one-line caption is placed either above or below the cut. It always should be in a face that harmonizes with the other headlines on the page and should not be so large that it attracts undue attention. If the caption is set flush-left, care should be taken to see that it is long enough to avoid too large an area of white space on the right-hand side. Generally, a line centered in the measure is more desirable, since the white space is balanced on either side of the type.

The tone of the cartoon should be in harmony with the rest of the type-dress. A study of the pages mentioned in this discussion will show that all of them have observed this rule quite closely. On the editorial page of the *Chicago Sun,* which is darker in over-all tone than most of the others, the cartoon also is heavier; whereas the *Rutland Daily Herald,* which has an editorial page that is lighter in tone, uses

[5] Rand, *A Study of Reader Interest in Thirty Editorial Pages,* page 98.

cartoons with finer lines that are much more subdued than those found in the *Sun*. In both papers, the cartoons provide more contrast than any other elements on the page.

In addition to cartoons, small line cuts are used by some newspapers in connection with special columns on the editorial page. Among the newspapers represented here, the *Chicago Sun* and the *Rutland Daily Herald* follow this plan.

Halftones also are used sometimes to add interest and color. For instance, the *Chicago Sun* employs them to illustrate other types of articles on the page. Frequently, large halftones are run by some papers to illustrate important editorials or feature stories.

Cartoons, small line cuts, and halftones are excellent aids in brightening the page and increasing reader-interest. In the Rand study, for instance, it was found that the readership of columns employing cuts was 5.3 per cent higher than for those in which no illustrations were used. Thus, illustrations are not only of exceptional value in adding liveliness to the page as a whole, but they also are extremely helpful in attracting more readers.

OTHER TYPOGRAPHICAL DEVICES

Several other typographical devices are employed to obtain special effects on the editorial page. One of these is the use of initial letters. The *Courier-Journal* and the *Chicago Sun* use initial letters in the editorial columns on the left-hand side of the page. Although more time and care are required on the part of the operator and printer in setting composition of this kind, the initials add a touch of dignity that is pleasing.

When initials are used, care should be taken to see that they harmonize closely with the body-type and the type used in other headlines. They should be of sufficient size to add color and variety to the general design. If too many initials are used in several columns on the page, they get monotonous and much of their effectiveness is lost. Furthermore, they are not well adapted to certain types of articles because of their connotation of formality, and consequently they should be reserved only for those articles that require a dignified treatment.

Another device employed to brighten reading matter and make it more interesting is the use of sub-heads. These should be set in the same kind of type as that used in the body-type or in other headlines on the page, and they should be placed at intervals in an article to break up the mass of gray body-type. Usually the one-line cross-line is used for sub-heads. However, some newspapers following a modern style of makeup set them flush-left, and others use two-line structures.

Running paragraphs set in boldface type at intervals throughout an article is not so widespread as it was a few years ago. However, a few newspapers still follow the practice in some columns. The main fault to avoid is causing the page to become spotted as a result of the contrast between the masses of light and heavy type used together.

Dashes also are used by many newspapers to separate articles. These always should be of a design that harmonizes closely with the head-dress. Newspapers using the modern flush-left headlines, with white space separating decks and used between headlines and stories, often follow the same plan on the editorial page, thus maintaining uniformity throughout the entire paper.

Use of Advertisements

Since the editorial page is regarded as one of the most important pages in the paper, the most desirable plan is to keep it entirely free from advertising. Traditionally, this page has been selected as the one place in the paper where the more serious, thought-provoking articles should be run, and many readers judge the character of the paper and its staff by the appearance and content of the editorial page.

In most communities, readers have been educated to expect a page that is dignified and somewhat more formal than other pages in the paper, and often they resent the intrusion of commercial advertising. However, on days when a newspaper is crowded and when the expense of printing an additional section or insertion can be avoided, an editor sometimes is forced to place some advertising on the editorial page. The choice frequently is narrowed down to seriously overloading other pages or taking care of the overflow on the editorial page.

Some newspapers run a small amount of advertising on this page regularly. Usually the same advertisers are given this preferred position in the paper, for which they are willing to pay a premium. The *Salt Lake Tribune* follows this practice.

When advertising is placed on the editorial page, it should be chosen with considerable care. In the first place, the type of advertising run should be dignified in character if it is to carry out the general atmosphere. Furthermore, it should be of a design that fits well with the other elements on the page. If it is too heavy or too light in tone, it detracts from the effectiveness of the over-all design.

EDITORIAL PAGES IN TABLOIDS

The tabloid page is considerably smaller than that of standard-size newspapers and consequently it must be given somewhat different treatment. However, most tabloids use columns of different widths on the editorial page, and in general it is given a somewhat lighter typographical display to add distinctiveness. Most tabloids follow a practice similar in many respects to that used by the *Daily Mirror* and the *New York Daily News.*

Figure 162. Editorial pages of the *New York Daily Mirror* and the *New York Daily News.*

The *Mirror* breaks up the editorial page into three columns, the widest of which is located on the right-hand side of the page and contains the main editorial of the day. This paper uses two cartoons. The largest usually ties in with the leading editorial and is placed near the center at the top of the page. The other is located on the left side at the bottom of the page. A special column, "Washington Merry-Go-Round," appears on the left side at the top under a specially designed, boxed headline.

The *Daily News* puts its main editorial in a wide column on the left-hand side of the page, next to a feature column which is brightened with several small halftone illustrations. The editorial cartoon is at the top on the right-hand side, with letters to the editor run in two columns underneath, headed by a modified boxed headline, "Voice of the People." On both of these pages, the leading editorials are set in a type that is larger in size than that employed in regular news columns, and the type is well leaded to increase readability.

The *Daily Mirror* also sets some of this reading matter in regular boldface and boldface Italic to give emphasis to certain statements.

Another small group of tabloids follows a plan similar to that used by the *Gazette and Daily*, of York, Pennsylvania. The editorial page of this paper has a more formal appearance and looks much like that found in many standard-sized papers, except that it is smaller and has a tendency to run quite gray in the lower area. All columns on the page are of the same width, but are wider than those used on regular news pages. The leading editorial is placed in column one, under a masthead of the traditional variety.

Figure 163. Editorial page of the *Gazette and Daily,* York, Pennsylvania.

The word "Editorial" is centered at the top of the page, where it is printed in connection with the running head. A cartoon is given the center position at the top of the page, and an article with a two-column headline is run directly underneath. The use of white space instead of column rules gives a modern atmosphere to the page.

Since the page-size is too small to permit the inclusion of all editorial material, the opposite page also is used.   It is headed by the same style of running head as that used on the regular editorial page and follows the same general style of makeup, except for the absence of the cartoon. Both of these matching pages are gray in tone because of the lack of display headlines or other typographical elements below the fold; but they are dignified and clean looking and present the news in an interesting manner.

Several of the standard-size newspapers also devote two pages to editorial material.   Usually the material written by members of the newspaper's own editorial staff appears on the main page, and syndicated, interpretative articles by outside writers, along with other feature material, is placed on the other.   Among the newspapers following this plan is the *Courier-Journal*, which frequently keeps this second editorial page free from advertising to make more room for interesting news of this kind.

ADVISABILITY OF CHANGES

There is no reason why the editorial page cannot be made one of the brightest and most pleasing pages in the paper.   The material lends itself extremely well to unusual and attractive treatment.

On most newspapers, little if any additional expenditure would be involved in making desirable changes, and many editors might benefit from re-evaluating the effectiveness of their present practices.   In some instances, the page might need to be completely redesigned; in others, only a few minor changes might be required to bring about improvement.

Some of the most valuable devices for obtaining effective typography and makeup on this page are: (1) moving the masthead from its top position on the left-hand side of the page, thus freeing this area for the most important editorial of the day; (2) designing headlines that are readable and attractive; (3) widening columns, especially those in which long editorials are carried; (4) using a somewhat larger body-type than that employed in the regular news columns; (5) using sufficient white space between lines and around column rules to let plenty of light into the page and to assure a maximum of legibility; and (6) using pictures and cartoons to add liveliness and interest.

If one or more changes brought about even a small increase in readership, several hundred additional readers would be gained on most newspapers, and on the larger ones, the figure might run into the thousands.   In addition, everyone seeing the page would benefit from any improvements made in readability and attractiveness.

XV

Other Special Pages

IN ADDITION TO THE EDITORIAL PAGE, MOST
newspapers departmentalize other types of news stories by placing them
on separate pages and giving them special treatment to set them off
typographically from all other pages. Because of limitations in size,
the smaller newspapers are unable to provide as many of these special
pages as their contemporaries in the large cities. However, practically
every daily, regardless of size, and many weeklies contain one or more
individualized pages (in addition to the one given over to editorials),
where certain kinds of news are handled differently from that carried
on regular news pages.

One of the most common is the sports page. Here all the important
sports news of the day is segregated and given special treatment as an
aid to interested readers. Some of the larger newspapers use two or
more pages for the sports section.

THE SPORTS PAGE

The nature of sports news, which breathes of the great out-of-doors
and healthful physical activity, is such that it demands strong, vigorous
treatment. In order to create the proper atmosphere, the types and
headlines employed on this page should be in keeping with the kind of
news which they accompany.

The use of Italic and Script faces—unless they contain strong, bold
lines—should be avoided, particularly in the main headlines, and when
used for purpose of contrast or unusual effects, they should be adapted
in tone and design to the other elements on the page.

A headline in a light airy type, when used in connection with a story
about a bulky, hard-hitting fullback, is ridiculously out of place. The
newspaper which makes the mistake of using weak, feminine headlines
of this kind for main headlines, or elsewhere on the page, is violating
one of the most important principles regulating type display—that

which calls for an adaptation of the types to the kind of message to be conveyed.

Of course, all headlines on the page need not be extremely heavy and bold, but the faces employed should be of the stronger designs. Enough variation naturally should be provided to assure that pleasing contrast is obtained.

Figure 164. Sports page of the *Chicago Sun* of December 26, 1946.

Most newspapers use the same family of type on the sports page as throughout the rest of the paper. The *Chicago Sun* uses Gothic faces exclusively; the *Chicago Daily News* and the *Washington Post* employ Bodoni Bold; the *Des Moines Tribune* makes use of Cheltenham. All these types are the heavier varieties of their particular families, and the resulting pages have a strong, bold tone.

Figure 165. Sports page of the *Chicago Daily News*.

Use of Nameplate

Most present-day newspapers label the sports page with some style of sports nameplate. The *Washington Post* sets its two-column page-label in a line of small Text type similar to that in the regular nameplate; it reads: "Washington Post Sports." The date of publication is printed directly underneath in Italics. The *Chicago Sun*, the *Chi-*

Figure 166.   Sports page of the *Des Moines Tribune*.

cago Daily News, and the *Des Moines Tribune* bury theirs in the area above the fold.

Each of these papers has a specially designed nameplate containing the word "Sports," the name of the paper, and copy for the running head. Without exception, the nameplates are two columns wide and take up approximately the same amount of space on the page, but none of them is run at the top of columns. On the other hand, they always are buried somewhere in the upper half of the page and are

Figure 167. Sports page of the *Washington Post*.

shifted from one position to another, according to the type of makeup required for a given edition.

Some editors contend that if a nameplate is to be used on this page, it should be placed at the top of columns, since it is an individualized unit that has a tendency to injure the over-all design when positioned down inside the page. This contention has considerable merit. If the "floating" nameplate is not handled skillfully, with close attention to harmonious agreement of surrounding elements, it may produce effects that are not pleasing. Furthermore, the value of a nameplate that is buried so completely that a reader has to spend several seconds searching for it is questionable.

Editors who use no label on this page undoubtedly do so because they feel that readers will be able to detect the sports page by means of the distinctive typographical treatment employed and the type of news carried. They feel, too, that the space required for a label can be used to better advantage in presenting interesting news.

Running High Columns

Another device used by several newspapers is that of running high columns on the outside of the page. The *Chicago Daily News* usually places a large illustration in top position on the left-hand side of the page; the illustration runs flush with the main headline on the page. The *Washington Post* uses a special column two regular columns in width, headed by its nameplate high on the left-hand side of the page. It achieves a very effective top-of-the-page makeup by balancing the nameplate with a two-column deck on the opposite side of the page.

Practically all newspapers run at least one special column on the sports page. The special columns generally are accompanied by distinctive headlines, which are often boxed. Sometimes this material is run in wide columns, as in the *Chicago Daily News* and the *Washington Post,* to add variety to the makeup of the page.

One main disadvantage of running one or more columns high on the page is that the amount of space at the top available for strong display is limited and that an undesirable rigidity of makeup results. If the plan is left flexible so that the head in these columns can be dropped to permit the use of banners and large spreads when the news warrants, the practice is not objectionable and often results in a modern effect that is attractive and inviting to readers.

Use of Illustrations

Most newspapers make use of pictures on the sports page. The number used is determined partly by the photographic and engraving facilities available. Many editors employ pictures generously to illustrate important sports events.

A study of the sample pages will show that every newspaper represented has at least one picture on the sports page, but the amount of space used for this kind of news varies widely.

The pictures in the *Chicago Sun* and the *Des Moines Tribune* are so large that they completely dominate the page. The *Tribune* handles its cutlines in a special box at the top of the page which is surrounded by heavy rules ending in arrows that point toward the illustration. Half-column cuts, as well as cuts of wider measure, are employed to give color and interest throughout some of these pages.

In most instances, pictures are used more lavishly on the sports page than on any other page in the paper. They are exceedingly high in reader-interest and are of great value in brightening up the center and bottom areas and in adding liveliness to the top area.

Plan of Makeup

Sports pages generally are headed by strong display at the top of the page. Banners and spreads ordinarily are used to accompany the leading stories, along with pictures that tie in with the news.

One of the most common faults is allowing the page to become top-heavy. Top-heaviness can be avoided by including headlines and other elements of sufficient size and tonal value in the middle and bottom areas so that the over-all design will be pleasing and interesting.

Another common error that reduces the chances for the most effective top-of-the-page display is that of running the special column of the sports editor under a "dead" standing head at the top of column one. The top of this first column is the most important spot on the page from the standpoint of readership, and it is here that a good starter headline over the leading sports story of the day should be placed. Furthermore, when a banner is desired, the use of a standing head in this position makes it necessary to place the story that accompanies the banner in column eight, rather than in the first column of the page, where it logically belongs.

Once a special sports column has established a readership following, it need not be placed in the most important spot on the page every day. A much more desirable plan would be to start off the page with a good headline over the most outstanding news story, which is much more dependent upon strong display for attracting readers. If a standing head is used for the sports column, it might be placed under this top head next to the news story carried in the first column.

Makeup editors of the sports page usually are provided with more devices and given greater freedom than on other pages in the paper. As a result, the sports page usually can be made one of the brightest and best-read pages in the paper if the rules governing attractive design are followed carefully.

An attempt generally is made here, as on the editorial page, to keep the page as free from advertising as possible. The most desirable plan is to select ads for use on the sports page that deal with coming athletic events, sporting equipment, sports wear, or other merchandise that is of special interest to the class of readers attracted to the page. It should be noted that all the advertisements on the sample pages logically fall into this classification.

THE WOMAN'S PAGE

News dealing with society affairs and women's interests is run on special pages by many newspapers. Some editors set aside more than one page, but the most common practice is to bring together most of this news onto one woman's page, where it is given special treatment.

One plan calls for labeling the page with a "society" boxed head, and running all items on the page under small one-line headlines. Frequently, a few one-column, boxed label headlines for use over "Personals," "Hospital Notes," and "Births" are thrown in to assist in the classification of the news carried. No attempt is made to brighten the page and to tempt readers by means of interesting or unusual display in any area. As a result, the over-all design is very gray and without interest from a typographical standpoint.

Although such treatment permits the crowding of many items onto the page, the use of some well-planned headlines would have a very healthful effect on reader-interest. Few editors are satisfied with such drab, quiet treatment.

The *Chicago Sun* uses some headlines in light versions of the Gothic race, the same general style as that employed throughout the rest of the paper; but the main heads are set in Bodoni Campanile, along with a light, decorative Script, which gives pleasing, harmonious contrast and contributes greatly to the effectiveness of the page. Unusual headline structures and some body-type masses set in generously spaced Gothic are used to give further variety.

Cheltenham light is the type chosen by the *Milwaukee Journal,* which has a complete headline schedule in the Cheltenham family. Although Cheltenham generally is regarded as too heavy and masculine for such purposes, this paper creates a highly attractive page with definite feminine appeal by the skillful combination of both regular and Italic versions.

The *Chicago Daily News* makes exclusive use of Bodoni in the lighter varieties for headlines on the woman's page. Partially boxed headlines and overlines are employed to give contrast. The *News* always begins the second section with the woman's page, a plan that

Figure 168. Woman's page of the *Chicago Sun* of October 24, 1946.

attracts many women readers to the paper. The *Milwaukee Journal* also frequently runs this page at the beginning of the second section.

In addition to the types found in the papers mentioned in this discussion, several others are very suitable for use on the woman's page. Goudy, Cloister, Caslon, and Garamond are particularly well adapted, and their use can result in pages that are attractive in design and very feminine in appeal.

Figure 169.   Woman's page of the *Milwaukee Journal.*

Nameplate for the Page

Many newspapers label the woman's page with a special nameplate to assist readers and to add distinctiveness.   The most striking nameplate among those on the sample pages is that used by the *Chicago Sun*. "The Feminine Angle" is an unusual title and the design is very interesting.   It will be noted that the large capital "F" has been toned down

Figure 170.   Woman's page of the *Chicago Daily News*.

to reduce its boldness, and plenty of white space has been provided around the lines to give contrast.

The *Milwaukee Journal* repeats its regular nameplate on this page, with the words "Woman's Pages and Society" in simple boxes on either side of the title to serve as page-labels.

The nameplate of the *Chicago Daily News* is distinctive in design and takes a space only four columns wide at the top of the page. It is not always run in the same position, but is shifted as required to fit in with the display of news on a given day.

Here again, the question of the need for a label arises. If one is used, it should be designed in such a way that it is in keeping with the atmosphere sought and in harmony with other types in the head-dress. The best way for a newspaper to test the worth of its nameplate is to find out from readers if they consider it of as much value as a news story occupying the same amount of space. The findings obtained should be useful in making a decision.

Use of Illustrations

Most newspapers use pictures of strong appeal to women on this page; the number and size of the pictures vary widely from one newspaper to another.

The *Chicago Sun* always uses one extremely large fashion illustration at the top of the page, and another, somewhat smaller, dealing with teen-age interests at the bottom for purposes of balance.

Pictures on the *Milwaukee Journal* page, which always contains several large illustrations, have more of a tendency to follow live news of local interest. In addition, this paper frequently employs attractive line cuts to illustrate fashions and other items of interest to women. Many other papers follow a similar plan.

The *Chicago Daily News* always brightens its woman's page with several pictures; it frequently prints a series of several "shots" dealing with the same subject, as shown in the sample page. The "Points for Parents" cartoon always appears at the bottom of the page.

Pictures are of great value on the woman's page, as on the sports page, for adding interest and variety. By selecting type faces, headlines, and pictures that are adapted to the nature of the news carried on the page, and by following the rules regulating good makeup, many newspapers today are providing women readers with special pages that are attractive and interesting. Those papers which do not departmentalize this news and fail to give it appropriate treatment are overlooking an opportunity that might result in more readers and greater interest.

PICTURE PAGES

With the invention of Wirephoto and other equipment for the transmission of pictures, American newspapers began receiving a greater volume of illustrations than ever before in their history. Increasing

Figure 171. Picture page of the *Chicago Daily Tribune.*

interest in this type of news led many editors to expand their photographic staffs in efforts to give more complete local coverage.

As a result, the use of pictures has grown tremendously within the last few years, and many editors have begun the practice of running special pages in order to give the pictures greater emphasis. Some of the methods followed in handling this type of pictured news are shown in the accompanying examples.

The *Chicago Daily Tribune* always heads its page with a boxed ban-

Figure 172.   Picture page of the *Milwaukee Journal*.

ner line which summarizes some of the more outstanding news carried. No other captions are placed over the cuts. Cutlines are set in generously leaded Cheltenham type that harmonizes well with the Bodoni Bold used in the banner. The Cheltenham is large enough and of sufficient color to fit in nicely with the tone of the half-tones carried.

Cutlines are set in two column widths under all cuts that exceed four columns in width so that high readability will be maintained. Under

Figure 173. Picture page of the *Chicago Sun* of December 26, 1946.

the cutlines accompanying a picture which ties in with the news on some other page in the paper, a special line is set in Italic type to direct the reader to the story involved. A credit line in small type is used either directly above or below the regular cutlines.

The *Milwaukee Journal* also uses a banner line at the top of the page, but it is not boxed. It usually employs another line, or spread, below the fold over pictures carried at the bottom of the page. Goudy Bold is used for both headlines.

Cutlines are printed below each picture; the first few words are set in boldface. Under halftones more than two columns in width, the reading matter is set in two columns. When there is room, the "credit" is included on the last line; otherwise, it is set in a separate credit-line following the cutlines. The credit-lines are always set in an Italic face. The running head is run in its regular position at the top of the page, with a headrule underneath it.

The *Chicago Sun* usually prints one dramatic picture which completely dominates the page in the upper left-hand section of the page. A distinctive touch is provided by a caption set in an attractive Script type over this picture. All other captions are in bold Gothic type, centered above the cutlines. When the makeup requires reading matter to be placed at the side of the illustrations, it is set one column wide under a three-line, flush-left headline.

The cutlines are in a light Gothic type that is well leaded and that gives pleasing contrast with the boldface captions. Credit-lines are in all-caps in a type smaller than that used in cutlines, and they are placed either under the cutlines or on the last line.

Additional variety is provided by the use of a border of light tone in a Ben Day pattern that is used around at least one picture and sometimes between type masses on the pages to set them off from other elements.

The *Des Moines Tribune* uses several devices to add variety to its picture page. The running head is the equivalent of four columns in width and is placed above a headrule at the top of the page on the left-hand side.

Small stars are employed to separate pictures in a series dealing with the same general subject; the pictures are set off from each other by means of specially designed borders. Arrows used under cutlines that are placed at the side of pictures point toward the illustrations which they accompany to prevent confusion on the part of the reader.

A large Gothic caption is put over the main picture at the top of the page on the left, and other captions on the page are set in Cheltenham

Bold Italic.   The picture in the top position on the right-hand side has been mortised to accommodate the caption, and the reading matter is made to run around the caption under the picture at the bottom of the page.   A credit-line in small type is run under each picture, on the left-hand side.

Many tabloid newspapers follow the same general plan as that used by the *Daily Mirror*.   This paper places its picture display on two

Figure 174. Picture page of the *Des Moines Tribune*.

pages, which are handled as a single unit.   This plan permits the use
of several pictures, which generally are smaller than those run by newspapers of standard size.   Cutlines are set in Gothic type; the first words
are in a bolder face than the rest of the reading matter.   The only
headline on the page is that placed over the three center pictures at the
top.

Some Points to Remember

The value of the picture page naturally depends mainly upon the
news-value of the pictures carried.   The size of an illustration also has
much to do with its appeal.   Pictures should be printed large enough
to make them easy to read, and their size should have some relationship
to their importance in the news.   If they are too small, they lose much
of their pulling power.

One common practice followed is that of including one "smash" shot,
which is printed larger or given more unusual treatment than the rest
of the pictures on the page.   The "smash" shot often is placed in the
upper left-hand corner, which is the most important area on the page.
However, if it is one of several in a series used to tell a story, it sometimes is positioned near the center, with the other related shots grouped
around it.   Usually a good plan is to run pictures dealing with the same
subject next to one another on the page.

Figure 175.   Picture page of the *Daily Mirror*.

If small pictures are used along with larger ones, care should be taken to see that they are not buried. Otherwise, they will lose their effectiveness, and the whole page-design will suffer.

Attractive, well-written cutlines are a great aid to the reader. The type should be of such a design and of sufficient size to be highly legible, and the lengths of lines should be carefully adapted to the size of type used. When pictures run more than two columns in width, the setting of cutlines in two or more columns rather than a measure equal to the width of the cut is advisable. The number of columns to be employed will depend upon the size of the cut. Furthermore, the cutlines never should extend beyond the limits of the printed picture.

Often photographs chosen for the page are of poor quality, with not enough contrast and detail to permit good reproduction. If the prints used for making halftones are flat and gray, it is almost impossible for the engraver to transform them into good halftones. Sometimes the fault lies with the engraver, who does not etch the plate properly, and consequently it cannot be made to print satisfactorily despite the greatest effort on the part of the pressmen.

A lack of enough packing on the impression cylinder of the press, not enough attention to make-ready before printing, or insufficient inking might account for poor reproductions on the printed page. Errors in making the stereotype plates also might be the cause.

Wherever the fault lies, it can be run down by making close checks of these causes and others that might be contributing factors. The careful editor will make every effort to see that pictures are well printed. Otherwise, the design of the page will be impaired and reader-interest reduced.

Second Front Page

Many newspapers run two or more sections in order to take care of the large volume of news. Some of them handle the first page of the second section in the same manner as other inside pages, with advertising pyramided to the right and with news displayed in the remaining area. Others give special treatment to the second front page, on which the nameplate is placed at the top so that it will have some resemblance to page one.

One common method is to display on this page much of the important news of the day that could not be run on the front page because of space limitations and to handle the makeup in much the same manner. The *Salt Lake Tribune's* second front page is an interesting example of this kind of treatment. The same style of flush-left headlines is used, and careful attention is given to the placement of cuts and other elements in order to create a pleasing design.

A great many other newspapers run a feature page at the beginning of the second section. The *Courier-Journal*, which usually follows this plan, places a special feature column, "Bill Ladd's Almanac," on the left-hand side of the page at the top, under a two-column headline that is partially boxed. This is balanced by a headline of similar width on the right, and a feature headline or one or more pictures are run in be-

Figure 176. Second front page of the *Salt Lake Tribune*.

tween. Pictures also are used in the bottom area of the page to give variety and interest.

The *Christian Science Monitor* follows a style similar to that used by magazines in designing its second front page. Several pictures are employed, all of which are generous in size and well printed, with one-line captions placed underneath. A banner line is printed at the top

Figure 177. Second front page of the *Courier-Journal*.

of the page.   Other main headlines are three columns in width; the ones placed on the upper half of the page are set in Bodoni Bold and those below the fold in Bodoni Bold Italic.

Headlines in the upper area consist of one line, with the by-line set one column wide at the beginning of the reading matter.   A second line in a smaller size is used under the main line in these headlines below the fold to add contrast and variety.   It includes the by-line copy on the right end of the line, which is balanced with three or four words

Figure 178.   Second front page of the *Christian Science Monitor*.

that give additional facts concerning the story placed on the left.   Dots are used in between to break up the white space.   All headlines are set in easy-to-read caps and lower-case.

The width of columns varies.   Two wide columns are employed for the feature stories carried on either side of the page in the bottom area, leaving two columns of normal width in the center for other news.   All stories starting above the fold are set one column in width.   Column rules are used on either side of the two center columns, but white space is employed for this purpose throughout the remainder of the page.

The *Monitor's* second front page has a modern appearance that is strikingly different from others carried in the paper.   Although head-lines and pictures are generous in size, they are handled in such a man-ner that the page possesses a dignified reserve that is in keeping with the rest of the pages.

When the *Chicago Daily Tribune* appears with only two sections, the second always begins with the main sports page, a practice that is fol-lowed by many other newspapers.   Another device for gaining atten-tion and adding interest is the "Moon Mullins" comic strip, which al-ways appears at the bottom of the page.

As mentioned previously, some newspapers, including the *Chicago Daily News* and the *Milwaukee Journal,* begin the second section with a special woman's page.

There is great merit to the plan of giving special treatment to the first page of the second section, and others, when included, since this gives an opportunity to gain attention and get readers off to a good start.   Since a break occurs in their reading when they come to the end of the first section, something is needed to pick up their interest and make them want to go on through the paper.   If the first page of the second section is filled with advertising or contains only a small amount of news with little attention given to news display, there is much less chance of the reader being tempted to the inside.

FEATURE SECTIONS

A few newspapers follow the practice of bringing together a large amount of feature material and running it in a special section.   Among them are the *Milwaukee Journal* and the *St. Louis Post-Dispatch.*

The *Milwaukee Journal* prints this section, which usually consists of four pages, on green paper stock and labels the page with a name-plate that carries the title, "Green Sheet."

Most of the headlines on the front page of this section are set in Goudy Bold, a different variety of type from that used in the regular newspaper. The use of Goudy Bold, combined with a somewhat different style of makeup, contributes to an over-all page-design that has little typographical resemblance to that found on other pages. A banner line is printed at the top of the page above the nameplate, and several pictures and line cuts are employed to add liveliness. Because of the unusual treatment, readers have no difficulty in locating this section.

Figure 179. First page of the *Milwaukee Journal's* feature section.

The *St. Louis Post-Dispatch* departs from the style of makeup followed in the rest of the paper in the design of the first page of its feature section. It labels the page with a nameplate carrying the title, "The Everyday Magazine," which is run in a specially designed type at the top. The date-line is printed underneath in the traditional manner between two parallel rules of light design.

A special column of wide measure is run on the left-hand side, with bold star dashes between long paragraphs to add distinctiveness. The rest of the page is given over to pictures. All headlines, captions, and

Figure 180. First page of the feature section of the *St. Louis Post-Dispatch*.

cutlines are set in Gothic type, and pointing arrows are employed to direct readers when cutlines are not placed directly under the accompanying halftones.

The practice of providing special feature sections regularly is not followed by many newspapers. A more common plan is to distribute this type of news throughout the regular newspaper, with special treatment being given to certain kinds of special pages.

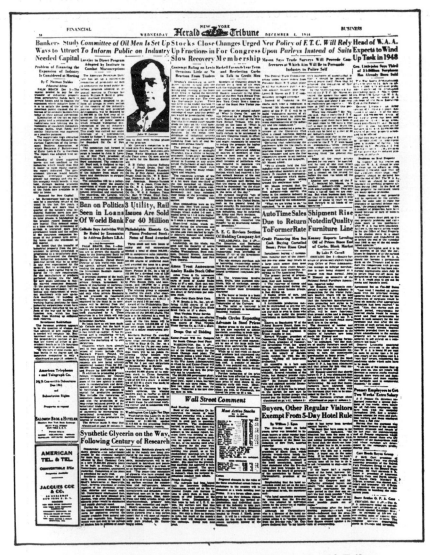

Figure 181.   Financial page of the *New York Herald Tribune*.

The Financial Page

Stories dealing with business and finance are departmentalized by most newspapers. If the amount to be run is small, it generally is carried on an inside page along with other news. However, many newspapers set aside at least one entire page for this purpose.

Newspapers in the metropolitan centers often print several pages of

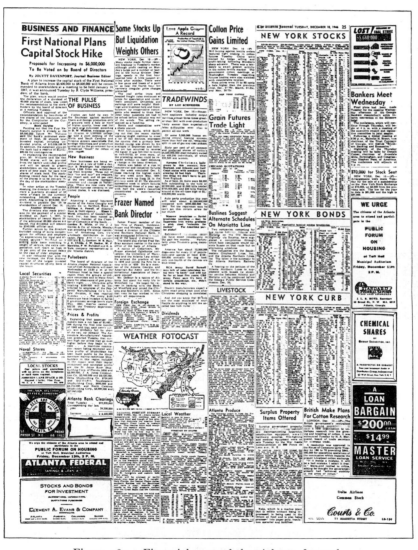

Figure 182. Financial page of the *Atlanta Journal*.

business and financial news. For instance, the *New York Herald Tribune* always carries two or more pages, the first of which is treated differently from the rest. This page is headed with a nameplate of the same general design as that used on page one, and it is printed along with the running head above the headrule. The words "Financial" and "Business," placed on either side of the nameplate, label the page. In general makeup, the page looks much like other inside pages, except that the amount of advertising included is very small. All the important stock quotations and other listings are reserved for other pages which follow, leaving this main one free for news.

Newspapers employing only one financial page include stock and bond quotations along with the news. These listings ordinarily are set solid, in type approximately six points in size.

The *Atlanta Journal* classifies its main listings under boxed headlines on the right-hand half of the page. The main story appears under a two-column headline at the top on the left-hand side. Above this is the line, "Business and Finance," set in boldface Gothic type to serve as the page-label. A small graph is run at the top of column four.

The two-column weather map is placed below the fold above the weather forecast for the day. This material undoubtedly attracts some readers who otherwise would not stop to read news on the page and is used by many newspapers for this purpose. It is also of high interest to some readers holding stocks that might be affected by weather conditions.

Financial pages, like the ones shown, are generally conservative, with the types and display adapted to the general atmosphere of the news carried. Advertisements are of a business or financial nature and should receive the same general kind of typographical treatment that is in keeping with the rest of the page, if possible.

One of the main pitfalls is failing to give display of sufficient strength where it is needed in order to maintain a conservative, quiet atmosphere. This failure causes the page to look gray and uninteresting, and often the reader finds it difficult to locate important stories readily. Here, as elsewhere in the paper, an effort should be made to give a story the kind of headline display that is in keeping with its importance, and small, hard-to-read heads should be avoided.

Most newspapers also overlook the fact that the people most likely to be interested in the financial news are in the older age groups who find it difficult to read small body-type. Many of them tire quickly if the type is hard to read, and as a consequence they often are unable to get the full benefits from the news.

The use of a somewhat larger body-type than that used in regular news columns, with sufficient leading to assure high legibility, is one important means that might be adopted by newspapers generally as an aid to current readers as well as a method of attracting more people to the page. It also should be remembered that pictures are one kind of news that is highly interesting to readers in all age groups, and the use of more illustrations is another valuable method for drawing readers and increasing interest in the financial page.

The Theater Page

In some of the smaller communities, the theater page appears only on those days when there is a change of bills; only a limited amount of news and ads of this nature appear on other days of the week. However, newspapers published in the larger cities generally carry a theater page as a regular feature.

The theater page of the *Courier-Journal* is typical of the kind run in many places. Ads are placed in the accepted pyramid style, with most of the top of the page left free for the display of news. Many of the stories tie in with advertising on the page and are given good display. Pictures are used in connection with the news.

In addition to the advertisements, a guide for theater-goers is printed under the "Today's Show Clock" heading. The body-type is slightly smaller than that used in the regular news columns. Although all papers do not follow such a practice, the *Courier-Journal* adds a modern touch to the page by setting all headlines flush-left and by using white space between columns in place of column rules.

The *Chicago Daily News* employs another type of listing on its theater page. The advertisements themselves are classified and run under small headings, such as "Downtown," "North," "South," and so forth. Ads for bills showing in the suburbs are carried under appropriate headings. In the smaller ads without illustrations, the name of the theater is given in boldface Gothic type to further assist the reader. Several show-houses have their names printed from reverse plates, which make very dark spots on the page.

The upper part of the first two columns is reserved for a special column entitled "Hollywood Chatter." This title is run as an overline in the two-column headline placed above the reading matter that is set the full two-column width. Small bold stars are used between items to add distinctiveness. All other news stories are run one column in width directly under the main feature article.

Most newspapers are unable to control successfully the kind of mats and cuts furnished them by the movie houses, and most theaters provide illustrations that are extremely heavy in tone.   In order to keep the space devoted to news in harmony with the area occupied by ads, many newspapers use bold headlines and other devices to create an over-all design that is darker than that on most of the other pages in the paper.

Figure 183.   Theater page of the *Courier-Journal*.

THE RADIO PAGE

Although the amount of space devoted to radio news varies widely, most editors run some information of this kind on one of the inside pages. Some newspapers place all such news, together with a listing of radio programs, on a special page and give it distinctive treatment.

Figure 184. Theater page of the *Chicago Daily News.*

The *Atlanta Journal,* which follows the latter plan, runs a two-column list of radio programs in small Gothic body-type under a special "Radio Clock" boxed heading. The information is given in tabulated form. Designations for stations, together with dial numbers, are printed over small columns at the top of the form, and the titles of all programs for each station are listed down the page under their respective headings. The time of the day for each show is given in the outside column on

Figure 185.   Radio page of the *Atlanta Journal.*

either side of the form. Morning, evening, and afternoon programs for each day represented are designated by cross-line headlines.

In addition to this condensed information, stories dealing with radio are run on the page under regular news headlines. Illustrations are used whenever interesting personalities are involved. A two-column cartoon, "Bobby Sox," is included to add interest. When there are not enough radio stories to fill the rest of the news space, other types of news are used.

Figure 186. Radio page of the *Courier-Journal*.

The *Courier-Journal* runs its radio news on a page which also contains other feature material. Four comic strips are printed in the bottom area of the page, running all the way across. In the three columns on the left-hand side of the page in the upper area, this paper prints "The Washington Merry-Go-Round" column under a one-line spread headline, along with a two-column line cut which is used to illustrate the article. Another special feature column is placed in columns two and three under that part of the "Washington Merry-Go-Round" that was carried over from column one.

A special radio article is printed in column four next to the program listings. All news columns on the page are wider than normal, and they are separated by white space. Initial letters and simple asterisk dashes are employed to add variety to the reading matter. Detailed information about radio programs is printed under a large headline on the right side of the page. A tabulated form is preceded by a list of selected programs of special interest.

CLASSIFIED ADVERTISING PAGES

No pages in the newspaper are less interesting typographically than the classified advertising page. The main reason is that most items are so small that little opportunity is afforded to give pleasing display. As a consequence, most of these pages are gray and uninviting, and unless the average reader is searching for a given article likely to be advertised in these columns, he generally will give the classified advertising page little, if any, attention.

Several devices are employed to make these pages more inviting and readable. One is that of starting the advertising on a page with news stories and other material of special interest to readers. The *Chicago Daily Tribune* always attempts to do this. In the page shown, a two-column cartoon, a halftone, and complete radio program listings have been included, along with news stories, on the upper half of the first page in the classification. Also, a want-ad index above the advertisements in the first column on the page is added to provide a convenient guide to readers.

The *San Francisco Chronicle* labels the first page with a "Classified Ads" nameplate of distinctive design and sets many of the ads in much larger type than the $5\frac{1}{2}$- or 6-point used by this paper and most others for many of the items carried in these columns.

By making effective use of larger type faces for display purposes and by opening up the gray masses with white space, classified ad pages can be made more attractive and more readable. The extent to which this improvement can be accomplished naturally is dependent upon the willingness of advertisers to invest more money in the material they want printed. In many communities, few advertisers will agree to pay the additional cost involved in running the larger ads on the classified page, but they much prefer to have all except the extremely small sales messages run on regular news pages in the ordinary manner.

Many newspapers run their daily comic strips on the classified ad-

Figure 187. Classified advertising page of the *Chicago Daily Tribune*.

vertising pages in an effort to brighten the design and to attract readers. Another device is running the weather map and forecast on one of these pages.

The use of bold display lines, reverse plates, and heavy borders is not the best solution for adding liveliness. Unless care is exercised, the page takes on a spotted effect that is not pleasing. However, the employment of heavier display in a portion of the page sometimes results in a design that is interesting and more readable.

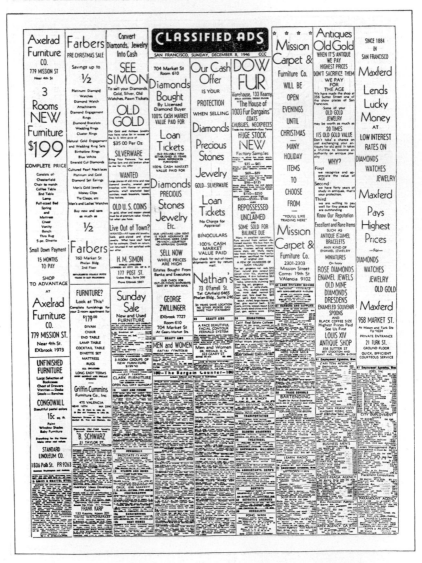

Figure 188.   Classified advertising page of the *San Francisco Chronicle*.

The *Alton Evening Telegraph's* classified advertising page is an example of this kind of treatment. Although the borders used on some ads are a little too heavy, the design of the page is interesting, and the pyramid of ads at the top of the page provides striking contrast with the grayer columns of type in the other area.

Kind of Format

Among the many changes made by newspapers during World War II in an effort to conserve newsprint was the conversion to a nine-column

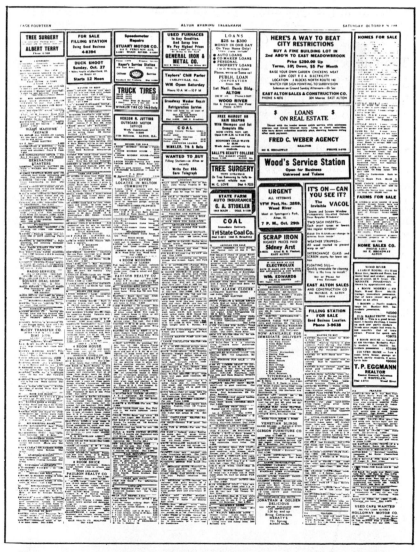

Figure 189. Classified advertising page of the *Alton Evening Telegraph*.

page for classified advertising in place of the normal eight. The change usually was accomplished by a reduction in type size and the elimination of display advertisements.

In a survey on newspaper classified advertising typography and style conducted late in 1945 by an organization of newspaper counselors in Miami, Florida, questionnaires were sent to 147 papers. Findings revealed that 18 of the 43 newspapers then using the nine-column format planned to revert to the pre-war style, and 15 indicated that they would delay the move to await developments. Over half of the 147 intended to reinstate larger type and display on the classified advertising pages.[1]

General Comments

The number of newspapers represented in this discussion of special pages is only a small percentage of those being published in this country. Many newspapers are doing an excellent job with their special pages, but no editor who is wise will fail to be on the alert for suggestions that will lead to improvement of his own newspaper, regardless of the high standards already being maintained.

Improvement is always possible even in the best-regulated institutions; perfection is never reached. Human tastes, in newspaper reading as in every other phase of life, are constantly changing, and editors who want to keep in step with the march of progress must be sensitive to the public's likes and dislikes in matters of typography and makeup as well as in the editorial offerings that are transmitted by means of printed words and pictures.

---

[1] Felix S. Towle, "Typography Survey Finds No Set Ideas, *Editor & Publisher*, 78:51 (December 15, 1945), 60.

XVI

From Infant to Giant

NEWSPAPER PUBLISHING HAS UNDERGONE TRE-
mendous changes since the establishment of the *Boston News-Letter*
by John Campbell in 1704. These have been brought about by a long
series of interrelated social and economic developments so closely knit
that it would be impossible for anyone to single out which ones have
contributed the most.

Outstanding among the greatest of these developments has been a
long chain of important mechanical inventions that have transformed
what was a modest one-man business at the start into a capitalistic
venture involving tremendous investments and corporate ownership.
The printing machinery alone required to produce an average daily in
a town of 10,000 represents an expenditure ranging from $25,000 to
$50,000, and the figures advance with the size of publications. The
value of newspaper properties in metropolitan areas runs into the millions.

To the editor-owner of our country's first newspapers, this would
sound like a fabulous amount, but it would appear no more fantastic
than the character of the modern newspaper, which bears little resemblance to its predecessor of two centuries ago.

Our first colonial newspapers consisted of only two or four small
pages printed on crude hand presses that were capable of producing less
than five hundred copies a day. The type of available printing equipment and the extreme scarcity of newsprint placed severe limitations
on the kind of newspapers furnished by these early publishers.

On the other hand, communities were small, and the "reading public" in many places consisted of less than 500 subscribers. For instance, the weekly distribution of the *Boston News-Letter* amounted
to only 300 subscribers; and by 1789, the total weekly circulation of
all types of newspapers had reached only 76,438 copies, which was less

than what many present-day daily newspapers produce in a single is-sue.[1]

As population continued to increase and communities multiplied, the need arose for better equipment. Faster presses and a much larger supply of newsprint were of first importance. However, not until after the beginning of the nineteenth century was any material progress made in satisfying these pressing requirements.

IMPROVED PRESSES

The first significant attempt at providing a solution came with the adaptation of "power," or steam, to the bed-and-platen press, in which the wooden frame was replaced with metal. This type of press was used for many years by the smaller newspapers. Eventually a maxi-mum speed of 1,000 sheets an hour was attained, but even this soon be-came inadequate for newspapers in the larger communities.

Relief came a few years later with the introduction of the flat-bed cylinder press, invented by Friederich Koenig in 1812, and during the 1820's, the Fourdrinier paper-making machine was put into successful operation in this country. As a result, the two main obstacles were temporarily overcome, and the stage thus was set for the appearance of the penny papers in the 1830's, the largest of which were printed at the rate of approximately 2,000 impressions an hour on flat-bed presses driven by means of cranks that had to be turned by hand. Later, steam power was applied; and in 1847, the type-revolving press, with still greater capacity, was introduced.

In the first flush of excitement over these new and revolutionizing discoveries, some editors started publishing the famous blanket sheets, but their exuberance waned in a few years, and the size of newspapers settled down to a more normal size.

STEREOTYPING AND HALFTONES

Meanwhile, attention was turned toward the perfection of other methods for increasing production. The discovery by Charles Craske in 1850 of curved stereotype plates and their adaptation to presses opened up new possibilities.

Then, in 1880, Stephen H. Horgan introduced the first halftone ever to be printed in an American newspaper, and the way was cleared for the development of modern pictorial journalism.

Another invention that was to have tremendous effects on the pub-

---

[1] Alfred M. Lee, *The Daily Newspaper in America*, page 16. New York: The Macmillan Company, 1937.

lication of newspapers was that of the Linotype in 1886, which was capable of casting automatically more type in a day than several men could produce by hand. It was followed by other type-casting machines, including the Intertype, the Ludlow, the Monotype, and the Elrod caster. Manufacturers of some of these machines, along with leading type foundries, since then have introduced hundreds of new type faces that have expanded greatly the possibilities of pleasing typography and design of advertising—and of newspapers in general.

COMING OF ROTARIES

In the 1890's, the first rotary presses, made possible by the aid of curved stereotype plates, were put into operation.

Thus, in less than fifty years, inventive genius had placed at the disposal of publishers the tools and equipment that were employed by Hearst and Pulitzer in their sensational splurge of "yellow journalism" at the end of the nineteenth century. Many of the new features in display and makeup employed by them in their battle for supremacy have had lasting effects on newspapers.

By the beginning of the twentieth century, tools were available for the production of a different type of newspaper at far greater speed than ever before, and engineers were busy designing precision machinery, equipped with special supplementary devices, that would assure further expansion.

Rotogravure was successfully used by the first American newspaper in 1914, and within the next few years, many editors had added magazine sections printed by this method to their regular editions.

FIRST REAL TABLOIDS

Fired with the idea that a newspaper of small format emphasizing pictures would strike the fancy of the American public as forcibly as had Lord Northcliffe's *Daily Mirror* in England, Joseph Medill Patterson and Colonel Robert McCormick in 1919 launched in New York City the first real tabloid to be printed in the United States. It was named the *Illustrated Daily News,* but within a few months the word *Illustrated* was dropped from the title. Making generous use of pictures and sensational news, by 1924 this newspaper had attained a circulation of 750,000, the largest of any daily in America; and by 1940, the figure had jumped to almost two million.

In an effort to successfully compete with the *Daily News,* William Randolph Hearst founded his New York *Daily Mirror* in 1924, and these two newspapers have engaged in a fight for circulation ever since.

Editors throughout the country gradually became more picture-conscious and photographic and engraving departments commenced to appear in an increasing number of newspaper offices. Many small dailies and weeklies, as well as newspapers published in the large cities, installed facilities to assure good local picture coverage.

This trend was strengthened when the Associated Press in 1935 introduced Wirephoto, which made possible the delivery of a daily flood of news pictures from all over the world into the offices of subscribing papers. A special picture-mat service later was made available to other members.

Several other picture syndicates soon were offering a similar type of service, and the results of their combined efforts were reflected in a gradual increase in the picture content of many newspapers.

OTHER INVENTIONS

Remarkable progress has been made since the establishment of the first newspaper in this country. In colonial times, the machinery employed was very similar to that used by John Gutenberg in printing his famous 42-line Bible. After a lapse of more than three hundred years, newspapers still were being set and printed by hand with equipment that was slow and crude.

From the mechanical standpoint, the newspaper publishing business was in its infancy during this early period. In the years that followed, it grew into a giant among industries and today it affects the lives of most of our people.

Of outstanding significance to the student of journalism should be the fact that a majority of the more revolutionary changes have come within a life-span. Many men and women living today no doubt can remember when the Linotype, the rotary press, halftone reproductions, and rotogravure sections first made their appearance in the newspapers they read.

They have had an opportunity to observe the vast changes in typography and makeup that have brought new life and interest into pages that for many years were gray and uninviting. They have seen small four- and eight-page newspapers grow into publications with many times that number of pages that today are printed in several editions during the day.

These improvements in design have come largely through the introduction of more efficient machinery and of types, styles of headlines, pictures, and methods of display that are much more interesting and readable. This increase in attractiveness and legibility has had a powerful effect on readership and, in turn, upon the usefulness and influence of the newspaper.

The tremendous strides forward that have been made, together with the great technological marvels that were the outcome of American ingenuity during World War II, hold great promise for even more astounding developments in the years ahead.

What the newspaper of the future will be like can only be guessed. Most publishers agree that there will be much more color within the next few years, with halftones and headline display, as well as advertising, receiving color treatment in more and more newspapers.

PROSPECTS FOR FUTURE

As newsprint becomes more plentiful, a large number of editors undoubtedly will discontinue some of the practices reverted to during the war in efforts to conserve space. They probably will adopt larger body-type, more generous leading of reading matter, more white space between columns, wider page margins, pages less crowded with advertising, and other devices aimed toward making newspapers more readable and attractive.

On the other hand, headlines with fewer decks, the use of white space in place of dashes and column-rules, and other desirable features that have been found more functional and contributing factors to better design probably will be retained. The trend toward greater departmentalization and toward papers of smaller format also may become more widespread.

At present, information is being circulated within the profession about new and revolutionizing inventions that are about ready to be placed on the market. Among what appear to be the most important are: a new printing process, requiring no type to be cast by machines, that makes use of light-weight magnesium plates for the production of newspapers; a photo-electric engraving machine that can scan photographs and make halftones on plastic material in less time than they can be produced by the photo-engraving method; and a photo-typesetting machine that is going through the final stages of testing.

The future appears to be bright with prospects for better-printed and more attractive newspapers. Editors and others interested in newspaper publishing should maintain a lively interest in the new developments as they make their appearance and weigh carefully the advantages of changes that would better serve their readers.

The infant now is a giant—but the giant is not full-grown! The healthy development of any member of the great newspaper family will add to his stature.

Bibliography ——————————————————————

BOOKS

Allen, Charles Laurel, *The Journalist's Manual of Printing*. New York: The Ronald Press Company, 1929.

Allen, John E., *Newspaper Makeup*. New York: Harper & Brothers, 1936.

Bleyer, Willard G., *The History of American Journalism*. New York: Houghton Mifflin Company, 1927.

Brucker, Herbert, *The Changing American Newspaper*. New York: Columbia University Press, 1937.

Carter, Thomas Francis, *The Invention of Printing in China*. New York: Columbia University Press, 1943.

Clodd, Edward, *The Story of the Alphabet*. New York: D. Appleton and Company, 1918.

De Vinne, Theodore L., *The Invention of Printing*. New York: Francis Hart and Company, 1878.

Dreier, Thomas, *The Power of Print and Men*. Brooklyn, N. Y.: Mergenthaler Linotype Company, 1936.

Hoe, Robert, *A Short History of the Printing Press*. New York: The Gilliss Press, 1902.

Hudson, Frederic, *Journalism in the United States*. New York: Harper & Brothers, 1873.

I. T. U. Lessons in Printing, Unit I, Lesson 5. Indianapolis, Ind.: Bureau of Education, International Typographical Union, 1931.

Kubler, George A., *A New History of Stereotyping*. New York: J. J. Little & Ives Company, 1941.

Lasky, Joseph, *Proofreading and Copy-Preparation*. New York: Mentor Press, 1941.

Lee, Alfred McClung, *The Daily Newspaper in America*. New York: The Macmillan Company, 1937.

Linton, W. J., *The History of Wood Engraving in America*. Boston: Estes & Lauriat, 1882.

Luckiesh, Matthew, and Frank K. Moss, *Reading As a Visual Task*. New York: D. Van Nostrand Company, Inc., 1942.

Mack, J. E., and J. J. Martin, *The Photographic Process*. New York: McGraw-Hill Book Company, Inc., 1939.

McMurtrie, Douglas C., *The Book*. New York: Oxford University Press, 1943.

Monotype Machine Typesetting. Philadelphia: Lanston Monotype Machine Company, 1939.

Murrell, William, *American Graphic Humor*, Vol. 1. New York: Whitney Museum of American Art, 1933.

N. W. Ayer & Son's Directory of Newspapers and Periodicals. Philadelphia: N. W. Ayer & Son, Inc., 1945.

North, S. N. D., *Newspaper and Periodical Press*. Washington, D. C.: Government Printing Office, 1884.

Olson, Kenneth E., *Typography and Mechanics of the Newspaper*. New York: D. Appleton and Company, 1930.

Oswald, John Clyde, *A History of Printing*. New York: D. Appleton and Company, 1928.

Partridge, C. S., *Stereotyping*. Chicago: Mize & Stearns Press, 1892.

Patterson, Donald G., and Miles A. Tinker, *How to Make Type Readable*. New York: Harper & Brothers, 1940.

Plomer, Henry R., *A Short History of English Printing*. London: Kegan, Paul, Trench, Trubner, and Company, Limited, 1900.

Presbrey, Frank, *History and Development of Advertising*. New York: Doubleday, Doran & Company, 1929.

Radder, Norman J., and John E. Stempel, *Newspaper Editing, Make-Up and Headlines*. New York: McGraw-Hill Book Company, Inc., 1942.

Rand, Robert R., *A Study of Reader Interest in Thirty Editorial Pages*. Evanston, Ill.: The Medill School of Journalism, Northwestern University (Thesis), 1941.

Stanley, Thomas Blaine, *The Technique of Advertising Production*. New York: Prentice-Hall, Inc., 1941.

The Newspaper As An Advertising Medium. New York: The Bureau of Advertising, The American Newspaper Publishers' Association, 1940.

Thomas, Isaiah, *History of Printing In America*, Vol. I. Worcester: Press of Isaiah Thomas, 1810.

Updike, Daniel Berkeley, *Printing Types: Their History, Forms, and Use* (2 vols.). Cambridge: Harvard University Press, 1927.

Watson, Elmo Scott, *A History of Newspaper Syndicates in the United States*. Chicago: The Publishers' Auxiliary, 1936.

Weitenkampf, F., *American Graphic Art*. New York: The Macmillan Company, 1912.

Winship, George Parker, *The Cambridge Press, 1638-1692*. Philadelphia: University of Pennsylvania Press, 1945.

ARTICLES

English, Earl, "A Study of the Readability of Four Newspaper Headline Types," *Journalism Quarterly*, 21:3 (September, 1944), 217.

Frank Leslie's Illustrated Newspaper, 2:124-25, 1856.

"Gannett Claims Invention Opens New Era of High Speed Newspaper Production," *Editor & Publisher*, 61:29 (December 8, 1928), 3.

Giegengack, Augustus E., "The Amazing Benjamin Franklin," *Who's Who in the Composing Room* (February, 1938, supplement).

McMurtrie, Douglas C., "Papers Must Modernize," *Editor & Publisher*, 74:10 (March 8, 1941), 40.

"Rotogravure Now in Media Limelight," *Editor & Publisher*, 68:21 (October 5, 1935), 5.

"The Development of the Intertype." Paper read by H. R. Freund, Chief Engineer of Intertype Corporation, before a group of New England publishers and printers in Boston, 1937.

Tinker, Miles A., and Donald G. Patterson, "Effects of Line Width and Leading on Readability of Newspaper Type," *Journalism Quarterly*, 23:3 (September, 1946), 307.

Towle, Felix S., "Typography Survey Finds No Set Ideas," *Editor & Publisher*, 78:51 (December 15, 1945), 60.

Index